# JOURNEY INTO THE HEART OF MUSIC

## Going Beyond the Notes to Sing *Your* Song

by

**BONNIE MANGOLD**

Printed in the United States of America

First Edition

November 2016

Published by Marisan Press, Teasdale, Utah

Edited by John Kadlecek: www.JohnKadlecek.com

Cover Design by Jim Hayes: www.Ha YesDesign.com

Library of Congress Number: Pending

ISBN: 978-0-9771232-8-5

www.facebook.com/Journey-Into-the-Heart-of-Music-1006739046118891

# DEDICATION

This manual is dedicated to three artists who have touched me deeply with their music and inspired me to reach for levels of communication such as theirs: Maestro Maurice Abravanel—profoundly passionate, longtime conductor of the Utah Symphony; my teacher Zara Nelsova—mesmerizing great cellist of her era; Sally Peck—principal violist of the Utah Symphony during the Abravanel years, who could move me with a one-note solo. I am grateful to them and to other teachers along the way for having awakened me to the soul of music and the heart of the cello.

Music is a metaphor for life. What is true in music is true in life. What is true in life is true in music. Every soul sings its own song and the capacity to create great music grows with one's soul. When you undertake to grow as a musician it *will* change your life.

To those who have nurtured my soul and inspired me to live my song I also give my thanks and gratitude.

# ACKNOWLEDGEMENTS

Books don't just write themselves or happen out of thin air, so I discovered. I had first contemplated writing a teaching book based on my own pieces in the late 1980s. The book I had in mind then is not the same book I have written. It seems life got in the way, and there were many lessons to learn before this manual could come to fruition. Even when I finally got down to serious writing, I had no idea that my initial ideas would evolve into what you have in your hands. It might have all stayed in my head, never gotten onto paper, if it had not been for meeting my editor, John Kadlecek, and his wonderful life partner, science writer Julie Rehmeyer. Together they convinced me that committing to an editor would jump-start the book. They were right. That this book exists is in large part due to them, so thank you John and Julie, and also for your supportive friendship ever since our first meeting.

Even when I started writing I had only a vague idea of the plan for the book. Only later did I see that it is a working manual—not a book to be read and put down—and in a way, a record of my own journey through life as well as music. Its creation reminds me a bit of the process used in Salt Lake City prior to the 2002 Olympics, when the freeway system had to be expanded and there were huge time constraints. It was a design-as-you-build approach. It worked, though there is one complex interchange that is not-so-affectionately referred to as the spaghetti bowl. Thanks to John, the strands of my thoughts got straightened out. His expertise, corrections, and suggestions have been invaluable, as well as his encouragement. The manual that this endeavor has become is a co-creation.

My sister, pianist Marilyn Mangold Garst, has shared much of this musical journey with me. The fact that I am still making music is due in large part to the opportunities that she has created for us to perform together in Durango, Colorado. As I say in the text, I now have the luxury of playing only what I want to play, but without her there really wouldn't be the opportunity to continue playing the wonderful cello-piano literature that we both love so much. That is part of what keeps my heart singing, so Marilyn, my eternal gratitude to you. I wish also to acknowledge and thank Marilyn for her willingness to read through the entire manuscript and for her consequent knowledgeable comments and suggestions for clarification, as well as catching mistakes.

My thanks to Nancy Green for the final proofreading and copy editing of this manual, thus helping her cello teacher avoid an 'embarrassment of errors.' Remaining mistakes I must claim as my responsibility. Additionally my thanks to Jim Hayes for his generous help and creativity with the cover designs.

There are several healers, all dear friends as well, whom I want to thank, because without their help I wouldn't be playing or writing: Natalie Clausen, profoundly knowledgeable about all things health related, who has helped me recover from autoimmune issues; Carol Lessinger, from whom I have learned many valuable Feldenkrais principles, and whose loving hands-on work has kept me free enough of pain to keep playing; Dr. Hallie Robbins, also for her brilliant healing work; Sylvia Nibley for her intuitive guidance, encouragement, and help in releasing unneeded beliefs.

I would also like to recognize another dear friend, Margaret Sanders, whose daughter Jill studied with me. (You will meet Jill in one of my stories.) During the years when Marilyn and

I lived 2,000 miles apart, and she would travel to Salt Lake City for some of our many concerts together, it was at Margaret's home—complete with the nine-foot Steinway—where we did our intense rehearsing and our 'dry-runs.' Margaret's support and faith in me have been instrumental in inspiring me to follow my dreams. My thanks to all these extraordinary women.

Perhaps I should acknowledge Mari (canine companion), as well, for being the bright spirit at my side, who throughout the writing of this book made me get out of bed in the mornings. That was her self-appointed job, a very important one, and one she did very well. She was relentless!

I'm of the opinion that friends are a treasure, and where I live now there are more priceless friends and students who have supported me in various ways, and to them also I owe and give my thanks. The list could go on a long time, so they shall remain nameless—here, but not in my heart.

What I've presented to you is a gestalt—an integrated whole—of a lifetime of study, exploration and experience. It is quite probable that there are few original ideas here, however many ideas were gleaned from experiences or studies from so long ago that I have no idea the source, so my apologies for not crediting someone if I have 'stolen' an idea. However I encourage you to steal all the ideas found here, make them truly your own, and continue to explore and create your own gestalt of playing from the heart.

# PRELUDE NO. I
## (from the heart)

Music is a language, a virtually unlimited one. Perhaps it is even the ultimate language. As with all languages, it is a tool for communication. Though written and spoken language can be beautiful poetry—communicating more than the words alone—music conveys great passion, emotion, attitudes, qualities, and... *that* which is beyond words. Composers, mystics, and philosophers alike have referred to music as the most divine of all the arts—it comes closest to expressing the inexpressible. Music existed before spoken language and goes further than what words can convey. It is indeed universal.

Rhythm and motion intrinsic to all life are intrinsic to music. Music can be a living thing!

Music can also be dead, boring, and uncommunicative, just as can poorly written or spoken words. Merely playing correctly what is written on a page is not the same as communicating the intentions of the composer. In speech if I say: every-word-correctly-with-the-same-emphasis-and-volume-and-pitch-and-don't-use-any-punctuation-and-run-my-sentences-together-and-fail-to-pause-at-all-and-have-an-attitude-of-uninvolvement, I will lose my listener quickly no matter the greatness or smallness of the thought I'm expressing. So it is in the performance of music. If a player renders exactly what is on a page, nothing more, nothing less, without personal involvement in the unwritten content that gives the notes shape and meaning, then that person will play like an automaton and fail to communicate to an audience. Just as the android character, Data, from *Star Trek: The Next Generation* is capable of 'executing' music 'perfectly,' many musicians today play with great precision and learned musicality, perhaps even quite beautifully, yet still fail to move their audiences. What is missing is the heart—the soul if you will—of the music. As musicians we have what could be considered a sacred purpose: bringing music to life. Playing music 'perfectly' is not the objective. Communication is. Changing the listener is. Touching the heart of a person is!

There are wonderful musicians who intuitively create the gestalt of the music—its overall meaning and beauty—and communicate powerfully to their listeners. Great artists do this naturally. Not all of us are so gifted. But we *can* develop that which may be intuitive in some. We *can* tap into this gestalt, or perhaps it is more accurate to say that it can be coaxed out of us, with the proper provoking.[1] And what better provocateur than someone who has struggled with this process?

The two great cellists with whom I studied were so intuitive that for the most part they were unable to communicate the 'how to' of transforming notes on a page into ecstatic, alive music. Fortunately something was passed on through a kind of osmosis. At the very least I was exposed to a high level of music-making. Nevertheless I struggled to bring music to life. Much of my struggle involved understanding the importance of my own deep desire to create and communicate beauty, to touch another's heart with *my* heart and being, and to do this through the vehicle of music. I had to journey to the understanding that this purpose outweighed other purposes I may have held for playing the cello. Creation and communication happen best when

---

[1] It was Plato who said: "The teacher can teach the student only that which he already knows."

the whole person is aligned with the purpose. This kind of communication has been my deepest purpose, and I have felt what it is like to truly touch another's heart.

Because I have had to learn how, I know it is possible to help others with the same desire. This opus is my offering to you, so that you too may touch another heart through music.

<>

## Working Definitions for Heart and Mind

For our immediate purposes 'heart' refers to that part of you that knows inclusiveness and compassion, is capable of feeling love and knows its absence as well as its presence, is the core of who you are. Later in the manual I will expand on this definition.

When I use the word 'mind' with a small 'm' I refer to the intellect, that part of you that analyzes things, thinks about things, solves problems, sees connections. This analytical function is important for understanding such aspects of music-making as form and structure, rhythm and other relationships, or for explaining the physical world. The mind is also very good at justifying our attitudes and beliefs, and rationalizing behavior—why it is OK not to practice today, for example. These are activities at which the mind excels (especially lawyer minds[2]).

I use the word 'Mind' with a capital 'M' to refer to something more akin to consciousness, something more than just brain function and intellectual capacity.

Prelude No. 1 (from the heart) was written spontaneously and quickly, very much coming from the heart. That could be sufficient to communicate my motivation for writing this manual, yet years of teaching have taught me that it is important to say the same thing in many different ways to accommodate different learning styles. Some of us learn most easily through verbal, analytical explanations, some through metaphor, some need examples to hear or to see or to feel, or all of these. Prelude No. 2 (from the mind) presents these same thoughts from a more analytical viewpoint.

Notice how you respond to these two Preludes—the different effects they have on you.

---

[2] See story on page 61

# PRELUDE NO. 2
## (from the mind)

There are many superb cellists and other instrumentalists throughout the world. In part because of refinements in teaching the technique of playing an instrument, countless musicians have now reached a level of competence that few could achieve in the near past, just as athletes continue breaking records and pushing the human body to new limits.

Does anything remain for an obscure cellist to contribute?

Despite this high level of execution demonstrated by many players, it often seems that "execution" is indeed what has taken place. Many performances may leave listeners cold. We can admire and even be somewhat overwhelmed by expertise, and yet be untouched and unmoved at our core. What is missing?

A good musician is far more than a good instrumentalist, a great artist more than a good musician. These are starting points, but we have to move well beyond competence, and even being a musically tasteful player, to touch an audience, especially in this age of flawless recordings and high technical standards. Can the more ephemeral aspects of music-making, which are impossible to notate in the score, be taught? Can a person learn to 'play from the heart' when it hasn't come naturally or has been trained out of a student in the pursuit of perfection?

I believe so. This manual is designed to help lead you, a cellist or other instrumentalist, to ways of approaching the making of music that take you beyond the symbols on the page to find and communicate the intentions of the composer through the act of your unique voice touching the hearts of your listeners. It is a guide for developing the qualities you need: the necessary attitudes of mind and Mind, the required understanding of the music, the finding of the feeling of the music, finding your interpretation, and ultimately in the playing of the music.

The idea, attributed to Plato, that you can only learn what you already know, has truth to it. What I am presenting in this manual is a path that could help you uncover what you already intuitively know and are capable of, but have obscured for some reason.

True music-making is not primarily an analytical activity; however there is a place for looking at the gestalt of music performance in an analytical way. Awareness and understanding of some of the often missing components can lead to finding a spontaneous, creative synthesis in the moment of performance that will deeply touch your audience.

# TABLE OF CONTENTS

# OVERTURE

## Nuts and Bolts of the Manual

# ABOUT THE MANUAL

In writing this manual I had in mind a rather broad spectrum of readers, encompassing music students studying to become professionals, moderately advanced players studying on their own, professionals looking to further advance their art, and teachers—for use with younger or less advanced students. I use some of my own compositions and other music as teaching vehicles. The principles involved in bringing music to life are true for all music, regardless of instrument or complexity of the music. Thus this manual can be used by non-cellists and the included music easily transposed or rewritten for other instruments. However, the sonorities and open string pitches of the cello have inspired me to write in a particular way, different than if I had been writing for another instrument, say, an oboe. My pieces, found in the Addendum, and most music work best on the instrument for which the music was originally intended.

This is not a book designed to be read then put aside. It is a *workbook,* which is why I refer to it as a manual. To receive what it has to offer, work through it in the sequence given, doing each of the 46 exercises as you come to them, not reading on until the exercises are complete. Each act builds on the ideas, understanding, and qualities achieved in the previous ones. If you skip to Act IV or V, hoping to apply that material, you will miss the foundation—the heart of the manual—and the heart of music-making.

Each section of this manual includes: concepts and ideas important to music-making including some critical definitions; exercises and instructions for applying the concepts; stories from my own experience; sometimes general suggestions that are of a more technical nature (Tips); and what I call *Musings.* There are also both music quotes and written language quotes scattered throughout the manual, which I hope you will find inspirational and will choose to spend some quiet time with—singing or hearing in your head the music and contemplating the thoughts. The written quotes came from many books, papers, and internet sources I've gathered over the years. I have endeavored to credit the authors within the body of the manual and to present information as accurately as possible.

You will notice that some of the music quotes complete a theme and some end in mid-stream, so to speak. Pay attention to how you respond when the theme doesn't come to completion as opposed to when it does. When a music quote is not immediately identified, as on the Overture title page, it is because I want you to hear it and sing it before reading what it is. These unidentified music quotes, or ones with a figure number only, are identified in Appendix A. Excerpts that go with the text or an exercise are numbered and identified just below the excerpt.

All the material is not appropriate for all ages, so teachers please use your discretion as to what you think appropriate for each student. Some of the concepts I discuss may be beyond the maturity level of children, however I am often surprised by the sophisticated thought that some children display, so take the liberty to disregard this opinion. The Review Section covers a few basics of music theory that are a necessary foundation for the understanding and intelligent practicing of music. Most readers, I hope, will not need this review.

I prefer to use the words that I think best convey what I mean. Consequently at times I use vocabulary (or concepts) that may be a stretch for younger students. This is why it is important for you younger students to have a teacher work through this manual with you. When there is a word you do not know or have only a vague understanding of, please, please, please… look it up! When you read and fail to understand a word or phrase, it's unlikely that you will be able to completely understand the information that follows; this is an important point in the study of anything. Given that printed music is a symbolic language representing sound—like the words or symbols of spoken languages—it is equally vital to understand everything that can appear on a page of music. Part of your tool kit should be a music dictionary of the symbols, such as accents, as well as the instruction words of music, which are more often in Italian, German or French than in English.

Access to a good English language dictionary is basic to any study—the older and bigger the better—as it is helpful to get to the root definitions of words and understand original meanings. The original meaning often gives a depth of understanding to something that current language use may minimize, thus my preference for the older dictionaries. For example, the word *concomitant* which I use in Act VI comes from the French *companion*, and implies a co-joining, as well as the concepts of accompanying, attending, association, and a synchronous existence. If you only consult the internet you will find a different slant on the word—one implying subjugation or a hierarchical relationship—not part of the original meaning. Every word has its own unique flavor, and no synonym has quite the same meaning. I prefer having many flavors to choose from. In my use of concomitant, the two synonyms companion and co-joined come closest to what I wish to express.

Also please acquire a journal or notebook before continuing on to Act I. Some of the numbered exercises require written responses on your part, perhaps lengthy ones. You will need the journal for recording your thoughts. Also in the main body of the text there are occasional suggestions or questions to ponder. Use your journal for all your responses.

The prerequisites for music-making include being able to read the printed music effortlessly and having adequate facility on the instrument to meet the technical demands of the piece in front of you. If you are still struggling with these things—not yet playing accurately and without effort—it is the struggle that will be communicated to the listener, not the music. Concurrently with building your technical skills and meeting these prerequisites for music-making, this manual can help you build the non-technical skills that allow you to put that technical facility in the hands of the heart.

The music used in the exercises generally does not make elaborate technical demands on a cellist. My intent is to help place your attention on finding and communicating the unwritten content, not having to learn difficult technical passages. My pieces are tools for focusing on one or two different ideas at a time. If played just as they appear on the page, they will sound as they appear: simple and uninteresting. But to play simple music beautifully, and to communicate its meaning, requires excellence in music-making. Played true to my concept of these pieces, and as I actually play them, it is quite possible to move people to tears. I know that this is so. When that happens I have achieved the real purpose of music: to touch the heart. I have found little in life that is more satisfying than that.

Ultimately it is difficult to separate technical issues from aspects of music-making, which is the reason for the practical tips about technique. However, the technique of playing the instrument is not my focus and is beyond the scope of any book.

Music does not happen in a vacuum; principles of life apply to music. Bringing the whole person to music-making means bringing all your understanding, experience and wisdom to bear on the art of creating and recreating the music. Follow my sometimes far-ranging digressions throughout this manual, and you will find that they apply both to music-making and to life in general. In my own struggle to communicate through music, it is this totality of life experiences and knowledge gained that has played a key role in learning to play from my heart. My own stories are included because I am going to ask you repeatedly to 'open your heart;' it seems only fair that I let you peek into mine.

And so, not everything is obviously about music. There will be suggestions for further reading and listening, those quotes to inspire you, perhaps the occasional poem, and anything else I think seems pertinent—maybe even the kitchen sink.

## HEART *AND* MIND

Though I differentiate between heart and mind (intellect), my comments are not intended to be value judgments. In and of themselves neither mode of functioning is bad or good—they are simply different. We need both heart and mind to function optimally in life. It is only when one function is ignored that there is an issue, because then we function less than at our best and are cut off from entire areas of experience. It is like trying to see with one eye: there is no depth perception and the view is limited. The mind minus the heart can lead to arrogance and lack of compassion, even cruelty; the heart minus the mind can lead to ineffectualness in the world.

We need the right balance of these two modes of perceiving and communicating. Throughout this manual I have attempted to balance the two in my writing. When my intent is simply to provide you with information, the writing will be in a straight-forward, factual manner, easily grasped by those with a verbal, mental dominance. At other times it is my intent to inspire you, provoke your curiosity, lead you to contemplate new spheres of possibilities. At these times my writing—often the *Musings*—may resonate more at the heart and emotional level than the mental.

We need both in the outer world. We need both in our inner world of music.

## MUSIC AS A HEALING ART

At age ten when I began playing the cello I didn't understand that music can be a healing art. I didn't consciously recognize that truth until more recent years. However, all the animals who have ever lived with me understood the healing or soothing properties of music. When I began the cello my first parakeet, inappropriately named Boots (his toes were actually well exposed and sharp) chose to ride on my bow, at least during my beginning stages of playing. As my bow speed picked up he decided to move, choosing between either my glasses or my shoulder, where he would chatter away for the entire practice session. At least these last two locations protected the cello if not myself from his effusive expelling of waste. He liked to stick his head in my ear to do his chatter, afraid I suppose that I wouldn't otherwise be able to hear him. I could. Occasionally he would go off to sleep and then there was blessed silence for a backdrop.

Later when I raised canaries they would go wild with song as I practiced. So did the room full of parakeets that I raised, though their chatter cannot easily be categorized as song. Nevertheless they responded to the cello with greatly increased vocalizations.

Then there have been the three dogs, all of whom have wanted to be close by when I played. Bastian, a Sheltie, liked to 'sing' (howl) along with me, but from across the room. He had his favorite music. He didn't sing to everything. Zachary, the Australian Shepherd, on the other hand, never sang but insisted on lying at my feet, actually touching the endpin, presumably for the extra vibrations. Mari is almost always in the room whether I am doing the playing or a student is. She seems to be the most discerning, and I said "almost always" because she has been known to get up and leave when something doesn't meet her standards. [4]

The qualities needed in the practitioner of any healing modality, to bring about healing—or more accurately to provide the environment in which one can heal—are the same qualities we need to make music from the heart and provide such an opportunity. The metaphor of music is applicable everywhere I look. It is a beautiful microcosm for studying the whole of life.

---

[3] Latin for the phrase *music soothes the savage beast*, originally *"Musick has charms to soothe a savage breast,"* a line in the play *The Mourning Bride* (1697) by English playwright and poet William Congreve (1670-1729).

[4] Lest you underestimate the awareness and consciousness of animals I encourage you to read *Beyond Words* by Carl Safina.

*"What is a person? Being a person is not a pat formula,*
*but a quest, a mystery, a leap of faith."*
—Jaron Lanier

## BRINGING ALL OF YOU TO THE MUSIC

Even without the innate, intuitive genius that makes a great artist, arriving at greatness in music-making is still possible, but it happens by achieving excellence with the components that make for greatness, step by step.

Physically, the necessary excellence on the instrument is commonly referred to as technique. This technical excellence requires: the ability to move freely on the instrument; the accurate playing of what is written thus producing the desired sound; and doing these things without unnecessary tension or effort in the body. If there is effort, excellence has not yet been attained. True excellence has the quality of effortlessness.

Ivan Galamian—extraordinary violin teacher of the 20th century—defined technique as: "the ability to direct mentally and execute physically all of the necessary playing movements of left and right hands, arms and fingers… What counts is not the strength of the muscles, but their responsiveness to the mental directive. The better the correlation the greater the facility, accuracy, and reliability of the technique."[5]

To complement the physical precision of playing the instrument, there must be a mental or analytical understanding of the music. This requires understanding the principles upon which Western music is based, the architecture of music—its form and structure, scales, keys (thus the Review Section)—and some understanding of the physics of sound. Some of technical excellence is dependent on this understanding of structure, primarily intonation. Intonation is governed by function, not by an absolute of physics. For example, does a note carry tension and motion such as the 7th—or leading tone—of a scale? Does it resolve tension, etc.? Expressive intonation, a term used by Pablo Casals, is dependent on this function of notes within structure. An understanding of the construction of a piece is a necessary component of technical excellence. Another aspect of the mental work is the discipline of knowing the piece so well that you could sing it, or even write it out, from memory. Both are more complex than simply playing from memory, when it may be mostly muscle memory that gets you through.

Then there is the emotional content of the piece, which is mostly un-notated. Having the understanding of this aspect of the music informs what you do physically and helps drive the decisions you must make about what quality of sound you want. Will you finger on this string or that string, cross strings or shift? How will you slur, if at all? Will you use vibrato or not? What quality of vibrato? What dynamics, tempos, rubatos, etc.? It is best to make most of your decisions by studying the music away from your instrument, before gaining facility with the notes on the instrument. And as your understanding of the music deepens, you always have the prerogative of changing the way you play the notes. When the mental and emotional understanding of the music combine, then how each note functions in the whole and the purpose each note serves, become apparent. It is the synthesis of these physical, mental, and emotional components that forms the foundation for making music. From this foundation you

---

[5] *Principles of Violin Playing & Teaching*, by Ivan Galamian, copyright 1985, 1962, Prentice-Hall, Inc.

can begin to communicate and express the entire content of the music. This manual addresses all these different aspects of music and how to communicate them: what is needed physically (including freedom from unnecessary tension); mentally (in part, a clear intention for the music); emotionally (closely related to the motions you use); and perhaps most importantly, what is needed spiritually.[6] We must examine purposes: the purpose of music, purposes for playing, who we are playing for and why, *who we are*.

### *We Should Talk About This Problem*

*There is a beautiful creature*
*Living in a hole you have dug.*

*So at night*
*I set fruit and grains*
*And little pots of wine and milk*
*Beside your soft earthen mounds,*

*And I often sing.*

*But still, my dear,*
*You do not come out. I have fallen in love with Someone*
*Who hides inside you.*

*We should talk about this problem---*

*Otherwise,*
*I will never leave you alone.*

Hafiz[7]
translated by Daniel Ladinsky

Notes lie on a page, nothing more than lifeless dots of ink. It is you who breathe life into them—or not. It is *your* playing that can animate them—or not. With understanding, you can recreate the music as sound in this physical dimension, all from symbols on a page representing an idea in the composer's Mind. Few things in life are closer to true magic.

---

[6] The original definition of Spirit is breath, breath of life or the life principle. Spirit, or the life principle, is also sometimes referred to as Mind—with the capital M—not just the analytical mind or intellect.
[7] Persian poet (c. 1320 – 1389)

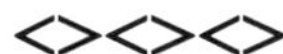

*Let us begin our talk.*

# ACT I

## The Philosophical  Underpinnings for Making Music

# MUSIC: ITS PURPOSE AND POWER
## —THEME A

There are specific physical things you can *do* to assist in playing from the heart so that your music touches the listener. We will talk about those—later. First, we will be talking about non-physical concepts and how you have to *be*. Through the written materials and exercises in this Act, I hope to ensure that you and I have the same understanding of key concepts—such as purpose—concepts which are not an aspect of our physical *doing*, but rather an aspect of non-physical *being*.

*"I have always considered music to be a very strange substance, a substance endowed with magical properties. Music is tangible, almost palpable, and yet unreal, illusive. Music is analyzable only on the most mechanistic level; the important elements—the spiritual impulse, the psychological curve, the metaphysical implications—are understandable only in terms of the music itself. I feel intuitively that music must have been the primeval cell from which language, science, and religion originated."*
—George Crumb (b. 1929)
American composer

## MUSIC

Music: An art over which the Muses preside.[8]

This ancient definition of music, from the Greek *mousike*, reveals something about its purpose to inspire: the Muses were godly sources of inspiration. As I mentioned in Prelude No. 1, music has been referred to as the most sacred of the Arts because it comes nearest to expressing that which can't be expressed. Other types of Art—poetry, painting, architecture— are limited by their own physically bounded forms. Music goes beyond discrete forms. Yes, form and structure are used as a container, but that container does not appear as a form in the outer world. Music expresses through form that is not material, not visible. Music is not fixed, frozen in time as a poem, painting, or building is. As with all living things in nature there is motion, rhythm, and harmony in music. And we find music in all of creation, in the movements of the planets and stars, the tides, flowers turning to the sun. There is no life without movement, which makes the illusion of movement in music so very important. Music *is* the language of that which we cannot describe in any other way.

---

[8] *Webster's New Collegiate Dictionary*, Copyright 1960 by G. & C. Merriam Co.

## PURPOSE

Purpose: The end or aim to be kept in view; intention.[9]

When you know your purpose, you possess a powerful tool—a criterion for evaluating the usefulness or correctness of other things. It could be a decision you need to make: Do I take this new job? Should I change how I hold the instrument? It could be a behavior you question: Is my use of drugs harmful? If something furthers your purpose keep it, if not discard it. Wise choices cannot be made in the absence of a known purpose. This pertains to music-making as well.

## "INTENTION" AND "TO INTEND"

*Intention* is one of the definitions of *purpose*. But the word *intention* is defined as "a determination to act in a certain way or to do a certain thing," with synonyms of "purpose, design, end, or aim."[10]  You will encounter both words in this manual, and I wish to distinguish between the two, as no two words have the exact same meaning, even when they are synonyms for each other.

*Intention* implies having in mind. *Purpose* is more over-arching than *intention*. *Intention* is less absolute, softer somehow, more casual, and situational. You might say: "It is my intention to learn this piece." Or using the verb *to intend*, you would say: "I intend to learn this piece." If I ask you why you play music, I am asking to know your overall purpose for playing, the reason behind it all. If I ask you what your intention is for this phrase, I am asking what you wish to communicate here. *Purpose* carries the idea of greater intensity or a larger scope. *Intention*, or *intent*, as I will use them, refers to what you are creating in your mind as it applies to a specific situation, i.e., "It is my intention to communicate sadness with that note."

---

[9] *Webster's New International Dictionary*, Second Edition, Unabridged, Copyright 1954 by G. & C. Merriam Co.
[10] Ibid.

## THE POWER OF FOCUS AND PURPOSE

Focus: a point of concentration, a center of activity, attraction or attention, as, focus of consciousness.[11] Focus does not allow distractions to exist. Nothing pulls your attention away from what you are focused on.

There is little as powerful as a single-minded purpose. Seeming miracles can happen when the focus never leaves that purpose. Maestro Abravanel came to the Utah Symphony as Music Director in 1947 when the Symphony was still a struggling part-time orchestra. He had a dream: to uplift people through the power of music, bringing great music to all of Utah and beyond. His passion was music; his love for the music spilled out to the players and the audiences. As members of the orchestra we were unable to sit back and withhold our own hearts and energy. We gave everything we had. We were pulled into the power of this purpose, his dream, and we could not help but resonate with it. (Resonance is an important concept. We will talk about it shortly.)

While many would have seen the mostly young, inexperienced musicians as an inadequate tool, Abravanel's intense focus on his purpose turned the orchestra into a whole greater than the sum of the parts, an orchestra that attained world-wide stature and recognition, one revered throughout Utah and the Inter-Mountain West. The Utah Symphony recorded all the Mahler Symphonies when few orchestras were even playing them, as well as many of the great choral works. All this was achieved because Maestro Abravanel's purpose was never to build his own career or a world famous orchestra, nor to become wealthy; rather he kept his focus on the purpose of making music that communicated. Everything else proceeded naturally from that starting point, as the following story helps to illustrate. Such is the power of focus on a known purpose, and just as inevitably, when that focus and intensity of purpose diminish everything falls out of place.

---

[11]Ibid.

**Figure 1**

## Mahler, Abravanel and a Friend's Story

I did not expect to find a sophisticated music-lover, least of all a Mahler enthusiast, in the out-of–the-way corner of Utah where I now live. But I did.

This woman grew up, "a loooong time ago," she often reminds me, on the East Coast. By the age of 15 she found herself captivated by music her older sister's boyfriend played on his French horn—music excerpts practiced rather too frequently for her parents' taste. She however found these excerpts compelling and unlike any other music she had heard. They were excerpts from the symphonies of Gustav Mahler, whose music was rarely performed at the time, even by the big orchestras in the eastern part of the country. It was indeed unusual for such a young person to be exposed to Mahler, but that exposure, even just to those excerpts for the French horn, was all that was needed to turn her into a lifelong devotee of his music.

She went on to a career in medicine, which eventually took her to Salt Lake City as head of the operating room at a prominent teaching hospital. She met her husband there, a respected surgeon, though not a Mahler enthusiast. But as a thoughtful gesture, on a trip to New York City he visited one of the famous Sam Goody record stores to buy a Mahler recording for his wife. A salesman knowledgeable about the music of Mahler began enthusiastically recommending a new release of the Mahler *Symphony No. 7*—the most extraordinary he had heard. The only drawback, he explained, was that the recording was by an obscure orchestra, somewhere out West, an orchestra that the gentleman would never have heard of. Laughing to himself my friend's husband bought the Utah Symphony's recording of the Mahler *Seventh* and returned to Salt Lake City—home of the Utah Symphony—with this gift for his wife. She loved it. Thereafter she was one of Maestro Abravanel's most ardent fans.

It is quite wonderful to have a friend who loves the music of Mahler as much as I do. I think of her as a non-playing musician: someone who plays no instrument, doesn't *make* the music, but whose heart sings and soars *with* the music. Without listeners who are this passionate, those who make music would be much diminished. Together we form the indivisible two sides of a coin. Gratitude for those who love to hear our music is essential.

My friend is equally passionate about animals. Helping them is now her single-minded purpose. Her home, a true oasis in the desert, is a magnet for homeless, orphaned, and abandoned dogs and cats. They show up on her doorstep in droves, sometimes on their own, sometimes dropped off by friends or strangers, all pulled there by some tug of the heart.

Some years ago she witnessed a passing motorist dumping a beautiful Border Collie on the highway, coincidently near her home of course. Predictably she brought the dog home, named her Mari, and decided that this was the right canine companion for me. Actually we auditioned Mari for the 'job.' I took my cello over, played for some time with Mari in the room, and when she did not get up and leave it seemed we had a match. I took Mari home with me where she listens attentively to all my practicing and teaching. Mari, too, is fond of Mahler. I am grateful.

**MUSINGS ON MUSIC**

In his book *Illusions II: Adventures of a Reluctant Student*, Richard Bach refers to stories as "written love." If you have read his book, *Jonathan Livingston Seagull*, you would probably agree. When a book or story can touch us deeply, when a character becomes part of us—haven't we been touched by an expression of love?

Music too is love, expressed in sound. There is the belief in many mystic and religious traditions that before the physical universe manifested in a material way there was only sound (vibrations), which we know from the discipline of physics is indeed what constitutes our universe, in various frequencies. Low frequencies manifest as matter, high frequencies as light and color, even higher frequencies as sound. All these frequencies can be measured and easily perceived. The highest frequency we can perceive is love. Love can be felt, even though scientists can't yet measure it with instruments. Love can be made manifest in sound. When sound is coherent and harmonious we call it music.

Music is love manifested as coherent sound.

*"Music should be healing. Music should uplift the soul. Music should inspire…*
*What makes us feel drawn to music is that our whole being is music:*
*our mind and our body, the nature in which we live,*
*the nature that has made us, all that is*
*beneath and around us,*
*it is all music."*
—Hazrat Inayat Khan

## MUSINGS ON THE PURPOSE OF MUSIC

Hazrat Inayat Khan was an Indian musician and a student of Sufism[12]. He was asked by his spiritual teacher to give up a performance career in India and go to the West to be "a musician of the soul and tune the hearts of men to the divine harmony."[13] In essence he was being asked to take on a larger calling, and his music was the tool to serve this purpose.

In the East, Sufis called music "ghiza-e ruh," the food of the soul, for "music fans the fire of the heart, and the flame arising from it illumines the soul."[14] In the West, according to Baroque composer Giovanni Battista Pergolesi, composers of his era felt their purpose was to create music pleasing in the eyes of God. High purposes indeed! We need such lofty goals to bring out what is greatest in us. It is no coincidence that the most moving and powerful works of classical composers—their masses and requiems—are an expression of spirituality. These works are not about *a* religion, they are about the yearning and longing in the human heart for something greater than our physical senses can know. These magnificent works are capable of inspiring anyone, regardless of views on religion.

Can anything truly great come from a lesser motivation than what Hazrat Inayat Khan describes: to heal, uplift the soul, inspire? People differ in what words they choose to express this high purpose, but the essence is the same.

When an artist does not aspire to these age-old lofty concepts of music and its purposes, no matter how great the skill level, you will know. The effect upon you will tell you. Depending on the intent of the performer, and that of the creator behind the music, the work will open your heart… or not. Open your heart and soften you, bringing you closer to love, or harden you and separate you from life and others. Which? Is the music-making about love, or its opposite—fear? (The opposite of love is not hate; it is the fear that precedes hate.) Of course music does not communicate only love and beauty. It can be suggestive of terror, ugliness or destruction. But when the intent is to open you to love and compassion, then light can be shed on these things. If the intent is to close you, then the music will drive you deeper into ugliness and darkness. Music is powerful. It can be made to do either.

As Inayat Khan says about every artistic creation: "there is always a voice hidden in it, continually telling for what purpose the work of art was created."[15] The same is true for the

---

[12] Sufism is a mystical path or way to draw the heart closer to the Absolute, but according to the Sufi teacher Radha Mohan Lal in Irina Tweedie's book *Daughter of Fire*, it is more a way of life than a religion or philosophy. Sufis say that this "way" has no specific origin, having appeared under many names in many lands. It is said that you are a Sufi if your heart is as soft and warm as wool. The word Sufi may come from the Arabic word sûf which means wool.

[13] Hazrat Inayat Khan, quoting his dying Sufi teacher in *The Music of Life*, Omega Publications, Forward page ix.

[14] Ibid., page 58

[15] Ibid., page 183

**18**

musical performance. The intent of the composer and that of the performer need to be in alignment; without that alignment there will be a confused response.

What would be the point of all the work you have done and will do to be a musician, if you don't then do something meaningful with the results of that work — if you don't touch hearts? What could be more important than illuminating another's soul?

We live in a time when many people no longer want music that opens the heart and touches the soul. Such high purposes are no longer prevalent in much of our culture's music. Music is often viewed as entertainment or used as a distraction, or as a drug.  But like my friend who loves Mahler, there are many who do still want what true artists have to offer, and they need the beauty we can bring to the world, as does our culture of violence. We do this by dedicating ourselves to making music that is food for the soul. It is an honorable purpose, one needed in the world as much as eradicating poverty or designing a new vehicle. There is truth in the aphorism: Beauty is not optional.

*"Music washes away from the soul the dust of everyday life."*
—Berthold Auerbach (1812-1882)
German novelist


## OF LOVE AND BEAUTY

My somewhat older sister and I grew up in a small family, just four of us, where there was little communication beyond the minimum necessary for day-to-day life. Certainly nothing that hinted of one's inner world, nothing personal or emotional, nothing of philosophy or ethics or social importance. But, and perhaps as a consequence, I became an avid reader. And… there was music in the house! Music and books kept my heart alive. They informed my inner world.

As a child of three I had witnessed two events that taught me that there was such a thing as evil and that the world was a dangerous place. The first of these experiences took place at our cousin's Christian church-school in the South, where we lived briefly before moving to Maracaibo, Venezuela. The teacher, presumably Christian, used a cane to beat a boy not much older than myself for being moments late returning from recess. *That* was my first experience of wrongness; both my sister and I recognized it as such. There was a deep knowing that what had taken place was wrong, no matter the strict discipline of Southern culture. I didn't have the words for it, only the knowing, but I remember that we adamantly refused to go back. Somehow we prevailed.

A short time later in Maracaibo, a boy, again not more than four or five, drowned in a swimming pool. This happened at the hotel for the international oil people, while we other children and the adults with their cocktails sat around, oblivious. I was sitting on the concrete surrounding the pool, close to my parents, coloring, and then I heard a cry that broke through the chatter when someone spotted the boy in the water. It was a chilling cry and froze me in place. I can still feel the hush that descended over everyone as the boy was brought out of the pool, not to be revived, though I remember a man working over the boy for a long time. Finally my parents told me that the boy was dead. I didn't really understand death, I just could see that the boy wasn't moving anymore, and I knew that was a very bad thing.[16] I felt smaller, diminished somehow. Witnessing such things before an age when one can bring any understanding or perspective to events destroys a certain childhood innocence and can leave a deep impression, in my case a negative view of the world, and a less expansive heart.

But as I said there was music in the house as I grew up, for which I will always be grateful. My parents had beautiful voices, and my sister and I frequently went to sleep at night listening to the two of them singing opera arias or songs from light opera/Broadway musicals, accompanied by my father on the piano or organ. Sometimes it was just my mother's glorious soprano voice with accompaniment. The music all spoke of *love* and *beauty*, and it had a huge impact on my young heart. Listening to this music, and the other wonderful classical music played on the phonograph, and to Texaco's Saturday morning radio opera broadcasts, awoke me to a realm beyond the physical, and to the possibility of something beautiful and good in the world.

---

[16] On a subconscious level this might well have been my first realization of the importance of motion to life and hence in music.

I didn't understand any of this at the time. Only in retrospect do I see what occurred. No surprise that my sister and I both became professional musicians. This early exposure to the uplifting effect of music and music-making was certainly instrumental (pun intended) in determining the direction of our lives. I often wonder though, if those of us who become artists, of various types, do so in part because of the lack of communication or inability to communicate in one's formative environment.

What is your experience? What do you think about the importance of communication in your own life? Was there a moment of awakening to its role? Perhaps some writing in your journal is in order.

*"If we treat people as they are, we make them worse. If we treat people as they ought to be, we help them become what they are capable of becoming."*
—Johann Wolfgang von Goethe (1849-1932)
German writer and statesman


## Exercise 1.

### Purpose: To have a clear understanding of your purposes with music

Do some deep thinking about your purpose in playing music.

- Why are you playing?
- What effect do you want to create for your listener?
- Why the instrument you chose… or didn't you choose it? If it wasn't your choice or if music wasn't your choice, do you wish to choose and commit now?
- For whom are you playing? Are you playing to please parents, a teacher, your ego, colleagues, critics?[17]

Having a clear understanding of your purpose is crucial. When you are only trying to impress you are playing to the critical,[18] judgmental aspects of people and that is what you get back (as suggested by the Goethe quote). Those listeners will not be touched or moved. But if you adopt the conviction that in everyone there is a sacredness, and you choose to play to that, the result is different. You will be completing the action of playing, like turning on a light switch to let the electricity flow and light up the bulb. Now you have the whole of the action: from the heart of the one who gives to the heart of the one who receives. Music becomes complete when it is truly received.

Examine your beliefs about the nature of the universe, and of human beings.

- Do we in some way reflect something greater than ourselves?
- Is there a part of humankind that 'reaches for the stars,' that strives to grow, to be better, to attain greater truth, understanding, wisdom, love?
- If you think there is such an aspect to a human being, then decide to play to that, play to give that part strength, energy, validation. The universe gives us more of what we put our attention on.

What the truth of the nature of the universe and mankind turns out to be is not the issue, nor is it important for our purposes. Whether there is a Creator or isn't, Divinity or not, God or not, what we mortals *believe* does not impact the Eternal. Truth is Truth and our beliefs are just that—beliefs.

---

[17] Music critics who are well-trained as musicians often have valuable insights, as did the long-time (1960-1980) critic for the New York Times, Harold Schonberg. He is the one who many times said words to the effect that it is not the critic who makes or breaks an artist's career; it is the artist who does that. I encourage you to read his book *Facing the Music*.

[18] In this case the definition I have in mind for the word 'critical' is the negative, destructive aspect of being critical, the act of looking *only* for what is wrong. Other definitions refer to the reasonable, careful, and discerning evaluation or thinking in regard to something, often art or music, as was the case with Schonberg.

However, when you play as *if* there is a sacred essence of the universe in each of us, and you play to that essence then you are likely to play your best, regardless of ultimate truth. I am not asking you to *believe,* in the sense that you *know* my words to be true. You merely have to imagine that it is so, and act accordingly. There is a best in you; there is a best in everyone, call it what you will. When the intent behind your actions, whether in music or otherwise, comes from that place in you and is directed to that place in the receiver, hearts are touched.

This attitude can serve you well in all of life. Understanding what works in the microcosm of music makes it easier to then extrapolate to the macrocosm. Perhaps you have had the experience that when you sincerely ask another human being for help, it is rare to be denied. The very act of asking assumes the best about another, and generally the response you receive will be coming from that same place—that best. And who has not experienced the great delight in helping another? It is similar to the exchange of music from heart to heart.

Do not skip or short-cut this exercise. Without the certainty and conscious knowledge of *your* answers, it will be difficult to release the innate artistry within you. This clear purpose for playing music may in fact be the only missing ingredient in your playing. When you are on stage you must know what you want to create with your music and for whom you are playing.

Please use your notebook or journal for writing your answers. Try reading your statements aloud. Do they ring true for you? If not, reexamine them.

To reiterate: the place you play from in yourself is the place you will touch in another. If what you discover through doing this exercise is not where you want to be playing from, you are free to change.

**Thanksgiving Dinner**

I was invited to Thanksgiving dinner by dear friends and asked to play a short program before the meal. I was happy to do so as I felt it would be my best possible contribution to the evening, and it got me out of cooking. I came early to set up and check out the acoustics. One friend was still in her kitchen work clothes. As I was warming up she said, "I have to dress now… for my ego." My response, which came unconsidered and spontaneously, was: "That's OK. I'm not playing for your ego; I'm playing to the god in you."

I had unwittingly said the truth about what it is that we must do as performers. I used the word 'god' in this instance because the person I was speaking to knew I was referring to that which is highest and best in all of us, rather than to a concept belonging to any particular religion. Call it what you will, that is what I play to—not the critical, judgmental ego, not the personality, social or intellectual status, but rather to that which is eternal, that which animates and inspires all life.

If you so choose—to play to *that*—you will never be "casting pearls before swine." No audience will be beneath you; any audience can be swayed by the magic of your music. Such is the integrity of a true artist.

## FOCUS AND PURPOSE—A STORY

In 1986 I had to quit playing for most of a year due to a repetitive-use injury to my right thumb and hand. When my hand first began to hurt while playing I didn't take time off from the Symphony. To my regret I didn't stop until I could barely hold the bow. By then I had lost most of the cartilage in several joints. These days professional players are a bit wiser, know what exercises to do, when to take time off. I wasn't wise. But I was fortunate that over time and with the help of remarkable healers, and some clever splints, I eventually regained strength and the mostly pain-free use of my thumb. As is the case with many adversities, it turned out to be a time of opportunity for discovery and learning.

First, I saw and heard a pitched African wood drum at an arts' fair. It was beautifully made of lovely exotic woods—lacewood and rosewood—and I loved the sound and resonance. I *had* to buy it. While my thumb and hand were healing I was able to practice rhythms with the lightweight drumsticks on my beautiful new instrument. This not only improved my rhythmic sense, equalizing the dexterity and rhythmic precision between my two hands, but the sound of the drumming was itself a healing element. It was delightful and kept me from being discouraged.

I also made a rather impetuous decision to study the art of bow-making, French style, with American archetier Lynn Armour Hannings, a wonderful teacher and bass player as well. Though I am naturally right-handed I learned to use many tools left-handed, such as planes. In retrospect I consider this to have been a wonderful challenge for my brain and muscles. I wouldn't recommend the injury aspect, but certainly the process of learning to do things with the opposite hand is useful. I adapted, and learned, and made myself light-weight bows with balance points closer than usual to the frog.

As I slowly returned to playing I found that sliding my hand up on the bow, closer to that balance point, allowed me to play longer with less pain. After returning to the Symphony there were still times I could not use my thumb in the normal way, so I experimented with substituting another finger under the stick, letting the thumb just hang. This was certainly not ideal but I made it work. We are adaptable, are we not?

Playing with right hand limitations did require me to think more deeply about sound production. I had to do more with bow speed and make better use of gravity. I also had to focus intently on mentally creating the sound I wanted before it manifested physically. Strength of intention (intention without reservation or purity of intention) can override many physical limitations; without that intention the physical limitations tend to win. I became more sensitive to how much I tightened the bow hair, realizing that looser bow hair gave me a deeper, fuller sound with less effort. I already had discovered that I preferred the bows that I made from softer wood, to those from harder wood, for the same reason: deeper sound, easier to control, greater capacity to change sound color, all with less effort. The bow hugs the string better, as is the case when it is not too tight. String players commonly over-tighten their bows, forcing the bow out of the string, thus requiring more bow and work to get the desired sound. Some players are deliberately going for more brilliance and bounce, which a tighter bow facilitates. But in truth, and particularly for cellists, we do more lyrical playing than off-the-string playing.

> **Tip:** Try less bow tension than you think proper and do some experimenting. It's subtle—perhaps less than a full turn of the screw from what seems optimum. Check to see if you can sustain a note for a longer period of time; that's one advantage. Can you get more dynamic variation on one note? Keep in mind there's no rule saying you have to keep the bow tension the same for every piece. Off-the-string writing or fast, loud, short sounds will call for a tighter bow.

During the period when I couldn't play my cello at all, I attended the International Cello Congress, held that year in Maryland, conveniently close to where my sister then lived. Wandering around the displays, listening to new instruments being played, and feeling rather sorry for myself, I stumbled across a small booth with a weird space-age-looking cello, a skeleton-like parody of the real thing. Or so it seemed at first. It was an electric cello, the first I had ever seen. Being curious I asked the maker to play it. It sounded lovely, not quite like a cello but still pleasing to the ear. I then tried it and discovered I could play with almost no right arm effort. In essence I could bow in miniature and simply turn the amplifier volume up. This was exciting. I ordered a five-string model like the one I tried, the fifth string being a low *F* that allows for a bass-like sound for jazz playing.

Eventually I found the right combination of speakers, amplifier, and digital signal processor to get the sound I wanted. It is an otherworldly cello timbre, perhaps closer to the sound of a pure sine wave, than to the complex sonority of an acoustic cello. I delighted in the fact that I could still play, and with so little right-arm bow effort. By reducing physical effort to almost nothing, not only was I pain-free, but suddenly my playing jumped to a higher level. (We will talk about effort elsewhere.)

I had already written some of my own music, and one evening, quite late, after all the day's duties were taken care of, I sat down to play through my pieces solely for the pleasure of it. That night I played as I had always wanted to play. It was beautiful; it was finally good enough. Nothing about it dissatisfied me—a first! It wasn't just that I was noticing what was right instead of what was wrong. There really wasn't anything wrong. The music flowed. It was effortless. My simple pieces came alive. The music soared, it wept, it caressed, it comforted. Only the music was there, no inner critic or ego. Perhaps for once I was too tired for the critical mind to get in the way. I was playing from the heart, not just notes but real communication, if only to the many plants in the room and the first of my wonderful dogs— Bastian, a Sheltie. I actually gave myself goose bumps, up and down my spine, and the hairs on my arms stood, as I listened to the music I was playing and let it touch me.

I played late into the night, not wanting to quit or lose this fulfilling experience. Eventually the thought of my early morning appointment intruded and I headed for bed. The plants and dog had long since turned in.

Sitting on my bed, I started thinking: what had just happened and why was it different? Why couldn't I communicate that way with my acoustic cello? My thinking mind eventually took me to the thought that this hadn't been legitimate music-making. What had happened didn't count, because I wasn't playing a *real* cello. The longer I let the uncontrolled thinking continue the more dejected I became.

Then I had the first of two experiences connected with music that I would call mystical. Sitting there, deflated, I heard, as if from an outside source and definitely in capital letters with an exclamation point, the command, "DON'T BE SO CONCERNED WITH THE TOOL. KEEP YOUR FOCUS ON THE PURPOSE IT SERVES!"

I was stunned, as this voice instantly cut off the prior thoughts with the completeness of a hot knife. It felt as if these words were being branded into me. They seemed to come from a very different place than normal thoughts. I could almost pinpoint the location of the prior critical words running through my head, but with this command—and it certainly felt like a command—it seemed as if my head were in the voice rather than the commanding voice being in my head. This voice was of a much greater magnitude than my normal thoughts, and it was indeed all-encompassing. The idea of debating this *thought* never occurred to me. It simply wasn't negotiable. The wisdom of this command about keeping my focus on purpose rather than on the tool, has served me well, not only in music but in all of life. And since then I have given several performances with the electric cello, which were indeed heart opening. Playing it has taught me a lot about playing without unnecessary effort, an economy I have been able to translate to the acoustic cello. The experience has reinforced my understanding that music can be served through many means.

### MUSINGS ON THE HEAD AND THE HEART

This use of 'head' is synonymous with mind or intellect as used earlier. And this musing might just as well be called: *Musings On Tools And Purpose.* I use "head" as a deliberate analogy to the hierarchical organizational and corporate structures where there is always someone at the head. The problem with this structure, and the head always running the show, is that often the head is out of touch with the heart, out of touch with the purpose. Input from the rest of the organization—the heart—is ignored. This can be as true for an orchestra as a corporation or a person, and once the head has forgotten the purpose held in the heart, things go awry. As I write this there are two prominent examples in the news: the peanut butter company that knowingly distributed tainted peanut butter, and the Volkswagen Corporation's falsified emission tests. The bottom line becomes profit or personal aggrandizement, not people or their well-being, or a product of true excellence and beauty.

The heart is the true CEO, not the head. The mind is always and only the tool of the heart—meant to serve and accomplish *its* goals. When there is enough love behind a vision and the communication of that vision, people draw together willingly to co-create the vision. When the reverse happens everything suffers, including cooperativeness and health.

I saw first-hand in the Utah Symphony what happened after Maestro Abravanel left and his heartfelt and single-minded purpose was diluted with extraneous goals. An extraordinarily physically healthy orchestra became a non-unified and very unhealthy one over a number of years, going from almost no need for sick leave to a high rate of illness. I do not think this was coincidence or due to modern health issues. For the most part, those players who had played with Abravanel and internalized a strong musical purpose stayed healthier than the newer players. Playing-related injuries increased dramatically, and I believe this had something to do with the level of soul satisfaction that accompanies fulfilling the purpose of music, or not. When the music-making is passionate, from the heart, the chemicals released in the body seem to protect against potential negative physical effects. When the heart at the head of it all (the conductor, CEO, etc.) is not involved, people suffer, regardless the activity.

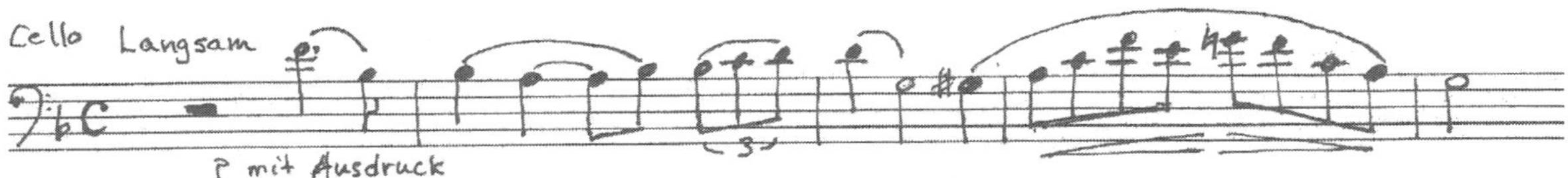


**Figure 2**

## The Decision for Music

My motivation for going to New York to study with Zara Nelsova at the Juilliard School of Music came from having heard her play in California while I was still in high school. Beverly Lambourne, my dedicated cello teacher, drove us two and a half hours to Los Angeles to hear Nelsova's recital. I was mesmerized. No one present could not *not listen!* From that moment on I knew I had to study with this woman. Nelsova was a figure bigger than life, and her influence on me was immense, though she had limited teaching experience when I first began studying with her. Like Maestro Abravanel, and a few other great conductors I have had the good fortune to play with, every time she picked up the cello the music got the entirety of her heart, mind, and body. Being exposed to this type of greatness has changed me, for life.

But during the years I studied with Nelsova I often felt quite discouraged. Her standard was what *she* could do, nothing less. "No, no dearie, that's ugly. Do it this way," she would too frequently say to me during my lessons. And then she would sit down with her Strad and play the most exquisite version I'd ever heard of whatever it was I was studying.[19] I thought about quitting entirely, and when I discussed this with Nelsova, she didn't disagree with the idea. She couldn't conceive of someone being happy as a musician if they couldn't play to her standard. She thought that indeed maybe I would be happier pursuing some of my other interests. I left New York for the weekend to contemplate the choice I needed to make.

When I returned, still uncertain in my decision, a colleague from school (whose passion for music-making was next to none) had an invitation for me to a dress rehearsal at Carnegie Hall for Verdi's *Requiem Mass,* with a chorus that she had helped prepare. This rehearsal was one of the most awe-inspiring performances I have ever heard, even to this day. It was non-stop goose bumps. At that moment I *knew* that I had to be involved in the playing of music. It wasn't a question of would I ever be a great cellist, or play to Nelsova's standard, or be successful. Simply put, I *had to* make music. I might not be happy with music as my life's work, but I certainly wouldn't be happy without music as the centerpiece of my life.

---

[19] The music quote at the top of the page is from the second movement of the Schumann *Cello Concerto in A minor*, which Nelsova demonstrated for me at one lesson—in its entirety. I have never heard that movement played more beautifully and soulfully than she played it that day. It was an immense privilege to be present.

## Treasured Listeners

In the 1970s, after a symphony concert in a small-town school gym in southern Utah, a friend and I were getting into my car. We were ready to travel on to the next little town and school gym for the next concert—each one *always* the most important concert, that was our standard—when a townsperson approached us. The middle-aged woman, relatively uneducated I surmised, had searched the high school buildings unsuccessfully for the Symphony manager. She gave us a message to pass on. It was two years since she had first heard the Symphony, she told us, and the experience had changed her life. A spiritual realm had opened to her that she now treasured. It was a brief exchange, but we felt well rewarded for our efforts. As a symphony musician, that was the most gratifying type of feedback.

## The Heart of Music-Making

Another memorable performance with an extraordinary musician was when Robert Shaw (then Music Director Emeritus of the Atlanta Symphony) guest-conducted the Utah Symphony and the Mormon Tabernacle Choir in Berlioz's *Requiem Mass*. We had done the same work with him ten years earlier, and the performance had been good though not earth-shaking. But ten additional years of the study of music, and of wisdom gained from life, made Shaw's leadership into something very compelling. This time the evening was totally about making music from the heart. We did. The audience went wild. The players went wild. And afterwards one of my Jewish colleagues commented: "That's enough to make a Catholic out of you." Indeed.

Ironically, it was another performance of this piece, which I had heard decades earlier at St. Paul's Cathedral in London, that had compelled me to reconsider my then-firm atheistic beliefs. It made me willing to consider—just consider, mind you—that there might be more to existence and the universe than meets the eye, more than science could yet prove. This was a monumental shift for me, since I had embraced atheism at the age of ten, not understanding that not being able (yet) to explain or measure something was not proof that it didn't exist. Reading Pierre Teilhard de Chardin's[20] *The Phenomenon of Man* further nudged me to reconsider my beliefs. (See Exercise 2, page 37.)

*"To anyone who is not a musician music may be comforting, healing, and soothing,*
*but to him who understands music it is a living thing; it speaks to him,*
*his soul communicates with it."*[21]
—Hazrat Inayat Khan

---

[20] Teilhard de Chardin was a rather heretical Jesuit priest, scientist and philosopher whose writings in the first half of the 20th century have had a major impact on religious, philosophical, and scientific thought.
[21] *The Music of Life*, page 16

**A Special Memory**

In our years of touring around Utah, the Utah Symphony touched many lives. In 1972, we arrived in Loa, population less than 400, county seat of Wayne County. Our late morning school concert was in the only building large enough to seat the children and the orchestra—the local church, with its good-sized gym on the lower level. We waited on our thrown-together platforms at one end of the gym, while *all* the school children in Wayne County filed in.

First came the kindergarten children, each child carrying a little chair. Next were the first-graders with their chairs, then the second-graders, and so on.  After the high school students arrived, we were to begin. But there were more to come. Adults began filing in, and soon the gym was standing room only. By the time the last listeners settled in, the room was filled to overflowing with about 900 people!

In typical Abravanel fashion our program was one of first-rate symphonic works, played by the full orchestra. As was always the case, Abravanel's love for the music, the musicians, and the audience was a palpable thing, felt by everyone there. As we played majestic works with full symphonic forces, with all the passion we could muster, the people of Wayne County remained absolutely silent and transfixed, all eyes on us. There was no fidgeting in this group, despite the length of Abravanel's selections and despite the assertions by experts that a child's attention span is no more than several minutes. No one had told these children that! I looked out at captivated faces of folks who had never heard a live symphony before—faces filled with wonder and amazement, both adults and children. I was six feet away from the youngest children, and the awestruck looks on their tiny faces are still clear in my mind.

Over the years, we played with Maestro Abravanel and other conductors in great halls around the world, in front of royalty and sophisticated music lovers. Most of those experiences didn't compare with what the music did for all of us that day. The responses of these folks, during the concert and afterwards, reflected to us the power of music. The importance of touring and performing school concerts was never so clear as on that day.

Loa is no mecca of restaurants, so the townswomen served up a potluck buffet for the orchestra players and all the Wayne County residents who had attended. We ate very well that day, nourished by the delicious food (I have never had so many varieties of potato salad) as well as the warmed hearts of our audience. As we left Loa behind on our way to our next location, we bussed through some of Utah's most spectacular, and least known, landscapes—landscapes that matched the grandeur of our music. That day, the performance and stunning beauty of the area touched me in a permanent way, so strongly that I now make my home in Wayne County. And what a reward that I call many of the people in the audience that day my friends, and they remember the concert as I do, with the same fondness and sense of magic.

**AFTERWORD**

When I 'retired' from the Utah Symphony I discovered I needed to continue being intimately involved in music-making. It seems I'm not finished with that making-the-music side of the coin. I'm not ready to sit only on the listener side. So I play—when I want, what I want, with whom I want, where I want, and how I want. The freedom to make music in this way is quite wonderful and has allowed me more consistently to play as I desire, and to explore new ideas, new technical approaches, and new music. And, to offer my music as a gift from the heart, free of concern for money. Recently I received a message from someone for whom I had played some of my pieces: "To Bonnie, who made my heart soar…"

I have been well paid.

# SPIRIT AND RESONANCE
## —THEME B

These two words, spirit and resonance, name two natural forces or phenomena present in life and in the art of music-making: unseen forces intimately intertwined with music and the ability to touch your listener with your playing. Understanding how they apply to making music will strengthen your foundation for playing from the heart. *Doing* (not just reading) the included exercises will help. The pertinent definitions included are from my invaluable, 3000-plus page, edition of *Webster's New International Dictionary*, Second Edition, Unabridged, Copyright 1954 by G. & C. Merriam Co.

*"What is music? This question occupied my mind for hours last night before I fell asleep. The very existence of music is wonderful, I might even say miraculous. Its domain is between thought and phenomena. Like a twilight mediator, it hovers between spirit and matter, related to both, yet differing from each. It is spirit, but it is spirit subject to the measurement of time. It is matter, but it is matter that can dispense with space."*
—Heinrich Heine (1797-1856)
German literary figure

## SPIRIT

Spirit: 1. The breath of life; life, or the life principle, conceived as a kind of breath or vapor animating the body, or, in man, mediating between body and soul. 2. The life principle viewed as the "breath" or gift of deity, hence, the agent of vital and conscious functions in man; the soul. 3. In the abstract, life or consciousness viewed as an independent existence; as, idealists maintain that the essential nature of the universe is *spirit*, pantheists that *spirit* pervades the universe. [ ] 14. Intent; real meaning; also, characteristic quality; prevailing tendency. [ ] 16. Act of breathing; inspiration.

*"To attain spirituality is to realize that the whole universe is one symphony
in which every individual is one note."*
—Hazrat Inayat Khan


## SPIRIT AND MUSIC-MAKING

Those definitions frequently apply when people describe how someone might play. It is commonplace to hear comments like: There is so much *soul* in her playing; His playing is *dead*; The music doesn't *breathe*; There was no *life* in her music; There was real *meaning* in his playing; It was *lifeless*; He doesn't play with any *spirit*; It was *deadly* dull.

Listeners know when this quality of spirit is lacking, just as they can tell when it is present. Spirit in music is something invisible but easily perceived by most people. Often the less musical knowledge a listener has, the easier it is to register such qualities. Normally when people hear music it is the right side of the brain that is activated. Right brain activity is associated with a wholistic response, one that is intuitive and emotional; spirit is readily perceived. However after several years of studying an instrument, brain activation when listening to music tends to switch to the left hemisphere of the brain—generally a more analytical response, one less likely to discern spirit. Integrating those brain responses in ourselves is one of our challenges as musicians.

Definition 16 of "spirit" (act of breathing; inspiration) provides an important connection with music. The root of the word inspiration is inspire, which originally meant to breathe, or blow upon, to infuse by breathing as in breathing life into something. Breathing properly and allowing the music to breathe is part of bringing music to life. You will not feel inspiration while holding your breath (often done when afraid) or while breathing shallowly. Singing the music while playing, either in your mind, or better 'under the breath' (sotto voce) with lips slightly open, is an important tool. That in itself releases unneeded effort. Your breathing becomes appropriate to the music and your phrasing becomes more natural. Much can be learned from the art of singing that transfers to the playing of an instrument. The amazing dramatic soprano Jessye Norman in her memoir *Stand Up Straight and Sing!* (page 182) said about singing (and she could have been defining all of music): "Singing, for me, is actually life itself. It is communication, person to person and soul to soul, a physical, emotional, spiritual, and intellectual expression carried by the breath. Life!" Norman and other great singers provide powerful examples of spirit in music-making.

*"Music is the smile of the soul. Being a musician allows me to enter people's souls."*
—Luis Szaran[22] (b. 1953)


### *MUSINGS ON THE UNSEEN*

A question that may be unanswerable is: what is the difference, if any, between spirit, soul, and heart (as I defined it earlier in the manual, the core of who you are)? What does it mean when someone "puts their heart and soul" into an endeavor? We use such phrases, but do we really understand what we are saying? Are heart and soul distinct from each other? Do they overlap? How is spirit different? Fortunately, for the purposes of this manual we don't need the ultimate truth, we simply can agree on a certain usage, so I will give you my understanding of these terms—how I use them.

Spirit seems something much larger than personal consciousness: not part of the individual self, rather something vaster, belonging to the unseen world. Spirit transcends that which makes each of us unique, yet we share in common the access to it. I liken it to an ocean to which each of us has access through our individual connecting channel—a stream, or rivulet or even a river—through which water (spirit) ebbs and flows. We can build dams of course and block the channel. Or, we can allow the water to flow freely and to steadily widen the channel.

What we call inspiration comes from spirit and enters into our hearts when we are receptive. The command I received about keeping my focus on the purpose something serves came from spirit. Spirit animates our bodies and is the unseen energy that departs when we die. My father, two dogs, and several birds (I raised parakeets and canaries for a time) all died in my presence, with my hands in contact with them. I felt something leaving and then there was a lifeless body—no longer animated by that which was life. There is such a stunning difference after life leaves the body that it is very difficult for me to think this is due only to the heart ceasing to beat. I call that animating force spirit. And that same force can animate our music when we are playing from the heart.

Heart is a more personal aspect of who we are than spirit; however spirit seems to work through the heart. It is heart that allows us to be empathic and connect with others on a deep level. It is that part of us that feels love and desires to express that love. It can be easily crushed by abuse, cruelty, and life traumas. A broken heart is not so easily healed. Scars remain. Yet the impulse to love is so deep that we go on.

Soul is something innate and unique to each of us, something we are born with, not the ego— or personality—that develops over time. Soul is the true self and comes from the unseen world into the seen, to merge with the body. What we resonate with, our unique expressions and inclinations, *what* we love are indicative of soul. *That* we love is of the heart. (We will be talking more about heart.)

We do not need absolute understanding of these terms to make use of the energies involved. We may not agree as to what these energies actually are, but they can be experienced. For our practical purposes consider them all to be in the realm of the unseen, with heart and soul more or less synonymous. Leave the fine distinctions to the philosophers and theologians.

---

[22] Director of *Sonidas de la Tierra*, the Landfill Harmonica—a Paraguayan orchestra of young people playing instruments made from recycled trash from the dump. Look for this on the internet.

## ANOTHER ASSUMPTION

In the first exercise I asked you to assume the presence of something sacred, or 'that best' in each of us, as I did in the Thanksgiving story, and for some the word *soul* is appropriate to describe this essence. Now there is another assumption I ask you to make, also useful in helping you to play to your highest potential, and again no one word will communicate to everyone. The assumption is that there is a higher creative force in the universe, one beyond knowing through the limited brain and sensory faculties. Let us agree that this force manifests in the physical universe as *Love*—not the sort of personal love for which there is an object, but an independent energy that just is—and let us assume that it is possible to channel this creative force in your music-making.

As before, put aside prior beliefs, including that there is no such thing as spirit or soul or a creative force, and act as *if* it were true that there is a higher force in the universe. This idea that you are manifesting the creative force, as *love*, through your music will aid you in playing from your heart to the hearts of others. Love *is* the most powerful connecting force, and this assumption is much more useful than the idea that you are merely sending sound from your instrument to someone's ears. Your assumptions will affect everything you do and how you do it. Check this out for yourself. Say "hello" to someone as if there were no *love* in the universe; then say "hello" to someone as if there were *love* in the universe. In both cases notice how you feel and how the other responds. Notice how different it sounds to your ears as well. Do you have a preference?

You can always let go of this or any other assumption at any time. What matters in this case, is what works to help your music touch the hearts of your listeners. There are things in this universe that work whether we can define them or believe in them or not. What *is*, is. What *is* doesn't require our understanding or agreement to exist. Gravity, for example, is. It exists, it is real, and has existed as a phenomenon of this universe, long before scientists ever began to understand it. Even the most profound of mystics has but a slim chance of knowing Absolute Truth, in this lifetime, so let go of the need to know whether something is *The Truth* and utilize the assumptions that work for you in life.

An example: I assume that kindness as a way to interact with the world is more desirable than unkindness. I prefer how I feel when I am kind to how I feel when I am unkind, so I choose to be kind—whether being kind is an eternal, absolute, desirable value or not. For me the hello with love is preferable to the hello without.

*"It is very difficult to elucidate this [cosmic, spiritual] feeling to anyone who is entirely*
*without it... In my view, it is the most important function of art and science*
*to awaken this feeling and keep it alive in those who are receptive to it."*
—Albert Einstein (1879-1955)
German-born theoretical physicist


**Exercise 2.**

**Purpose: To free up your beliefs**

You don't want a belief structure overlaid on your experience of life. You want to experience life and love flowing through you, unobstructed. A rigid belief structure blocks love and inspiration, and you need both of these to express music.

Essentially beliefs are ideas you have assumed to be true, often at an unconscious or subconscious level.[23] They are like garments that you put on. They can also be taken off. Like a particular piece of clothing, perhaps it does not enhance you or it is outdated, or it's simply too restrictive. In this exercise I ask you to examine your beliefs.

Use your notebook to make a list of all the beliefs you can spot. Many will be very hard to identify as they underlie how we habitually relate to the world and are virtually invisible. We confuse them with truths. They are particularly difficult to see if you "put them on" when you were very young, and if they were laid on you by an authority figure such as a parent or teacher.

Beliefs can be helpful or destructive. An example of a helpful belief is: I can learn anything. A destructive belief might be something like: I can't draw. Either of those beliefs if held strongly, or unconsciously, will affect how you learn or draw.

Make a list of your beliefs. To help you see them, ask yourself questions such as the following:

> Are people basically good?
> Is there life after death?
> Do audiences want you to succeed?
> Does diet matter as a factor in health and well being?
> Do you consider people of one political party as all bad, or all good?
> Do you believe your parents loved you?
> Can you teach yourself?
> Are people different from you dangerous?


Spend some time examining your answers to these questions and others you come up with.

Do the beliefs you have spotted serve you well? Perhaps it is time to let go of some of them. Just consciously examining a belief may be adequate for getting its tendrils out of your unconscious mind where it can control your life. However, traumatic events can often deeply

---

[23] These two terms are differentiated by many psychologists, but the important aspect that I am referring to is the lack of conscious awareness or choice.

impress beliefs into the unconscious, controlling behavior thereafter. You may need professional help to uncover or release beliefs acquired in this manner. An approach such as *Psyche-K*[24] can help to release unwanted beliefs and adopt more useful ones.

An example from my own experience of a deeply embedded belief was my unreasoning terror of needles. As a child of three, very ill, in a hospital in a foreign country where I didn't understand the language, my subconscious mind concluded that people with needles intend to hurt me. It was decades before this deep-seated belief surfaced and I could release it.

Perhaps there are beliefs that you would prefer to have, and to act on as if they were true.

One of my conscious beliefs is that most musicians become good musicians not because of a gift that enables playing the instrument and music without dedicated work, but because of a great deal of hard work and practice. I believe the gift is in loving music enough to foster the willingness to do the needed work.

I disagree with people who say, "I don't have a gift for music." I usually respond with, "I don't either. The difference is that I loved it enough to do the needed work. That is the gift." Nevertheless I recognize that this is my belief and it may not be true.

Fill several pages in your journal doing this exercise. If you have trouble filling them, please look more deeply. Deeply buried beliefs are difficult to bring to light, but often can be revealed by looking at an aspect of your life with which you are not pleased, and asking, what belief must I have for my life to look like this? Perhaps you have a belief along the lines of "everyone is against me" and a resulting semi-conscious assumption that "the audience is just waiting for me to make a mistake." This is merely a belief, but in believing it, you have lumped everyone in the audience together with an identical assumption about each person, which is sloppy thinking. True, maybe a few in the audience are watching for mistakes—unfortunately usually colleagues—but most audience members are there to enjoy what you do. Audience members do not all walk into the hall with negative attitudes, so examine your assumptions and look deeper for what underlying belief this assumption hints at.

When you consciously choose your beliefs, they become tools to further your purposes. I think of them as my current working tools.

*"Kindness is the language the blind can see*
*and the deaf can hear."*
—Mark Twain (1835-1910)
American author and humorist

---

[24] *Psyche-K* (Robert M. Williams, originator) is one of a growing number of approaches that can be used to essentially replace or override non-useful beliefs deeply seated in our unconscious minds, with useful beliefs (see www.psyche-k.com).

## RESONANCE[25]

Resonance: 1. Act of resounding; quality or state of being resonant. *2. Physics:* The phenomenon which results when, in the case of a forced vibration, the period of the force equals that of a natural vibration of the system to which the force is applied. It consists of a vibration of large amplitude in the system. If the force is due to a tuning fork in vibration, and if the system is a second fork of the same pitch, the latter will be set in vibration as a result of the waves emitted by the former, and consequently the sound heard will be louder. [ ] 5. *Music:* The intensification and enriching of a musical tone by supplementary vibration, either sympathetically or mechanically induced.

"Resonant" is defined as: producing resonance; increasing the intensity of sound by sympathetic vibration.[26] Also: resounding; ringing; re-echoing. Intensified and enriched by or as if by resonance.[27]

(I select the definitions from various dictionaries that are most pertinent, but exploring further on your own is recommended.)

Definition 5 of "resonance" is the one we most often think of as applying to music. On the cello this definition can be demonstrated by playing a low *D* on the *C* string. When well in tune the open *D* string will also vibrate, enriching the sound and demonstrating the phenomenon of resonance. The underlying principle at work is that described in definition 2 from the field of physics. The application of that concept is vitally important for finding 'right' intonation and sound production.

---

[25] *Webster's New International Dictionary*, Second Edition, Unabridged
[26] *Webster's New World Dictionary*, Second College Edition, Copyright 1970
[27] *Webster's New Collegiate Dictionary*

## UNSEEN RESONANCES

Author's Note: *A broader understanding of the concept of resonance is of value in understanding many of the phenomena we encounter in the field of music-making. However, some of the following material might be difficult for younger students to understand and can be skipped over, provided definition 5 (of resonance) is explored and understood.*

In the science of biology the concept of resonance is increasingly in use. The terms morphic resonance, morphic field and morphogenetic field are used to refer to phenomena previously unexplained. British scientist Rupert Sheldrake has been studying these fields,[28] which are as real as gravitational fields, electrical fields, or magnetic fields. An understanding of or at least an acquaintance with these concepts helps in comprehending some of the phenomena—unseen but nevertheless perceived and experienced—you encounter in music performance, both within groups of musicians and between performers and audience.

The definitions that follow are paraphrases of Sheldrake's words, drawn from the suggested reading: *The Sense of Being Stared At*.

*Morph* as a noun means form, similar to a pattern or blueprint; *morphic* is the adjective derived from morph and means pertaining to form.

*Field* refers to a region throughout which a force is exerted, as in a gravitational field.

*Morphic fields* are the fields that contain the information needed for development, that is, the forms or patterns or blueprints for organizing something into a discrete structure.

*Morphic resonance* is the process by which the instinctual memories in a species are transmitted across space and time, from past to present, to inform the development of an organism. Every member of a species draws upon and contributes to this collective memory. In human psychology the Jungian concept of archetypes is an example of collective memory created through morphic resonance.

Morphic fields are of various types. The field responsible for the individual shape of an organism is a *morphogenetic* field. Social morphic fields organize or coordinate the actions in animal groups such as ants. Behavioral morphic fields account for instincts such as the herding behavior of some animals. Mental morphic fields are involved in human connections, through

---

[28] Suggested reading: Rupert Sheldrake's *The Sense of Being Stared At*

attention, intention and resonance. The concept in someone's head of a piece of music could be called a morphic field. The emotions created in an audience through the performance of the music constitute a field. An archetype such as "the teacher" is a morphic field.

As mentioned above, the morphic fields involved in the development and shaping of the physical forms in animals and plants are called morphogenetic fields. Sheldrake considers this field akin to a construction blueprint for a building, a spatial idea or pattern of information, certainly not the bricks and mortar of the building. Each life form's development is shaped by a corresponding field: piñon pines are shaped by piñon pine fields, cats by cat fields. The field itself exists as energy only, an energetic blueprint, not yet physical reality—something that precedes genes and determines physical construction. Though morphogenetic fields are part of the unseen world, there does exist a technology (Kirlian photography), which when used in its intended manner is capable of recording the energy traces of these fields. The photographic results remind me of my electric cello, as they resemble skeletal outlines of basic structure.

Sheldrake additionally theorizes that certain difficult to explain human abilities, such as telepathy, are not paranormal but normal. He believes that they are aspects of mental morphic fields that are part of our biological nature, and that we share these powers with many other species in the animal kingdom in whom they are often more highly developed. It is interesting to note that in testing for the ability to receive telepathic transmission of images, a study done of Juilliard students found a 50% success rate, as compared to a normal rate of 32% to 37%, with random chance being 25%. This finding was confirmed at Edinburgh University for both musicians and artists.

Does music, as a practice, develop the brain in ways that enhance parts of it that most people do not exercise and develop adequately? There is certainly evidence for this. And music itself is so intertwined with morphic fields and resonances that as musicians we certainly become better at tuning into these invisible fields. Such on-going studies tell us that these phenomena are real, just not fully understood yet.

All this research is still in its infancy, but I borrow these terms and apply them to music to facilitate the discussion of our unseen phenomena. For example, I liken the morphogenetic field to the concept for a piece of music, as yet only in the mind of the composer. The written notes would be the genetic blueprint—like the genes for a piñon tree. The actual performance with its invisible but audible content would be the physical manifestation—like the physical piñon tree. Music seems very much a living thing, and any one composition a potential living entity, making this an appropriate borrowing. Various morphic fields and resonances are at work in music, in sports, and no doubt in most other activities. These fields will play an important role in your music-making.


*"The field is the only reality."*
—Albert Einstein

*"The true mark of genius is not perfection, but originality, the opening of new frontiers; once this is done, the conquered territory becomes common property."*
—Arthur Koestler (1905-1983)
Hungarian-British author and journalist


## RESONANCE AND MORPHIC FIELDS MANIFESTED

Is it morphic resonance and morphogenetic fields that allow each generation of human beings to attain a higher skill level, whether in music or athletics, than the previous generation? Once the runner Roger Bannister broke the 4-minute mile in 1954, suddenly many other milers were doing the same thing. Similarly, the superb technical facility demonstrated in the early 1900s by cellist Emanuel Feuermann now seems commonplace for young musicians coming out of music schools. These physical accomplishments appear to become part of a field or reservoir that later individuals in a specific pursuit can draw upon or tap into.

An orchestra formed by a strong architect, such as was the case with Maestro[29] Abravanel and the Utah Symphony, develops a powerful 'morphogenetic field' that envelops any new player coming into the group and molds that player accordingly. That field can also slowly decay, which it did with us after Abravanel was gone for some years. But it took a surprisingly long time. We did eventually lose that quality that had made us unique.

Thanks to Abravanel we also had a strong Mahler 'morphogenetic field,' and heaven help the guest conductor who might come in and attempt to go against that field. Big mistake! It was like telling us, "Stop being an orchestra, be a band." Sensitive conductors are aware of these fields in any given orchestra (even though they may be at a loss in naming the phenomenon), and choose to enhance the existing fields rather than attempt to override them.

It's not only a strong interpretation that can create a morphic field, the very body of music of a composer can create a morphic field, as I've experienced with the music of different composers. Through morphic resonance new generations of players tap into that field and thereby have a level of comfort with the music that prior musicians could not attain. I think of when Prokofiev and Shostakovich symphonies were first being played, and how different that was from today. Now those works are part of fields that can be tapped into with ease by today's orchestras. It's not just increased familiarity with the music. There is an ease that didn't exist before, that wasn't possible before, regardless of technical proficiency.

Jungian psychology describes concepts of archetypes and archetypical energies, each archetype being a distinct morphic field common to humanity. Carolyn Myss, intuitive medical diagnostician, author and lecturer, describes these fields and their power very well. In one lecture I heard, she identifies an archetype of marriage. She describes how two people may get along very well, even live together very harmoniously, but the moment they get married it is no longer just Jane and John who sit down together at the breakfast table. It is Jane, John, and the archetype of marriage—an energetic form or entity in its own right—all of whom now share the table. The relationship is no longer so simple.

---

[29] I have a story for you about the honorific *Maestro*, but will save it for later. It belongs in the kitchen sink category (Act VI).

In the physical world it has long been observed that a less strong vibration or oscillation goes into harmony or resonance with the frequency of a stronger one when placed in the vicinity of the more powerful oscillation, as in the case of a small pendulum becoming synchronous with a larger one. This is a manifestation of the pertinent physics definition of resonance, and it has huge implications for emotional fields.

Both the success of demigods, such as Hitler, and the behavior at some sports events or rock concerts when fans fall into irrational, herd-like actions, demonstrate resonance in behavioral fields and the strength of the influencing force.[30] Today it seems that very few morphic fields that engulf large groups of people are positive. In my experience live music performances (those meant to uplift) constitute one of the few instances where the end result created by resonance with an emotional morphic field is indeed positive.

All of this has implications as to what happens when we create music with strong intent, strong emotion, strong spirit. Essentially we and our music are the larger pendulum creating a powerful vibrational field, and the audience will begin to resonate with those vibrations. This is the phenomenon I was describing in the stories about the impact of music. What happens with a great performance of great music is very moving and powerful, and it happens because of resonance.

One such performance was the final time I heard Artur Rubenstein, playing the Brahms *Piano Concerto No. 2* with the Utah Symphony. He was magnificent, truly one of the great pianists of all time. In part it was memorable for me because it was the first experience I had of being consciously aware of resonance in an audience, and how powerful that unified field felt—everyone feeling the awe, reverence and appreciation due this great artist. We were of one mind, and it was a loving mind.

And then there was Gregor Piatigorsky's last performance with us of the Dvořák *Cello Concerto in B minor* (keep reading).

---

[30] The new field of Socionomics investigates the unconscious herding behavior of humans in masses. I believe it is morphic resonance that accounts for this phenomenon. For more information read: *The New Science of Socionomics* by Robert J. Prechter Jr.

**Figure 3**

## Piatigorsky: A Story

Mstislav Rostropovitch was scheduled to perform the Dvořák *Concerto* with the Utah Symphony at the Mormon Tabernacle in Salt Lake City, which seats at least 6,000 (more if folks squeeze together on the wooden pews). That night there were at least 6,000 present, 6,000 who had come to hear the great Rostropovitch, then unparalleled as a cellist. But, to the surprise of the audience, it was Gregor Piatigorsky who was announced as the soloist. At the last moment Rostropovitch had cancelled. Piatigorsky was his replacement. He had agreed, as a favor to his friend Maestro Abravanel, to come out of retirement from public performance and play the Dvořák. This wasn't more than a few months before his death in August 1976.

Piatigorsky was noted for his dramatic, expressive vision of the works he played. The validity and the authenticity of his interpretations were rarely questioned, in part because of his close association with many great composers of his era, who showed their respect for him by their dedication of music to him. When Richard Strauss conducted a performance of his *Don Quixote* tone poem, with Piatigorsky playing the solo cello part, he is said to have remarked, "Now I've heard my Don Quixote as I imagined him."[31]

A large man, an impressive man, Piatigorsky came striding out on stage, cello held horizontally at shoulder height, as he had always done. Yet his once vibrant, dominating physical presence now had an undertone of fragility; there was a hint of unsteadiness, a slight hesitation. Still, as he began playing it was clear that he knew the concerto with great intimacy.

The intensity with which he created the emotions of the music, including the nobility of the opening theme, which he personified, made his vision of it powerful and clear. However his body was failing and his physical execution of the piece was flawed. Accuracy suffered— intonation was off, bowing not always controlled—but so convincing was his understanding of the spirit of the music and so powerful his intention, that those of us willing to be touched heard his intent more than the actual sound. You could feel his passion, almost see his vision, hear what was in his heart and mind.

Those who were poised to be critical, heard only the sloppy execution, and so went away disappointed; the reviews were caustic. However the majority of this great mass of people, and certainly the entire cello section, was united in awe at the magnitude of this soul. We exulted at the magnificence of his artistry, even when it could no longer entirely manifest in sound. His spirit, the spirit of the music, the spirit with which he played, all these created a resonance and field that the audience both synchronized with and further enhanced. Some of us were moved to tears. These moments leave indelible marks on the heart.

---

[31] Strauss' comment is an excellent example of the musical equivalent of the biological morphogenetic field. The composer has acknowledged that the notes on the page are not the same as and cannot by themselves capture what was in his mind: the concept, his idea of the character of Don Quixote. Piatigorsky tapped into that field and expressed in sound what Strauss attempted to capture through written notes. Not all cellists succeed in this way.

**Exercise 3.**

**Purpose: To increase the sense of life force**

What are the things in life with which you resonate, which increase your sense of vitality, that give you more access to spirit?

Is it walking in nature? Sharing your dreams with someone who truly listens? Playing with your dog? Swinging on a swing (very good for grownups)? Meditating? Dancing? Singing at the top of your lungs when no one can hear you?

How can you increase what gives you vitality, what energizes you?

List as many activities as you can think of that are life supporting and make you feel more alive. Then, be sure to do some of those daily. It might mean a half hour less in the practice room—probably a good thing if you are attending a music school. There is *not* a direct correlation between hours of practice and artistry (technical excellence, yes, but not artistry).

Being in nature, walking in a beautiful environment, are effective for many people. Whatever it is that works for you, be present and mindful during the time you devote to that practice. Listen to the sounds, smell the smells, feel with your body, be aware of your environment, let go of your thoughts. Above all, enjoy!

**The Great Salt Lake**
When I lived in Salt Lake City one of my most joyful activities was kayaking on the vast waters of the Great Salt Lake, at sunset and into the night. I would go with my kayaking buddy and once we got some distance away from the stink of mud around the marina it was like being on the ocean. We felt as if we could paddle forever into the disappearing horizon, where the blue of the water faded into the darkening sky. To the east the city disappeared, becoming a blur at the base of the Wasatch Mountains—mountains lit with the purple and pinkish-gold of the fading sunset.

Our paddling would fall into a rhythm, each with her own cadence. It was an experience of resonance: becoming one with the kayak, one with the water, one with the surrounding silence.

When we would tire and begin the long paddle back to the marina, we always knew where to head in the otherwise pitch black blending of sky and water; behind the marina were the lights of Kennecott Copper, with its huge smoke stack. What a contrast to the natural environment we had basked in—but there were times on dark nights when we were grateful for those lights leading us back.

People belonging to the dominant faith in Salt Lake City used to ask me what ward I was in (ward is the term for a geographically defined congregation). I would generally respond, somewhat 'tongue in cheek' but with more than a kernel of truth, that I attended the Church of the Great Salt Lake. We each must find the activities that touch and expand our own hearts.

If you ever have the opportunity to kayak on still water (i.e. lakes, broad flowing rivers, or an ocean bay), grasp it.

### *The White Kayak*

*Lake of Salt*

*Largest moon*

    *through darkening clouds*

*Ghostly stack –*

    *dark silhouettes behind*


*Encapsuled in silence –*

    *Kayak and I*

*Dipping rhythmically –*

    *port to starboard*

*Gliding through velvet swells*

    *of murky sea*


*As one*

*With the vast stillness*


Bonnie Mangold
1998

*"An ancient musician informed me, that there were some famous lutes
that attained not their full seasoning and best resonance
til they were about fourscore years old."*
—Robert Boyle (1627-1691)
Anglo-Irish natural philosopher


**Exercise 4.**

**Purpose: To experience mechanically caused resonance**

How many instances of resonance can you find on your instrument?

This is easiest on a string instrument because open strings resonate with fingered pitches. Pianists can easily perceive this too. It is useful to feel and watch the vibrations of higher or lower octave strings (to the pitch being played) under the lid of a grand piano.

It is more difficult for wind and brass instruments to find obvious instances of resonance. Instead, you can try playing with crystal glasses filled to different levels with water. Get the crystal singing by running your moist finger around the lip of the glass. It may take some time before you get the knack of it. Don't force it—let the glass sing with a light touch. Can you set another glass to vibrating without touching it? Experiment with this. Get some friends and tune the glasses with different amounts of liquid so you can have some fun. If you don't have water, wine will work fine. (Adults only please.) OK, I've never actually succeeded in getting the un-touched glass to sing, but it is a lot of fun to try, and theoretically possible.

> **Tip:** As you learn to pay attention to the resonance of your instrument, to hear and feel it, you will find that what I call "right intonation" increases that resonance, giving a more vibrant sound. Thus listening for the resonance becomes a tool for being able to play with good intonation. When a note is not in tune resonance decreases. Resonance also diminishes when you use force on your instrument, as opposed to allowing the instrument to sing, just as with the crystal glasses.

**Exercise 5.**

**Purpose: To be aware of *non*-mechanically caused resonance**

How do you resonate with different morphic fields?

When you are with a friend, what is her mood, what is yours?

Does one of you fall into the field of the other?

Does your mood go down or up to match the other person's? Do you want it to?

The act of writing often adds clarity, so note your observations about these questions in your journal. Regularly revisit your writings and notice if and how your responses to exercise questions have changed. Write down new responses.

During a performance (but not while you are playing) notice the audience's prevailing field.

Does it seem negative, critical, daring you to do something good, or does it seem supportive, expectant, anticipatory of a positive experience? This is apt to be an intuitive perception rather than analytical.

Comedians become particularly sensitive to the morphic field of an audience. From them we get expressions such as: It was a tough crowd; The crowd came with me. They not only become very aware of the field, they also learn to work with it and to pull the crowd to where they want it. When you are in groups of people tune into what the morphic fields are, and make a conscious choice to join in or not. But what matters most, is noticing that such things exist.

By being conscious of morphic fields and how you are resonating with them, you do not have to be pulled down into a more negative mood. Perhaps you can pull a friend up, or allow yourself to be pulled up.

## More Water Stories About Resonance

We were off the coast of Vancouver Island in kayaks on a whale-watching trip. I was in a double kayak, paired with a friend who was twice my weight and taller by a foot. He had never kayaked before, but after only a few minutes exclaimed, "This is what my body was made for." He was indeed a natural at paddling. He also had a *very* fast and *very* powerful stroke.

There was no way I could keep up with him, so our stroking rhythms were at odds (as in zero resonance). The movement of the kayak was erratic and inefficient. His solution was for me to quit paddling. Sit back, he said, enjoy the ride. That wasn't exactly efficient either, but slowing down to my pace didn't seem to be an option.

An afternoon came when he slipped into my rhythm, inadvertently perhaps, and suddenly we were soaring through the water. We were paddling into a breeze and the setting sun—just skimming the tops of the glistening wavelets, it seemed. The sun sparkled off the water like flying bits of glass. Now, the wind was our friend, not an obstacle but providing lift, as if our paddles were wings. Or so it felt. Falling into resonance at last, effort had vanished. What remained was joy.

This same magic can happen when you are in resonance with your musical partners, and as in the quote above, music too is a symphony of motion, illusory motion which allows you to soar. (That illusory motion is the subject of Act IV.)

The book *The Boys in the Boat* by Daniel James Brown, is a story about resonance in the physical realm. Not only do you get an engaging true history of what it took for a crew of boys to win the 1936 Olympic gold, but you gain more insight into the negative herd behavior (also an example of resonance) that was occurring in Hitler's Germany. One of the important figures in the story, George Yeoman Pocock, makes that statement (quoted above) about the art of rowing. It is a beautiful summation of what resonance can bring about.

Resonance, in whatever guise it comes, is a quality that we human beings respond to and seek. Resonance can mean being in harmony with the laws of nature, or with the laws of our own body and soul, or with our instrument, a car, the place where we live, or the people who surround us. When resonance occurs enhancing 'the good' (as in a musical performance versus a violent crowd), it is virtually irresistible. This experience of being 'at one' with others or the universe is perhaps our natural state. It is what the mystics talk about. Indeed it can be an ecstatic experience.

## METAPHORS
## —THEME C

Much of the art of teaching is in the ability to find the right metaphor to enable that particular student, at that particular moment, to *grasp the concept* being imparted. For the moment you are that student and since you will never really be holding a *concept* in your hand, even if you *grasp* it, this is also a metaphor. In this manual I make use of metaphors and similes; you can make use of them to help in finding the way to express what you intend.[32]

*"All the world is a stage."*
—William Shakespeare (1564-1616)
English poet and playwright

## METAPHOR

The oldest definition of metaphor is to carry over or transfer. Music performance is a metaphor for life because the principles that work in playing an instrument and making music are also true and workable in our day-to-day existence; they carry over. For example, on a string instrument if you are making a long shift from one note to another, to arrive at your exact destination you have to be very aware of both your starting point and your ending point, that is, aware of the sound you are producing now and simultaneously hearing in your head where you are going next. In ordinary life the same principle applies; if you wish to drive to Los Angeles you need to know your starting point. If you start off in Salt Lake City but think you are in Phoenix and attempt to follow the map from Phoenix to Los Angeles you are in trouble. The principle is the same; this need to be aware of both starting and ending points carries over from music to life or vice versa.[33]

In common usage "metaphor" refers to the use of a phrase or word—which can represent an object, activity or idea—as an analogy or likeness to something else. Shakespeare's "All the world is a stage" is a metaphor. Metaphors, unlike similes, relate two unlike things without using *"like"* or *"as."* A simile would be: The world is *like* a stage. Both metaphors and similes are powerful tools for creating and communicating concepts or feelings, and can assist in getting the right feeling in your body to express the music. Don't confuse this with thinking that music can be communicated by words. It most definitely is not a language of words. As American composer Ned Rorem said: "If music could be translated into human speech it would no longer need to exist." It is however related to the language of metaphors and how they function. Metaphors are useful to facilitate playing from the heart, and in teaching. They act as shortcuts, communicating a concept with a minimum of words, as you will see.

The power and effectiveness of metaphors came to my conscious attention through watching an episode of *Star Trek: The Next Generation*. In this story Captain Piccard and crew encounter an alien race, previously unknown and potentially dangerous. There is no language in common. Piccard has to figure out how to communicate with these intelligent beings. In an

---

[32] Did you notice in my story on page 45 that I urged you to *grasp an opportunity*?
[33] Shifts are most often missed because of the lack of awareness at and of the starting point.

50

effort to spur communication the alien captain sets up a situation where he and Picard are transported to a primitive planet where they must work together to solve a problem—defending themselves against a dangerous creature. The alien's intent is to force Piccard to understand, through the need for repeated cooperative action, that his species communicates entirely in metaphors. Picard comes to this realization and then has the android Data research all the known metaphors of different intelligent species. They eventually succeed in communicating—through metaphors. Piccard explains to his crew the usefulness of metaphors by giving an example of how much can quickly be communicated by just a phrase such as "Juliet on the balcony." All those sharing the same culture will instantly have an entire gestalt of meaning and information from those four words. In this case those who know Shakespeare will understand that you have warring factions, and a tragic love attempting to cross those boundaries.

Many of these *Star Trek* episodes set in alien universes and cultures are beautiful metaphors for issues that exist in our world. Having a dramatically different setting allows us to look objectively at issues that may be so highly charged that we can't easily think about them in a rational way. Unexamined beliefs easily get in the way.

There is much research occurring currently on how metaphors function. Linguists have shown that metaphors are pervasive in all languages and perhaps crucial to memory. There is evidence that we think primarily in metaphors, that the brain is designed for that, and that given unfamiliar metaphors the right hemisphere does a better job than the left in processing or understanding the metaphor.

A metaphor is *like* a morphic field or morphogenetic field (this is a *simile*). Think about it. They are both non-physical and both contain information, enough in the case of "Juliet on the balcony" to construct an entire situation or scenario. Enough in the case of a piñon morphogenetic field to construct a piñon tree.

Make use of them.

**Excerpt 1  Schumann *Fantasy Piece No. 1***

## Schumann Metaphor

An effective and memorable metaphor, or in this case more of a simile, was provided by my first cello teacher. I was studying the Schumann *Fantasy Pieces* and having difficulty with the long, slurred, flowing phrases of the first piece (see above excerpt). I couldn't quite get the smooth flowing sound the music demands. My teacher likened the music to a broad river: quickly flowing but unperturbed by rapids, shoals, or turbulence of any sort, so that the water seems calm and languorous as it flows to its destination. Once she suggested this image I was able to create the needed smooth flowing lines.

I still make use of this metaphor of the broad, unperturbed river; however I also like the metaphor suggested by the wonderful cellist Steven Isserlis in one of his master classes: the music is a love duet between the two voices—piano and cello. This metaphor helps you to bring out the tenderness of the music. As he repeatedly emphasized, the first of the three pieces is the dreamy one, not the passionate one. Now my broad river is a gentle, loving, broad river.

## Mahler Metaphor

Maestro Abravanel provided a striking metaphor the first time we played the Mahler *Symphony No. 1*. We had begun the last movement, and shortly into it (see bar 42 of excerpt on following page) there is a series of emphatic chords over eleven bars. The cellos play a middle *C* staccato eighth note. The first one is marked triple forte, the remaining ones merely fortissimo. When we played that first *C* Abravanel stopped, turned to the cellos and thrusting his hand hard against his chest as if he were stabbing himself, said in his heavy accent, "It is a knife stab through the heart… terrible heart-rending betrayal." As a reminder I penciled in a heart around the note with a knife stabbed through. My stand partner and I from there on gave everything we had to making that one note communicate the entirety of the concept, as did all the rest of the section. Long after Abravanel was gone from the podium the cello section remembered and gave our all to that note. However no other conductor ever even noticed we were playing there, let alone what our note was communicating. From the audience our sound may have been covered by other instruments, but there was an energy we created that communicates to listeners even when it is impossible to pick out the sound of the cellos.

It is a mark of Abravanel's understanding of and passion for the music that he would take the time to ask for such things. It is a way of bringing to life the notes on the page. He was a genius at evoking feeling and emotion from the musicians. *And* this happens best through love and respect, not through fear and harshness. There is a difference between evoking and demanding, and the sound of an orchestra reflects that.

# IV. Satz.

**Excerpt 2** Mahler *Symphony No. 1*, beginning of the fourth movement, cello part

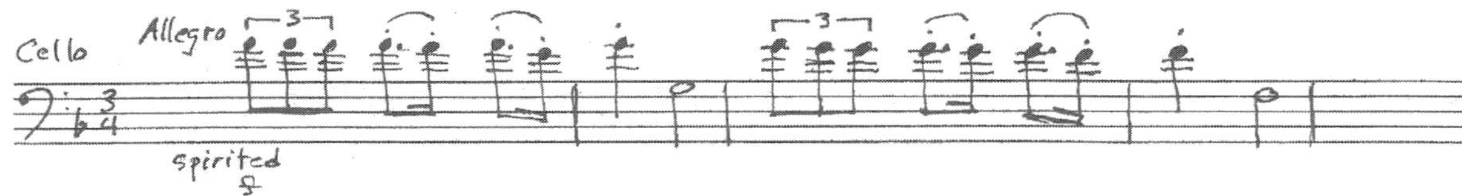


**Excerpt 3** *Off-Leash*, **first four bars**

## *Off-Leash* Metaphor

I have had three wonderful dogs, all of whom have wanted to be close to the cello while I play. Zachary, a sturdy Australian Shepherd, was the second of the three. After his death I wrote *Off-Leash* as part of the *Suite of Songs for Zachary*. The title and music represent the literal, physical-world experience of Zachary, untethered, running freely in the dog park, being tackled endlessly by the two lovely lady Aussies who seemed enamored with him. He would fall, tumble, and be up running again with them in hot pursuit. Exuberance unlimited! (Until time to be back on the leash.) This was the literal experience of Zachary off-leash.

But I also had in mind the metaphorical meaning, that having died he was now free from the limitations of the body, truly unlimited. This metaphor presupposes that there is some essence of a being that survives bodily death and is now unrestricted by physical universe laws. I don't *know* that this is true, and it doesn't matter whether I know. It is true or it isn't, and as I have said before what I think won't change what is. But I chose to believe it to be true as I was writing this piece, and so when I play it I have in mind both the literal and the metaphorical meanings. I want to communicate the excitement of the physical running, and I want to communicate the joy of a being unleashed from the restraints of the physical world; yet there is the touch of sadness at leaving a loved one behind that interrupts.

Understanding that there is a metaphorical meaning, as well as the literal, changes how you will play the piece.

<><><>

**Excerpt 4** **Beethoven** *Piano Concerto No. 4*, **beginning of the second movement**

## Beethoven Metaphor

The extraordinary second movement from the Beethoven *Piano Concerto No. 4* provides an instance where the music enables you to understand forces and principles in life. Here we have the orchestral introductory theme, full of bluster and fury, played loudly, forcefully, with great energy and aggressive articulation. After five bars of this the piano comes in with the most serene, molto cantabile, quiet melodic line. The orchestra enters again with more sound and fury; the piano answers pianissimo, totally unperturbed by the bluster. The orchestra continues to interrupt with interruptions coming ever more quickly, but by the eighth orchestral interruption it is the orchestra that has been worn down, and is worn down further until reaching a pianissimo dynamic. Then the interruptions cease altogether and the piano continues on against a silent backdrop. Throughout all of this the piano line never wavers in its unperturbed, steady flow of serenity. It takes a true artist to have the patience to follow Beethoven's markings and maintain the pianissimo (without the high *G* downbeat in bar 47 sticking out[34]) until the bar of trills, when the music then crescendos mightily to a fortissimo.

What a powerful metaphor this can be! If only we humans could behave thus in the face of aggression and force. If only we were not changed by those things! If instead, we could maintain the steady, quiet flow of love. Those who do, we generally label saints. And it is those beings whose love endures thus, unchanged in the face of great wrongs, whose impact on humanity endures.

There are metaphors with nature too, like the small persistent stream of water that eventually wears down hard rock and leaves its imprint. Persistence in a quiet, loving way overcomes force. My neighbor, whose background is in physics and hydrology, likens this Beethoven movement to 50,000 or 60,000 years in geologic time where the gentle stream eventually becomes the roaring cataract canyon that then in many more thousands of years is filled in with sand and the raging river is once again a gentle stream. It is like the adage: the pen is mightier than the sword. This movement encompasses all that. It is *must* listening. But not every pianist proves to be imperturbable. Listen for the ones who are.

---

[34] Examine the score, which you can find online at www.imslp.org

**Exercise 6.**

**Purpose: to become comfortable with creating mental images appropriate to the music**

1. Create some metaphors or similes or images for music you know well (half a dozen at least), then try playing the music with that metaphor in mind. Make sure you have some variety in the type of music you select. Remember: the metaphor contains the information you need to evoke a particular energy or emotion.

2. Now try the reverse. Get an image in mind and then find music that suits the image. This is great preparation for improvising.

3. As you encounter new music consider if there are images, metaphors, or stories appropriate to the music.

> **Tip**: Often, finding the right metaphor (right for you) will bring greater technical ease to your playing and even vanquish technical issues, as it did for me in the Schumann.

*"What is the heart? It is not human, and it is not imaginary.*
*I call it you."*
—Rumi
(translated by Coleman Barks in *The Glance*)


### MUSINGS ON THE METAPHORICAL HEART

I have used the word "heart," and the phrase "playing from the heart," assuming that you, the reader, have understood from the beginning of this manual that I am not referring to the physical organ, but to something non-physical: the metaphorical heart. It is possible however that there is a closer relationship between the two 'hearts' than we typically think. Current scientific studies indicate that the electromagnetic field of the physical heart may be more powerful than that of the brain. That is, the feelings we associate with 'heart' coincide with frequencies produced by the physical heart that are stronger than brain frequencies. They can therefore influence brain wave frequencies to go into resonance with the heart and associated feelings.[35] Perhaps our metaphorical meanings and uses of the word 'heart' are more closely tied to the physical than is commonly acknowledged.

Non-physical meanings of 'heart' are frequently used. For example: There's no heart in her playing; She knows the poem by heart (already two very different meanings); He lost his heart to her; I have no heart for this battle. Most people have a pretty good idea of what is meant by each of these uses, but it is worth exploring this word more fully. In my favored 1954 dictionary the definitions of heart take up an entire twelve-inch, small-print column. Most of the space is given over to the non-physical definitions, such as: "vital part, secret meaning, real intention," or "the seat of life or strength," or "the seat of spiritual or conscious life," or "the emotional as distinguished from the intellectual nature." From *Webster's New Collegiate Dictionary*, 1960 edition we have: "the inmost or most essential part of any body or system." From the 1970 *Webster's New World Dictionary*, Second College Edition: "the central, vital, or main part; real meaning; essence; core."

In this manual the word "heart" refers to your deepest, innermost self, the "you of yous" in George Pocock's words. It is the part of you that reflects the light of the Divine, the part that remains when you take away the ego. The part of you that is not limited in the love that can be felt. This heart is a portal—an opening to something vaster, to the infinite, to the realm of the unseen, to the part of you that is vast beyond measure. Certainly it is the conduit between spirit and your consciousness and it can be opened or closed just as the wings of a butterfly can be. It can be dull and non-reflective of love, or it can be polished and reflective of something greater than you. The quote on the next page from the *Qur'an*,[36] captures the magnitude of what is meant by heart.

Do any of these definitions resonate with you? Do you recognize something in yourself that you would call heart? *That* is what you need to cultivate, nourish, treasure.

---

[35] The HeartMath Institute has been researching and documenting this. Their website is www.heartmath.org
[36] The holy book of Islam.

## ON THE UNSEEN

Spirit, resonance, fields, metaphors, heart, these are all part of our unseen universe, yet they can be felt, and perceived through the effect they have on us in the manifest universe. Ask yourself: how much of my world is unseen? Have you thought about that before? The point here is to ask questions and be open to possibilities beyond what you have previously accepted. There are always more questions than answers, and the more questions you ask the deeper you will go into your music-making.

Studies of these phenomena have not been as robust in the United States as in Europe and Asia, though recently there is more interest in both studying and denying the existence of such things. The biologist Bruce Lipton, for example has been making waves, with his book *The Biology of Belief*. (Did you notice the metaphor *making waves*?) The idea of fields however is not new. The 19th- century scientist Michael Faraday extensively studied electromagnetic fields and postulated that there had to be some unseen organizing force behind the pure matter (meaning energy only), which then takes on form and mass in the physical realm.

According to Faraday, Sheldrake, Massimo Citro,[37] and others, it is this unseen organizing force (morphogenetic field in Sheldrake's terminology) that accounts for an arm becoming an arm and a leg becoming a leg even though they contain the same proteins encoded in the same genes. Perhaps it is why people who have lost a limb have the experience of the arm or leg still being there and can have sensations including pain in the missing limb (phantom pain). It is clear that there is a field that organizes development in the physical world, and that it is always there. What isn't clear, is how. But it is only a matter of time until these fields are thoroughly understood, as scientists constantly are developing new tools with which to record and understand more of the workings of the unseen world.

---

[37] Italian doctor Massimo Citro has written a book *The Basic Code of the Universe* that both documents and speculates on much of the work and research done on fields. Reviewer Marc J. Seifer, Ph.D said: "This is the kind of book that gets the mental wheels to spin…" I encourage you to read it.

**Exercise 7.**

**Purpose: To examine *your* thoughts and responses**

Did you think about how much of your world is unseen? Did you ask other questions of yourself?

What thoughts have you come up with about the nature of heart, soul, and spirit? Is heart the same as soul or spirit? If you think not, can you describe or feel a difference? Is it possible that what some call *soul* might be the field that organizes humans in physical form? Or that perhaps this field is an intermediary between the body and something else that might be soul or *spirit*? Perhaps soul is a meaningless term for you? How do the definitions of spirit relate to these ideas? And *heart*? Might any of them refer to fields? Some philosophers refer to the unformed energy in the universe, what scientists have called "pure matter," as spirit. What are your thoughts? If some of your responses feel quite rigid, consider whether you are willing to set your certainty aside and entertain the possibility that the definitions I have given might be useful.

I have suggested that metaphors also constitute a field of some sort, perhaps akin to that of archetypes, one that can be tapped into. What did Maestro Abravanel's metaphor of a knife stab through the heart create in your world? Was there a body sensation, an emotion, a mental concept, a gestalt created in your unseen world? How similar might that be to the field created in another's mind by this metaphor? Have you noticed how much of your speech is made up of metaphors?

What about your resonance with various periods of music, or periods in history? What kind of music do you most resonate with? Is it Baroque, Romantic, Classical, Modern, Contemporary, Jazz, Indian, Middle Eastern, something else?  Why do you think this is? Does the *why* matter? Might it be enough to simply notice what is? What else in life have you found that you resonate with?

In your examination of your thoughts don't be limited by my suggestions. Your thoughts can travel anywhere. They are part of the unseen world.

**Figure 4**

## MEANDERINGS (from the mind)

It is worth looking in greater depth at Strauss' comment about Piatigorsky and *Don Quixote*. No matter how carefully Strauss wrote down his tone poem in the language of music—symbols on a page—it was impossible for him to capture or represent in these symbols the totality of the character of Don Quixote as envisioned in his own mind. Yet Piatigorsky captured his vision. How does this happen? Resonance between fields makes this possible. Strauss' vision constitutes a field of some sort and Piatigorsky tapped into that field. Likewise Zara Nelsova was able to tap into the field created by Ernst Bloch with his Hebraic-themed music, such as *Schelomo*. He said about her: "Zara Nelsova *is* my music." High praise from a composer.

Consider an analogous situation that you probably have experienced many times. When you read an engaging book you construct a mental image, a rather complex idea, of a character. If you then see a movie based on the book does the movie depiction of the character generally match your mental image? Not too often, I suspect. Resonance is not automatic between different minds. Do you think one vision may be closer to the creator's field, more in resonance?

As a child I was enamored with the *Black Stallion* series of books by Walter Farley. Aside from *the Black,* as the horse was known, the teenage boy Alec is the main character and he became quite real to me, as real as any of my friends. My images created a morphic field. Having so loved these books, as an adult I *had* to see the movie that was made in 1979 based on *The Black Stallion*. I was horrified! They got Alec all wrong! I was sure that the movie depiction of Alec would have equally horrified the author, but I never got to ask him. My mind and those of the screenwriters and director had the same information to work with. Why such contrasting results?

All languages are limited and are incapable of capturing the subtleties and the gestalt of an artistic creation. Each of us forms a concept of the original creation through the interaction of our fields with the fields behind the created work. It is most unlikely that any of the resulting interpretations will be the same or identical to the creator's; however the greater the resonance between these fields the closer we will come to the creator's vision. How then do you consciously set about tapping into an artist's field, resonating with their creation?[38] There is of course always information to start from, whether it is words, notes or images, but it is never strictly through the analytical mind that we arrive at resonance; often the analytical mind tends to get uncomfortable when dealing with the unseen world. What then?

Until we have more understanding of what we are dealing with we rely to a great extent on what is called intuition… which reminds me of a story.

---

[38] We will talk about this in Act V Singing *Your* Song.

A preeminent, now retired, water law and natural resources lawyer, Owen Olpin, gave a talk on water rights issues in western states. Olpin is a wonderful teacher and storyteller with a great sense of humor. He started his lecture by 'deputizing' all of us in the audience as Supreme Court Justices, and then he gave us a water case to adjudicate. He 'trained' us to be judges with the following story, which may or may not be apocryphal. (Olpin claims it is true.) An ordinary, legally untrained citizen was pressed into service as a judge in the absence of a properly appointed and qualified person. Naturally this citizen was reluctant and nervous about taking on such a serious responsibility. He was given the following advice by an experienced judge who told him: It's simple. You listen carefully to both sides, gather all the facts you can, and then you follow your gut instincts about what is fair and decide according to that. Your instinct for fairness will be correct virtually all the time. But whatever you do, do not say how you arrived at the decision and why it is correct! That's for the lawyers to figure out. (There's that "lawyer mind" I referred to back between the two Preludes.)

It is for the scientists to figure out these unseen things discussed in this Act, but in the meantime we make use of them.

Before we go play in the unseen world there are some practical matters to talk about next.

> *"Logic will get you from A to B.*
> *Imagination will take you everywhere."*
> —Albert Einstein

# ACT II

## Practical Underpinnings for Making Music

### The P Words

# P x 3 = THE THREE PART THEME

The three "Ps" could stand for patience, patience, patience or, as the concierge answered the tourist who asked, "How do you get to Carnegie Hall?" "Practice, practice, practice!" There are many "p" words that could fit this section heading, but for now let's look at your pre-playing preparation: the things that need to happen prior to lifting the instrument.


*"By failing to prepare, you are preparing to fail."*
—Benjamin Franklin (1706-1790), American inventor, statesman, scientist


## PRACTICE—the right understanding

If you have any aspirations to improve as a musician, then you know that you have to practice, but have you ever looked up the word Practice to understand all its meanings? I capitalized the word "Practice" because what it represents should be regarded with reverence, not dread, so let us look at various meanings of the word—meanings that will make it deserve a capital P and make it conjure up a sense of appreciation and reverence rather than obligation, pleasure rather than punishment (hmm, more "p" words).

Practice (noun)[39] 1. Actual performance or application of knowledge.  2. Repeated or customary action; usage; habit; as the practice of rising early.  3. Usual mode or method of doing something.  4. Stratagem; a scheme; plot.  5. Systemic exercise for instruction or discipline.  6. The exercise of any profession or occupation.

Practice (verb)[40] 1. To do, perform, carry on, or exercise, especially often or habitually. 2. To perform or work at repeatedly; to acquire proficiency (*the definition normally connected with music*). 3. To follow or work at, as a profession; as, to practice law. 4. To train, drill.

Definition 1 as a noun is pertinent to *how* you practice. Practice is an application of knowledge. Practice is not just repeating something endlessly. There are two things here: knowledge and the application of it. In the field of performance one is worthless without the other. You need musical knowledge, which requires study away from the instrument. If you then practice without applying that knowledge—just mindlessly going through the notes—you are wasting your time. You might as well leave the practice room and go have fun.[41] Knowledge has little value if it just sits in your head and never reaches the physical world through your body and the sounds coming from your instrument.

Consider these usages: You practice, not the law, but music; Your Practice is music. Just as Buddhists or Catholics have certain practices, from now on your practice is music (or at least one of your practices). Consider the words of Hazrat Inayat Khan that music *is* a spiritual practice, and that it can elevate a human beyond any other practice. He thought that someday music will be the universal religion just as it is a universal language. You are a Practitioner of Music. Choose to have awe for the magnitude and importance of your Practice.

---

[39]*Webster's New Collegiate Dictionary.*
[40] Ibid
[41] See the following *Musing.*

*"A bird does not sing because it has an answer,*
*it sings because it has a song."*
—Maya Angelou (1928-1980)
American poet

## MUSINGS ON WORK vs. FUN

I often use the word "Work" in the same sense as Practice, as in "music is my Work"—not just my profession.

Shortly after I moved to this rural area, which never ceases to stun me with its beauty, a fine though inexperienced young violinist asked if I would like to get together to play through some music "just for fun." My spontaneous response was, "I don't play for fun." That sounded strange, and it wasn't until she began studying with me that I had the opportunity to adequately explain what I meant.

Music is not what I do for fun. If I want fun I might play pickleball[42] with friends, watch a movie or throw the ball for my dog, whose joy is quite contagious. (That would be resonance.) Music is my life's Work; it's my passion; it's my Practice; it's not amusement; it is not for relaxation; it is not my entertainment; it is not background for something else. It is a way of life, sometimes it is my solace, sometimes my meditation. It was what got me through a time of terrible physical pain and illness. But when I practice, or perform, that activity gets my full attention and my greatest involvement—nothing less than one hundred per cent. That doesn't make it 'serious'[43] in the sense of heavy, dire energy. There is great joy in the Work; nevertheless it is not what I do for fun. Fun is a different level of attention and involvement. It is of the outer world. Music is of the inner world.

---

[42] A fairly new sport, a very active but not physically debilitating one, which can be played by all age groups. Try it—it's great.
[43] 'Serious' is a state that usually includes worry, and unnecessary effort.

## PRESENCE—the mental preparation

What you habitually do in practice is probably what you will do in performance. Mere repetition does not make something perfect, rather it makes it permanent. You get more of what you practice, not only on your instrument but in all of life. If you practice seeing people as being unfriendly you will encounter more and more unfriendly people. If you practice a mistake over and over, you will become good at making that mistake.[44] If you practice with a distracted mind or with tension or with a closed heart[45] that is what you will get more of, including during performances. So, before you begin playing you want to be sure to show up. By that I mean: be present, be centered, have all your attention free for what you are going to do, be in the 'now,' be mindful, be mentally where you are physically, have a calm mind and body.

Choose your word or phrase that best communicates this concept of presence, and find a technique to realize it if you don't already have one. Perhaps you meditate or will learn some form of meditation[46] to enhance your practice and performance. Perhaps you become present by just sitting there with your instrument, feeling the instrument in your hands, feeling the floor beneath your feet, your behind[47] on the chair, feeling your breath going in and out, or hearing the sounds in the room or hall without mentally commenting on them. Perhaps you will include a few minutes of deep breathing. Check in with your body and notice what's happening internally. Just noticing is usually enough to let any tension go. 'Working' at letting it go doesn't work.[48]

Without your presence any practicing you do will be wasted effort and probably detrimental. I wasted many hours of practice as a child because I practiced while surreptitiously reading a book I had on my music stand. Not only can I not remember the books, but my scales certainly didn't improve. The need for presence also applies to the physical body warm-up procedure you will use and is one reason I like the Feldenkrais approach.[49] It requires your presence and awareness. Those times when you're just not able to become present, go take a walk or do something lighthearted, something that makes you smile.

As you regularly practice becoming present before playing, presence will become the state you associate with playing, and it will become easier and quicker to attain. Presence is also part of what your audience needs to sense coming from you. Like most things it is a skill that can be learned—a vital one. Great artists all have a commanding presence; you can too.

If this preparation becomes a regular part of your practice session you will get to the point where you *can* become fully present in moments. There are times when you may have only a few brief moments to achieve this state, as the story that follows demonstrates.

---

[44] Albert Einstein defined insanity as "doing the same thing over and over again and expecting different results."

[45] A closed heart will feel emotionally and physically contracted, unloving, cold, critical, disconnected, at odds with life and other people.

[46] For our purposes meditation means bringing your mind to a quiet place—a still point—thereby leaving space for inspiration to enter.

[47] See Ray Conrad's poem page 69.

[48] One of the simplest and most effective ways of becoming present is through what is called *Intentional Resting*. Check it out at www. intentionalresting.com

[49] More on this under The Physical Preparation, page 72.

*"I am always doing that which I cannot do,
in order that I may learn how to do it."*
—Pablo Picasso (1881-1973)
Spanish painter, sculptor


### *La Valse:* **A Story**

In concert, just prior to the downbeat of Ravel's magnificent waltz, my *C* string slipped and snapped off the peg. Had I been the principal cellist I would have walked off-stage to re-thread the string and tune it in the relative privacy of the stage wings, and the conductor would probably have waited. That not being the case, the music proceeded without me.

And there I was, sitting at the edge of the stage closest to the audience, fumbling to get the string threaded through the small hole that I couldn't even see, given that the focal point of my eyeglasses was not inches away but feet away (the distance to the music being shared with my stand partner). The peg was entirely a blur. Feeling way too many eyes on me it seemed forever before I got the string threaded and properly wound. It wasn't forever, but we were a substantial way into the piece before I accomplished this and had the string more or less in tune. I took a moment to then center myself and orient to the music before beginning to play. Fortunately that near infinitesimal moment was adequate to become present and be able to compensate for the not-quite-right tuning of the *C* string, and to play as if a breath earlier I hadn't felt like a lone fish on display in a goldfish bowl.

There are many stories of renowned musicians who have had distressing or humorous things happen on stage in the middle of the music, including serious memory slips and clothing disasters, bringing everything to a halt. (Nelsova told me of one such disaster when she was offering me one of her voluminous gowns, which were her trademark. I won't share it here—sorry.) Those who have cultivated the art of being present deal with such events with great aplomb. One famous pianist, when a memory slip brought her playing to a halt, simply turned to the audience and said, "Pardon me. These things happen sometimes." And began again, playing even more beautifully.

Such things *do* happen. Be prepared!  Make presence a part of your Practice. When you maintain presence, the audience will remain unperturbed.

### ***Behind In My Work***

*My sermon for today considers cats, and where they lurk.*

*Mostly they do lurkage in the spot you want to work.*

*Like, on your desk, among your high priority transactions.*

*That's where any normal kitty will concentrate his actions.*

*You have to make the mortgage payments or you lose the house!*

*Kitty has the check now, thanks, pretending it's a mouse.*

*Perhaps you need some postage stamps to mail the check away with!*

*Good luck! Those stamps are just the thing the kitty wants to play with.*

*As for the only pen you have, all rollable and messable,*

*Kitty, in a New York minute, makes it inaccessible.*

*Cats are soft and sweet, but it is sometimes hard to focus,*

*When the document you need is hidden under kitty's tocus.*

*And if you have a box of stuff to search in for a minute,*

*There just ain't no doubt that there will be a cat-butt in it.*

*Papers don't just disappear. Things like that don't happen.*

*Where the paper is is under where the kitty's nappin'.*

*So if there's something urgent that you really have to find,*

*Don't get all distracted. Look under the cat's behind.*

Ray Conrad
2004

I had to include my friend Ray's poem, with his permission, just in case you were feeling too serious.[50] He plays various instruments by ear, paints, and writes cowboy poetry. This poem is included in his book *Fence Lines* (2009).

---

[50] Another book to read for a bit of diversion is *An Exaltation of Larks* by James Lipton. This title and my made-up expression in the Acknowledgements ('an embarrassment of errors') are examples of collective nouns. In the 15th century these expressions were known as *Terms of Venery* and applied mostly to animals: "a lepe of leopards," "a parliament of owls," "a swarm of bees." Lipton has made up many of his own including: "a parenthesis of cellists." You and your friends might come up with some.

### MUSINGS ON AN OPEN HEART

The pre-requisite for having an open heart is presence. The two can seem synonymous, however it is quite possible to be present without an open heart. A mugger, for instance, might be incredibly focused in the present moment, but only a closed heart would allow him to harm you. Whereas when you are admiring a beautiful mountain scene you are present, or you wouldn't notice the surroundings, and you are open-hearted, as admiration requires openness. You will be cultivating these two states in tandem, along with awareness.

An open heart is that feeling-state you have when you experience gratitude, love, or compassion. It is what you feel when you look at a sleeping puppy or baby. It is what you feel when you listen to great music-making, or breathe in the crisp, clean, deep blue air on a beautiful desert morning. It is what you feel when you grieve the death of a dear friend or the death of the dolphins in a polluted ocean. It is the longing in our hearts that keeps us striving for something we can never quite name.

You want to be playing to listeners whose hearts are open or will be opened by your music. For this to happen you too need to be in that *space* or place of open-heartedness. Space is a good word because it contains the implication of expansiveness. An open heart does feel expansive and helps the body to be that way as well. More on this in Act III.

Your heart will not be open if you are fearful, tense, distracted, caught up in thoughts and emotions of the past or the future, or are busy judging how you are doing. That is why being present is the first prerequisite. I help myself get into an open-hearted place through a variety of ways. Sometimes I just say to myself, "yes, yes, yes, yes," until that affirmation opens my heart. Perhaps I will think of someone I truly love, or feel the presence of my dog lying at my feet eagerly anticipating the first wonderful vibration of the instrument. I want my heart to be smiling before I begin playing. Find what makes your heart smile, and make that part of your Practice.

**Exercise 8.**

**Purpose: to be able to become present quickly in an open-hearted state**

Find a technique that works for you to become present and open-hearted. You will be going back and forth between a closed-hearted state[51] and an open-hearted state until you can readily feel the difference and consciously put yourself in either.

Because we are likely to spend much of our time in a closed-hearted state, that will probably be the condition most familiar and easiest to deliberately create. First, exaggerate this consciously, making yourself feel more and more unloving, before trying to change anything. Focusing on things you dislike, repeating to yourself "NO, NO, NO..." or remembering unpleasant incidents, will all tend to put you in a closed-hearted condition. Amplify that as much as possible. Notice what your body feels like in this state. (Of course as soon as you notice, the noticing will bring you back to the present.) Now do the reverse: think of what you like or love, say "YES, YES, YES..." or remember a moment of exhilaration. Continue this until you feel a shift. Notice how your body is now, how it feels.

Now try approaching this from the physical side. Tighten your body and see what that does to the sense you have of being in your heart. Slump over and see what effect that has. Lift your chest. What does that do? Focus your eyes on something very close. Change that focus to a distant object. Play in these various postures and notice differences.

Keeping your head upright instead of hunching over the cello and burying your head in the strings will make it easier to maintain an open heart. It also allows you to hear with greater objectivity and to play with less effort. You play to the audience not the fingerboard. You want to include your audience in your heart space and that tends not to happen when you exclude them on the physical level. Use your eyes to encompass the entire hall and extend yourself into it, permeate it, hold the audience in your heart. We are integrated beings—body, heart, mind, emotions. What you do on one level permeates the whole.

Challenge yourself to achieve a level of presence and open-heartedness where *you* determine how you respond to the audience, rather than being the puppet whose strings are pulled by every stray thought or emotion or sound from the audience, without conscious choice. This skill applies to all aspects of life, and thoroughly developing it puts you in the position of being causative so that you respond to life rather than reacting—a significant difference. Though there may be deep psychological issues interfering with this ability, it is surprising what can be achieved just by doing drills like this. Knowing that you can be the puppet master, not the puppet, is a starting point.

You can harness these energies or states without full understanding of the phenomena, just as we have long used the power of electricity without full understanding of this invisible force. As you no doubt know, if you have ever received a shock from an electrical device, it too can be experienced without any understanding.

Practice presence!

---

[51] Refer back to footnote 45 on page 67.

## THE PHYSICAL PREPARATION

On the physical level before you ever set foot on stage or go into your practice studio there is a very crucial "p" to deal with. If you are going to be on stage for any length of time without a break, such as for a performance of a Mahler symphony, you will want to include this "p" in your pre-playing preparation. (You'll be sorry if you don't.) Equally important are the warm-up stretches or movements you do before you enter the room or hall. There are many good sources of information to help musicians prevent playing-related injuries. Don't wait until you hurt to address this aspect of your physical well-being. Find a routine that works for you. I prefer the *Feldenkrais Awareness through Movement* approach to ready myself to play, primarily because these movements emphasize the awareness skills we need, and it is a gentle approach. Unlike as can happen with other techniques, in utilizing the Feldenkrais principles you will never hurt yourself by overdoing a stretch your body isn't ready for. The saying: "no pain, no gain" is not appropriate for musicians. Rather go with Moshe Feldenkrais' principle that if there is strain, there is no gain.[52]

Essentially, you want to eliminate the potential for unpleasant body sensations distracting you from your purpose. Your body is one of the tools you will be using to make music. It is the interface between what you create in your mind and the instrument you play. Care for your body please, as you would the cello or other instrument that you use. Your body is your manifestation in the physical world, the only one you have, and (trust me) after-market replacement parts are not as good as 'original issue.'

After these initial preparations, you are ready to play the instrument.

---

[52] A good YouTube video for more information on this approach is at https://www.youtube.com/watch?v=-GD28QBKyNU
Another video more specific to musicians is at https://www.youtube.com/watch?v=00aUXpLCZ9c

## AS YOU WALK ON STAGE

Part of your permanent Practice as you walk into your 'hall'—your special space devoted to music—or actually on stage for a performance, whether the first or hundredth time, is to remind yourself why you play and what your purpose is. Remind yourself of your longing to bring beautiful music to your listeners, to 'the best' in everyone, and your desire to open and touch their hearts. Include the entire space of the hall, or room, within your awareness. Fill the space with the unique energy of who you are, your gratitude, and the appreciation you have for this priceless opportunity to create beauty. Know that there is nothing more precious. And do not wait until you are in the performance venue to practice this! Make it part of your pre-playing preparation.

# ACT III

## Connecting the Seen with the Unseen
## (the practical and the philosophical)

### The 'E' Words, 'C' Words and More

# EXECELLENCE
## —THEME A

There are one or two threads—interrelated qualities or attributes—that run throughout each theme of this Act. Like a fine weaving, if you remove one of them the fabric, the whole, falls apart. Look for them.

**Figure 5**

## EFFORTLESS EXCELLENCE

In referring to technical excellence and effortless excellence in the Overture, I intentionally did not use the phrase *mastering your instrument*, because the verb *to master* carries connotations of dominance and subjugation, which do not belong in the field of music. The concept of excellence is more useful. It implies wholeness and a high level. A synonym for excellence is worthy.

Effortless excellence means the comfortable technical proficiency adequate to express the musical content.[53] When you have achieved this necessary excellence you are worthy of entering the arena of music-making. This level of proficiency is, as my colleague Kay puts it, *the price of admission*. The work to acquire adequate tools has to be done. *Now*, the music can begin. Nothing in the way of inadequacies should distract your listener from receiving the content of the music. I assume you have paid the price of admission, or are doing so, and will continue with this aspect of playing the instrument. But, as I have said, the technique of playing the instrument is not the focus of this manual.

What is generally thought of as technique can of course be so stunning that it alone can take someone's breath away, convince the listener that he or she is listening to a genius with capabilities beyond what's normally considered human. If one attains *that* level of technical excellence it could be tempting to stop there; after all a very high price has been paid. Unfortunately (or fortunately for the sake of this manual) I have never been faced with that dilemma, nor are most of us who desire to make music.

But music-making doesn't happen if you are struggling to play the notes, or if there is unnecessary effort (tension, rigidity) in your movements and body. Excess effort kills awareness, kills physical ease, kills joy, kills excellence. Unnecessary effort will be noticed by those listening and will override what you intend to communicate.

---

[53] The playing of pianist Artur Rubenstein is the zenith of effortless excellence. Watch a YouTube video of him playing the Brahms *Piano Concerto No. 1* and you will see and hear effortlessness in action. The music quote above is the beginning of the first theme as played by the violins and cellos in the opening tutti of the Brahms.

My friend Carol, one of the people who helped me through the various injuries that put a stop to my playing at times, is a practitioner of the work of Moshe Feldenkrais.[54] What follows is one of his pertinent teaching stories as related by her, commonly known as the bird turd principle:[55] If you are carrying a heavy stack of books and bird poop lands on the top book, your physical effort will be such that you won't be aware of the added weight; on the other hand, if you are carrying a thin piece of paper the effort needed to do this is so minimal that if bird poop happens to fall from the sky onto the paper, you *will* notice the added weight, not just the impact.

In other words awareness and sensitivity are in inverse relationship to the effort used. More effort equals less awareness. Less effort equals increased awareness. Applying this to our art, awareness decreases when there is more effort and tension in your body than is actually required to make the needed movements. When you're tense, it is more difficult to hear what is really happening with your intonation and quality of sound; your perception of bow contact will be diminished, and the presence needed to create will be lacking.

---

[54] Check out her website for additional information on the *Feldenkrais Method* and related approaches: www.carollessinger.com

[55] More properly this is referred to as The Weber-Fechner law, resulting from the research in the 1800s by Ernst Heinrich Weber and Gustav Theodor Fechner.

*"If people would only do what they think they are doing,*
*the world would be a better place."*
—Moshe Feldenkrais (1904-1984)
Israeli physicist and founder of the *Feldenkrais Method*


**AWARENESS**

I encourage you to read the book *The Brain's Way of Healing: Remarkable Discoveries and Recoveries from the Frontier of Neuroplasticity* by Norman Doidge, with particular attention to Chapter Five. In this chapter he discusses the work of Moshe Feldenkrais and how simple awareness of—just the *act of paying attention to*—what is actually happening with your body and motions can change your brain and resultant compulsive movements and patterns. In other words awareness alone can rewire your brain.

Slow, conscious, small movements, free of effort are the key to organizing your movements optimally. This is why when I begin the physical learning of the notes of a new work, or reworking something I have played before, I do so slowly, softly, and with awareness of any unnecessary effort. I want to practice effortlessness, not tension and anxiety. Beginning the physical process in this way allows me to hear far more accurately and objectively than if I practice loudly or too fast, (too fast being faster than I can play accurately at this stage in my learning process). Feldenkrais emphasized that it is when muscle tension is at the minimum actually needed that the brain is most available for learning.

> **Tip**: To fix any non-optimal movements in your playing, you first need to become aware of them, and then sometimes you may need to consciously do them until they are not compulsive—that is you now have control of those motions you have been making—then gently explore other possibilities until you find the effortlessness. Awareness and removing effort are the keys to fixing most of what we consider to be technical issues.

**Philippe Petit**

Philippe Petit (b. 1949) is a French high-wire artist (aerialist). He tells the story in his book *On the High Wire* of how he surreptitiously strung a wire between the twin towers of the World Trade Center in NYC in 1974, shortly after they were built. Not only did he walk the wire multiple times, he sat down on it, lay down on it and virtually danced on it before he walked the wire back to the north tower and jumped into the arms of the waiting police who arrested him. Fortunately a District Attorney had the good sense to get him off with the penalty of having to perform in Central Park for children. This book is quite arresting, as are some others he has written. His attitude as expressed in the following quote from *On the High Wire* captures how we want to approach our music-making: "You have to work so hard and yet you can't force it. The tendency is to want to calm (the wire) by force. In fact you must move with grace and suppleness to avoid disturbing the song of the cable."

**Exercise 9.**

**Purpose: to make levels of effort conscious and be able to change them**

You will always solidify what you practice, so if you are unconsciously practicing playing with effort, you *will* make that a part of your performance, and you *will* communicate that effort to your audience, and your awareness and sensitivity will be limited. Do not confuse effort with the emotional and physical energy needed to communicate the musical content. My piece *Protest* requires enormous emotional and physical energy, as well as physical motion, in order to communicate this feeling of protest. When I wrote it I envisioned the protest as being on the order of protesting some immense injustice; likewise that is what I feel when I play it. It is no casual thing. As is the case with *Protest*, the music you play may call for a great deal of energy; do not waste your energy on effort (unnecessary tension).

1. Take a passage that you can easily play and play it while noticing, on a scale of one to ten, what level of effort you are using. How much tension there is in your body? Note how open you feel, how much you can be aware of. Make ten the maximum effort level; make one the minimum effort needed to actually play. Play the passage with the maximum effort level; now jump around using various levels of effort: eight, three, seven, nine, two, five, etc. Get so you can do this at will. Notice what changes.

2. Take a passage you are struggling with; notice your level of effort as you play it. Increase the effort level to your maximum. This will always involve the mouth and jaw being tight as well as knee joints and every other joint. Once you can consciously use the maximum effort to play this passage, reduce it level by level, until you are at your minimum. Keep noticing, as in step one.

3. Skip around between various effort levels; then see if you can play at an even lower effort level than you reached in step two. Get really curious about this and see how high and low you can go. For string players, when you are at a minimal effort level your left hand fingers will feel rather floppy (not sloppy), with no rigid joints, and your right hand will barely be holding the bow—again no rigid joints. (Someone could easily pull the bow out of your hand even if a great deal of body weight is going into the bow through your hand. For wind players, the instrument itself could be removed from your hands.) Keep noticing.[56]

> **Tip:** Before a passage that we *consider* to be difficult, invariably we tense up. Be alert to that tendency. Instead of fearing the notes, try bringing love to them. Your body naturally relaxes and goes soft when you are coming from love. Except for you unfortunate keyboard players, instrumentalists generally play just one note at a time, and in truth there is all the time in the world to be present on that one note. Even keyboardists still just have one position of the hands in the present moment.

---

[56] Again, Rubenstein provides a worthy example. Notice how he uses his hands. The fingers aren't curled into claw-like, rigid digits. They look relaxed and floppy, with no unnecessary tension present.

*"When you are courting a nice girl an hour seems like a second. When you sit
on a red-hot cinder a second seems like an hour.
That's relativity."*
—Albert Einstein


### MUSINGS ON RELATIVITY

When you are present, time expands: an eighth of a second seems leisurely. Talk to anyone
who has raced cars about how time expands with presence and awareness. One hundred fifty
miles per hour can seem slow! You probably know this phenomenon from your own
experience in a car: after traveling for a time at seventy miles per hour that begins to feel
comfortably slow, and when you suddenly need to drop to thirty-five miles per hour it seems a
snail's pace. You think you have slowed way down, yet you are going fifty-five miles per
hour, and now there are flashing lights on the car behind you! (I hope you have been more
fortunate—or careful—than I have been.)

> **Tip**: This phenomenon is also why it is important at some stage in learning a work to
> practice music at tempos way faster than you ever intend to play in performance. The
> music then will seem easier at the slower tempo. But, when you practice faster, do not
> practice being sloppy or using greater effort. Practice with the same effortlessness you
> have been developing.
>
> We have such things as fast twitch and slow twitch fibers in our muscles, generally
> about 50% of each in the muscles used for movement. It's possible to have more of one
> type than the other, but both types need to be trained.

## EXCELLENCE, PERFECTION, AND CREATIVITY

Perfection is not the goal. The effort to be perfect will always limit the freedom to create. Excellence and perfection are not synonymous. Excellence gives you freedom to focus on the music. It is a tool you need to fulfill your purpose. Striving to play perfectly is a goal, an intention that usurps your purpose to touch the heart of the listener.

A goal of perfection traps you in the fear of making mistakes, and this will kill your *creativity* (the bringing into being of a new idea or presentation). Being obsessed with perfection is what makes playing music 'serious' as opposed to joyful. If it is your desire to play something perfectly, there will be increased tension in your body, you will be less aware and you will not take the risk to be creative. Creativity demands that your attention be in the present moment. You can't be looking backwards, as it were, at the idea of a flawless performance. You don't know the outcome in advance when you take the risk of creating anew in the present moment. Perhaps you will do a fingering you have never tried or make a crescendo where you stayed pianissimo before. Maybe you will color the emotions slightly differently than you did the previous time. You want to leave room for the inspiration of the moment, and that doesn't happen when you are trying to play perfectly.

Committed musicians must attain excellence, yet resist the siren call of perfectionism. We do walk "the razor's edge." Sometimes we fall off.

## A Vocalist's Thoughts

Here are some thoughts from another remarkable artist, soprano Renée Fleming, from her book *The Inner Voice* (pages 174-175). They are pertinent to the themes of presence, achieving excellence, and releasing creativity. "If everything is going right, there are moments in a performance when the audience is absolutely silent… I know I have reached them, and with that knowledge comes freedom, the absolute freedom to go where my imagination leads me. That is the goal, the purpose of all those years spent working to develop a strong technique. Freedom means that I'm able to be spontaneous with a phrase… The more skill I have, the more I can trust my voice; and the more I trust my voice, the more risks I am willing to take… Because these are moments of inspiration, they are ephemeral, and the next performance will never be exactly the same."

What singers go through to achieve excellence with both the instrument and the music they sing is so complex that it is not surprising that teachers of other instruments advise their students to listen to singers. Because pianists are at a distinct disadvantage in not being able to change the quality of a note once it has been sounded, they particularly benefit from this listening to all the ways that lines and phrases can be created. My sister studied with a number of noted pianists, and she tells me that they all advised her so. I encourage you to immerse yourself in the art of singing. Listen to as many recordings as you can find of great artists from the past as well as current favorites. Make use of all the internet tools to hear them, watch them, listen to their master classes and read their books.

### *MUSINGS ON CREATIVITY*

Creative expression is essential to life; perfection isn't. Creativity is really the energy of who and what you are. If you are alive you can't *not* create. And it isn't just about being an artist. We express this fundamental attribute in different ways. One person may write poetry, another arrange flowers or create a beautiful garden, another may create a beautiful relationship, or a weaving. But not all the results of our innate ability to create are beautiful. It's equally possible to create an ugly relationship or destructive music. Everything we bring about in the outer world is a result of our creativity, including what will be your unique understanding of a musical work.

If you have ever been told that you aren't creative, or you think you aren't, it's time to know: *it's a lie!*

Return to your journal and Exercise 2, page 37. Add any beliefs about creativity that you didn't document before: creativity in general, your creativity, what you've been told about your creativity that you might have believed, and other thoughts that come up on the subject. In Act V there is an exercise providing additional tools for letting go of or replacing any beliefs that don't serve you well. For now simply note down the ones you can spot.

## CONTROL, COHERENCE, CONGRUENCE

By "control" I refer to that fine-tuned use of your physical body in conjunction with the body of the instrument that allows you to reach excellence, the way Philippe Petit did as an aerialist. The synonym "guiding" gives a useful sense of what control is. Control is not the same as domination, which is *imposing* your intent or will on something else, as in the concepts of master and mastery previously mentioned. Having control over what you are doing simply means that your body and instrument are carrying out your exact intention, and that you are not at odds within yourself, i.e. you have coherence, congruence.[57] *No* control would be a situation where you intend one thing and something else happens. For example, you wish to pick up a glass of water and instead your hand goes to the salt shaker, or knocks the water over. This isn't bad control; it is lack of control—no control—and lack of awareness.

Control is free of unnecessary effort. When there is more effort than needed, the result is lack of control, and you will be neither congruent nor coherent. At times you worry so much over a difficult passage that you attempt to do it with force—domination rather than control. The results are rarely pleasing or musical. Your body is tense, you can't move your fingers as fast, can't hear as well, etc. If you are an aerialist, the wire may very well dump you.

Refer back to Ivan Galamian's definition of technical proficiency that I quoted on page 8 and compare that to the concept expressed by the Sufi teacher Hazrat Inayat Khan: "Our mind governs the body; our mind should have every muscle, each atom of the body, under its command. When we move upward, all must come up; when we turn to the right, all must turn to the right; when we turn to the left, all must turn to the left." He spoke these words in reference to dance, but it is a wonderful description of the congruence needed for true control in any activity.

---

[57] Coherence: a sticking together, cohesion, consistency
Congruence: in harmony, in agreement, consistency, correspondence between things

The desire for perfection is at odds with the trust you need in yourself to do what you intend. When that conflict arises do your best to let go of this impulse to dominate the passage, and allow your intentions to happen, without laboring (efforting) to get it right. Quit trying,[58] cease thinking about technical issues, trust that your body will do what you have trained it to do. When you let go of the conscious need to dominate every aspect of the physical and simply intend what you want, effort ceases, you relax into the music, you trust.

Consider what Renée Fleming has to say about confidence and trust: "Trust has everything to do with my ability to go onstage certain that when my mind tells my voice to do something, it's going to happen. It's hearing a phrase in the mind's ear and then knowing the body can reproduce that phrase a split second later." [59]

Once the work has been done and the effortless excellence is there, intention and trust can now do their job, which segues nicely into my other 'mystical' experience.

---

[58] Trying implies effort and lack of trust.
[59] From Fleming's book *The Inner Voice*, page 138

## A Mystical Moment with Shostakovich

Years ago I was preparing the Shostakovich *Sonata for Cello and Piano* for performance. In the last movement there is a sixteenth-note passage that didn't sound as clean as I wanted. I had used all my tricks to get it accurate at our desired tempo, but it had not reached effortless excellence. In the dress rehearsal with pianist Marilyn Mangold Garst, (my sister—my good fortune), at the very moment I began the passage the following words flashed into my mind: "*Let Me do it!*" (We receive our moments of wisdom and inspiration through different senses. Mine often come through the sound of words in my head.) I let go of something, which was replaced with trust, and the passage went flawlessly. I don't know with certainty what the "Me" in that command was, but I relaxed, allowed *it* to take over, and *it* certainly did a good job.

The entire scene was indelibly printed in my memory. As soon as I let go of the effort, awareness increased exponentially. I know exactly where I was sitting, the direction I was facing, the lighting in the room, the time of day and so on… It wasn't an experience to be sloughed off, ignored or forgotten.

I have great affinity for language and the concepts behind words, which makes language a good vehicle for information to be imparted to my consciousness. For some, information or instruction or wisdom come as bodily sensations, maybe visual images for others, or just vague impressions of something. Regardless of the means through which you receive inspiration, you want to be alert to its arrival, pay attention to and honor such messages.

### MUSINGS ON TRUST

I particularly like the word *trust*—what it represents. It has many meanings. One meaning is "to go or act without fear or misgiving." Another is "to commit or consign, as to one's care; entrust." Also, "ground of reliance."  Another usage is, "That which is committed or entrusted to one, as a duty, task, or charge." Then there is the idea of "a property interest held by one person for the benefit of another." [60]

The house in which I am privileged to live I call TrustHouse. I named it that because of three applicable definitions of the word trust: The previous owner and I trusted each other and did the sale on a handshake; The money came from a small trust that my parents left for my sister and myself after their deaths; I felt that the true legacy from our parents was a type of trust— the charge to carry out our purposes in music. Thanks in part to that financial trust my sister and I both live in locations that we love and that are suited to carrying out that charge of making music together.

As I mentioned in Act I, there was little communication in our home as we were growing up, but there was always an appreciation for and love of music and beauty. When my sister and I, as adults and professional musicians, began playing together our parents were very supportive. They were our biggest fans in fact. They helped make it possible for us to explore in concert the wonderful literature for cello and piano, for which we will always be grateful. The trust they left has allowed us to carry out the trust they charged us with, and trust in life and the universe gave me the courage to leave Salt Lake City and follow a new path.

---

[60] These definitions all come from the *Webster's New Collegiate Dictionary*.

Imagine the trust Philippe Petit must have—in himself, his tools, and even in that which can't be controlled. That level of trust doesn't happen without an open heart and awareness, as well as the needed excellence. Recall the times in your own life when you truly trusted. What qualities accompanied that trust? (Use your journal.)

Remember you get more of what you do, so make trust your companion in life. Practice, practice, practice!

## COMMUNICATION
## —THEME B

Music is communication, so we will look thoroughly at what this is and what makes it work.

*"You are not just playing the instrument in your hands, you are*
*'playing the lute that is in every heart.'"*
—Hazrat Inayat Khan

## COMMUNICATION

The verb "to communicate" is defined as: to impart; convey; to make known; to converse; to be connected; to share in common; to participate in; to bestow.[61]

Definitions of communication include: interchange of thoughts or opinions; means of passage from place to place; connecting passage.[62]

For communication to occur between humans there has to be an idea, concept, intent, or feeling that originates with one person, the desire to give or send that, and, to have it received and understood by another. This desire to give or send something takes us back to the purpose behind our music-making. We want our music to be received, and we want it to change the heart of the listener, touch the soul, in the way we intended.

There are prerequisites for successful communication, and we have already addressed some of them. Before any content can successfully be communicated there must be attention on the part of both the sender and the receiver: awareness. That means we have to 'show up'—be fully present, in all the ways discussed previously. We may not be able to control the attention of all the audience members, but by our own powerful presence we will capture the attention of most. Zara Nelsova had an immense presence on stage. She commanded the entire space in every way: how she walked on stage, her dress, her posture, her sound, the content—total congruence. There was no question that she had her audience's attention. Additionally, complete silence and stillness just before we begin to play creates the expectancy we want in our audience. (Theme C in Act IV addresses silence as an integral part of music.)

---

[61] *Webster's New International Dictionary*, Second Edition, Unabridged
[62] *Webster's New Collegiate Dictionary*

## COMMUNICATION AND CARRIER WAVES

Communication also requires a means or vehicle for transmission. Sound waves created by our voices or instruments are vibrations that travel through the air. Those physical sound waves seemingly are the vehicle to convey the content we intend to send: words with meaning if we are speaking, notes with meaning if we are playing. These are the waves produced by physical, mechanical vibrations. But there is something more: the waves we humans emit—not heard but present in every communication. Each is analogous to a carrier wave.

In physical-universe terms, a carrier wave is a high-frequency wave used in telecommunications to convey either video or audio signals. High-frequency waves are modulated by low-frequency signals in order to encode the information being broadcast. Such waves are independent of the content they carry. Any content being broadcast—whether signals for a comedy, a romance, a tragedy, or a mystery—is piggy-backing on this carrier wave.

The existence of a similarly acting wave, present in all human communications, is not commonly acknowledged. As mentioned previously, the HeartMath Institute and other researchers are doing experiments to physically document the existence of and effects of such waves. Frequencies emitted by a person, which are not part of the visible or audible spectrum, act like carrier waves. They underlie the audible sounds intentionally produced, and have an impact on the person receiving the communication, separate from the meaning of words used or sounds from our instruments. There will always be such a carrier wave involved in communication between humans.

It is the absence of that carrier wave that we sense when we listen to an electronically produced 'voice.' This inaudible wave that we knowingly or unknowingly broadcast will have the frequency of our underlying attitude or feeling, which is largely dependent on the purpose we are serving. The waves produced by such frequencies are perceptible to humans, belonging to the 'you know it when you see it' category, or in this case 'when you feel and hear it.'

In music performance the desired wave is that quality or frequency of love and open-heartedness that we have been cultivating.[63]  The frequency of our carrier wave, whether it is love or something else, will dominate the communication with an audience. If this carrier wave is something other than love—disdain for example—even the most eloquent technical execution will not prevail over the negative impact of the carrier wave. Remember Khan's words: "There is always a voice hidden in it, continually telling for what purpose the work of art was created." This is true for every type of communication, whether it be speech, music, dance, or other arts such as that of pottery or architecture.[64]

---

[63] I do not think that a recording, digital or analog, can capture the carrier wave present in a live performance. My experience is that all recordings are a bit akin to the stuffed head of a dead animal on display. The life has gone out of it; the real thing has qualities that can't be captured by ones and zeros on a computer, or by bullets and taxidermists.

[64] With architecture consider the difference you perceive between a prison and a cathedral. The hidden voice is not so hidden.

Antoine de Saint-Exupéry writes in a passage from *The Little Prince*: "'Here is my secret,' said the fox to the little prince, 'a very simple secret: It is only with the heart that one can see rightly; what is essential is invisible to the eye.'" We might say: It is only with the heart that one can play or hear rightly; What is essential is inaudible to the ear. An open heart gives and it receives; it is expansive; it reaches out and includes the other. It transmits love and that is the most powerful carrier wave.

Again quoting Hazrat Inayat Khan:[65] "The earnest feelings of one heart can pierce the heart of another; they speak in the silence, spreading out into the sphere, so that the very atmosphere of a person's presence proclaims his thoughts and emotions. The vibrations of the soul are the most powerful and far-reaching; they run like an electric current from soul to soul."

His simile of the electric current captures the concept of this carrier wave that connects performer and audience. Be aware of what your underlying carrier wave is. It will reflect your purpose for playing.

In Act IV of this manual we will talk about how to include the emotional content of the music in our communication. However the heart of the music is in our carrier wave of love. That is our 'pack animal.' It has a lot to carry; it needs to be well developed and strong and a bit stubborn, not easily knocked off the path.

---

[65] *The Mysticism of Sound and Music , The Sufi Teaching of Hazrat Inayat Khan* , 1991, pages 125-6

**Exercise 10.**

**Purpose: to understand barriers to communication**

Find someone to experiment with. If no one is available simply observe the communications that occur routinely in daily life.

1. Your responses to how others communicate to you.

    a)  Notice what happens when someone faces away from you while talking to you.
    b)  Notice how you respond or what effect has been created.
    c)  Notice what happens if someone speaks too loudly, and your response.
    d)  Notice what happens if someone speaks too softly, and your response.
    e)  Notice what happens if someone speaks to you without really being present, (when that person's attention is elsewhere), and your response.
    f)  Notice what kind of carrier wave is present, independent of the words, and what effect it creates on you.
    g)  What effect is created when someone's words are not congruent with their body language?
    h)  In any of these situations did you feel that a successful communication took place?

2.  Others' responses to you and your reactions.

    a)  What happens if someone interrupts you while you are speaking?
    b)  What happens when you speak and the other person pays no attention?
    c)  What happens if you say something and the other person does not respond in any way, neither verbally nor with body language (motion, posture)?[66]
    d)  Do you feel heard in these situations?

3. Now turn it around.

    a)  What happens when you begin to speak without first getting the listener's attention?
    b)  What happens if you begin to speak without knowing what you wish to communicate?
    c)  What happens when you face away, or speak too loudly or softly, or have your attention elsewhere?
    d)  What happens when you interrupt, or don't give the other person your attention?
    e)  What happens when your carrier wave is something other than love?
    f)  What happens when your words are not congruent with your intent and body language?
    g)  How do you feel in these situations? What do you pick up about the other person's feelings?

4. In each of these situations did you perceive that the communication was received as intended, or did it get misinterpreted?

5. Did you find that you intuitively know exactly how much effort is needed to reach another person with your communication, or is it something you need to practice?

---

[66] This is why we have the tradition of applauding a performer or speaker, even though the sound of applause breaks the mood created by the music in a very harsh and abrupt manner. Still, it is way to let performers know they have been heard.

I think this is a skill not unlike my dog's ability to know exactly where the ball is going to land; with some dogs it seems innate, others need to learn. But perhaps the more accurate analogy would be: knowing exactly how hard to throw the ball to have it land where I want, and that really starts with knowing *where* I want it to land. It's the same in the game of pickleball I might add. Knowing where you want the ball to go and then keeping your focus unwaveringly on the ball is the crux of being a good player.

> **Tip:** With communication, once your intent to reach the recipient is present, then you will tend to use just the right amount of effort to get your communication across. And, by knowing exactly the content you wish to communicate, the right words (or notes) will follow—effortlessly.

6. If you are inclined towards sports, particularly those involving throwing a ball to someone, you might experiment with throwing a ball, rather than delivering words, under the different circumstances suggested in this exercise—or imagine doing so. Our common errors in verbal communication when translated onto the ball field become glaringly obvious.

Being aware of your responses to others and their responses to you should help you to apply good communication practices to your playing. Once again, the principles hold true in both the macrocosm of life and the microcosm of music.

*"Music is always the language which permits one*
*to converse with the Beyond."*
—Robert Schumann (1810-1856)
German composer

## MUSINGS ON UNSEEN COMMUNICATIONS

There are many types of communication that are not yet understood, but which are very real and a common part of our experiences. There are the invisible communications between species, between members of a species, our carrier waves, what we term telepathic communications, etc.

Two days ago it was snowing where I live—despite being mid-May. And yesterday while I was in my study writing, I finally became aware of motion at my window. There, in our frozen landscape, was a lone hummingbird—beautiful greens, blacks and purples—hovering, virtually tapping at my window to get my attention. Its message was clear: I am back, the others are on their way, where is the food? I acknowledged it; it disappeared. I saved my work and went to the kitchen to prepare the requisite food.

So far just the one bird has been chowing down, but clearly this bird had been here before and was impatient to replenish its weight, down by half from the beginning of its migration up from Mexico. How did he know that for the food to appear he needed to make himself known to me, and how did he know where to find me?

Three weeks ago a friend—a harpist—and her young dog, Duke, were visiting. As is the case with most of my visitors she chose to hang out on the window-nook day bed—the place with the stupendous view—and watch the beautiful landscape from there. It is dog-friendly territory so both her dog and my dog Mari joined her. I wanted to read some of this manuscript to her, so I joined the pack. While reading the Carrier Wave section in order to demonstrate the concept, I sang a bit of one of my favorite cello solos, the opening of the slow movement of the Schumann *Piano Quartet in E-Flat Major*. When I sang *just the notes*, like a robot, as much as possible without that carrier wave of love, Duke ignored me, preferring to spread out over as much of the territory as possible. When I sang with an underlying carrier wave of love Duke bounded up to my face to give me a puppy kiss. In fact he was all over me with enthusiasm. We let him calm down and I went on with my reading and demonstrations. Once again I sang a passage in the two ways, and once again he responded with great enthusiasm when that vibration of love was there. Be assured that if a puppy can feel the difference, we humans can too. We just don't respond so overtly.

Think about the various communications you have observed in your life, visible and invisible. It will make it easier to understand my next two stories.


92

**A Story of Resonance: Cello Duos and Mozart**

Years ago my cellist colleague Suzanne and I did a lot of playing together, thoroughly investigating the duo literature. We found that if we *each* took the attitude that we were *each* responsible for playing both parts, everything went better—in fact more than a little better, stunningly better. From my point of view it was as if every sound that came out of both cellos was my doing; she experienced the same thing. What was at play here? Clearly we had resonance, aided by being good friends to start with, but there were other elements too. With this approach any judgments we might have had about the other's playing had to go, which then allowed the carrier wave of love to be strongly present. Awareness and visible communications (eye contact for one) were heightened, and no doubt other elements were involved.

I took this experience and applied the idea as best I could throughout my career, though usually unilaterally—I wasn't always comfortable risking being labeled weird. But once, when I was having trouble playing to my liking a solo cello line in a Mozart Quartet, I set aside my ego and asked my colleagues, who were all people of good will, to mentally play the passage with me as I played. To everyone's surprise, it went effortlessly and beautifully. The principle here is that if all involved take responsibility for creating (imaging, intending) the same thing, there is no room for judgment, ego, fear, etc., and the combined carrier waves of love can give a boost to performance capabilities. This certainly happened in the Symphony those many years with Maestro Abravanel. We were all co-creating his vision of the music. We were in resonance with the morphic field. It is like adding more horsepower to a vehicle, sending it up a hill easily.

*"In the sweetness of friendship let there be laughter, and sharing of pleasures.*
*For in the dew of little things the heart finds its morning and is refreshed."*
—Khalil Gibran (1883-1931)
Lebanese artist, writer


**MUSINGS ON RESONANCE WITH OTHERS**
*Choose carefully with whom you play!*

We don't always have a choice of course, but making music with others is a very intimate activity. You do expose your soul when you play from the heart, and it behooves you to play, when possible, with those people who won't trample on that. In her book, Fleming speaks of that exposed heart and soul as follows: "When I'm close to an audience, I feel as if I am completely open to them, and in turn, they can see me for who I really am. With my heart and soul expressed through my voice and the music, all else fades away."[67]

Unfortunately because of the competiveness in our profession, colleagues are not always as malleable as audiences. You want the best possible communication and resonance with your music partners—not necessarily the best players technically, but the players with whom you are in tune so that your hearts can soar together, like the way we soared in the cello duos and in the double kayak. It's all about recognizing the beauty in each other and in the music and saying "I love you" with music in infinitely different ways.

When this doesn't happen life can be painful! I had a most miserable experience when I failed to listen to my intuition and agreed to play in a piano trio with people and music someone else selected. It was early in my career and I desperately wanted to play the selected repertoire, and so I said yes. The violinist and I could have achieved a nice resonance, but the pianist was of a very different energy and mindset. We had an initial read-through before either the violinist or I had a chance to prepare the music (second mistake). It wasn't going well, and immediately the pianist wanted to go into detailed fixing of everything, though an overview was needed to get a sense of the work ahead of us. The pianist, who knew the pieces well, had her attention on everything being correct, now. The violinist and I weren't at that stage of excellence, and the more the pianist picked at the imperfections the worse we played, and the more critical the pianist became. We never did play the concert.

It really was a horrible experience for me, since at the time I had no real understanding about things such as resonance, spaciousness[68], and the necessity of maintaining an open heart and a carrier wave of love. I didn't understand what was happening to me and my playing. In retrospect I realized that the pianist was not coming to the group with an open heart, but rather a very judgmental attitude—a rather negative carrier wave—nor were we the people she would have chosen. We did not start as a team and didn't become one. What happened with both the violinist and me was that with every comment from the pianist our hearts closed further, and every aspect of playing got more difficult with the increased tension and need to play *perfectly*. Ideally we would have maintained presence, spaciousness, open hearts, and focus on making music, and we would have played well anyway. It just didn't happen that way. It was an important lesson.

---

[67] Page 179
[68] We will talk about that on page 101.

If you do find yourself in that type of situation, recognizing the dynamics of the situation will help you through it. Having done the exercises suggested in this manual, you will have the tools to feel, quickly, what is happening and the tools to respond as you choose, rather than unconsciously. You don't want to be a puppet as I was.

Think before you say yes. Know whether you can maintain an open heart regardless of colleagues' attitudes. If you are not ready to do that, say no.

But there was a happier outcome another time when I played in a different trio with two unchosen colleagues.

Immediately after graduating from Juilliard I had taken a job in Bogotá, Colombia, as principal cellist of the National Orchestra. One of the responsibilities accompanying the position was to play in a piano trio with the concertmaster and the orchestra pianist. Three more unlikely people for a trio would be hard to find. Ages, nationality, musical training, life experiences, all these could not have been more different.

The pianist was an older Jewish-Austrian refugee from World War II—a prodigy in her youth—her career in Europe cut short due to the necessity of escaping Hitler's persecution. The concertmaster was German-Spanish, Catholic, perhaps fifteen years younger, who as a young child had encountered near starvation growing up in those two countries and cultures during the war. He had the least formal training of the three of us and had done a lot of playing in restaurants over the years, very different music than the classical trios we were to play. Though to some extent he was self-taught he also was very good. And, he had family connections with more than one former Nazi. Then there was the young American cellist—an additional fifteen years younger—who spoke neither German nor Spanish and who had no experience of such hardships. Despite all these differences we forged the most wonderful resonance and played happily together for several years. The pianist was vastly more experienced than the violinist and myself, and knew how to guide us to become better, not worse. We truly played with open hearts and the love we shared was quite special.

The moral here is: don't make assumptions as to what can work. Trust your inner knowing, not analytical judgment as to what you think is possible. Logic would have told us that we were unsuited to each other. Shared purposes for playing music brought us together. (Rehearsal breaks with tea and pastries helped too—highly recommended for building resonance.)

In truth, the sharing of food and drink with colleagues does go a long ways towards building resonance. We used that tool over many years to create and keep a unified, friendly cello section in the Utah Symphony, taking every opportunity to party together. The tuba player once asked if he could be an honorary cello section member as we actually talked with and liked each other! Don't wait for others to initiate this sort of socializing. Be the one to bring the goodies or at least to suggest it. The idea will catch on.

When playing in an orchestra your choices are few, and you have had or will have experiences of playing with a conductor, or sitting with or close to someone, with whom you have no resonance. This can go on for years and be very distressing. If for example conductors are most concerned with their careers or the reviews, there is little likelihood of their making music from the heart. If you are in this situation, to walk away from the stage still in love with music, you must either quit or focus even more strongly on creating within your own small sphere. Maybe you can't play the dynamics or shape the line as you would like, but still you can be absolutely present and play every note with love. Other choices are disastrous to the heart, to the body, and to your playing. I have had colleagues who would intentionally play badly to demonstrate their disapproval of conductors or other players. They are not happy people. Your integrity to the music is paramount.

To end this musing on a happier note, the most precious resonance I have experienced in music-making is with my pianist sister. As I have alluded to previously we have played much music together, and I feel fortunate to have had that opportunity. Not every pianist would be willing to learn some extremely difficult piano parts, such as the Kurt Weill *Sonata* (1920), for no monetary reward. But even more important to me, is that we seem to have a built-in resonance, perhaps due to being siblings, definitely due to sharing the love of music and our many years of playing together. (This didn't just magically happen during our teen-age years.) We have often been told that we "play as one," which of course is the ideal. I owe her much gratitude.

Never miss an opportunity to feel gratitude. It's part of becoming a person in the way that Jaron Lanier spoke of in the initial quotes in the Overture.

## CONGRUENT COMMUNICATION

Before continuing on, revisit the definitions of coherence and congruence in the footnote on page 83. For maximum aesthetic effect all aspects of our being and our performance should be coherent and congruent.

We are complex creatures, not robotic machines, though certainly at times we behave that way. Our bodies are the offspring of Mother Earth, made of the elements of the physical world: minerals, water, oxygen, sunshine—no different than the bodies of other creatures with whom we share this earth. We can learn much about motion and bodily congruence from the other inhabitants: dogs for example. The motions of a dog's body are coherent with the dog's feeling-state. When a dog is happy to see you, she doesn't just bark a hello. She wags her entire body in pleasure. Every atom in her body joins in greeting you. She doesn't hold back— her head and tail are full of motion. A lion leaping to capture prey is one hundred per cent aligned physically, mentally, and energetically for a successful jump. He wouldn't survive long if he were not—certainly not long enough to reproduce. Everything in his body is focused towards the same end.

It is this way with humans as well, when we are functioning optimally. Body language *is* a part of human communication, and there is a certain amount of natural, intrinsic motion that must be allowed to happen, motion congruent with and part of the expression of emotion. Whoever saw a purportedly happy person holding perfectly still and was convinced of the authenticity of the emotion? Who would be convinced of your great sadness if you were gyrating wildly? We *are* hard-wired to read body language, so let us use it to our advantage as communicators, just as a fine actress will use the body motion congruent with the lines she is speaking.

Some schools of thought however would have you eliminate all but the essential body motion when playing music. One could point to Artur Rubenstein who sat very quietly at the keyboard using almost no extraneous body motion while producing exquisite music. Joshua Bell uses an extreme of body motion, also producing exquisite music. Paradoxically, both artists seem to be congruent within themselves and with the music—who they are and how they conceive the music. Rigid rules don't apply.

Appropriate motion is also dependent on your body structure and the instrument you play. If you are a pianist or cellist with a smaller frame, to get the power you need there will be more upper back and shoulder involvement. You simply may not carry enough weight in your arms to get the needed sound. My sister says this can be the case with pianists, and I think it is a factor for cellists, and more apt to be true for females. Evidence of this is in the statistic that the most playing-related injuries among symphony musicians occur with small-framed, female cellists. Also with string players there is the entirely asymmetrical use of the arms, which requires the body to shift, support and balance for that usage, rather than being static.

Natural body motion coherent with the motion that we impart to the bow and vibrato can help to communicate the emotional content of the music. It can be an integral part of music-making.

Later in this manual there will be an exercise addressing body motion. In the meantime notice what various performers do and become aware of what your tendencies are. If you find yourself wanting not to watch as someone plays, it could be that there is too little motion, a perceptible stiffness that doesn't match the music, or that there is too much or wrong motion that fights the musical content. Either extreme, when not congruent with the whole, becomes a distraction for the listener, and defeats the purpose of making music.

Another aspect of congruence pertinent to performance is attire—that too is a tool of communication. Our exterior physical presentation should be congruent with the intent to uplift; hence there is really no place for a sloppy look that is not congruent with the intent to create the beauty that touches the heart, even if the occasion calls for informal clothing. A word of caution to women: the sight of exposed arm, shoulder, and back muscles at work while we play is not necessarily pleasing to the eye. Remember to keep your focus on your purpose when you choose your clothing.

The aesthetics of your entire presentation ideally should match your intent for the music.

### More from Jessye Norman

In an interview for the Chicago Humanities Festival, published May 22, 2014 (YouTube), Jessye Norman speaks of the need for singers to sing the words and deport themselves in a way that listeners will be able to understand what is happening even if they don't speak the language the music is sung in. This is a situation where congruent body motion is crucial to the communication. A singer who stands on stage perfectly still does not achieve optimum communication, particularly in opera—at least not these days where audiences have an expectation of understanding something of what is occurring. The intent behind the words must be communicated regardless of language.

Also of interest are Norman's comments, similar to Fleming's, about the need for excellence with the physical technique so that her mind is at ease (effortless excellence) and she can "concentrate on the work at hand, which is for you to understand what I would like you to understand about the music, and my energy goes out to you and your energy comes back to me and we have a beautiful circle and we call that music." What a delightful description of a true communication and the two sides of the musical coin.

*"The essence of communication is intention."*
—Werner Erhard (b. 1935)
controversial American author of *EST*
and other transformational models[69]

---

[69] Whatever you study—particularly if there is a cult of personality involved or a requirement that you be a 'true believer'—take the good and leave the rest. True enlightenment isn't found in the marketplace, and a wise teacher will not restrict your exploration of other ideas—unless of course you are venturing into waters well over your head.

**LOVE**
**—THEME C**

To live lives of excellence, love is a necessary ingredient in all that we do.

*"Love assumes many forms; sometimes it is peace,*
*sometimes it is happiness, sometimes bliss or joy. Restlessness or sorrow.*
*Love is the Root, and like a tree it has many branches spreading around..."*
—Sufi master Radha Mohan Lal (Bhai Sahib) (1893-1966)
quoted in *Daughter of Fire* by Irina Tweedie

## ZARA NELSOVA'S WORLD

Prior to her death in 2002, Zara Nelsova was interviewed by Tim Janoff of the Internet Cello Society. "When I watch you play, I can't help but sense that you are showing the audience how much you love music and how much you love people. Am I on the right track?" Her response: "Absolutely. For me, playing music is about sharing, sharing my love for music and sharing my love for what we are as human beings. The minute I start to play, I'm in a different world, and I'm so caught up in the music and my desire to share it with the audience that all else fades away. The overwhelming feeling I get is a sense of connection with each person in the audience; I want the audience members to know how much I love what I am doing and how much I love them. And how do I do it? I do it by trying to communicate my love through beautiful music."

If I were to choose the most precious thing Nelsova offered as a teacher, it would be this attitude. Do you remember my story of the first time I heard Nelsova play? I was so drawn to her music that my attention could not wander. That magnetic, attractive force of love was present as the carrier wave. In my own conversations with Nelsova, years later, she told me as soon as she begins to play she finds herself out of her body and listening from the back of the hall. She was not saying this metaphorically—it is an example of an *unseen* ability. Some aspect of her consciousness was at the back of the room. When she told me this, she was surprised at my surprise, that this wasn't an ordinary occurrence for me too!

She also spoke of her sense of an overwhelming mission or calling or purpose, which drove her to continue performing and creating the music she so loved, as long as she possibly could. Though we cannot literally see another's purpose we can witness the results of that purpose, and it was crystal clear with Nelsova. She didn't need to think about it, make lists, ponder; she knew her purpose while yet a small child. This sense of purpose is critical, but just because it hasn't been clear or innate early in life, doesn't mean it can't be discovered and brought to fruition. Knowing and remembering purpose is the starting point for greatness.

There is a moving tribute to her available on the internet written by another wonderful cellist and teacher, George Neikrug.

**99**

### *MUSINGS ON LOVE*

Like the word heart, love is used in many ways, with the particular usage rarely defined. As used in this manual, the concept does not refer to what we think of as romantic love, though it too is a force with great attractive powers. Love creates a field, not unlike a gravitational or magnetic field. We all experience the need to draw closer to what we love, but love is a power, not an emotion. Love belongs to the essential self, the heart, not the personality or ego. Emotions are like clouds that obscure the blue sky, for a time. They come, they go, they shift into something different. Love is eternal. When the clouds are gone the blue sky remains.

The nature of love is merging and oneness. It is said by mystics that love is the force that holds all of creation together, from the tiny atom that would spin itself apart without it, to the totality of our known universe. It all holds together through the power of love. Every cell in the universe is permeated with love. Love made manifest is a wave form, a high frequency. It doesn't discriminate: no qualifications, reservations or conditions. It is all-inclusive. Love requires no reciprocation. It just is. That is the love we want as our carrier wave.

This is the magnetism of a Nelsova or Fleming. Great artists from all genres of music, from Leonard Bernstein to Miles Davis, when they talk about what happens between the audience and themselves, often use the words of love, describing that relationship as akin to a love affair.

How does this love happen? One concept is that the heart is a portal between the seen and the unseen worlds, where our sacred nature and human nature meet, the place from which we have access to the infinite, to spirit, to love. We don't own love, we don't create love. Love flows through us, through the heart. It comes from the unseen into our hearts. We can be the channel that allows it to then flow outward through our music.

For that love to flow, the heart—our channel—has to be receptive and expanded, what I refer to as *spacious*. When you are present your heart has the potential to open. When your heart is open love can be present. The more open and spacious the heart the more love can flow.

### More from Renée Fleming

She describes her goal when performing, regardless of audience size as: "communicating with the audience. When the evening is going well, I feel larger than myself. It's as if the boundaries of my body have dissolved and I can reach out through my voice and touch the audience in an almost physical way. For me, the singer's art is the art of expression—expressing the music, expressing the text, projecting my voice into a large space, and then using it to make that space between me and the audience grow smaller and smaller. My voice becomes a wide net, which I spread out across all of us to draw us closer together."[70]

---

[70] *The Inner Voice*, page 174

*"What was said to the rose that made it open
was said to me here in my chest."*
—Rumi


### MUSINGS ON SPACE AND SPACIOUSNESS

The extent of our awareness is what I mean by the space we occupy. In some instances awareness may not extend beyond our brains, not even to our own bodies—in which case our space is very compacted. When our space is compacted, it becomes difficult to do anything well. Our ability to perceive suffers, our reflexes suffer, breathing suffers, effort increases, facility diminishes, mood gets serious, etc. Whether it is making music or playing pickleball our space has to extend at least to the edges of the 'playing field.'

A spacious or open heart, though unseen, by nature occupies more space than just our own brain or body. If our presence stops at the edges of our bodies, or the edge of the instrument, our hearts will not be sufficiently open to allow a flow of love to reach a listener. Spaciousness, presence, love—all of these aspects are intertwined in an inseparable manner, and when we develop one the others increase as well. Likewise, the diminishing of one diminishes all.

You permeate or occupy with your energy and awareness a certain area around you, and one of your tools is your ability to expand and contract the amount of space you include in your awareness. The smaller it is the less likely you are to feel love or communicate on a carrier wave of love. It is as if your heart shrinks or expands with that sense of space, and vice versa.

Nelsova's experience of being out of her body and in the back of the hall is related to the concept of spaciousness, though as she described it, it was a true out-of-body phenomenon. Not having experienced this phenomenon, I have only other people's accounts as to what it is like. Some describe it as their essence (soul?) leaving the body, yet still being able to control the body from a distance. An expanded space that includes all the audience and the entirety of the hall is how I understand Fleming's experiences, which seem more like expansion *from* the body rather than moving *out* of the body.

This sense of the space you hold within your awareness is a wonderful tool to play with. When you do increase your space the effort to do anything decreases. Everything simply happens with greater ease, and this coincides with an expansive heart. As performers this means we want to hold within our sphere of awareness the entire audience and hall while we are controlling our bodies to do what we intend—with love of course. (That's all!)

**Exercise 11.**

**Purpose: to become aware of and be able to change at will the perimeters of the space you occupy**

This is not a goal likely to be reached the first time through the exercise. Expect to come back to it many, many times, each time increasing your abilities. The first six steps should not take you very long, but it is useful to limit yourself on step seven to a period of time through which you can stay focused and alert—long enough for some change to happen, but not to the point of fatigue. Awareness itself does not require time. It is there or it isn't. It is in the realm of a decision.

1. Sit with your instrument and have your awareness extend only as far as the bridge (of a string instrument) or comparable distance for other instrumentalists. Use your eyes to just focus on that much. Often we restrict ourselves to this amount of space when we play. Notice how this feels.

2. While keeping your eyes focused as in step one, feel your feet on the floor and become aware of the floor underneath them. Notice how this feels.

3. Use your eyes and other senses to become aware of the entirety of your instrument as well as your feet and the floor. Again, notice.

4. Extend your space, or awareness, out to include the entire room. Be aware of the wall and the space behind you as well as what your eyes can see. Continue to notice.

5. Close your eyes and continue to sense the entire room. You can develop this sensory ability, as blind people constantly demonstrate. Continue to notice.

6. Use your eyes to focus on the most distant point you can see (for me it is the mountain-top across the way) and get the sense of occupying all the intervening space. Again, notice how you feel.

7. Go back and forth between the differing occupied spaces, with eyes both open and closed, until it seems effortless. You may not get to "effortless" the first time through or even the thirtieth, but do continue with this step until there is some change. There is no 'right way' to perceive this; experiences differ. Stay attentive.

8. Now go through all the steps while playing something simple. Notice differences with each step. Do not do this to the point of mental exhaustion. Continue on when you feel you have attained a new level or awareness.

9. Do the same while playing something difficult. Notice differences, and stop playing at a positive point.

> **Tip:** Stopping on a positive note (pun intended), is advisable for any practice session or segment of a session. Take whatever you are doing to a new level or several new levels and stop at completion of such a step. You don't want to leave a learning process in the middle or at a point of discouragement. There are many completion points within a process. Stop when you feel good about what you are working on. If something isn't

getting better, simplify it and take that simpler step to a greater level of ease and excellence.

In that vein, in passages that are giving you trouble try practicing just the right arm bowing patterns on the appropriate open strings until the bowing is accurate and effortless. Difficult passages often resolve simply by being more aware of your bow contact.

This exercise will help to hone your skills in communicating across a distance. For example to talk to someone across the room you have to reach out with your invisible attention and awareness to include them in your space. Only then will you reach them with your voice or your cello. Your communication will stop where your space stops. Don't let it be at the end of the fingerboard. The greater the extent of space you occupy the less effort there will be in your playing, and the more successful your communication.  Listen as if you were somewhere else in the room, the further away the better. Notice when your space decreases (often before a difficult passage) and expand it. Get very comfortable with this willful expansion. You want to be able to apply this ability in performance.

**ANOTHER ANALOGY… this time with the art of pottery**
My artist friend Marion, one of my closest neighbors, is married to my physicist friend Bob (he had the brilliant analogy or metaphor of a vast geological time span with the second movement of the Beethoven *Piano Concerto No. 4*). Marion makes exquisite pottery, both functional and beautiful. She has shared with me some of the concepts and techniques she uses, and not surprisingly there are correlations with music and other disciplines, including physics. She tells me that an important tool in her art is a mirror set up on the far side of the potting wheel, so that she can *see* from a distance, see the form that is truly taking shape. As in music performance, if her space is too condensed due to her proximity to the wheel, she can not accurately judge what is happening with the clay. The clay is her sound, and she plays with it just as we do our sound. There are other similarities of course, which we will talk about later.

Another artist, Nancy — my multi-talented cello student, editor friend — mentions the same tool: a mirror at the far end of her painting studio. (There are perks to having artist friends: beautiful works by these artists adorn my home, and there is always something to learn from them.)

*"You gotta have heart*
*Miles 'n miles 'n miles of heart!"*
from the song *Heart*
(Broadway musical *Damn Yankees*[71])

## ON SPEAKING FROM THE HEART

Communicating from a spacious heart with a carrier wave of love is helpful in any arena of life. For some years in Salt Lake City I was deeply involved in community issues where there was great polarization between community members and the various "powers that be." There were continual stalemates with neither point of view winning out. It was often a battle, rarely a cooperative, creative effort. This discord began to take a tremendous toll on my peace of mind. Eventually I discovered that when I advocated passionately for what our community loved—as opposed to fighting what we didn't want—then people got it, they understood the differing point of view, and progress was made. My heart had to be open to see clearly; I had to look at the issues from all the various points of view, find solutions that helped everyone, and communicate effectively, including everyone in my space. Once I began speaking from the heart—that is, with a carrier wave of love—speaking my truth passionately instead of communicating antagonism and resistance, adversaries became friends. Magical!

---

[71] Music and lyrics by Richard Adler and Jerry Ross

## AN EXPERIENCE OF UNCONDITIONAL LOVE

Did I mention that I once raised parakeets? A friend was moving to New York City and 'gifted' me twelve beautiful parakeets to care for. I built a large cage for them, provided nesting boxes for colony-style breeding (where nesting pairs are not in separate cages) and often left the cage door open so they could have the run (flight) of what became the bird room.

They did pair up to some extent, and several pairs successfully nested and raised chicks. One pair—Whitey and Lady—had not yet hatched a clutch but were quite devoted. Blue Boy, however, was also smitten with Lady and pursued her relentlessly, much to Whitey's discomfort. One day apparently a challenge was issued for her affections, and the three of them dropped to the floor in a triangle with the males facing off.  Blue Boy and Whitey closed like boxers and pecked and clawed at each other. In some manner not visible to me it was eventually determined that Whitey had prevailed, not without injury to an eye, however. His minuscule eyelid was torn and required intervention. The vet gave me an ointment to apply several times daily.

When you have a large cage and many parakeets living together they do not become pets. I had not made a practice of handling them, so to catch Whitey was very difficult and impossible to do without upsetting everyone. The need to treat his eye required that he be separated from the others, so I put him and Lady in a smaller, separate cage—one in which I could easily pick him up. Three times a day we went through the same struggle: me picking him up despite his best efforts to escape my hand—a hand larger than his body; he biting the fingers that held him; me putting a drop of ointment on his eye and everywhere else it seemed.

A parakeet's beak is very sharp and very strong. Every time I picked him up he would bite my finger, draw blood, then hang on and worry it as well. My fingers became a mess and I really didn't look forward to these encounters. Gloves were out of the question as it takes a sensitive hand to hold a small bird without doing harm. But I was responsible for these birds, and I could understand his terror, and with that understanding came empathy, compassion, and what I came to realize was unconditional love. I never got angry, I was never rough, I never gave up on him, and I felt an immense connection to this little life form. It didn't matter how much blood he drew or real pain he inflicted; what I felt was love from the heart—not an emotion but an all-embracing love.

Indeed this was the oneness aspect of love. There was no sense of separation and I could totally put myself in his position. He had no means of understanding what was happening or why. If a 500-foot-tall creature were capturing me thrice daily, putting something in my eye, and making sounds with no meaning to me, I believe I too would be terrified and would struggle with all my strength and use any available weapon to try to escape. I could empathize! I came to see that fear is behind most destructive behavior, and that it needs to be countered with compassion—action, too, at times—but always with compassion.

Whitey's eye healed and he and Lady went on to successfully raise many chicks over the years. Whitey's devotion and assistance in child-rearing were remarkable and Blue Boy's covetousness persistent. (These creatures do have their personalities.) Always during nesting season I had to place Whitey and Lady in a cage separate from the others, which did allow me to easily handle their offspring. Consequently these birds became quite comfortable with the gigantic hand that would pick them up from time to time, and they even considered my hands—in particular my fingernails—to be toys. (Trust, perhaps?)

There was more to learn. The just-hatched baby parakeet is a featherless, reptilian-looking creature, which I first found to be remarkably ugly. But there came the occasion when I needed to remove a dead newborn from the nest. After actually having to pick it up, and studying it a bit as it lay in the palm of my hand, I could no longer understand how I ever thought it ugly. It is amazing what being present with something can do to take away fear and aversion.

Our life lessons may come in unexpected ways and our teachers in unexpected forms. When we're present, all of our experiences have the potential to become our teachers. The beauty of music, so utterly inexpressible in words, has perhaps been the greatest teacher in my life. How grateful I am.

**AWARENESS OF YOUR TOOLS
—THEME D**

This could also be titled "listening," as that is the common denominator with all of our tools.

*"There is always music amongst the trees in the garden,
but our hearts must be very quiet to hear it."*
—Minnie Aumonier (1865-1952)
English artist, poet

## COMMUNICATION WITH THE INSTRUMENT

Richard Bach, eloquent writer about all things to do with flying, has the kind of passion for flight and his tools—airplanes—that we need in our music-making. In the short story *Steel, aluminum, nuts and bolts* from the book *A Gift of Wings*, he tells the story of a pilot who, despite the loving care he had given his small plane, was forced to make an emergency landing in a mountain meadow not large enough for a takeoff. He writes that all the evidence of physics and mechanics was against the possibility of a pilot doing the impossible and taking off in a space too small to fly out of. Nevertheless, he relates, after duct tape and plastic sheeting repairs, plane and pilot *did* take off—safely. He concludes: "Not one voice said that if conditions are right, that if a pilot loves his airplane and shows this in his care, then an airplane might just one time and for the briefest of moments become a thing alive, that can love in return and show this in its flight. There was not one word that said this could be so." But it was so!

This kind of love, born out of responsibility, caring, and communication, is what we must have with the instrument we use for making our music. Then the impossible can become possible.

In the development of effortless excellence on your instrument, a crucial aspect is being in superb communication with it. You need to *be* in your fingertips, *be* at the point of contact where bow hair meets string. (For wind players that means *be* in your lips and in your fingertips.) This means you are aware of and really *feel* the contact, which helps to ease many technical issues. You need to resonate with the instrument, be in tune with it, to get optimum results. When you are in communication you will know what the instrument's own voice is, and can allow that to sing forth, rather than forcing your concept of a cello, viola, or oboe sound onto it. Respect your instrument as if it were a living thing, as vocalists must, and the two of you will flourish together. That attitude is congruent with the concept of *effortless excellence* rather than *mastery over*.

There are many fine instruments that have fallen into the hands of players who insist on getting their preferred sound or response out of any instrument. They begin by having the instrument altered until there is nothing left of its own voice, its own free vibration. I would not want to be that instrument. Unfortunately this happens with vocalists too, who force their voices towards a type of sound that is not innate, either ruining the voice or shortening their careers. It is our obligation to discover how each instrument needs to be played and then to

**107**

honor that. Developing a sound is different than forcing a sound, and it takes time and patience. As famed violist William Primrose said about the viola, it has to be "wooed and won and resents manhandling and outrage."[72] We all have unique aspects to our sound, based on our concepts, but ultimately it is a partnership between you and the instrument. It's the same principle as a conductor honoring the morphic field of an orchestra.

Pianists are good at quickly discovering what is needed and adapting to that. Since they rarely perform on their own pianos they do not get much choice. (Great pianists can take their pianos with them, but they are few in number and likely not reading this manual.) Pianists have to play the instrument they are sitting in front of, whatever it is, wherever they are.

Each instrument has its optimum adjustment and condition of course, and we develop a sensitivity for when our tools are out of sorts and need 'tune-ups,' just like with our own bodies. We should be able to discern whether an instrument is vibrating at its optimum or not, even an instrument that we are playing for the first time. It is a question of first being quiet and listening, with ears and body, not jumping in with *your* ideas.[73]

It is possible that you truly do not have the right instrument for you, but before you abandon it for another, be sure to consider and implement that command I received about keeping your focus on the *purpose* the tool serves. (Remember my story, on page 25, about the mystical experience?) As we progress, yes, we do need to upgrade our tools, but for most musicians there comes a point where financial considerations prevent buying a more expensive, presumably better instrument. Like with your own body you might just be stuck with the one you have, and at some point the *more* you already have has to be *enough*. Our culture of constant growth fails to recognize this, and so it has become rare for people to be happy with what they have. The desire for *more* is pervasive, and yet *more* doesn't seem to bring happiness or contentment. Don't obsess over upgrading!!

If you still believe you cannot make music with the instrument you have, I encourage you to find on the internet the video (if it is still there) of a man making a clarinet out of a large carrot, a saxophone mouthpiece and a funnel. He simply cores the foot-long, fat carrot, drills holes through it sideways for the fingers to stop, sticks a funnel in the bottom to form the bell and slips the mouthpiece over the top. He makes it in a matter of minutes and then he plays it—and makes music![74] It's amazing. It really sounds like an instrument.

Resonance and communication with the instrument are an important part of music-making.

Bottom line: Care for your instrument—with love—and know the purpose it serves.

---

[72] *Strings* magazine, Summer 1988, from an earlier interview by David Dalton.

[73] This reminds me of the joke: *How do you make god laugh? Tell god your plan for your life.* If you live long enough to see your life take unexpected turns this joke becomes quite funny, regardless of any belief in a supreme deity.

[74] The link if still available is at http://youtu.be/BISrGwN-yH4

*"Do not spoil what you have by desiring what you have not; remember that what you now have was once among the things you only hoped for."*
—Epicurus (340-269 BCE)
Greek philosopher


**Exercise 12.**

**Purpose: to increase your love for and communication with your instrument**

Our brains devote a great deal of capacity to processing visual input, at the expense of input from our other senses. Therefore if we cut off the visual input by closing our eyes, there is increased awareness of other information coming into the consciousness. For that reason—to heighten awareness of touch and sensation—do this exercise with eyes closed.

1. Initially, *do* look at your instrument, more carefully than you have ever done before. Notice all the dimensions, shapes, lines, curves, seams. Notice the materials used. Notice the colors. Now, close your eyes and proceed with the remainder of this exercise.

2. Run your hands, with particular awareness of what your fingertips feel, all over the instrument. Feel the entire instrument, slowly with maximum awareness of what you perceive. Can you feel the dimensions and shapes, lines, curves? Can you discern textures of different parts? Do different materials have different temperatures? Are they warmer or cooler than the ambient room temperature? If you tap a surface does it resonate? Does it resonate freely? Does it have a pitch? Do you associate a texture with a color, or a pitch with a color? (Some people do.) Explore!

3. Now experiment with touching the instrument in many different ways: sometimes with tenderness, sometimes with harshness, coldness, sometimes with great affection, or neutrality. Run the gamut of emotions you can conjure up, staying away from actual violence to the instrument, please. (Coincidentally the main definition of "gamut" is a recognizable series of musical notes, as in a scale. Emotions do form a scale of sorts, as each emotion has a different frequency.) End by truly caressing your instrument with all the tenderness you can muster.

4. Bring the instrument to playing position. With your hands in playing position go from touching it coldly to touching it with gentleness, compassion and love. Back and forth. Notice how differently you feel when you change the quality of your touch. If a string player, cuddle the neck of the instrument as if it were that fragile bird you would not want to crush, and the bow something to be cherished. Hold and touch with the same level of love you would use with someone you dearly love. All instrumentalists, including singers, do the same.

5. If you were to talk to the instrument, what would you say? Do you have questions for it? Try asking; see what response comes to mind. Are you willing to express gratitude to it and its maker for being a tool that is serving you well? If it hasn't served you well, this exercise might just improve the situation. Go ahead, talk to it. But you might want to be sure no one else is around.

*"It is the supreme art of the teacher to awaken joy in creative expression and knowledge."*
—Albert Einstein


### Jill's Story

I had a wonderful teen-age student who would get rather exasperated with me for continually haranguing her about being in her fingers, feeling the contact, being aware of the vibrations at the point of contact of bow hair and string. Over and over I would say, "*Be* in your fingertips." Years later she told me a story that I relish.

She had gone on a hike up a mountain with friends, and they had not completed the descent before dark. And it was dark—apparently very dark—with no flashlights at hand. Jill began feeling anxious but then she thought to apply to her current situation that concept of being present in her fingertips and sensing from that location. She decided to *be* in her feet and to feel from there. She let her feet do the seeing. That took care of the anxiety, the stumbling, and uncertainty, and got her down safely. She was a student who truly understood a principle and applied it to life. I am grateful that she thought to tell me the story.

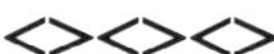

### "The Wood Speaks Only When You Have Nothing Left to Say"

Violin-maker James N. McKean writes in his book *Art's Cello:* "The art of making a violin is learning to disappear. You have to banish thought. You have to banish you. You can't be the wizard, the master craftsman, working your magic… the wood moves from here to there, and the violin happens. The silence is what counts, the spaces in between are as important as the strokes of the tools. The wood speaks only when you have nothing left to say."

I liken his thoughts about violin-making to the ideas we have been exploring. The ego-self has to disappear, the considerations have to disappear, the technical aspects have to disappear. *Your* excellence becomes invisible so that the music can speak. Applying James McKean's thoughts to music: Music is the space between the notes as much as the notes themselves; It is defined as much by silence as by sound.

### More from the World of Clay

Marion tells me that before she ever begins to work a hunk of clay (highly technical term) on the potter's wheel—and every hunk is different—she spends time "listening to it": working it with her hands, kneading it (wedging is the professional term), feeling it, getting a uniform texture throughout, playing with it. She becomes present with it, gets to know the clay, lets it tell her what it can do, what it can become. The clay and the wheel dictate what is possible. Can it be a vase, a bowl, some shape for enclosing space? Or need it remain a flat piece—a plate or tray? She pays attention to the inner space as well as to the outer form as she creates. She doesn't force the clay to become a shape that isn't inherent in it.

As with James McKean and other fine makers of the tools we use in life and for making music, she imbues each piece with love and caring, never destroying the clay's own voice. This concept has ramifications for us when we begin to look at our interpretations of music.

# ACT III Reprise





## *MUSINGS ON CONNECTING THE SEEN AND THE UNSEEN:*
## *THE PRACTICAL AND THE PHILOSOPHICAL*

In Themes A, B, and C we looked mostly at the unseen tools we either already have or will develop within ourselves. These include the necessary excellence, effortlessness, awareness, control, coherence, and trust, as well as the various skills of communication: the carrier wave of love, spaciousness, congruence in all aspects. I trust that by now you have fully heard and integrated the message about keeping your focus on the purpose that these internal tools serve.

In Theme D we examined our relationship with *external* tools—the tools we create or use that seem separate from us. Here there is an additional challenge. To maintain good communication with our tools we must listen to the voice of the tool or raw material, as well as staying aware of the purpose it serves. The airplane, a cello, the clay, a piece of wood, the high wire, your vocal chords, your feet, they all have a voice that speaks to us when we listen.

Every hunk of clay is different, every piece of Pernambuco bow wood is different, every piece of maple or spruce that will become an instrument is different, every airplane or machine or wire fashioned by someone's hand is different. Every human voice is different. The clay speaks to Marion through her hands; the wood speaks to the violin-maker through the hands and ears (what is the pitch of the wood, how resonant is it, how dense, how flexible). To hear that unique voice we must be *in* the tool, as Jill was *in* her feet. Resonate with it—permeate the tool with love, essentially and ultimately become one with the tool—as Philippe did with his wire, as the pilot did with the airplane that he so loved, which allowed them together 'as one' to do the impossible.

The threads woven throughout all these factors that are needed to make music from the heart—essentially the common denominators—are intention and awareness and the qualities of open-heartedness and love. There is much research yet to be done regarding how the brain and physical heart interact with these aspects of the unseen world. Don't wait for science, or religion, or philosophy to provide you with all the answers; the more you communicate, the more you interact, the more you share, and the more you take responsibility, the more empathy, compassion, and love you will experience. Your unseen heart will know its purpose.

When you perform *be* in your heart. It is very large and it knows how to listen. It can contain the entirety of the music, the instrument, your colleagues, the audience, and more.

### *How Does It Feel to Be a Heart?*

*Once a young woman asked me,*

*"How does it feel to be a man?"*
*And I replied,*

*"My dear,*
*I am not so sure."*

*Then she said,*
*"Well, aren't you a man?"*

*And this time I replied,*

*"I view gender*
*As a beautiful animal*
*That people often take for a walk on a leash*
*And might enter in some odd contest*
*To try to win strange prizes.*

*My dear,*
*A better question for Hafiz*
*Would have been,*

*'How does it feel to be a heart?'*

*For all I know is Love,*
*And I find my heart Infinite*
*And Everywhere!"*

Hafiz
translated by Daniel Landinsky

# ACT IV

## The 'Melody'

### What you have been waiting for

# PRELUDE TO ACT IV

*"Music is the divine way to tell beautiful poetic things to the heart."*
—Pablo Casals (1876-1973), Catalan cellist and conductor


## MELODY

We humans seek out the 'melodies' in life and we seek them out in music. They are what 'speak' to us and what we find meaning in.

The melody generally dominates the attention of concert-goers. It possesses the greatest potential to come alive, to be expressive. It is what audiences wait for and what they remember. This Act is called The 'Melody' because it is probably what you've been waiting to hear (read). What we will examine in this Act forms the melody of the manual: the understanding needed and those physical, concrete things you can do to bring music to life. How we play the melodies in music will be the biggest factor in whether we succeed. The foundation you have been creating is important to successful application of these Act IV materials. In a symphonic work a melody in the violins often rests on the foundation that the basses and cellos are creating. Smart conductors make sure the foundation is in place and that those who play the melody are aware of what supports it. It is hard to fix what is on top if the bottom is weak, just as for string players it is hard to fix left-hand issues if the bowing is not sound. Nothing in this Act will be of much help if you are not present with an open heart, creating anew in every performance, so please continue building your foundation for bringing music to life. Like everything to do with music, this is an open-ended pursuit: no definitive arrivals or end points. Perhaps that is why Casals was still practicing at age 93, and Sergei Rachmaninoff said: "Music is enough for a lifetime, but a lifetime is not enough for music."

The melody is where our conscious attention tends to go when we listen to music. It is "the only element in common to music of all times and all peoples..."[75] Often it is the aspect of music we can't get out of our heads. Melody is vocal in nature; it can be sung. The singing of melodies may predate spoken words, and sometimes song and speech almost overlap. There are languages where pitch change is an important aspect of the language, and so they sound more musical than English, though in most cultures speech tends to be primarily a function of the left brain. People who have had injuries to that hemisphere, leaving them unable to speak, may however still be able to sing. This is because music tends to activate, perhaps even be inherent in, the right hemisphere of the brain—the hemisphere that activates with emotional responses. Melody is paramount in providing the emotional content of the music, and something about melody is indeed so intrinsic to being human that for some of us life without it is unfathomable. Song (melody) is so powerful that the master farmers of the Native American Diné tribes feel compelled to sing to the seeds they plant. They sing traditional songs "that the souls of the seeds long to hear in order to grow,"[76] words that remind me of my own experiences as a child and how important it was to hear the beautiful melodies my parents sang. Just perhaps, all of life responds to the beauty of song. In truth I think there are melodies so beautiful that indeed you would have to be thoroughly dead not to respond.

---

[75] *Harvard Dictionary of Music*, Second Edition
[76] *Advocate*: a magazine of the Grand Canyon Trust, Spring 2015 issue, page 21.

## MOTION AND LIFE

All life is characterized by motion. Everything in the universe has a vibration of a specific frequency, including those things we call dead, but the vibrations must be within a certain frequency range for us to recognize life and to see motion. The speed of vibration in living things is greater than in dead things, and allows for motion, animation. Motion is defined as a changing of place, position, or direction of movement. It happens in the dimensions of space and time. A table has a low, slow frequency and we don't expect to see one moving about on its own. We don't consider the table to be alive. We do however recognize motion in the daily rhythms of life: seasons, tides, waxing and waning of the moon.

To animate something is to bring motion to it. When we animate music we bring motion to the lifeless symbols on a page. There is in fact no actual motion on the printed page where the blueprint of music is stored. Nor when music is played are the notes traveling to, or found in, new locations in space. Yes, the *sound*, as waves, travels through space, but as each sound is created it exists for our ears a mere infinitesimal moment—the present moment only. It is not this wave motion of air per se that brings music to life. There is no literal physical space involved in the music itself, so we are left to work with time. When we wish to have life in our music we have to create the sense of motion, and it is the perception of time that allows us to create the illusion. If the ear, actually the brain, can be tricked into thinking that there is a progression of sound through time, then we have the sense of motion and the music becomes a living thing.

## WORKING DEFINITIONS

Rhythm: the pattern of movement in time.

Harmony: the chordal or vertical structure of music as opposed to the horizontal structure of successive notes.

Tonality: loyalty to a tonic or keynote to which the music orients.

Melody: in the general sense, "a coherent succession of pitches."[77] Melody is differentiated from harmony in that it refers to successive pitches rather than simultaneous sound. It is differentiated from rhythm as it refers to pitch rather than duration or emphasis.

Melody most certainly is the heart of music; it *is* the melody that makes music music. However a random sequence of pitches, all of the same duration, does not constitute a melody. Rhythm, that pattern of movement in time, is intrinsic to melody. Every pitch has a duration, and it is how the sequence of pitches progresses through time that turns it into a melody rather than just random sound. Additionally, in the tonal systems of music, successive pitches and their relationships to each other suggest chords, harmony. The relationships in monophonic music with its single melodic line are generally described as melodic, not harmonic; however *the harmonies are often implied in that single line of melodic writing*. Musicians playing non-keyboard instruments need to be aware of this. The Bach *Six Suites for Solo Cello* are a superb example of implied harmonies without underlying written chords. More complex relationships exist of course in harmonized music.

Motion: the technical definition of motion in the language of musicians refers to the sequence of changing pitch levels in a melody; hence motion is viewed as going up or down, which is an idea of verticality applied to space, rather than a movement through time. There are additional technical ways the word "motion" is used in music, but unless otherwise specified I'm going to use motion to refer to the *perception of motion in the physical universe that we associate with life*.

Melody cannot truly be separated from rhythm and harmony. Our understanding has to encompass these aspects to bring the greatest possible life to the melody lines we play.

---

[77] *Harvard Dictionary of Music*, Fourth Edition

## ON THE IMPORTANCE OF RHYTHM TO MELODY

I have played the game with colleagues where someone taps out just the rhythm of a familiar theme of music, and the rest of us guess the piece. The easiest and most obvious is the opening motif of the Beethoven *Symphony No. 5*. Even non-musicians tend to know that one. But it is quite possible to play those same motif pitches, with a drastically different rhythm, and have the motif go unrecognized. (Prove or disprove this for yourself. Experiment.)

A melody might actually be graphed with two axes like other physical universe phenomena. The horizontal axis would represent time, divided into equal segments (as in beats, measures or seconds). The vertical axis would represent pitch frequencies, going from low to high. A melody looks something like the diagram below when graphed.

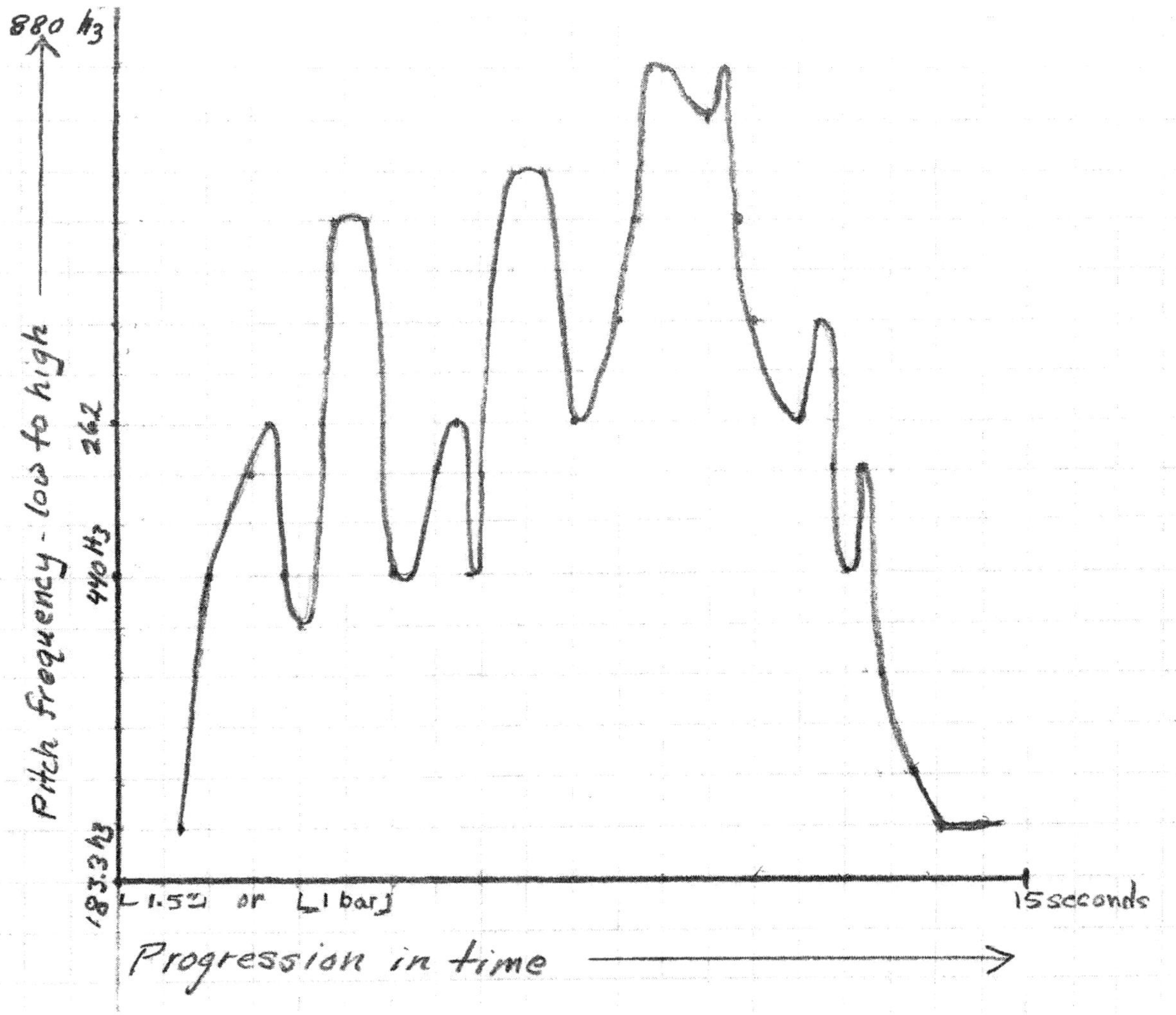


**Figure 6**

If I were to compress the vertical axis more, or stretch the horizontal axis, then this graph would appear less jagged.

Take away the axis of time and it is meaningless. Take away changing pitches and it is no longer music—just rhythm, which of course has its own power. This graphed representation of a melody is not unlike our actual notation system, and the similarity is what allows my brother-in-law, who doesn't read music, to be a good page turner for my pianist sister. He is seeing the contours of the sound through time.

## ON THE IMPORTANCE OF HARMONY TO MELODY

The morphic field formed by tonally-based music gives us the framework to make sense of what we hear, to make sense of a melody. Without that framework, listening to a melody would be "like listening to a poem being read in a language you don't know,"[78] an apt analogy. We need an understanding of the harmonic foundations of the music we play. It is through the relationships between notes and actual or implied chords within a specific tonality that there is a feeling of tension and release—another way of creating a sense of motion.

Due to this morphic field of tonality that has informed our 'ears,' hearing just a fragment of a melody (such as the fragments included in this manual) creates a feeling of incompleteness. Our response of sensing that incompleteness is evidence of the intimate connection between harmony and melody.

As soon as you create the perception that something else has to happen, that there is some place you must go next, that you are not finished, not at rest, you have created the need for movement and then the illusion of motion when you come to completion. This *tension and release,* as it is often called, comes from the harmonic framework of music. It is the relationships between notes and actual or implied chords, *within a tonality*, that help create the illusion of motion. This is why you need an understanding of tonality and the harmonic foundations of the bulk of the music you will play.

But, tonal music is only a portion of the music you will encounter. In the twentieth century and into the present, there was and continues to be a great split in the evolution of music, with one road following the path of tonality, and one road abandoning tonality. This latter road of atonal and avant-garde music I refer to as *the road less travelled*[79] and is the subject of Theme E. The bulk of this Act deals with music that still fits in the tonal framework.

---

[78] A quote from my brother-in-law, Ron.

[79] Also the name of a wonderful book by M. Scott Peck, which is recommended reading. That title is itself a play on the words of poet Robert Frost in the poem *The Road Not Taken*. The last lines of the final stanza are:
"Two roads diverged in a wood, and I—
I took the one less traveled by,
And that has made all the difference."

## THE ILLUSION OF MOTION

Music that we perceive as being static is boring. Despite the lack of movement of music through space—what we normally perceive motion to be—we still have the sense of either the presence of motion or the lack of it in music performance. It is through our perception of time and its forward progression that we sense music's motion, motion perceived due to the change in sound in every moment. This is the illusion we manipulate to bring the music to life.

We create the illusions by using physical motion: such things as bow speed, speed of vibrato, dynamic changes, emphasis, rhythmic distortion, etc. The amount of change per second in the sound determines whether the motion is perceived as slow or fast, yet even when a passage is fast it may not have forward motion if the only change in the sound is pitch. Sameness shuts down perception. We will isolate and analyze components of the music that contain the greatest opportunities for physically creating the illusions. But paradoxically, in the end it will be about *being* not *doing,* and how that will drive your physical motions.

Ultimately the most successful way to create the appropriate movements that communicate the sense of life is to simply 'be' the music. Your body will then know what to do, without you going through analytical decision-making with every note. The congruent physical motions with our instruments and bodies resulting from *being*—or becoming—the music, then create the illusions of motion and emotion.

But there is justification for analytically examining this gestalt of illusory motion and for understanding which physical motions to employ, and when to do so. Common human functioning is that your mood determines how you move your body; however it is also possible that by deliberately changing how you move your body, your mood will change.[80] Deliberately creating the illusions that communicate motion will help you to feel the content of the music. Eventually you will be comfortable simply *being* the music, having the strong intent that will then drive, without conscious thought, everything you do physically to communicate the music.

---

[80] For advice from a biomechanist on the natural, appropriate body motions needed to improve health and mood read *Move Your DNA* by Katy Bowman, M.S. and *Alignment Matters.*

## RELATIONSHIPS—THE COMMON DENOMINATOR

Bringing the melody to life is about understanding relationships between notes from multiple points of view: the harmonic and structural relationships including pitch, the rhythmic or time relationships, that of sound and silence, those between voices, the relationship between motion and emotion, and more.

The intention behind the exercises in this Act is to help you understand and use those relationships to make the melody more expressive, to touch the listener to a greater degree. The material on harmony, tonality, structure/form, intervals and rhythm will include information that may be well known to some readers. Regardless, look through the material to see how it is being applied in the exercises, and do the exercises too. Perhaps you are advanced enough as a player to move quickly through these sections, but I encourage you not to skip anything. Harmony and rhythm are empty without the melody, yet understanding the interplay between all three gives you tools to create illusions.

In summation, what we do with the melody ultimately determines whether the music seems dead or alive. Giving the music a sense of direction and movement, as if we were dealing with space-time, is crucial. In much of this Act we will be looking at various ways of approaching a melody that strengthen this sense of moving through time and space.

# HARMONIC AND STRUCTURAL RELATIONSHIPS
## —THEME A

The study of how music has been constructed, known as harmonic analysis, is the province of the mind. This analytical understanding is important in its own right and is an entire field of study, one worthy of exploration to a greater extent than we will do here. Like many aspects of analytical understanding its greatest value to a performing musician comes when you use it as a tool to help realize your purpose of bringing music to life and communicating to your audience.

The following cursory discussion basically just examines how harmonic relationships apply in our playing of the melody. If you have a limited understanding of the harmonic and structural aspects of music (that is, concepts of tonality, keys, triads, scales, intervals, chord progressions, cadences, and key signatures), then now is the time to go to the Review Section, which follows the Addendum, and acquire a working understanding of these basics on which much of Western music is built.

**Figure 7**

## HARMONY

As defined on page 117, harmony refers to the chordal or vertical structure of music, in contrast to the melodic or horizontal structure. Chords create a simultaneous complex sound— notes stacked on top of each other—as opposed to the succession of single pitches in a melodic line. Harmonic analysis defined more fully is: "the study of the individual chords or harmonies in a piece of music together with their use in succession to form larger units of phrases, periods, sections, or whole compositions. It is applicable to all Western music that has a harmonic aspect. Although such study is necessary to understand music of other periods, it is particularly applicable to the tonal music of the 18th and 19th centuries; in this area it still forms the initial basis of training for the young musician."[81] I would add to this quote that it is equally necessary for understanding music from the 17th century.

## TONALITY

Tonality is defined further as: "Loyalty to a tonic, in the broadest sense of the word. One of the most striking phenomena of music is the fact that, throughout its evolution—in non-Western cultures, in Gregorian chant, and in harmonized music—practically every single piece gives

---

[81] *Harvard Dictionary of Music*, second edition

preference to one tone (the tonic), making this the tonal center to which all other tones are related."[82] This assertion however is not necessarily true for music of *the road less traveled*.

Tonic and keynote are basically synonymous. Tonal center has a somewhat looser meaning, but mostly I will use them interchangeably.

Tonality derives from the harmonic or overtone series, which is the acoustical or physical relationship between frequencies whereby consonance and dissonance can be understood. In a harmonic series the tone of lowest frequency is referred to as the fundamental, and the tones that are derived from the fundamental are exact multiples of the fundamental's frequency. It is this relationship that gives us, for example, the harmonics that we can play on a string instrument. The harmonic pitches above the fundamental are referred to as overtones. This relationship of tones is rooted in the physical universe; it is not a matter of opinion as to how tones are related. It is however, familiarity that determines to some extent whether *you* find various relationships to be consonant or dissonant.

Keyboard instruments are generally tuned to the equal-tempered system, which is not acoustically correct or 'pure.' Rather it divides a true octave into twelve equal semi-tones or half steps, spreading the inaccuracies that would be present in some keys in the pure system over all the tones and keys. Part of the beauty of a string instrument is that we can play intervals that sound right—'just' tuning, it is sometimes called—rather than being restricted by equal-tempered tuning. Our instinctive just tuning sounds better and resonates more freely. Thirds can be played where they sound best. When you are not playing with piano you can adjust your intonation accordingly. Your ear is the guide here—not some definition.

There is a trend today towards greater tuning flexibility, away from equal temperament only, so perhaps by the time you read this, other tuning systems will be commonplace alongside the equal temperament system. Harpsichords, in solo playing, are often tuned to different 'historical' temperaments, that is, reflective of the era from which the composition comes.

Please refer to page 374 in the Review Section for a discussion of the technical difference between notes on the piano keyboard that are the same key and sound the same, but that are written differently—called enharmonic notes, such as *C#* and *Db*. On fixed-pitch instruments, the pitch is not differentiated, but ideally these enharmonic notes should sound subtly different, and we can and should make those differences in pitch on string and wind instruments.

---

[82] Ibid.

### *MUSINGS ON HARMONY, RESONANCE AND MELODIES*

Harmony is organized resonance, in reference to what we experience as musical sound. It is resonance organized according to the principles of physics involving the frequencies of sounds: how those frequencies augment and enhance other frequencies (consonance), or conflict with other frequencies (discordance, or a lack of harmony). Two tones in perfect resonance create a sense of aliveness and vibrancy. Resonance is being in harmony: with the laws of nature, the laws of our own bodies and souls, and with other frequencies. Being in resonance with all the tools we use in creating music brings a magical, effortless experience, as in the kayaking story.

The study of the relationships of successive notes in a melody is generally considered the purview of melodic analysis, not harmonic analysis. However debating the relative *merits* of a melody line, as is apt to happen in melodic analysis, in terms of whether it is a scaler[83] (step-wise) progression or a chordal progression, an ascending or descending line,[84] is not particularly useful to us. Understanding how things function is, and that requires harmonic knowledge. Though the horizontal or successive relationship between notes will be what primarily determines whether we find a melody beautiful, a composer would be hard put to create a beautiful melody on the basis of an analysis of the horizontal relationships of beautiful melodies.[85] Inspiration is needed.

All types of melodic constructions are found in great music and all are found in mediocre music, but we are in the business of bringing to life the melody in front of us, not judging it. What is useful to us is noticing the relationships. Noticing their existence and understanding the harmonic context gives us tools to increase the sense of motion.

We make music by playing the relationships between frequencies. We do not just play a series of unrelated notes. A composer can create the most beautiful relationship between notes, but if the musician does not play with the understanding of those relationships, then the music will sound dead. *We are recreating and playing relationships.* They help create the sense of motion. We need to know what it is we want to express and then use the relationships between notes to help communicate that intent.

We do not need to have 'perfect pitch' to be good musicians; rather we need the well developed sense of relative pitch—being able to hear the optimum relationship of one note to the next. In many cases that relationship will be one that is as harmonious as possible; in other cases it will be a discordance that demands resolution, and so we often emphasize the dissonance to increase tension, heightening the demand to resolve.

We will look first at melodic relationships within this framework of harmony, tonality, and resonance.

---

[83] Also spelled *scalar*

[84] Some theorists assert that an ascending line creates more tension and that a descending line is a more natural movement for a melody.

[85] A corollary to trying to write a beautiful melody based on analysis of beautiful melodies would be attempting to write an inspiring fugue based on the rules derived from successful fugues. By following all the rules I did pass the exam on writing a fugue in my theory class at Juilliard, but it certainly was boring (my fugue). Let's leave room for inspiration. It is not bound by rules.

## INTERVALS AND INTONATION

The simplest relationship is that between any two pitches. The distance between those pitches, or frequencies, is referred to as the 'interval.' The mathematical ratio between the frequencies of two tones determines whether we call that interval an octave, fifth, major[86] third, minor third, major second (whole tone or whole step), minor second (half step), etc. The intervals that are our building blocks are really major and minor seconds (whole and half steps). Every other interval can be defined in terms of those, as can the structures of the predominant scales used in Western music.

Each interval has a unique quality that helps to identify it for the ear; hence you can recognize the interval regardless of what the two pitches happen to be. For example, a major third could be from *C* to *E*, or from *F* to *A*. The relationships are the same—a distance of two whole steps between the pitches—and it is the familiarity with the sound of a particular interval that allows you to sing on sight, or hear correctly in your inner ear the written pitches once you know the starting point. This is the sense of relative pitch. Being able to hear, sing, and reproduce those intervals optimally is the foundation for excellent intonation, which then allows your instrument to resonate or vibrate freely, helping to create aliveness in the sound.

This is part of technical excellence of course, and intonation must be pristine not to mar the beauty of the music. The word pristine wonderfully captures the quality of intonation needed. Hearing pristine intonation is like walking outside into crystal clear, sparkling air. It is invigorating, creating a sense of aliveness. Hearing approximate intonation is like walking out into smoggy air; it has a life-robbing quality.

### *MUSINGS ON INTONATION*

A pair of doves recently set up housekeeping in the huge Ponderosa growing out of the base of the cliff behind my house. Today they were quite busy either calling to each other or complaining; I'm not quite sure which. But one of them could use more practice on its song. It didn't much resemble a typical dove call. (Bird songs are not innate, so perhaps this bird grew up in a dysfunctional family and never learned a proper dove song.) Its call was very out of tune, to my ear, (or according to the morphic field I am attuned to). It was attempting something like a minor third up, then a half step down, but the minor third was too squashed and the half step down very approximate. Hearing this motivated me to include what I call the Dove Drill as Exercise 13.

---

[86] The 'm' in major is often upper case when combined with an interval or scale name, and the 'm' in minor is left lower case. I will use upper case 'Ms' when combined with a specific key or chord, as in *C* Major or *C* Major chord, or in the title of a work. Upper case is also used with P for perfect and A for augmented. Other usages in abbreviations are shown in the Review Section.

**Exercise 13.**

**Purpose: to become more observant about note relationships**

**Figure 8   The Dove Drill**

As you play this pattern hear and think in intervals. Start with the open *D* string if you are a string player, which will keep that pitch constant and allows you to check the next pitch against the open *A*. Now play that major third (two whole steps) up to the *F#*. As you are not restricted in this exercise to the equal-tempered tuning of the piano, find the *F#* which sounds best with the open *A*. Listen for maximum vibrancy. Now play down a major second (whole step) to the *E;* then down a perfect fourth (two and a half steps) to the *B* natural, which you can check against the open *D*; a minor third (step and a half) up to the *D;* then down a minor second (half step) to the *C#*. As this sequence has not resolved on a tonic chord note (*D, F#* or *A*) of what we could presume to be a *D* Major tonality, the tendency will be to repeat the sequence over and over, just like the dove did with its pattern, which is exactly what I want you to do.

What I wish you to hear (besides the beautiful resonant major third from *D* to *F#*) is the relationship between the *F#* going down to the *E*, as opposed to the relationship of the *D* down to the *C#*. As you repeat this, listen for what seems the most satisfying relationship for each. Eventually you will hear that the whole step down cannot be compressed or it loses effectiveness and beauty, whereas in the half-step-down scenario pushing the *C#* close to the *D* adds more interest, encouraging you to repeat the pattern by returning to the *D*.

## NOTE FUNCTIONS

Specific notes, or pitches, in a melodic line (and corresponding chords within a harmonized melody) function differently depending on the tonality you are in: They can be stable points, like when a note is the tonic of a scale or key; They can carry motion forward with great tension when the note is the 7th of a scale (a discordance) and the ear needs it to resolve. Notes can carry the motion forward with somewhat less tension as in the 2nd of a scale. They can create a sense of harmony and resonance if the 5th of a scale. In any given passage you must understand what the notes are doing: are they urging you forward or completing something—moving or static. Does a note behave as a jumping off point, or is it a landing? We use different techniques to help a note accomplish its job within the line we are playing, such as appropriate intonation, bow speed, quality of sound, vibrato.

> **Tip:** Pushing the 7th of a scale higher does increase tension and is part of what Casals called "expressive intonation." As with most everything there is no rigid rule that can apply, but paying attention to the specific function of the note will help you to know when to close up that half step interval and when not to. If you have a sequence where you go on down from a 7th, rather than resolving up to the tonic, you may not want to increase tension that demands resolution, so you would not push it closer to the tonic. But if you go from the 7th to a lowered 6th you may want to emphasize the "tugging at

the heart-strings" quality with close half steps bracketing the step-and-a-half interval (minor third sound[87]). Always consider what you want the music to communicate and what best achieves that. Also keep in mind that when we play with other instruments we are constrained by the other pitches being played and how our 7ths fit in. See page 131, Tonally-Based Movement Illusion for some specific examples.

## Exercise 14.

### Purpose: to listen for the resonance between pitches

To give notes their best sense of function within tonality, you need to hear and be able to create the beautiful resonance between pitches dictated by the intervals. This exercise builds on what you did in the Dove Drill.

There is a tendency to compress intervals when they go from a higher to a lower note, and particularly when there are two whole steps in succession. The second of the two intervals tends to be get compressed, especially if the melody then goes back up. This also seems to happen frequently with the sequence of a half step then a whole step down, and back up. The whole step gets compressed. Even if one has intentionally made the half step narrower, the following whole step has to reflect the appropriate distance from the starting point.

**Excerpt 5  Rachmaninoff *Vocalise*, transcribed for cello and piano**

The music quote used in this excerpt and on page 123 provides an example. It is the opening of Rachmaninoff's *Vocalise*, a wordless song written for voice on a chosen syllable, usually 'ah.' The cello version, shown here, is in the key of *E* minor, and the starting note is the third of the tonic chord. We will call it 3, so the sequence becomes 3-2-3-1-2-3, then 2-1-2- 7-1-2 (or *G*, *F#*, *G*, *E*, *F#*, *G*, *F*, *E*, *F#*, *D*, *E*, *F#*). When intervals get compressed as I have described, it is often a case of lack of presence, particularly on the bottom notes, as attention has gone too quickly back to the top note. The lack of presence disturbs as well as the questionable pitches. Even current, highly acclaimed sopranos in their performances of *Vocalise* lose some of the beauty of this melody because they compress the descending thirds, both the initial minor third (the third down to the tonic) and then the major third from the 2nd down to the 7th. Though listeners may not be attuned to small discrepancies, some of the beauty has been lost. Beauty is enhanced through appropriate resonances and dissonances. Approximates add nothing.

Play or sing the notes of the *Vocalise* excerpt being fully present on each pitch and listening for the right relationships, the optimum resonance.

---

[87] Technically we can't call this a minor third, even though that is the sound, because within the scale it is still spelled with adjacent note names, as in *G#* to *F*. If it were written as *Ab* to *F* we could correctly call it a minor third.

**Exercise 15.**

**Purpose: to increase awareness of interval relationships**

For this exercise we will use the last ten and a half bars of the third movement of this Brahms *Sonata*. I have written out just the notes, without articulation or dynamic indications.

**Excerpt 6  Brahms *E minor Sonata for Cello and Piano*, ending of the third movement**

1. Start by observing the first note of each beat and the relationships between them: first the half note *A*, then *G, F#, E, D#*, back to *E, D* natural, *C, B*, back to *E, D, C, B, C, A, G, F natural*, then *G, F#, G, F#, G, F#* an octave higher, *G, F#, G, F#, G*, then *E, C, A, F natural*, *C*, then *A*, and then a chord on the fifth of the *E* minor scale and finally the *E* minor chord to end. The relationships are: whole step, half step, whole, half, half, whole, whole, half, a perfect fourth, whole, whole, half, half, minor third, whole, whole, whole, then 10 half steps as you go back and forth between *G* and *F#* (ignoring the skip to the higher octave), and finally m 3rd, M 3rd, m 3rd, M 3rd, P 4th, and m 3rd.[88]

2. Play or sing these notes with attention to the sequence of intervals.[89] This is one of the lines that the ear needs to hear.

Notice that the note on the 4th beat of each measure, through the end of the bars of triplets, is the pitch that propels you forward to the next downbeat. Be sure to make a clear distinction between whole and half note intervals. Don't let the difference get minimized as you proceed, the way my errant dove did.

3. Pay attention also to the final descending pattern of *G, E, C, A, F natural, C*, and *A*. What chord do those notes create? If you have a keyboard at hand play those notes altogether to hear the sound relationship that you must hold in your mind. When you play just those notes in sequence perhaps you will sense that it is a bit like falling down stairs, missing every other step. Don't hold back. Let these relationships propel you to the bottom.

---

[88] If you are confused by the abbreviations, go to the section on intervals in the Review Section.

[89] If you are not comfortable with singing these intervals, or recognizing them through their distinct sound, then drill yourself on intervals until it is effortless. This may be a lengthy on-going process.

4. Now look at the relationships between the notes within each beat: in the four bars of eighth notes there are only thirds—*G* to *B* is a major third, then a minor third, minor, minor, minor, minor, major, minor, minor, minor, major, minor, major, minor, major, minor. As you sing or play these, pay attention to what the interval relationship is and be sure to find optimum resonance, as you did for *Vocalise*.

5. In the triplets notice that the music goes back and forth between two patterns: the first triplet has two whole steps between the notes, the next a half step and then a whole step. Sing or play with awareness of these alternating patterns.

6. In the final eighth-note sequence notice the pattern within each beat: m 3rd, M 3rd, m 3rd, M 3rd, m 3rd, M 3rd, then a P 4th. Sing or play these notes with the interval awareness, bringing extra emphasis to that final fourth.

7. Play or sing the entire passage while maintaining awareness of all these relationships as best you can (and remember: awareness of something is not the same as thinking about it). Just having noticed and understood all these different relationships should help you give the music a sense of shape, direction, and motion. This awareness will also make it physically— technically—easier to play the passage well and with ease. Always, the more aspects one understands about the music the easier it is to play.

This type of study could be done with any passage in a piece of music—it is worth adding to your daily practice routine. Passages you are having difficulty playing will particularly benefit.


**Exercise 16.**

**Purpose: to be able to transpose relationships to other keys**

1. Do the Dove Drill starting on different pitches. Having understood the pattern of relationships you should be able to both sing and play the sequence beginning on any note.

2. Do the same thing with the *Vocalise* excerpt.

3. Do the same thing with the Brahms excerpt.

The Brahms is more difficult, but simply maintain all the same relationships. Speed is not the goal here—being able to replicate the pattern is, thus allowing you to transpose the passage to another key. If this is at all difficult, and most likely it will be on your instrument but maybe not so much when singing, make it an on-going drill. Don't stall on this exercise. The ease will come as you continue doing it.

## TONALLY-BASED MOVEMENT ILLUSION

I mentioned the possibility of pushing the 7th (tone or degree) of a scale higher to add tension to a relationship. For example, in the tonality or key of *C* Major the ear will hear the note *B natural*—the 7th of the scale—as needing to 'move' or resolve to *C*. Within the single line played by a string or wind instrument we can exaggerate that tension and create a greater need to move by pushing the 7th (in this case the *B*) just a bit higher than it would sound on a fixed-pitch instrument such as the piano. The sense of motion will be heightened.

Look next at my piece *Cry Of The Earth*, page 361 in the Addendum, for some examples of tension. You will also find additional comments about playing the piece in Act VI.

**Excerpt 7** *Cry of the Earth*, **first three bars without markings**

The piece is written in the key of *D* harmonic minor using the lowered 6th (*Bb*) and raised 7th (*C#*). The mournful quality of the minor-second and the minor-third sound relationships when they occur in succession, as they do in the first bar, is exaggerated by pushing pitches closer to the notes they belong to or want to resolve to. The *C#* to the *Bb* is our minor third sound. Pushing the *C#* up closer to a *D*, and the *Bb* down, closer to an *A*, will maximize the emotional impact of the note relationships. The *C#* is the 7th of the scale and will benefit from being closer to the *D* everywhere in the piece. Lowering the *B flats* towards the *A* when preceding or following the *C sharps* adds to the tension. The first *Bb* in the first bar stays neutral; the next one is slightly lower. The *Bb* in the third bar played against the open *D* sounds best when it remains neutral.

*G#* is the augmented fourth of the scale, and increases the sense of dissonance and tension. I push all the *G sharps* to the high side to exaggerate that tension. In the places where a descending minor-third sound relationship occurs with the *G sharps* going to *F natural*, as in bar two, I do push the *F*s down a bit, but otherwise the *F*s (the third of the scale) need to be neutral, not too low—as at the end of bar two. These *G sharps* add significant tension when played against the tonic *D* or dominant *A* later in the piece.

Chordal relationships behave the same way, including implied chords. Within a key there will be some chords that create for the ear a greater need to hear the movement to the tonic chord than others. When those chords are emphasized in some way, the need to move or resolve to the tonic or another resolution sound becomes greater. More tension is created. The greater need to resolve creates a greater sense of movement. The note or chord that the music resolves to however is *not* what carries the motion or gets the emphasis. In the melodic lines within a tonality we need to distinguish the notes that carry tension from these resolution notes. Understanding the fundamentals of tonal relationships allows us to discern the differing functions. Then we can make apparent to the ear this tension in numerous ways: by giving emphasis to the tension notes through a slight crescendo, bending the pitch slightly, stretching the note, using a more intense vibrato or sometimes no vibrato, or otherwise changing how we use the bow.

**Exercise 17.**

**Purpose: to be able to identify in tonally-based music which notes form the tonal center and which carry the harmonic tension**

Use my piece *HeartSong* for this exercise. It is a simple monophonic piece, but with the notes tracing out obvious chords. The version shown on the following page is without dynamics or other indications as to how I envision it. The full version is in the Addendum.

1. First, just play the written pitches, all with the same value, ignoring the rhythm, until it is clear to you which notes carry some sort of movement or tension and need to move on or resolve. There is very little in this piece other than the tonic chord, which tends to be static. It is in the key of *D* minor, therefore the tonic chord *D-F-A* is the scaffolding on which the piece hangs. These notes function as stable or static points or points of repose. They are not the notes that create or carry the tension and motion. There is in fact very little motion in this piece, (implying an emotion that is calm). You need to make the most of what motion is inherent in it or the piece will indeed seem dead.

The scaffold needs to be sound: stable, unmoving. As with any piece, you want the tonic note and the chord notes built on it to have an ideal relationship with each other. Those three notes—*D*, *F*, and *A*—must be impeccably in tune with each other. Other notes might be pushed one way or another, but not these. If you are a string player, find this relationship by playing an open *D* or *A* string with every pitch in the piece, like a drone, starting with finding the right *F*. Listen for the optimum resonance—that pristine intonation. Once you have these three pitches stable you will hear how the other pitches want to move to one of them. In the first eight-bar phrase it's the *C* and *G* that carry this tension of needing to move. In the second phrase it's *C*, *G* and now the *E*. In the four-bar tag before letter B there is a *C#* as well and in bar 30 finally a *Bb*. That's it. Out of all the notes in the entire piece, only 43 have the potential to create this type of illusory motion. Notice that in the second half of the first phrase—bars 5 through 8 with pickup—there are only the tonic chord notes, so no potential here for creating a tonally-based movement illusion.

2. Once you have established excellent intonation, effortless of course, try playing this piece exactly as it appears on the page. There are no markings in this version, so one might think that all notes would have a certain equality of importance. So play it that way, with the *Cs*, *Gs*, *Es*, etc. having no extra significance. Totally dead and boring, right?

3. Now try doing something different on the non-tonic chord notes. The first *C* for example could have extra weight in the sound, or perhaps be stretched slightly, or add some vibrato (the first *A* and *D* need none), or all of these. Are there places where these non-tonic notes should *not* have extra significance—perhaps the quarter-note *G* in the third and similar bars?

What about the bars with eighth notes? Is there another means of creating the sense of motion that has priority here?

Copyright © Bonnie Mangold 2016

**Excerpt 8**  *HeartSong* **without slurs and markings**

4. Do this same process on other simple pieces. Use my pieces *Inner Reflections* and *Improvisation in G*[90] for this purpose. Note that the *Improvisation* goes back and forth between *G* Major and *G* minor.

5. When you are comfortable with simpler pieces take a section of a Baroque work and apply this same process. Eventually you want to be able to look quickly at a piece, identify tonal centers and understand which notes create the tension and need to move or resolve.

---

[90] Addendum: pages 317 and 327.

## MORE ON TONALITY

Tonality codified around the mid-17th century and was dominant into the 19th century. Mostly it is in the music of 18th-century composers where a simple and obvious tonality is present. The use of a single tonal center then gave way to increasingly greater harmonic complexity, with the use of elaborate chords of five, six, or more notes, and frequent changes of key. A less definite feeling of tonality prevailed, and as mentioned, in the 20th century some composers moved away altogether from the tonality associated with keys and scales.[91]

The focus in the previous exercise on a clear tonality and the tonic chord was to help train your ear to be sensitive to those pitches that need to be stable, which are not the pitches carrying the tension. In more complex music, especially that of the late 1800s and 1900s, it might be difficult for those not highly trained in harmonic analysis to be sure what key any segment of the music is in. However your ear will be your guide as to the pitches and chords *acting at the moment* as tonal centers, to which other notes are oriented and drawn, like a gravitational pull, or moths drawn to a flame. This is one potential for creating the illusion of motion.

These crucial notes can just be thought of as pitch centers or focal points. Your ear, as well as your study of the music, will lead you to understand that you are not just playing sequences of unrelated notes. You may tire of hearing this: *you are playing a series of relationships and it is those relationships between notes that allow for the illusion of movement.*

In music of greater complexity the focal point will change frequently, and so your orientation must change with the music. If you play a series of notes without this orientation there will be no sense of movement generated by this tonal quality of the music. In the next exercise you will look at this aspect in a more complex piece. First, let us revisit the Brahms passage on page 129 to consider it from the point of view of these tonal center relationships—only one of many types of relationships in the cello line, but one I didn't ask you to notice earlier.

Once again paying attention to just the notes on the beats, notice that from the starting *A* through the four bars of eighth notes, this descending line has as its tonal center or focal point the note *E*, so that is your orientation pitch.[92] After the last *F natural* the ear anticipates going to an *E*, resolving on this tonic pitch—but the music doesn't do that, at least not in the cello line. Rather, on the next downbeat the *E* appears in the piano part instead, and the cello goes to the third of the tonic chord: a *G*, which is nicely set up by the *F* and *A* immediately before it. In the cello line we don't get another *E* until the last beat of bar 7. By keeping the *G* as the focal point in the cello line in bars 5 through 7, the anticipation of finally arriving at the tonic *E* in the last measure is heightened. The cello ends with the entire tonic chord (*E-G-B*). In this passage the *D sharps*, the *F sharps*, and the two *F naturals* that are on the beat carry the most tension and requirement to move. This is an important relationship to be aware of in this excerpt. And then, of course, there are all the relationships between the cello line and the piano voices!

---

[91] *Harvard Dictionary of Music*, Second Edition (paraphrase)
[92] The music is in the key of *E* minor.

**Exercise 18.**

**Purpose: to expand your ability to recognize shifting tonal centers and to create tension and release**

Use the beginning of the Bach *Concerto for Violin in A minor* on the following page for this exercise. (As you will often have to do with Baroque music, disregard all dynamics and slurs in various editions. There are no dynamic markings for the solo violin in the manuscript, and Bach's slurs are often hard to decipher and very inconsistent. You will do well to approach Baroque music with an empty mind and come to your own views regarding dynamics and slurs.) The title tells us that it is in *A* minor. Were it not for the title we would need to look at the key signature to conclude it is either in *A* minor or *C* Major. Examining the first few measures of the solo part it is clear that this phrase is built around the pitches *A-C-E*, the tonic chord of the *A* minor tonality, rather than *C* Major. These notes then will be stable in terms of intonation and more static in terms of energy or motion. (I have transcribed it for cello through letter B, but without showing my bowings here. It is basically just an octave lower.)[93]

Play the first eight bars, establishing excellent intonation with these notes. Be sure you come back to the identical pitches with every *A*, *C*, and *E*. Now play and notice which other pitches create the need to move to one of these tonic chord notes, especially to the *A*. The *G sharps* are the obvious candidates, but the *B* and *D* at the end of bar three lead the ear to the *C*. Again play these bars, keeping in mind this knowledge. Quite possibly how you play and emphasize these non-tonic notes will change simply because of your awareness of how they are functioning. When you intend[94] that they have more importance—to draw the ear to them—your body may find the way to do that without conscious analysis of *how* to do it. Play the passage again and notice whether you in fact have changed how you play the passage. If you don't hear a change, then begin experimenting with ways to emphasize the tension: give these notes more sound through more bow weight or speed, stretch them slightly, move a bit closer to the bridge to give a note a denser sound. Baroque music needs very little vibrato, but perhaps a hint of vibrato on these notes will be appropriate. Keep experimenting until you really hear the tension and resolution it is possible to create.

As you continue on, notice that in bar 8 the tonal center seems to change. It becomes apparent that the notes of the chord *E-G#-B*, alternating with *E-G-B*, become the focal points about which the music orients. There is a clear resolution on the note *E* at the beginning of bar 20, the emotional, energetic[95] ending for this section. But the music continues with a four-bar codetta[96] (or tag ending), again on an *E*—the first note of bar 24—at which point we have arrived at the literal end of the section. The sense of forward motion must be maintained from the beginning until here. (The character of the music changes dramatically as the next theme begins.) Without looking at what is in the orchestral accompaniment, we might consider the music in bars 8 through 24 as exploring sounds built on the fifth of the *A* minor scale, or we might conclude that the composer has modulated to the key of *E* minor.

---

[93]Later in this Act, I include these bars with bowings and other marks to suggest how it might be played. It is best to first study a work without being influenced by others' opinions.

[94] See the Revisiting Intention comments on page 148.

[95] See *Musings on Energy* page 154

[96] Codetta is Italian for *little tail*, meaning a brief concluding section following a part of the formal structure such as this initial exposition of the theme.

Excerpt 9  Bach *Concerto for Violin in A minor*, Breitkopf & Härtel edition, opening of the first movement

**Excerpt 10  Bach *Concerto for Violin in A minor*, opening transcribed for cello**

In harmonic analysis terms we would call the chord at the beginning of bar 8 the dominant of *A* minor. (In order to be called the *dominant* chord there will be a raised third—*G#* in this case.) Then we move through several bars in which Bach is modulating to the key of *E* minor. The chord at the beginning of bar 20 creates a deceptive cadence.[97] The ear expects the *E* minor tonic chord, but it is actually a chord built on the sixth of *E* minor—due to the *C* in the bass line of the accompaniment. Finally there is the tonic chord at the downbeat of bar 24. Despite the *G#* this *is* the tonic chord of *E* minor.[98] For our purposes we do not have to have the correct labels, but the ear has to recognize that the tonal center has shifted to *E* since the beginning of the piece, and we need to play accordingly. In these bars the notes that carry the most tension and demand movement are the *D sharps*. Also some of the *F sharps*. Play bars 8 through 24 going through the same process as with the first eight bars, giving emphasis to the appropriate notes.

Work through to the first half of bar 43 in this way, finding the chord notes that form the tonal centers. Look at patterns, look at resolution notes, look for a recognizable scale, like the descending *E* minor scale notes back in measures 20 thru 22. Notice that starting in bar 32, then again in bar 34, again in 36 and in bar 38, we have sequences of 13 notes starting on the 7th of a scale, going up to the tonic, then descending to the tonic note of that scale. Notice that at bar 43 we clearly end in *A* minor. Looking backwards from an end or resolution point often makes it easier to figure out or see these things. You want to use this harmonic tool to come to an understanding of an entire piece in terms of what are the resolution notes and what are the notes propelling the illusion of forward motion.

---

[97] Cadence: "a melodic or harmonic formula that occurs at the end of a composition, a section, or a phrase, conveying the impression of a momentary or permanent conclusion." From *Harvard Dictionary of Music*, Second Edition

[98] It was commonplace in Baroque music and even in later periods, to brighten the mood of a minor key by raising the third of the tonic chord in a cadence—known as the Picardy third.

If you have difficulty creating this illusory sense, try playing through a section giving no emphasis at all to any note over the others. Notice how mechanical and dull this sounds. Now play it with an awareness of which notes carry tension and which resolve the tension. Alternate between these two approaches until you hear some sort of shift in what you are doing.


## Exercise 19.

### Purpose: To be comfortable finding tonal centers in modern music

You will encounter music where you cannot easily identify a key or true tonal center. Perhaps the composer did not use a key signature or the music modulates so frequently that you are unsure of what is happening harmonically, or it is atonal music such as that of Anton Webern. In that case look for what I call a pitch center. A passage may be oriented around a particular recurring pitch, causing it to act temporarily as a tonal center, or at least as a stable point around which other notes orient. Like the tonic note of a scale, this pitch will act as the magnet to attract other notes to it, creating the sense of tension and release and thus motion.

*Schelomo* by Ernest Bloch (following page) is interesting to examine. (For non-cellists who don't read tenor clef, the clef sign centers on the second line down on the staff, designated as middle *C*; hence the initial pitch is *A*.) There are two flats in the key signature, indicating music either in *B-Flat* Major or *G* minor. As you will quickly hear from the emotional character of the music it must be *G* minor. However looking at just the cello part it is unclear that either key applies, as throughout the first section, up until the end of the cadenza in measure 19, the cello line is based on a *D* chord (*D-F-A* or *D-F#-A*). If you know your fundamentals of harmony you will quickly recognize that this is the chord built on the fifth of the *G* minor scale.

This analytical understanding is valuable, but for the ear it is most important that we establish the *D*, and the *A*, as the tonal centers. These are the two pitches around which the entire section focuses. To give you a visual, metaphorical image, the *D*s and *A*s are the fragrant flowers that the bees circle in their desire to get to the pollen. To begin with, the *E flats* and *B flats* exert the most tension. Later the *C sharps* and *G sharps* create tension. The *D* and *A* must remain impeccably in tune, but it is quite possible to put the half step pitches above or below the *D* and *A* just a bit closer (to the flowers), to exaggerate the tension and compelling need to move.

Examine other music you know well, from the late 19th century on, with the intent of identifying tonal centers and these aspects of tension and release. Remember the point of all this is to be able to create the illusion of motion, and for that we need departure points and destination points,[99] creating a sense of flow and motion, not only within an entire work, but within each successively smaller section.

---

[99] See *Musings on Departure and Destination Points and More* page 167.

# Schelomo
## Rhapsodie Hébraïque

**Excerpt 11   Bloch** *Schelomo for Cello and Orchestra,* **G. Shirmer, 1916**

"Really there is something in this; the tone of mind<br>
produced by architecture approaches<br>
the effect of music."[100]<br>
—Goethe


## STRUCTURE OF THE WHOLE OR STRUCTURAL MOTION

We don't want to plod through a piece note by note or one measure at a time, getting caught in the tyranny of the downbeat where every bar gets an emphasis on the first note, leaving the music thudding along lifelessly. We need to look at the musical equivalent of syntax: the way words are put together to form phrases, sentences, paragraphs and chapters to communicate. In music we have these same principles, and we use some of the same language to describe this grammar of structure  how the music is put together, how it is assembled. When the ear is made aware of these relationships, this additionally helps to create the sense of movement. We are building something and are continuously moving to its completion.

We can use the analogy of building a cathedral. The cathedral is made up of individual stones (the notes), but we will put three stones together (a measure) and then another three on top of those, all in a frame, and then lay all six together on top of another six, and so on until we have an entire wall, then a different wall, until we can create a roof to complete the structure.

This is again the province of analysis: identifying the structure of the entire piece, referred to as *form and analysis*. We are examining relationships, on various scales from the entire movement down to a two-bar or four-bar unit. How the small sections fit together to create larger sections, and how those larger sections work together to create something larger, until there is the whole—all this helps to create a sense of movement through time from the beginning to the end. This structure is reminiscent of the patterns found in fractals: the pattern of the whole is found in the parts.[101]

Several pieces I have played recently, such as the Turina *Piano Trio No. 2*, have as the basic building block a unit of two bars. This is almost constant throughout the three movements, and is not uncommon. Usually a two-bar unit is combined with another to make a larger unit of four bars, then this is combined with another four-bar unit consisting of the two two-bar units, to make an eight-bar unit, or phrase. And then two eight-bar units combine to make up a sixteen-bar unit, and so on. This is a classic structure or form, and it is prevalent in music from all periods, not just what we think of as the classical period. Understanding how the composer has put the music together helps identify where the climax of the entire movement or piece is. We want to know where the peak of energy and emotion is, so that all the music before the peak leads to it, and the music after the peak falls away from it. Again, this is part of what will bring life to the music. There is a container—the form—and it shapes the music, leading the listener effortlessly through the music.

---

[100] Goethe's words reference his own comment that architecture is "petrified music."

[101] If you aren't familiar with fractals, research them a bit. Try the fractalfoundation.org site. Fractals are natural phenomena or mathematical constructions that have never-ending, repeating patterns at every scale: self-similarity. When represented visually they make exquisite and beautiful images.

140

**Exercise 20.**

**Purpose: to become aware of the form in music**

Use my piece *Inner Reflections* on page 317 of the Addendum for this exercise. Just by looking at the score you can see that the entire piece is composed of two-bar units. The physical, visual contours of the printed music tell you this—even if you don't read music. If it is not immediately apparent then sing it, play it on a keyboard or on your instrument, until you hear that each successive two bars form the building blocks for this piece.

Now observe that each group of two two-bar units (four measures) always relate closely to each other, creating and completing a short musical thought. Those first four bars constitute the theme. They provide the musical kernel on which the rest of the piece is based. If it were a verbal construction there could be a comma after the first four bars, tying them to the next four bars, to complete the first eight-bar 'sentence.' The next eight bars relate in the same way, completing a 'paragraph.'

The next four bars, which are in six-four meter instead of five-four, create a bridge to the second half, which follows the same pattern as the first half, completing another paragraph. The final four bars, like an epilogue, are again in six-four meter. They simply constitute a tag or coda to allow the music to wind down further, bringing it to a standstill—the music having lost all forward motion and energy by the final tonic note.

Examine the piece more closely for the dynamic and energetic peak. The dynamic markings indicate that the composer intends bar 26 to be the climax of the piece. In the first half there is a peak in bar 9, but it doesn't reach a forte level, it is merely louder than what came before, and the *E* goes gently to the *A*, rather than emphasizing the arrival on the *A*. In the second half each two-bar unit begins at a higher volume level than the previous one, culminating in the forte bar, with the *G#* adding the emotional intensity missing from the first half. From there the volume and energy step down. The little crescendo at the end of bar 30 ties that two-bar unit more closely to the next two-bar unit, so that the ear becomes more aware of the four-bar unit. The coda with its extra beat per bar is a calmer, pale reflection of the earlier material, almost static now.

It doesn't take much examination to determine how to shape or pace a piece this simple in its structure, but it is always critical to do so to help bring any music to life. Longer and more complex music will require significant thought and analysis to understand how it is put together, and to know what illusions you wish to create to give an entire work a sense of movement from beginning to end.

The understanding you gain from examining the structure enables you to communicate through your playing these relationships and sense of progression or movement. Then you can intend for the listener to hear the two-bar units (or whatever unit forms the basis of what you are playing), not just single bars or beats in succession. Awareness of the unit structure will naturally make each first bar lead to the second, and the first two-bar unit lead to the second, and so on. You will know where the music needs to breathe, and how deeply. You will know where it has to grow slightly to lead onwards, where to lose energy to bring something to an end.

### *MUSINGS ON FORM AND FORMLESSNESS*

Form in music helps to keep the attention of the listener. In Theme E we will talk about the atonal music written since the 1920s, which in addition to abandoning tonality also often departs drastically from prior rhythmic forms, or has no discernible structural form.

Music written without traditional forms or structure may simply meander with no destination, causing the listener eventually (or quickly) to lose interest and stop hearing it. Here, I speak of some of what is called New Age music, which affects me negatively because of this lack of form. The music may consist of sounds pleasing to the ear, but often there is little beyond that. The original purpose of the genre was to help the physical body relax and find ease, and some composers, Stephen Halpern for example, did that well. However this type of music has become ubiquitous in those situations where people want you to be calm and relaxed, as in waiting rooms or on massage tables. But given how the bulk of this genre has developed, I often find myself becoming irritated, rather than relaxed, with the aimlessness and lack of intention and the incessant looping of the material. This may not be the case for those who have no inclination to actively listen when music is played as background to something else, like a massage.

I rarely hear New Age Music that compels me to listen to it again, and again, and again and again… There is of course music falling within the New Age genre—by composers such as Paul Winters—that is intriguing and well worth listening to. When I do resonate with such music it seems that there is additional purpose to it, beyond keeping me relaxed.

Lest I influence you unduly I will admit to having a definite prejudice against the genre, a prejudice I haven't chosen to give up, at least not yet. (Maybe next year.) What about your response to music of this genre? Do you enjoy it? If so what is it that speaks to you? If not, have you identified why?

**Exercise 21.**

**Purpose: to recognize form in more complex music**

We look next on the following two pages at the exquisite second movement of the Brahms *E minor Cello Sonata*, just the first *Menuetto* section. (The *Trio* section changes key and character, becoming more dreamy and improvisational in sound and considerably more complex.)

This section, though very cleverly written with the voices trading material back and forth, still has a simple basic structure based on two-bar units. Even without looking at the piano part this is apparent to the eye and ear if played with this awareness. I have heard it played with equal emphasis on every downbeat, destroying the sense of movement and forward progression. Including the piano part in your examination will confirm this building block of the two-bar unit.

The two-bar units begin at the double bar, after the piano and cello upbeats. The first two units combine into a four-bar phrase. The next four bars—related in the same way—combine to form an eight-bar unit. This completes the first musical sentence with the cello's half note *E* resolution. It is followed by a two-bar tag. (These two bars have been tagged onto the theme.)

Now the four-beat upbeat material that was in the piano part occurs in the cello line (just prior to the double bar before bar 16). The two instruments reverse parts and play an additional similar sentence plus tag, bringing to an end what could be called the first paragraph.

In the next paragraph there is the initial eight-bar sentence, made up in the same way, a second eight-bar sentence, a third eight-bar sentence, then four bars leading to the peak of the *Menuetto* on the downbeat *E* in the cello on measure 58, and the downbeat in the piano a bar later.

This resolution bar in the piano also becomes the upbeat music, as in the beginning, returning us to the original eight-bar theme, which gets stretched a bit. Then the *Menuetto* winds down through the last eight bars to finish gently, setting up the change of mood in the ensuing *Trio*. From where it begins to wind down in measure 71 to the end of the section no retard is indicated. The music is not finished, and though the energy winds down the sense of motion must continue. Only the last chord (possibly two) needs to be 'set' a bit, (delayed just slightly) to bring the section to a quiet close.

Even a quick examination of the music (such as what we have just done) should allow you to make determinations about dynamics and pacing, which notes lead onwards, when they finish something, when the music needs to breathe, etc. It is also quite possible to intuitively understand all these aspects, never looking at the structure. However having the conscious awareness of how the music is put together can save you a lot of time while your intuition is developing.

**Excerpt 12   Brahms *Sonata No. 1 in E Minor,* Schott edition, second movement (continues on the next page)**

cresc. poco a poco
cresc. poco a poco
pizz.
arco
Fine

## 15

Let's look at one way to play the first twelve opening bars of the cello line, keeping in mind that both cello and piano lines are marked *piano* and the word *dolce* is additionally in the piano part. Later the cello line is marked *grazioso*. The upbeat note, marked with a dot, can create the feeling of both lift and the expectancy of leading somewhere within the gentle, dolce feeling indicated in the score. I give it more weight, thus a bit more bow speed and sound, than the ensuing downbeat, and only the slightest separation. Too short or brusque a note will break the sense of leading motion. The last three eighth notes of bar 2 lead to the second bar of the unit, requiring a bit more energy leading to the $G\#$—so an increase of sound is called for, best produced by each eighth getting slightly more bow (that is, bow speed and sound) than the previous one. After the downbeat ($G\#$) of bar 3 (the second bar of the unit), the two $E$s can be a rebound from the $G\#$, so lighter (less bow). I treat that second $E$ not as an upbeat, but as losing energy in that rebound effect. In the next two-bar unit, which I start softly again, I allow it to gain more sound than the first unit had, thus creating the sense of building something, yet giving the notes within the two bars the same internal relationship. In bars 6 through 9, I let the music grow to the $D$ in the third of those four bars so that they will flow together without the sense of two plus two, moving all the way to the half-note $E$ in bar 10 without the motion and flow being held back in any way. I view that downbeat $D$ as the peak of this phrase in terms of dynamics and emotion, the music falling away from there to the half-note E.

Played in this way the music will have a sense of forward motion. If, on the other hand, you play every bar with the same emphasis on the downbeat, it will sound very pedestrian. Experiment—just singing the passage, or playing it if you are comfortable with it—and find out what happens with varied approaches. You can also create a sense of forward motion by making every third beat in the second, fourth, and comparable bars play the role of an upbeat, rather than the rebound effect I suggested. That will be determined by the nature of the mood you find in the music and what best expresses that mood. I like the not-quite-real effect produced by the rebound. If I choose to play the theme a bit more mischievously, then I would make those notes feel like upbeats. String players have the advantage of being able to change a plethora of factors to create the sense of movement. Wind players too have many tools. Keyboard players have to be true magicians of illusion, but it can be and is done.

Bring the ideas from this section to each piece of music you study, and even if the complexities of the music are beyond your ability to analyze and label appropriately, look for how the distinct parts relate to each other and where the peaks of motion and emotion are. Trust yourself.

Theme A has dealt primarily with aspects of harmony and structure applicable to tonal music that inform how we might approach the music physically. As stated previously this is a cursory view of the vast subject of how music is constructed. You could spend years studying all the tools and devices used in composition, even during the relatively straight-forward Classical period of music. If you want to have a clue about what composers such as Stravinsky and Hindemith and Shostakovich are doing in their music then it behooves you to understand what Mozart and Beethoven were doing that we find so very beautiful: all the ways you can play with a theme, the importance of repetition, the presence of ambiguity. The more you analyze how music is constructed the deeper your understanding of a piece becomes, but ultimately it is not the inversion of the theme, or augmentation of it, or some other device the composer has used that you are playing. It is what these *represent*—the feeling-state that they create in you—that you must play. You are not playing the form of the piece or the technique used. You are playing what the music means to you. The blueprint has communicated something to you and now you become that something. *How* that happens remains a bit of a mystery.

**INTERLUDE**

*"Determine the thing that can and shall be done, and then we shall find the way."*
—Abraham Lincoln (1809-1865)
16th President of the United States

## REVISITING INTENTION

In Western culture perhaps the best known example of an intention is from the *King James Bible*: "And God said, Let there be light: and there was light." Intention is a statement of what shall be. It is not a 'doing,' not a process—rather a *fait accompli*. Whether it is the composing of the music or a performance of the music it all begins with an intention held in the mind. This is how music incarnates: first the intention, then the manifestation. Intention is effortless and virtually instantaneous. It is not something you work at. The idea forms in your consciousness and it is done. The intent to touch another's heart is simply there in the background when you perform. It doesn't require attention or work. It just is. The intent to create a relationship within the music may be all that is needed. Now it exists.

Having an intention does not require that you receive proof that you have carried out your intent; it doesn't require validation; it isn't attached to results. Attaching your intent to feedback from listeners pulls you out of the present moment and prevents you from *being* the music, creating in the moment. Being attached to results is an ego manifestation that interferes with playing from the heart. You are not *trying, using effort,* to get the audience to react; you are not trying to impress. When you walk on stage you know your intent; it is already set, and then you let it go. And you play from *your* heart. How others respond is not your business.

Aspects of computers and their programming mimic aspects of our minds and how we function. Our purpose for playing music, our intentions for a piece, our carrier waves, are all analogous to background programs on a computer. They are always running, like a basic operating system or security system, without needing conscious attention, while consciously we are doing or using something else. It is the same in the rest of life. Once you have decided something or formed an intention—for example, to drink a glass of milk—you don't have to consciously orchestrate every move of that process. Instead, your body walks to the refrigerator; your arm and hand reach out to grasp and open the door; your hand goes to the milk bottle, which your eyes have spotted and focused on; you pull it out, pick up a glass, pour some milk, return the bottle, and probably begin drinking the milk with no conscious thought at all on how to accomplish this. You may in fact have been absorbed in a phone conversation while carrying out this action. You never gave conscious thought to when to move your arm, how far to extend it, how much effort it would require to pick up the bottle, and so on.

As infants we go through learning processes where we explore and learn to control our bodies to achieve our desires. Once the intent is known, actions proceed appropriately unless there are barriers to that smooth flow from intent to realization, such as brain damage, excess effort, trauma, or… fear.

In Act I there was much emphasis on keeping your focus on your purpose, yet the human tendency is to focus on what we don't want. It is difficult to fix anything when that happens.

**148**

For example, if there is a shift that you have frequently missed, the tendency at the moment you again make the shift is to be fearful of missing it, thus focusing on what you don't want. That generally ensures you will miss it. If all of you is creating what you do want—hearing the desired sound—the shift is apt to be accurate.

> **Tip**: If you still have problems, apply the principle mentioned in the tip on page 79 of taking conscious control of what has become a habitual pattern—missing the shift—until you can deliberately go too high or too low at will. Then go back to intending the correct pitch.

In preceding exercises describing how to create some of the illusions, I have used and will continue to use various words or phrases to encourage you to do something physical to bring out the importance of a note in leading the ear onward. In the process of teaching I have found that it is important to find the meaningful words to describe the physical actions needed. I have said "emphasize the note," which can imply louder, though it is never just a question of playing a note louder. It has to start with the intention to lead the ear somewhere, which is not achieved by accenting a note or being suddenly louder. The expressions that I like to use to clarify the idea of emphasizing are: "lean into the note," "sink into it," "give it more weight," "let it grow" or "bring it out." I like these because they have a physical, visual connotation that helps get the needed sound. When I am with a student I can use my own body motion to demonstrate these ideas. Leaning into something is very different than accenting something. An accent is a punch, there is an initial impact. When you lean on something the initial contact is gentle and then it gets heavier. You let your weight rest on something, which we can do with a note.  "Louder" doesn't capture the concept as it references a strictly physical decibel change that misses the aspect of intention and emotion behind making something more important. I prefer to avoid using the word "stress" (as in the phrase "stress the note"), as it can carry negative connotations. When I do suggest to stress a note, it simply means do something to bring that note to the attention of the ear.

In the process of writing this section I have had to analyze what I do when I play the referenced passages, and then put that into words. Originally I didn't decide to increase bow speed here or there, rather I decided what *shape* I wanted the music to have and what I wanted to communicate. Then, my body carried out that intent with all the tools I have at my disposal. Clarity as to your intent—knowing and focusing on what you want—is always the easiest and quickest way to achieve something. Deciding how to use your bow on every note is the long way and the hard way, as it will require vast amounts of time to integrate this into a whole. Nevertheless you must have acquired the needed tools—know and understand what is available to you. If you aren't getting the musical effect you want, you may need to change the tool you are using.

Ultimately what you do physically simply flows naturally and harmoniously from your intention, so that the motions your body makes carry out those intentions.

Awareness is another magical tool. Like intention it is not a matter of working at it, nor does it require time. It is just there—or it isn't. And it simply requires a decision. You intend to be attentive to something, and so you are.

# VOICE RELATIONSHIPS
# —THEME B

**Figure 9**

## SWITCHING 'VOICES'

'Voice' refers to any sound that can be likened to a human utterance or speech—a means of expression, such as a melody line for the cello, or the right hand part in a work for piano. It is not just the human voice. When you have complex music you may have many voices present at the same time.

Another aspect of relationships and motion, even in a single melodic line, is the illusion of there being more than one voice 'speaking' and possibly coming from different locations in succession—easy enough to do in an orchestra where there is an actual change in space from where the sound originates as the music travels from one instrument to another.[102] For a single instrument this is a more difficult impression to create. It requires that you clearly understand and communicate when there is a change in the voice 'speaking.' You can't just switch from the cello to the clarinet or transport yourself to the other side of the stage.

Often you will encounter a dialogue in the music where one voice or quality of energy will 'speak' and a different voice responds. These two differing voices may represent masculine and feminine energies in dialogue, the quality of a statement or question and a response, or an antithesis. Steven Isserlis' description of the first of the Schumann *Fantasy Pieces* as a love duet between the cello and piano implies a dialogue between voices, and as one takes over from the other a sense of movement is created. This is in addition to the actual change in the physical location from where the sound originates. The dialogue is like the differing lines in the two staves of piano music, the right hand and the left hand on the piano trading off with the important 'words,' or contrasting energies. In a single line of music, as in the case of a solo instrument or the human voice, there are still differing voices 'speaking' and a switch of voice needs to be obvious to the ear to communicate the composer's intent.

It is particularly vital to make this apparent in the music of the Baroque period, which does *not* feature long singing melodies with accompanying harmony. In the *Six Suites for Solo Cello* by Bach there is mostly the one line of music, with occasional double stops or chords; nevertheless there are multiple voices needing to be heard. When musicians play as if there were just one voice going on and on—a monologue—it gets very boring indeed. One of the problems with many of the editions of Baroque music is that 19th-century editors, influenced by the writing and performance styles of their own period, added extensive slurs that obscure this aspect of the structure of the music. Whenever possible look for Urtext editions, which

---

[102] Ravel's *La Valse* is a prime example of the swirling effect of sound moving through the orchestra.

150

generally come closest to replicating the original manuscripts. Having several editions of a piece for comparison is always a good idea.

The music of Bach is full of examples of alternating voices. Often there is a sense of interruption, as if one voice can hardly wait to say something and jumps in before a decent pause—rather rude-seeming for some of us.[103] These alternating voices do need to be slightly on the rude side to interrupt the flow and create the illusion of a change—hence motion.

> **Tip**: Imagining how a pianist would play a single line of notes (which notes must be taken with the left hand, which with the right), helps to clarify how the voices divide. Singing the music helps too, as does practicing without slurs and other editing marks, such as dynamics, that might obscure the voice changes. William Pleeth, wonderful cellist and teacher with whom I had the good fortune to study all the Bach *Suites*, suggested I practice them single bow and legato until I could hear the structure and voice changes, then decide what bowings (slurs, staccatos) would help make these features apparent to the ear.[104] It was a laborious task as I first had to get out of my head the sounds from many years of playing and hearing the *Suites* with all the romantic-style editing. Many hours of gentle, quiet single-bow work eventually led to hearing how notes were grouped, where something started and where it ended, where slurs were appropriate and where they were not. Pleeth didn't share his bowings until after I had decided mine. To my great pleasure it turned out that my choices were very close to his. The consequence of all that work is that I have my very own edition of the *Suites*.

---

[103] People in different cultures wait varying lengths of time before beginning to speak following another person. If someone violates what you subconsciously consider to be the appropriate wait, you will find yourself annoyed. If someone waits too long, you will probably begin speaking again.

[104] My experience with the *Suites* also showed me that this was an effective way to hear the tonal centers and find the right intonation, which is why I advocate this process for the initial practicing of any music.

**Exercise 22.**

**Purpose: to be able to differentiate voices**

To apply this concept of switching voices we will look again at passages from the same Bach violin concerto, from the end of bar 4 through bar 8. If written for piano it might look thus:

**Figure 10**

In this example the right hand plays the ascending notes and the left continuously interrupts with the repeated *A, G#, A.* In bar 7 the right hand might take three notes before the left takes over, instead of just the one. See what you think.

<><><>

**Figure 11**

In this second passage, from the end of bar 24 through bar 28, one hand, perhaps the left, starts with the six-note pattern; then the other hand plays a five-note response. To me (today) the six-note pattern represents a gentler, questioning voice and the response a more assured answer— so two different voices. It could be played the other way around and be just as convincing. Sing it both ways and see which resonates most with you. Since the voices are in the same range, on the piano the hands will be crossing over each other.

If a comparable passage were by a later composer, say Brahms, most likely we would not hear those four bars as two voices, but as just one continuous voice or line. However, it was written at a time when music was more like speech—less like song—and longer note values were played as much as fifty per cent shorter than the written value. There were definite silences in the music and constant interruptions of one voice taking over from another. Creating two voices in this passage brings greater life to the music.

How to make these voice changes apparent on a string instrument primarily involves how you use the bow, and of course your intent. The intent always comes first.

In Figure 10 the notes given to the right hand must have a slight separation from the three left-hand notes. On a string instrument taking these 'right-hand' notes down-bow using plenty of bow for a faster bow speed, and having the slightest break in sound before the three 'left-hand' notes, which could be slurred, will differentiate the two voices. Pleeth referred to this stop in sound as closing the lips of the note, just as you close your lips between words you speak, when there is a need for clarity. Try singing this passage closing your lips after the right-hand notes, but without losing tempo. Then emulate that on your instrument.

In Figure 11 the three notes starting both patterns need to grow just a bit to propel you to the next note, which in both cases is the peak of the respective pattern. The dynamic falls off slightly from there. The tied notes in both patterns need to fade and be cut short so that we hear the other voice coming in. Each pattern interrupts the other and may do so by coming in slightly louder than the previous group ended. If you were to sing this you could take a very quick breath between each pattern, or at least make a break in the sound. Try it, and again emulate this on your instrument. Most important is to give each voice a slightly different character. Conceive of them with different emotional qualities. Try singing them with varying attitudes and emotions. Find what resonates with you.

<>\<>\<>

Look again at this score (my cello version without markings) starting in bar 24 and consider how you might divide the notes following bar 28 between the voices.[105]

**Excerpt 13  Bach *Concerto for Violin in A minor,* first movement excerpt, transcribed for cello**

---

[105] See page 189 in Theme D of this Act for a version with the slurs and markings I use to help show these ideas. There is also the possibility of the left hand taking only the three 16th-note upbeats and the right hand taking the rest. But this is where the solo violin diverges from the tutti violins, and I hear it as being a suddenly more intimate and lyrical theme requiring different treatment. The ambiguities are marvelous.

# INTERLUDE


*"I would rather die of passion than of boredom."*
—Vincent van Gogh (1853-1890)
Dutch painter


### MUSINGS ON ENERGY

Energy: 1. strength of expression; force of utterance; life; spirit;—said of speech, language, words, style, etc. [ | 3. Power effectively and forcefully exerted; vigorous or effectual operation; [106]

Energetic: Exhibiting energy; operating with force, vigor and effect.[107]

The energy we use to communicate music goes beyond the biological, metabolic cellular energy of the physical body that we draw on for our physical movements. This is an energy that we create—through purpose and intention. *If* your physical body is functioning properly yet you think you don't have the energy to do something like take a walk, oftentimes this inertia is simply due to lack of purpose or intention. As soon as you make the decision to do something the energy magically appears.

It is an energy of spirit and Mind that you call upon, and it is that energy we use when we create and play music. It will be reflected in the motions we use, and it has to vary constantly to communicate the content of the music. When I say that the music loses energy or winds down I am referring to the diminishing of the sense of power or force in the music ('force' in the interprctation of music is not to be confused with excess effort). The music might get softer, it might slow down, it might get gentler, it might do any combination of thesc, or something else.

Look at this image of Camille Claudel's sculpture *La Valse* and notice how much motion and energy is captured and communicated. Ravel's *La Valse* contains a similar energy and motion. The sound swirls, it grows, it recedes, it grows again and again, always with forward motion and propulsion, culminating in a paroxysm of energy. To play this without bringing a high level of energy to your physical motions misses the meaning of the music. *We* decide what energy we will bring to something, and it manifests. To play *La Valse* true to the composer's intent requires this tremendous expenditure of energy. The parceling out of energy in a miserly fashion as if you couldn't create more doesn't belong in this work. The music *is* the feeling of abandon: wild abandon of good sense and carefulness, come hell or high water! *That* is what the music demands! Being careful is the antithesis of the energy inherent in *La Valse*.

Being careful is the antithesis of creating anything.


---

[106] *Webster's New International Dictionary*
[107] Ibid

**_La Valse_, by French artist Camille Claudel**

Camille Claudel (1864-1943), French sculptor and graphic artist, was often considered to be the muse for Auguste Rodin. During her turbulent life, the work officially attributed to her never received acclaim equal to his. There is significant evidence that many sculptures attributed to *him* were actually created by *her*. *La Valse*, from 1893, is undisputedly her work. She captures the same free, dynamic, swirling and turning motion that Ravel's music—written some 30 years later with no apparent connection—communicates. In my mind they both tapped into the same morphic field, expressing very similar concepts of a wild, passionate, and grand waltz. The same sense of motion and life has been captured by both artists within their different mediums.

Silence is a tool we can use to indicate a switch of voices. Silence is also a part of structure. Silence or emptiness or space is as much a part of structure as are the visible or audible physical parts.

> *"No more words.*
> *In the name of this place we*
> *drink in without breathing,*
> *stay quiet like a flower.*
> *So the nightbirds will start singing."*
> —Rumi
> from *Night and Sleep*, translated by Coleman Barks

## SILENCE

"Silence" is defined as the absence of sound or noise, stillness.

Silence is integral to music, as stillness is integral to life. Silence is the canvas on which we paint our sound. Stillness is the canvas on which we paint the motion of our lives. When the music stops we hear the silence. When the motion of our lives stops there is stillness.

There is the necessary silence of the mind (ego) in performance, so that something else—intention, inspiration—can be present. There is the silence of the body: the freedom from *incongruent* effort and motion. Silence creates a feeling of expectancy, anticipation: what will come to fill this container? Without the silence and emptiness nothing new can come into the space. This is why stillness before you begin to play is so important. It is for both you and your listener. You are creating the empty vessel which will be filled—with love.

When my potter friend talks about her art, she too speaks of the importance of the silences. With the vessels that she makes—the vases, bowls, cups—the silence is the empty space that the outer form of clay contains. The inner space is as important and real as the outer form. The clay contains the nothingness that can then be filled. Even the shape of a handle is guided by the absence of something: an emptiness that can be filled by the fingers of your hand. Negative space, akin to negative sound. Like the empty space of the pot we enclose silence with sound.

Consider again James McKean's words about violin-making: "The silence is what counts, the spaces in between are as important as the strokes of the tools." In like fashion Debussy is purported to have said "Music is the silence between the notes," and similar sayings are attributed to jazz composers Thelonious Monk and Miles Davis. This idea that much of the music occurs between the notes has persisted for a long time. The music is not the notes; the music is something the notes and the spaces between attempt to express. Again, the written music is a blueprint, a morphogenetic field, quite different than the realized structure. As we flesh out the blueprint—bringing it into physical existence, bringing it to life—like a cathedral or other vessel, the spaces are as important as the walls.

*"At the still point of the turning world,*
*there the dance is."*
—T. S. Eliot (1888-1965)
American-born British poet, essayist, playwright
from *Burnt Norton*

### MUSINGS ON SILENCE

Out of nothingness, out of silence, our universe burst into existence… into sound, light, vibration, motion, life. I call that nothingness The Vast Stillness. This silence—no sound, no vibration—is the 'ground' for all of creation.

In life there is both motion and silence. Life breathes. There is space or silence between breaths, between movements, silences in our speech, the silence before the storm, still points in the natural motion of life. Before a pendulum reverses direction there must be that momentary suspension of motion—stillness—prior to the opposite motion occurring. And when all motion of life stops, that is the end of physical life. Only stillness remains. We are born out of stillness and we return to stillness.

Without silence and stillness, and the spaces between the notes—the moments of no motion— motion becomes invisible, inaudible. That which you are immersed in disappears to the senses. Without shadow we would not understand light. Without exposure to air fish would not be aware of water. Unexamined beliefs and patterns of behavior are so pervasive we cannot see them; they disappear to our consciousness.

Strangely, the very lack of *something*, whether sound, motion, or thought, leaves a nothingness that can be observable and palpable. When I meditate I can feel the stillness. When I paddled on the Great Salt Lake I could perceive the envelope of silence surrounding me, yet also hear the distant sounds from that dead, gray ribbon (Highway I-80) bisecting the desert towards the west. We know the one because of contrast with the other.

We perceive motion because we know stillness.

***The Vast Stillness***

*Into the Vast Stillness*

*My beingness ebbs and flows*

*Silence is my nature*

*Silence is my home.*

Bonnie Mangold
2010

## Exercise 23.

### Purpose: become aware of your still points

Think about the moments when you get some sort of inspiration, and notice when those have occurred: what are you doing, or not doing? For myself I realized that the times I am most likely to get good ideas are while meditating, driving, or when I am in the shower. These moments have in common that I am not doing anything very active or that requires much attention. In most respects I have come to a still point; now something else can enter.

But let me qualify the inspiration-while-driving piece. This is not city driving. Have I mentioned that I live in the middle of *nowhere*? Even on the more populated road to the nearest town with a grocery store, 18 miles away, the traffic isn't much. (I do avoid rush hour however, when the traffic easily doubles: four cars instead of two.) There are times I have driven a lonely hundred-mile stretch of road and haven't seen even one car in either direction. I generally don't play any music, books, lectures, or the radio (who wants to listen to static anyway?). I like silence. I once drove three thousand miles in silence. It is wonderful. It serves me well. I have learned to keep paper and pen handy to make notes when ideas or themes for a piece come up. If I am meditating I still go ahead and make notes. Otherwise my attention will be caught in not wanting to forget the idea and struggling to remember. Better to break the meditation, write the thought, then go back to the meditation unencumbered. As for the shower, that is when most of the themes for my pieces have come to mind, and then I do engage in a bit of singing, enough to set the theme in my analytical mind. True, I sometimes get carried away with the glorious shower stall sound, but eventually I go back to my still point.

Go to your journal and record those still points of your own that you are aware of. What inspirations or realizations or greater clarity have come at such times? Under what circumstances do your mind and body quiet down sufficiently for inspiration to come in? Could you create more opportunities for that to happen? What might they be?

## THE MISSING SILENCE

Our contemporary performance style has been much swayed by what has been referred to as
Wagnerian song: lush, smooth, sustained sound, continuing on and on without breath, without
pause, without silence. Listening to this way of playing is like traveling on a highway on the
East Coast of the U.S. where the road becomes a tunnel through beautiful but never-ending
green trees. It is unrelenting. Only if you look up do you see open space: the sky directly
overhead. As a westerner, it becomes quite claustrophobic to me, and when I finally get far
enough west to see open spaces and distant landscapes, there is palpable relief. Ah, space, I
can breathe again.

So it is in music. We have been trained to conceive of music as if it were these beautiful green
trees that go on endlessly without a break. But the canvas on which we paint our sound is
silence. Without the backdrop of silence and empty space, what we create in sound loses
meaning. It is the contrast between sound and silence that is so powerful.

Nowhere in music has silence been so important as in the music of the Baroque period—until
some composers took that road less traveled in the 20th century. [108]

---

[108] John Cage has written pieces that are entirely, or almost entirely, silence. There is purpose behind these—they are not a joke—nor was he
the first composer to do this. The 1897 *Funeral March for the Obsequies of a Deaf Man* by Alphonse Allais consisted of 24 blank measures.
Cage, in part, has wanted to draw attention to ambient sounds from the environment.

*"The space within becomes the reality of the building."*
—Frank Lloyd Wright (1867-1959)
American architect


### MUSINGS ON SILENCE IN THE BAROQUE PERIOD

In the Baroque period it was understood that silence and space were part of music. As much as half the value of a note might be silence (i.e. a written half note might sound as a quarter note of sound and a quarter rest of silence). Performance styles today allow for very little silence, regardless of the period of music being played. The idolized, sustained, lush sound can be appropriate for music of the Romantic era; nevertheless all music benefits from and needs opportunities to breathe.

Perhaps the incorporation of so much silence and space into Baroque music is a reflection of the often-stated ideal of writing music *beautiful in the eyes of God,* music inspired by Spirit (Breath)—that Nothingness out of which all Creation has been formed—that Vast Stillness that is the container for all that is.[109]

Or, is it that Baroque music is really speech, every note a word rather than being the rich song of Romantic-period music?[110] When treated as speech it communicates on a deeper level. As William Pleeth said, "closing the lips of the note" at the end of a group before continuing on is necessary to create this sense of speech. It creates a momentary silence, just enough to differentiate one 'word' or 'word group' from the next. He was noted for his understanding and playing of the music of the Baroque period, and as I mentioned earlier his approach to the Bach *Suites* was a revelation to me, converting what I had heard played as 'dull etudes' into ecstatic music.

### Bach *Chaconne* and Breathing

I recently heard a performance via radio of the well-known Bach *Chaconne,* from the *Partita No. 2 in D minor*, by a world famous and mechanically flawless violinist. Unfortunately in this performance of the 15-minute movement, the only breaths and silences were when the violinist did a series of down-bows on the big broken chords. There would be just a moment almost free of sound during the retake of the bow. Otherwise the artist could have been a Wagnerian opera singer with an infinite supply of air. It was like seeing the beautiful cathedral stuffed full of lush, over-padded furniture. I kept thinking, when is this person going to come up for air? Even whales have to come up for air. When the performer was announced I was surprised. Normally I respect this artist's playing, but I found the performance of the *Chaconne* to be empty of meaning. The incredible intimacy of the music is lost when it is played in an over-bearing, domineering fashion, without breath. Yes, the beauty of Bach's external structure is still there, those outer walls of the cathedral, but all the inner spiritual content, all those variations that speak of love, are obscured.

---

[109] The Hindi word *Sura* means both breath and sound.
[110] Nikolaus Harnoncourt, Austrian cellist and conductor, pioneer of historically informed performances, wrote an informative book titled *Baroque Music Today: Music as Speech.* It is suggested reading.

Too few instrumentalists of our time, or past times, have bothered to learn about performance styles in different periods. Even in the 20th century, composers like Prokofiev and Bartok played their own music with much more spacious silence than do most interpreters of their music.[111]

> **Tip**: String players can learn much about breathing and silences from listening to singers and wind players. Singing the music you play is crucial to understanding about breath and silence. If possible take singing lessons or sing in a chorus. It is very rewarding, and can counter our tendency to be seduced by the possibilities of never-ending sustained sound. Yes, there is music calling for this lush, sustained sound, but that tool should not be applied indiscriminately. Shortly we will look at the post-romantic composer Strauss' beautiful and intimate song *Morgen!* with these thoughts in mind.

*"Silence is God's first language;*
*everything else is a poor translation."*
—Father Keating (b. 1923)
American Trappist monk

---

[111] Listen to the Anne-Sophie Mutter/Lambert Orkis performance of the Beethoven *Sonata in C minor, Op. 30. No. 2* for a superb example of artists who bring out the changes of voice, allow for silence, and play with the transparency of sound appropriate to this fairly early Beethoven sonata. (Available on YouTube—Paris performance)

**Exercise 24.**

**Purpose: to attain a sense of the non-sustained nature of Baroque style**

Listen to recordings of Baroque music by early-music period instrument chamber groups. You will hear how communicative the music can be. Notice that the sounds are more feathered: The beginnings and ends of notes are not so well defined; The sound does not start with an accent nor end abruptly except at voice changes.

Find an excerpt from a Baroque work, or just use scales you know well, to experiment with this style. William Pleeth taught a way for string players to approximate this sound while using a modern instrument and bow. The feathered sound can be produced by using your bow arm 'improperly.' Move out to the upper half of the bow and do not use motion from the elbow, but rather use a whole arm motion from the shoulder joint (a ball-and-socket type joint), as beginning students are apt to do. You will find yourself moving closer to the fingerboard as well. Above all think of talking with the notes, and breathing as you would need to do if speaking or singing, instead of playing a string instrument. Find a mix of running fast notes interspersed with longer note values to practice this technique. To avoid muscle and tendon inflammation, do not overdo this practice. It is hard on the arm.

This sound is not the rich, complex sound we want for music of the Romantic period, rather it is a purer, simpler sound. Leave off the vibrato and only add it on the occasional longer notes. Suit the speed and width of the vibrato, if used, to this other-worldly sound that you are creating. It is more like the sound of a child's voice than an adult's voice, or an innocent's as opposed to a worldly voice. Shorten longer note values. Depending on tempos, play eighth and sixteenth-note passages truer to their written value than the longer notes. Start without slurs and add them judiciously if they make clearer which notes belong together. Often fast passages should be played separate bow, not slurred, to create a flurry of sound, requiring more bow speed than seems appropriate. Nevertheless still attempt to do this with the whole arm from the shoulder joint. Build your endurance gradually.

Once you have some comfort using your bow this way, apply this style to the short *Preludio* from *Sonata in D minor* by Arcangelo Corelli (1653-1713). This sonata originally was written for violin and cembalo and the old Augener's edition in *E* minor is shown here. The later Lindner arrangement for cello and pianoforte kept the same slurs as in Augener's violin edition, but changed the key, presumably to make use of open strings, which are quite appropriate for this music. Subsequent arrangers introduced Romantic period influences, with elaborate piano realizations that are too busy, and slurs in the cello part that obscure the spoken nature and inherent silence in the cello part.

**Excerpt 14   Arcangelo Corelli (1653-1713)** *Sonata No. 8 in E minor,* **Augener Edition, first movement**

I've written out the first eight bars below as arranged for cello—in *D* minor—showing typical slurring that has been introduced.

**Excerpt 15   Corelli *Sonata*, first movement arranged for cello and piano**

Cellists, for the rest of this piece read from the violin score. To play it in *D* minor you simply have to play everything an octave plus a whole step lower, so you will be starting on an open *A*. If you wish to avoid thinking down a whole step and can't yet see and think quickly in interval relationships, you can simply pretend the entire piece is written in tenor clef and play accordingly. You imagine a flat in the key signature (*B* for *D* minor), and then only two notes will read differently in tenor clef. In bar 21 the treble clef *C#* half note will be a tenor clef natural, and in bar 27 the treble clef natural becomes a tenor clef flat.

Compare how the solo lines are written in the two versions. Now remove all slurs and begin to play it single bow. You could even remove all the rhythms and simply play all notes the same value. This should help make the structure clear to you: where the beginnings and endings are, what notes lead where, where the resolutions are, where the emotional peak is, etc. For now, accept my sense that the mood we are after is one of internal contemplation of a wondrous truth. It is introspective and quiet, not bold, not driven by human passions, not sensual. The music asks to be played with a sense of marveling, wonder, worship. It has a quality of being self-contained. You could be alone in the universe, contemplating what is. Experiment with bringing those attitudes to your playing to help bring the music to life.

Once you understand the relationships, add the rhythm back in and decide if you like the printed slurs. This original violin version is quite close to how I like to play it. Most editions include trills on some of the longer notes and at endings. Experiment. Ornamentation was expected by the composers of the period.

I have included the initial eight bars once again with markings that approximate how I tend to play it.

**Excerpt 16   Corelli *Sonata*, beginning of first movement with my markings**

I have used a line with a dot over it to indicate that a note still has space before the next sound but is a little heavier and proportionately a trifle longer than the notes with just dots. The dots indicate that I do not play the note full value, but it is a feathered ending to the note, not an abrupt cessation of sound. These are not meant to be staccato markings where the bow stays on the string and the sound clearly ends. There is a bit of a lift to the bow, out of the string, to keep a more vibrant, resonant sound that does not rely on left-hand vibrato. The commas indicate even a longer break between sounds, proceeding on very deliberately.

If you adopt the style suggested by William Pleeth—staying in the upper half of the bow and using your arm as a unit from the shoulder joint—all this will happen fairly naturally. This is not very comfortable, but gives you more of the Baroque sound.

## SILENCE IN STRAUSS' *MORGEN!*

Later you will be listening to the beautiful recording of Strauss' exquisite song *Morgen!* with Renée Fleming and the English Chamber Orchestra (Jeffrey Tate conducting, Paul Willey solo violin, Ossian Ellis solo harp). There is a stunning, almost pause in sound near the end that is a wonderful example of the power of silence, or in this case near-silence. (Played at a low volume it will seem to be a true break in sound.) Between the second and third of the final six notes for violin, the violinist makes a lovely diminuendo on that second longer note, stretching thc diminucndo to almost nothing, creating the illusion of a brief silence before continuing on with the last four notes. That moment absolutely captures your attention.

Following is one translation of the German text of this poem by Strauss' contemporary, John Henry Mackay, who was of partly Scottish descent but brought up in Germany.

### *TOMORROW!*

*And tomorrow the sun will shine again,
and on the path where I shall walk
it will reunite us, the blessed ones,
amidst the world that breathes in the sun…*

*And to the wide shore, lapped by blue
waves,
we shall quietly and slowly descend,
silently we shall look into each others' eyes
and upon us falls the silence of true bliss…*

# INTERLUDE

*"Life without music is unthinkable. Music without life is academic.*
*That is why my contact with music is a total embrace."*
—Leonard Bernstein (1918-1990)
American conductor and composer
quoted in *Dinner with Lenny* by Jonathan Cott


### *MUSINGS ON DEPARTURE AND DESTINATION POINTS AND MORE*

It has been about a year since I began the serious writing of this book, and once again the hummingbirds are back, early. This year there are two in the advance guard—it has been a week now and others have yet to appear. I marvel at how accurate they are in arriving year after year in the same backyard thousands of miles from where they start their journey. (And we string players have difficulties making a two-octave shift!)

In the Metaphor section I mentioned that difficulties in shifting accurately, or going from any note or chord to the next, are often due to lack of awareness of your starting point. It is easy to let your attention jump forward to where you want to be next, and thus lose the awareness of where you are. This makes it difficult to arrive accurately. Using the analogy of driving to a known destination: you are unlikely to arrive at your desired location if you don't know where you are *now*. This translates for musicians into the necessity of having both the physical awareness of the touch sensations of your fingers on the instrument and the inner hearing of where you are and where you are going.

The same principle applies to the entire structure of the music: where does this group, theme, phrase, section, etc. start and where does it end? When you have the answers, then you can plan the 'route' that will get you there. Nelsova said, "You should have the whole work within you." Casals emphasized the importance of never doing anything illogical such as making accelerandos or ritards that have nothing to do with the music. Part of the genius of Maestro Abravanel was his ability to envision the 'route' for an entire Mahler symphony, creating an inexorable flow from the beginning to the end of these gigantic works. He brought a wonderful pacing and sense of timing to them. But this understanding didn't come without intense study of the scores. At the time of his death there was an open score of the Mahler *Symphony No. 9* on his desk, even though he hadn't conducted for years. He was still studying.

The Practice of Music is open-ended. You are never finished; you never arrive at the ultimate understanding, or performance, of a piece of music. Whenever you pick up a piece again, whether it's two months, two years, or two decades after first playing it, always revisit your concept of the music. As you grow and change, your concept of the music will also change. You will see and hear things that you didn't perceive before, find new relationships to bring out for the ear, new ways to communicate the illusions of motion and the many voices of love. This is why the contributions of older musicians and conductors are so valuable, even when physical facility may be diminished. The impaired Piatigorsky's Dvořák was more commanding of attention than versions from young prodigies. There are exceptions of course when the interpretation of a young artist has the depth of an "old soul." When that happens it is indeed something to marvel at.

I had that experience in the early seventies when an eleven-year-old violinist played the Tchaikovsky *Concerto in D Major* with the Utah Symphony. Her performance had a maturity beyond belief. Maestro Abravanel later said that had he known her capabilities he would have asked her to play a work of greater depth and breadth. Sadly, at least for the music world, she disappeared from the music scene.

There is a difference in studying music for the purpose of playing it and touching someone's heart, versus the intellectual satisfaction of knowing how a piece is put together. The purpose is quite different. In the former, understanding the composer's concepts and discovering how best to realize and communicate the music in the physical realm is the purpose. In the latter case the study is to understand how the music has been constructed for the sheer joy of appreciating the work of a brilliant mind, without the concern of how to best manifest what you have understood. Seeing relationships and actually manifesting those relationships in sound are two different endeavors.

Again, there is an analogy with magnificent cathedrals, which, along with the great works of music, I find to be the most beautiful of all humankind's creations. The performer is akin to the person who sees a beautiful cathedral and is compelled to go inside to feel the energy, or pray, or gain inspiration. Another person stays outside to examine the architecture in great detail so as to appreciate the genius of the creator.

In a similar vein there is music that is written for the eye (or mind) as opposed to music written for the ear. Music written for the eye may be very cleverly constructed; it looks good on the page. It may follow all the rules of harmony and form as taught in music theory classes, or avoid those rules as with atonal music, but if it lacks inspiration, usually evidenced by an insipid melody, it will stay on the page, in the realm of academic exercises, rarely to be heard in the concert hall, written by the mind without the heart. It is the "music without life" referred to by Bernstein in the quote; this applies to both composing and performing. And it is not just students who end up writing or performing in this way; unfortunately even great composers have written such failed works and yet those do get performed, due to the composer's fame. I'd love to tell you which they are, but you won't hear it from me. Find out for yourself—they're out there.

# RHYTHMIC RELATIONSHIPS
## —THEME D

*"Pulsation. Breathing in and out…it contracts and expands, like the universe.
And that's what great music does. Each piece in its own way."*
—Leonard Bernstein[112]

## RHYTHM

Rhythm is defined as "the whole feeling of movement in music, with a strong implication of both regularity and differentiation. Thus breathing (inhalation vs. exhalation), pulse (systole vs. diastole), and tides (ebb vs. flow) are all examples of rhythm."[113] Rhythm can be perceived through other than just the aural sense, as the examples show. We can see rhythm, we can feel rhythm, we can hear rhythm.

Meter is defined as: "the pattern of fixed temporal units, called beats, by which the time span of a piece of music or a section thereof is measured."[114] It also plays a part in the understanding of rhythm. The basic beat of a piece is the steady underlying pulse which may remain regular and is implied regardless of how it is divided into parts. Up until about 1900 meter tended not to be varied, but from then on it became common for composers to experiment with the changing of meters within a piece, for example going from 5/4 to 3/4 to 6/8. In the case of music from some of the road-less-travelled composers, meter may not exist at all, at least not for the ear.

The more classical definition of rhythm in music refers to music where the number of beats in each measure is the same and each downbeat gets accented. This way of composing, based to a great degree on dance forms, dominated music for a lengthy period, and the downbeat emphasis is still appropriate in the performance of some music. But this definition of rhythm, as it was used between the 1600s and early 1900s, is inadequate for understanding how to perform much of the music we encounter. If it is a waltz to be danced to, then perhaps the clearly emphasized downbeat of each measure is desirable. If it is the second movement of the Brahms *E minor Cello Sonata*, which we looked at previously, then beware of tromping on all the downbeats. The music will become heavy and dead. However, using this definition of rhythm, the Brahms movement, which we described in terms of structural units of two bars,[115] can also be described in terms of rhythm with the identical understanding that two measures are a unit—a rhythmic unit—then four and so on. So what was called measured music was another way of looking at the form created by measures of the same time duration, often getting emphasis on the down beat, and thus measuring time and dividing a longer piece into regular time units. Marches are good examples of this classical definition.

In Western music, note values have specific durations relative to each other, i.e. an eighth note is half the time value of a quarter note, a quarter is half the value of a half note, etc. This

---



[112] *Dinner with Lenny* by Jonathan Cox

[113] *Harvard Dictionary of Music*, Second Edition, Willi Apel

[114] Ibid. Meter is indicated by the time signature showing the number of beats per measure and what note value gets a beat, as in 4/4 time where there are four beats to the measure, and a quarter note gets a beat.

[115] I will be using the terms *bar* and *measure* interchangeably.



**169**

system is not used throughout the world. There is something called "free" rhythm, used for example in Indian music and traditional Hungarian folk songs, that cannot be expressed in our Western notation system. In it, there is no common unit of time: notes do not relate proportionately in terms of beats and fractions of beats, as happens in most Western music with the quarters, eighths, sixteenths, etc.

The music of the 1600s and 1700s had the greatest emphasis on regular meters, heavier downbeats, and long passages of same-duration notes. Nevertheless when playing music of this period it is important to avoid a sameness throughout that deadens the listener's ear and mind.

Rhythm and meter are not exactly equivalent to the patterns of note values within a measure or over multiple measures. Once again it is a matter of relationships. The arrangement of note values offers many opportunities for enhancing the illusion of motion. Measures, meter, and tempo create a framework. The way in which the note values within that framework group together or relate, provides an opportunity for creating a feeling of motion.

We will work with these patterns as well as other aspects that help to create that "whole feeling of movement in music…"

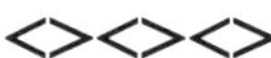

## RHYTHMIC TENSION

Rhythmic patterns in music carry a lot of the responsibility for creating the illusion of motion. If all notes were of the same time value and got the same emphasis, there would be a stationary quality, rather than a sense of tension motivating movement, regardless of whether all note values were 32nds or quarters. Change and contrast are needed for a sense of motion. The accented downbeat of each measure in dance music is a suggestion to the body to move through the dance steps, but as I have said before, that can become a trap. Sameness for extended periods tends to make things become essentially invisible, or inaudible in the case of music, encouraging us to stop registering the input. In the Brahms second movement if the downbeat of every bar were equally accented you would certainly feel and hear the music as being in 'one' (that is a feeling of one beat to the bar, regardless of tempo), which is desirable as it does help the music to flow. But soon the sameness would weary the ear and the sense of forward motion would be lost for lack of additional and more complex relationships. Fortunately there are other ways besides accenting every down beat to communicate the feeling that music written in 3/4 or 4/4 or 6/8 time really has just one or two beats to the bar, as opposed to a stodgy three, or four, or six beats to a bar. Bringing the attention of the ear to various rhythmic features and relationships in the music helps to create the illusion of movement. It may be a question of emphasizing something other than the beat, or it may be a deliberate and essential slight alteration of the printed rhythm to give forward motion to the music.

The way you play a note will determine whether it will be perceived as leading somewhere or resolving what has come before. I think of it as notes facing forwards or backwards, with backwards being a still point that finishes something. Your awareness of how the notes relate (form and structure) is essential for knowing the difference. When music seems dead it is often because notes that should propel the music forward are played in a way that holds it back.

Most obvious are pickup notes that lead to the next beat or note. But the same principle occurs in many rhythmic figures that we will examine shortly. The notes that face forward or propel the music onward communicate that direction by being emphasized in some way. They require a change in the energy you are using, usually an increase. It starts with intention, of course, and may manifest physically through such things as an increase in bow speed, weight, vibrato, volume. Something different has to happen than with the previous note. There has to be an urgency in the intention to move forward.[116] It is not a passive playing of the note. But if you want something to feel static, or very deliberate, then you would not do any of this.

A long passage of notes of the same duration should not be played absolutely straight, exactly equal in every way, though they might appear that way on the page. There has to be a give and take, the gaining of momentum, the losing of momentum, rising to a peak, falling away, leading, resolving. Perhaps there will be dynamic changes, a slight bit of rushing, an increase of energy to reach a peak and then a losing of energy or slowing in the process of falling away from that peak. At times there will seem to be a correlation with physical universe laws of gravity and motion.[117]

There is great value in practicing with a metronome, so that you *are* capable of doing exactly what is written, and any unconscious deviations from that are made conscious and brought under your control. (There are always temptations to alter the printed rhythms to compensate for technical difficulties.) But ultimately you must leave the metronome—the "evil mistress" as one of my students refers to it—behind and find the appropriate shaping of the printed music. What is in print is not unlike the potter's clay; it has to be massaged and molded before it can say something.

---

[116] This is discussed further in Physical Implementation, page 175 and Extreme Motion, page 182.
[117] Discussed in Tempo Alterations, page 194.

## WHERE TO PUT THE EMPHASIS

The development of bar lines and measures with a fixed number of beats came out of the practical problems of how to perform music written for two or more voices. They allow for music to be notated so the performers understand how the voices line up with each other in time. But there is an arbitrariness to this system that developed, which may create a deceptive idea as to which notes need emphasis and which don't. The look of the printed music can easily override the sense of how notes relate.  What became the written downbeat of the measure, or the initial sound (note) of a sub-divided beat—visually emphasized with the Western notation system—took on more rhythmic importance than the part of the beat or measure that may actually carry the motion.

Abandoning the idea that the downbeat of a bar *must* be brought out, there are decisions about which other beats or parts of a beat can be emphasized to help create the sense of leading somewhere. Rhythmic relationships vary greatly in music of a singing, melodic quality, and they can be used to facilitate the motion illusion. In general, and this is most applicable to music of the 19th and 20th centuries, the notes that occur off the initial part of the beat or off the initial beat of the bar—often those notes with a shorter time value compared to the previous note value—act as upbeat notes or leading notes[118] belonging to the next note or measure. These need to be given more emphasis. For example, in Figure 12, to be expressive and create the sense of motion the sixteenth needs more emphasis than the dotted eighth.

**Figure 12**

I think of it as giving such notes more significance; they are more important to the ear in creating movement. Just the *idea* that they inevitably lead to the following note may be all it takes for you to do something physical that will express this relationship. It will be something that gives this note more importance or intensity than the previous note, and creates for the ear the expectation that it will lead somewhere, i.e. to the following note, an arrival point.

Figure 13 is an example of the often used and visually misleading representation of this long-short pattern of Figure 12 where the long note is on the beat. Using beams to connect the dotted eighth and sixteenth visually groups the sixteenth with the previous note.

**Figure 13**

---

[118] The use of the term *leading note* in this section is not to be confused with *leading tone* which refers to the 7th tone of a scale. However leading tones generally act as leading notes in this sense of propelling the music onwards.

Slurs are sometimes added, connecting the long and short notes, grouping them in the same manner, as in Figure 14. This addition may be to facilitate ease of bowing. When not original the intended sound is altered.

**Figure 14**

These patterns consequently tend to get played as in Figure 15,

**Figure 15**

with the short note (16th) almost swallowed. This is appropriate in music of the Baroque and Classical periods. An original two-note slur, whether of equal-value notes or a dotted figure as shown here, indicates that the second note should be subordinate: softer and falling off in sound, somewhat shorter than written.

But in later music generally the shorter note (16th in these figures) is the note that carries the sense of motion and is the one in need of emphasis, as in Figure 16,

**Figure 16**

whether played with or without slurs. My use of accents in Figure 15 and Figure 16 is to indicate emphasis, not an actual hard accent.

For the pattern to look to the eye more how it needs to sound to the ear it would be printed as in Figure 17.

**Figure 17**

Convention dictates otherwise and tends to lead to laziness in the sound and a lack of the sense of urgency of the shorter leading note.

Compare two vocalizations of the word *fire* in Figure 18.

**Figure 18**

Which version creates a sense of urgency and movement?

When played to sound as in Figure 17, different bowings can help to give this emphasis. The pattern could either be played with a slur from the short to the long note as in Figure 19,

**Figure 19**

or played single bow—the long note up-bow and the short note down-bow—as in Figure 20.

**Figure 20**

This is a favorite bowing asked for by some conductors for extensive, fast passages. If the left hand motions are complicated it can sound rather messy, since it is not as familiar to players. It's a good pattern to practice and become comfortable with. Use it on scales. *When* this principle of the shorter note needing more emphasis does apply, it applies to long-short patterns of any note durations and in any tempo (slow or fast), whether with dotted eighths and sixteenths, or longer note values such as dotted quarter plus eighth, or half note plus quarter, or dotted half plus quarter, or in triplet form as in Figure 21.

**Figure 21**

When it doesn't apply will be discussed further on page 184, but often in Western music notes of shorter value generally need to be emphasized over the longer notes they come from and lead to. These shorter value notes are often the upbeats to the next beat, like an in-breath leading to the more relaxed out-breath. Likewise, there will be upbeat notes to the next measure needing the same treatment. Rather than thinking in terms of time relationships within a bar or a sub-divided beat, it is often more useful to think in terms of the grouping of notes— which notes belong together. Sometimes those groupings will be of same-duration notes as we will see in the Vivaldi *Sonata in B-flat Major* example.

## PHYSICAL IMPLEMENTATION

If a note is to lead the ear onwards, the energy you use must increase during the note so that there is more energy at the end of the note than the beginning. We want to compel the ear to anticipate motion to the next note. Something different happens with this note than with the previous note.

Use the motion of your bow (or the air column if you are a wind player) as you would your voice in speaking. For example in speech if we want to convey that we are not stopping, that we are not at the end of a thought or sentence, our voices go up in pitch and have a bit more energy or emphasis. If we have ended the thought our voices go down. Check out the difference in how you say the word "brave" in the following two sentences.

> You have to be brave.
> You have to be brave, courageous, a true hero.

What we do with our voices translates into what we do with bow speed to communicate this difference. If it is appropriate for there to be a brief silence between notes, as the commas dictate with the words, then by letting the bow come off the string while speeding it up, we create the sound that lets the listener know that there is more to come, despite the slight break in the sound before continuing. The thought is not finished.

Slowing the bow speed as you finish a note conveys an end to something—a group, a phrase, an entire musical sentence, just as does the dropping of the voice on "brave" when it ends the sentence. Ending with the *same* energy or bow speed can let the sound hang in the air and create somewhat of a mystery.

Possibilities to communicate that the music leads onward (besides an increase in bow speed) include: more volume (a slight crescendo into the following note); more intensity, which could manifest as more or faster vibrato; a sense of urgency, which might come primarily from your strong intention; or a slight delay of the note without a change of tempo, thus shortening it, to increase the feeling of motion, speed, excitement. There could be a change of tone quality or color, which might mean going closer to the bridge and using less bow but more weight, or a slight stretching of the note thus delaying the resolution note and increasing anticipation, or perhaps something else we can't easily put into words. A long note held for many beats must also be brought to life by some change of the energy in it from beginning to end. A rest, too, has to have the appropriate energy. Silences follow the same principles: are they arrival points, leading moments, or truly static? Your intent during a silence is important. The music hasn't stopped. Don't go on vacation!

In terms of energy, an arrival point is communicated by having more energy at the beginning of the note than at the end, and it may begin with less energy than the leading note before it. After the note is started the energy drops off, so perhaps the bow pressure lets up a bit and you let it glide. As you back away from the note dynamically, bow speed might lessen by the end of the note. It becomes less intense, maybe vibrato slows. Again, how you accomplish these effects starts with your intent, and the intent must be to show that this note completes a group.

There may be longer duration notes in a pattern that serve double duty—facing both backwards and forwards—as do the dotted quarters in the opening of the Barber *Cello Sonata*, which we will be looking at in Exercise 26, page 179. Such a note may be an arrival point requiring backing off after it is started, but then during the latter part of its duration the sound begins to pick up energy again before the next true leading note.

> **Tip**: In a legato passage when you need to change bow directions and do not want to imply an end or a beginning, the bow change must be seamless. For a bow change that is inconspicuous and doesn't disturb the flow of the music, imitate what a competitive swimmer does to make the turn-about upon reaching one end of the pool. It is done with curves, more of a figure-eight-type flow than anything linear. Let your bow arm have that feeling of flexibility and suppleness. Nothing should be rigid and fixed. For inconspicuous string crossings a bit of extra bow weight may be needed to get the string to speak.

**Exercise 25.**

**Purpose: to see the relationship between structural motion and rhythmic motion**

What I term "structural motion" is very closely related to this idea of rhythmic motion and emphasis. These two ways of looking at the music and the awareness you gain will often lead to the same end result: using the same notes to create the illusion of motion. The non-tonic notes that need emphasis are often the notes with a shorter time value, or those that are off the beat, leading to or belonging to the following note or bar, requiring emphasis to make that relationship obvious. In this exercise we will look at *HeartSong* again (refer back to page 133 in Theme A of this Act or the full version on page 319 in the Addendum) to see and hear the correlation between non-tonic notes and their placement within the bar or beat. Whether you look at this music from the harmonic and structural point of view or the rhythmic point of view, the decisions you make about how to play it are going to be very similar.

From the rhythmic point of view, and following the principles outlined in the prior section, we are looking for the notes, probably of shorter duration, that lead—those notes with rhythmic tension that create a sense of movement.

In *HeartSong*, the rhythm is rather static (as is the case with the pitches). The few dotted-quarter/eighth-note patterns and the pickup quarters at the very beginning and at the ends of bars 4, 8 and 12 are opportunities to create movement illusions. The quarter notes at the ends of bars 24, 26, and 35 are also pickup notes, already getting special attention because of being non-tonic-chord notes. The notes before them are longer, but not just static resting points, rather part of the onwards flow, different in nature from other bars where pickups follow a resolution. Whether considering them from a harmonic or rhythmic point of view, these third beats need to lead. The half notes before them do not act the same as the half notes in bars 4 and 12. (They face both backward and forwards as discussed on the previous page.)

Some of the isolated eighths are from the tonic chord, some are not. They all need special attention or emphasis. Sometimes that will mean just being absolutely present on the note. When I play this piece I create the propelling-forward effect with a bit more weight (sound) on the eighth notes. I do not delay them—playing them later and shorter—because I do not want to create any sense of hurrying or real urgency. I just make sure that they are heard and carry forward what motion is inherent in the piece. They group with the following beats.

Try playing this piece while ignoring this rhythmic tension, so that the eighths sound the same as longer notes and consequently more or less disappear to the ear, and the quarter upbeats are static.

Booooring! For lack of rhythmic tension you might even have fallen into the "tyranny of the downbeat" so that the music really plods along one bar, or even one beat, at a time.

Now play it with your special love, presence and attention on every note and especially those notes that carry the music forward rhythmically. Make every note speak to the listener.

Did the music change? Did you notice what you did physically to play in this way? It doesn't matter if you didn't notice what you did. That's for teachers to be able to identify. You just have to create the desired effect.

How often did the harmonically and rhythmically important notes coincide?

Before we leave *HeartSong* there is one more grouping pattern to look at: those two places with a series of eighth notes, bar 17 and bars 29-30.[119] In these cases the six eighth notes in each bar have to flow as one big beat leading to the next bar. In bar 17 there could be a slight crescendo throughout the bar leading to the next downbeat. If you break those six notes apart, you will hear that you must *not* accentuate the first of each two eighths. If anything, it is the second of each two—the offbeat pitch—that needs more presence. If you emphasize the first of each pair you will create a plodding sense of three unrelated beats in the bar and lose momentum and flow. Again, with bar 29 the whole of the bar leads to the *Bb* in bar 30, a non-tonic note that can be emphasized—perhaps by lengthening it a bit before hurrying down to the following *D*. In bar 30 notice that the tonic notes are on the offbeats and the reverse situation exists. Do not emphasize the offbeats. The eighths on the beat are actually more important to the ear. Here is a case where the structural emphasis and rhythmic emphasis diverge.

---

[119] I play these bars very freely—out of tempo—usually in considerably less time than would happen metronomically. The version in the Addendum contains the *ad libitum* markings.

**Exercise 26.**

**Purpose: to hear the difference in illusory motion when emphasizing different parts of the beat or measure**

**Excerpt 17   Barber** *Sonata in C Minor for Cello and Piano*, **opening of the first movement**

Notice that this opening theme of the Barber is based on intervals of a sixth and the rhythmic figure of a dotted quarter followed by an eighth or two sixteenths.

1. Play or sing this theme making the overall crescendo as marked, but within that crescendo emphasize the longer notes, more or less 'swallowing' the eighths and sixteenths, including a weak pickup eighth to start the melody. Experiment. Exaggerate. Make it subtle. Notice the effects you have created.

2. Now play it with the emphasis on the shorter eighth and sixteenth notes, including the pickup eighth. To do this, speed the bow and give it more weight on these shorter notes just prior to the bow change. Experiment as before. Exaggerate. Do not accent the beats. Notice the differences.

3. Now play the passage with no emphasis, but rather just growing steadily as indicated from the opening note to the arrival at *Ab*, as if it were all under one long slur. Notice the effect.

With the emphasis and attention on the long notes the music is plodding and jerky. It is the eighth note (or equivalent two sixteenths) that needs emphasis, growing each time to draw the ear onward to the next note a sixth above. Played in this way the music moves forward in a powerful fashion; it easily builds in intensity and leads to the top dotted-half *Ab*, a momentary arrival point. When played with no differentiation, rather just as one long steady sustained crescendo, the music loses excitement and energy. The forward motion is gone, the passion and intensity are gone, subsumed in beautiful sound,[120] displaced by sameness—the evenly spaced trees in a tamed forest. The wildness only comes across when the second halves of the second and fourth beats have more energy and importance than the notes they lead to. I believe that the slurs in the score actually obscure what the composer intended. They may be needed for bowing purposes—where to change bow directions—but they don't highlight the note groups. Fortunately you can create the needed intensity within the marked slurs.

This opening line is a good example of notes that face two ways. In this case the dotted quarters begin as arrival notes. After the initial sound it is necessary to back away from them slightly, but before you get to the leading eighth notes (or their equivalent), the dotted quarters begin to pick up energy, turning around and continuing forward.

4. Play the line once more with this in mind.

---

[120] The ability to produce a beautiful sound is very important and a great asset—as long as it doesn't go unchanged for long. Beautiful sound alone does not communicate musical content. Like every other aspect of playing, you want it to be a conscious choice not just a 'default setting,' though as defaults go, it is obviously preferable to a non-beautiful sound.

5. Let's look at more of this first section of the movement.

**Excerpt 18  Barber *Sonata in C Minor for Cello and Piano*, opening of the first movement**

Once you have arrived at that *Ab* in bar three, let the volume back off just enough so that you can again grow into the shorter *G* and then grow through it (it's a vital upbeat and gets lengthened as well, as indicated by the *poco rit*) leading to the arrival note—the *Eb*. Once again the arrival is momentary. There is a *Gb* to be emphasized, carrying the music through the *Fb* and to the final *Eb* of that phrase. But again, you can't stop here. So that the ear knows the music goes on, you want to increase the intensity of the *Eb* as you end it, which you will do by increasing the bow speed as you lift the bow from the string for the rest. (More on this tool in Extreme Motion.)

The music goes on with all the volcanic intensity that has been building. In the second line, the second note of each slurred group of two needs emphasis to propel it forward.

The first three bars of the third line follow the same principle but starting softly; "soft" in this case is neither lazy nor gentle. In no way should the urgency of the shorter notes diminish. This line might start as a whisper, but it is a passionate one. The music builds with the emphasis on the shorter notes of each slurred group, getting ever more fervent. On the notes before the eighth rests, in bars 12, 13, and 14, the bow once again has to leave the string with an increasing bow speed to keep the forward motion going through the rest, as with the *Eb* that ended the first line.

In bar 15 the *Eb* falls heavily into the *D*, and both the *Eb* and the following three triplet notes lead as a group to the third beat *A*. Let the final eighth or two of that bar pull back time-wise just enough to really 'set' the *C* at bar 16. I lift the bow out of the string to have the slightest break in sound before attacking the *C*. It is an attack here, with great power, and the lower octave *C* has to sound just as strong. The next two half notes and the following three quarters are equally emphatic. They stand on their own in a way—being static relative to motion but not emotion. A little separation in sound between all of them will help to communicate this. Then the slurred eighths return to the leading/arriving concept. In bars 20-22 the two half notes and the tied-over whole note maintain sound and energy. With the *Bb*, somehow the ending of the note has to grow, and the bow must come off the string with the increase in bow speed. It is not a polite ending. It is ferocious. Due to the length of this *Bb* I arrange to take it on an up-bow to maintain the volume and facilitate this quality. I bow as needed before bar 16, in order to start up-bow on the *C*, which also helps keep the lower two half notes as strong as the higher ones.

When you bring this awareness of the relative importance of note values and their appropriate groupings to your playing, you will communicate more of the unwritten content of the music. You will move your listeners to a greater extent, even if they are unable to say why.

7. Find music that you have played before and reexamine it from this point of view; see if you have intuitively applied these principles. If not, consider if you can apply these ideas to make the music come alive.

## EXTREME MOTION

Sometimes we want to be extreme in compelling the listener to anticipate the music moving onward. I alluded to this in the discussion of the Barber. My piece *Protest* also provides an opportunity to look at an energy extreme and how that is reflected in the bowing motion.

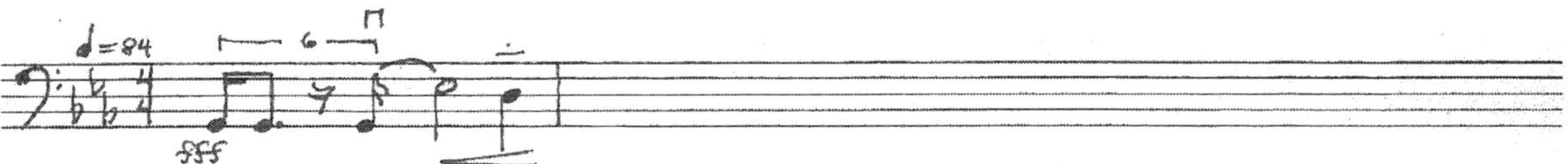

**Figure 22**

This motif (a short element or fragment of a theme) is the basis for *Protest,* and has to end in a manner that will create anticipation of more and greater motion. To do this, let the bow come off the string at the end of the last note of the group, with that increase in bow speed. Like an airplane leaving a short runway, it has gathered momentum and now surges into the air, not on the same even trajectory but with a sudden angling upwards (in flight, very disturbing to the stomach). Then, the briefest of silences before the bow returns to the string. We refer to this as 'throwing the bow away.' It has a purpose; just be sure when you utilize this technique you are serving a known purpose and not doing it unconsciously at the wrong places and times.

Orchestras have a tendency, with any piece that ends loudly with great energy, to make this sound-surge at the very end as the conductor cuts them off. It is also known as 'goosing' the note. A final note that ends while the sound is still expanding in an organic sort of way—the bow lifting off the string at the same speed rather than surging—is generally more effective as an ending, unless the composer requests otherwise. This organic ending to a sound has a wonderful way of hanging in the air and even expanding, whereas the surge has the sudden increase in intensity. A surge tends to propel the music forward, so use it appropriately.

Let's talk through *Protest*. The complete piece is in the Addendum (page 349). The motif, both in its brief form and expanded forms, occurs seven times with ever increasing volume and energy, before it begins to lose energy and momentum over the following seven iterations. The first ten times, the last note of the motif can have a bow surge with the bow coming off the string, followed by the briefest of silences before the motif repeats. Finally in bar 16 the dotted-half note *C* is sustained through to the next downbeat, the bow not coming off the string with a surge, but maintaining sound and energy into the following four bars, which then continuously lose energy, sans surge, until reaching the soft dynamic indicated in bar 21.

As I mentioned in Act III this piece is meant to communicate a sense of protest of some immense injustice, the sort that after an explosion of energy you are left saddened and exhausted. It demands a high expenditure of energy. It starts with as much sound and fury as possible. And then it grows! Until that energy peak in bar 11. Then volume and energy diminish steadily until that exhaustion point is reached at bar 21. Though the music returns to the energy of protest in bar 30, it is now minus the over-the-top insane energy and forward propulsion of the first eleven bars, and no more surges are needed, just sustained sound. Most days. Sometimes I feel it differently and the return of the protest motif gets as much energy as at the beginning, with surges. Being present and creating in the moment is important. Don't rigidly fix every detail.

Experiment with what you can communicate with this tool.

When I originally wrote *Protest* I subdivided the first beat of the rhythmic motif into a typical sixteenth/eighth/sixteenth pattern. But I didn't play it that way. I exaggerated the shortness of the first and last notes. The middle note, though held slightly longer than the first, cut off abruptly with the bow lifting off the string (but without the surge of the longer note at the end of the bar) to leave space before the delayed final note, which was as close to the next beat as I could play it. Eventually I ended up notating the figure as the sextuplet that you see, which is as close as I can come to representing how I conceive of and play it. I actually play the entire piece rather freely in terms of rhythm—sometimes holding notes longer than printed to exaggerate some quality, or making other alterations, being governed by the spirit of the moment and the acoustics of the venue.

This experience of having difficulty finding within the written language of music the right notation to represent my concept, made me more aware of the need to bring my own musical understanding to everything I play and not get caught in a literal reproduction of what's on the page. In speech, the use of the more formal written version of a language may at times seem stifling and inadequate to express what we wish, and so we invent idioms, slang, new words and other alterations that don't appear in the written language—all in the name of communication. The language of music requires the same freedom to depart from what is proper or correct in order to communicate intent.

## WHEN DO THE OFF-THE-BEAT NOTES NOT PROPEL THE MUSIC FORWARD?

Lots of places. How does one know the difference? By applying several criteria. Do the stylistic practices from the time period of the music dictate otherwise? This is more often the case in music of the Baroque period than of the Romantic, and we will look at some Vivaldi next for some examples. The composer may indicate otherwise by the use of accents on the beat or on the longer notes, or the music may be written so that the leading notes *are* on the beat. Most importantly, the emotional content may drive it otherwise, though this upbeat stress is an element usually found in music and performances that are expressive. The upbeat feeling is not the source of the expressiveness, but a tool for expressiveness. If applied unthinkingly as a rigid rule, this too can become a mechanical-sounding device that loses its effectiveness quickly. Remember, you are the source of the expressiveness! And, as always, experimentation and singing what you are studying should give you the answers. The bottom line is that this principle doesn't apply if the emotional content you find in the music dictates otherwise.

Recall that with the Brahms second movement I said I might play it differently depending on the mood I am feeling. With the dreamy mood, I don't apply this concept at the ends of bars two and four; rather I treat the repeated quarters as rebounds from the downbeat. If I want the more 'upbeat' mood I treat the third quarter in these bars as a true upbeat leading to the next two-bar unit.

I have analyzed in some detail how I apply these principles to the pieces used for these exercises. However, this grouping of notes and upbeat feeling have been integrated into my playing to a degree that I no longer think about it. I just do it, so this analysis is after the fact. Obviously I can't be thinking about and calculating these details in performance: that would take me out of the present moment and preclude creativity and playing from the heart. What happens in performance can never be an analytical, deliberate application of these or other principles, rather your creation in the moment is informed by all the knowledge and understanding you have gained by studying the music from all the different perspectives.

Nonetheless, I do want you to experiment and hear the differences when you apply these principles and when you don't. Hearing the differences in music played this way versus renditions treading heavily on the beats or longer notes is the first step. Eventually it will simply become how you hear in your mind's ear the music you see on the page, and you will move it out of the analytical realm and into the kinesthetic. At some point you no longer need to think about this at all; you just do it as needed. But first you have to hear the difference.

Let's compare two examples, one where this principle is obvious and one where it isn't.

Throughout the extended opening theme of the first movement of the Brahms *E minor Sonata* the shorter notes of each bar clearly lead and carry the sense of motion.

**Excerpt 19 Brahms** *Sonata in E minor for Cello and Piano*, **Schott edition, first movement**

<> <> <>

It is not so clear in the first three bars of the opening theme of the Barber *Sonata*, third movement.

**Excerpt 20 Barber** *Sonata in C Minor for Violoncello and Piano*, **opening of third movement**

The shorter notes still get more emphasis then the longer notes, yet some of them occur on the beat. Barber has made the beat coincide with the needed emphasis. By the second line it is once again the eighth notes at the ends of the bars or half-bars that carry the motion.

As we proceed, continue to keep in mind that first definition of rhythm: "The whole feeling of movement in music…"

## A Detailed Look at Note Grouping

We will look at this Largo from the Vivaldi *Sonata No. 6* in terms of silence and note leading or grouping. I have written out the solo line for the first half of the movement, including the bowings and markings that most closely approximate how I like to play it. These markings are my personal shorthand, not to be interpreted by other standards but rather in the way I indicate below the excerpt. I have written this in treble clef, an octave higher than it should be played, for several reasons. Cellists often encounter orchestra and even solo music where composers have done this, for reasons I don't understand (Dvořák and Haydn are two culprits who come to mind). It behooves us to become comfortable reading music in the treble clef and playing it an octave lower. For this manual it also facilitates other instrumentalists being able to play the part without translating from the tenor clef, which would be the easiest clef to write this in. Finally, putting it up the octave in treble clef facilitates my writing out the part with the fewest leger lines. There you have it.

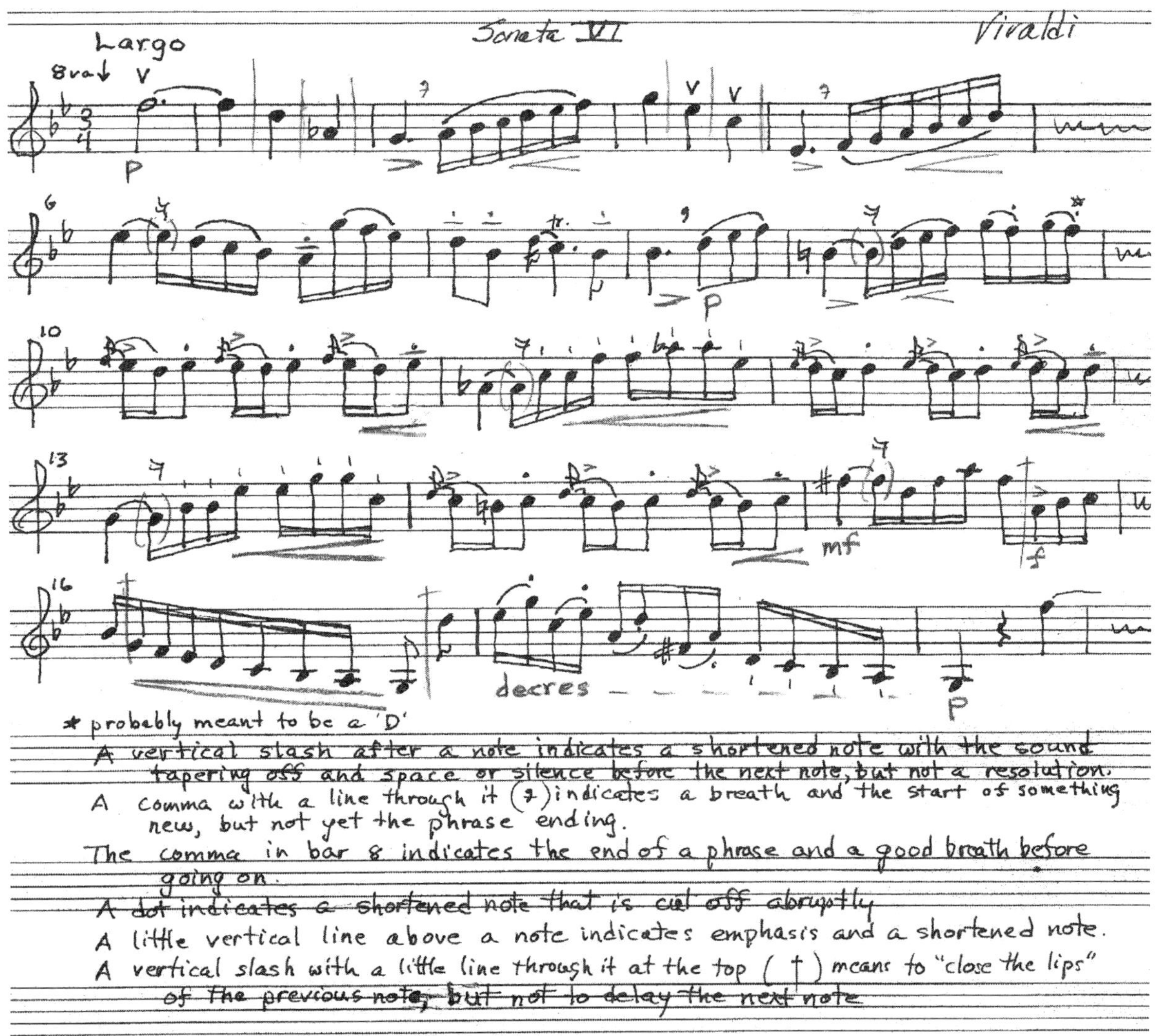


**Excerpt 21  Vivaldi *Sonata No. 6 in B-flat Major for Violoncello and Basso Continuo***

This is the opening movement of the sonata and immediately sets a quiet, thoughtful, inner tone, rather similar to the Corelli movement we looked at. (Vivaldi was born just 25 years later in 1678 and died in 1741.) A tempo of approximately quarter equals 46 on the metronome works well. It may be easier to think in eighth-note beats, thus an eighth equals 92.

You can find editions that have turned this work into a lush, romantic version with elaborate keyboard realizations of the simple continuo part Vivaldi wrote. The keyboard player was expected to realize this bass line in a manner befitting the Baroque style, not into something that didn't yet exist, that probably was not even envisioned. Bach, on the other hand, whose life encompassed almost the same time period, was pushing the limits of Baroque style, leading music into the future.

Applying the ideas about silence in the Baroque, I do not sustain the long opening note full value or the following three notes. However they still have a relationship. I sneak into the first note, let it swell a bit, then feather off and put space before it falls to the *D*—a landing. I view that first note almost as a long upbeat to the quarter-note *D*, despite the silence before the *D*. This means that it is my *intention* that mostly carries the illusion of going to the *D*. For the ear the *F* leads nicely to the *D*. They group together. Then the *Ab* quarter becomes a pickup to the *G* in bar 3, grouping those two together, though I still put space between the two. The *F, D* and *Ab* as a unit all lead together to the *G*. The following six 16th notes are grouped with and lead to the next *G*. Within these six 16ths there is additional grouping with the subtle sense of the 2nd, 4th, and 6th being weightier, leading to or belonging to the following 16th. The slur over the 16ths is Vivaldi's, so I believe this interpretation is valid, as opposed to it being a case of the second of each two notes falling off (softer and shorter).

In bar 4 the *G, Eb* and *C* going to the lower octave downbeat *Eb*, an arrival point, relate as did the notes at the beginning. The following 16ths going to the octave higher *Eb* relate as did the previous 16ths, and that *Eb* is a temporary arrival point. Then we have a three-note upbeat group leading to the 16th-note *A*, then another three-note group leading to the next arrival point, the downbeat eighth-note *D* in bar 7. In these three-note 16th groups (and subsequent ones) the first and third notes are more important than the second, they being the offbeats of a sub-divided beat. Try it both ways. It is subtle but you will hear the difference in the sense of motion imparted. To make it obvious try really emphasizing the other note—the third 16th within the beat (second of the three-note slur)—and you will hear how plodding it is that way, how it stops the motion. Check this out with those six 16ths as well.

After the downbeat *D* in bar 7, the next note (the *Bb*) faces both ways. The *D* has resolved comfortably to the *Bb*, which seems to be finishing something, but then that *Bb* becomes an upbeat for the real cadence that actually finishes the first thought. This first *Bb* both finishes and leads. How to make it do that is difficult to put into words. The beginning of the note needs to feel at rest and the end needs to have a lift—that upbeat feeling, all within its short time span. It starts in the mind and happens in the bow. Experiment. Much of it is attitude, but you might find it effective to start the note gently and then at the end lift the bow out of the string with a touch of extra speed with a pregnant silence following before the trilled *C*, which starts from the note above (the *D*). The *Bb* at the end of that bar has a definite upbeat feel to resolve more quietly on the downbeat dotted quarter. There is time for a good breath before going on with the next three eighth-notes upbeat to the new thought.

These three eighths lead to their resolution *B natural*; the next three 16ths lead to four 16ths at the end of bar 9 that for the first time follow a different pattern. Here is a typical Baroque example of two-note slurs where the second note is subordinate. In this case these four notes group as two and two, with the emphasis on the first of each two, the second note falling off and being played short, more like a 32nd. These are not part of an ascending or descending melodic scale pattern and they have a unique look to them. You will learn to see these, though the pattern can be obscured by editing that adds slurs over four notes. The same pattern happens in the first two beats of bar 17. The notes are grouped in twos, with the second off-the-beat note falling away, played shorter. *However,* be alert to the fact that the second group of two 16ths within the beat (that is the second half of the beat) might still act as an upbeat to the following beat. See if you think it does in this instance.

Bar 10 proceeds in a similar manner with the second half of each beat, an eighth in this case, being weaker than the initial part of the beat—falling away and played short. However within the two 16th-note groups beginning each beat, the second 16th goes with the following eighth but without emphasis. Both fall away from the first 16th with its preceding grace note; the short eighth allows for silence before the next beat begins. With all three beats of the bar the same, something must be differentiated. The second entire beat can act as a bit of an echo to the first beat, and the entire third beat can be an upbeat, leading to the next bar.

After the *Ab*, in bar 11, the first of each two repeated notes acts as an upbeat to the second, receiving more emphasis. The music continues in like fashion until bar 15, where once again the 16ths organize starting after the beat and leading to the first note of the next beat. Starting after the first *Bb* in bar 16 the following seven 16ths fall quickly to the bottom *G*, then there is the upbeat *D* to the pattern we previously discussed in the first two beats of bar 17 (the second and fourth 16ths are lighter and shorter than the first and third, but the second and fourth groups of two can lead). The final beat into the resolution on the *G* in bar 18 might be divided as one 16th (a resolution) and the following three leading to the downbeat *G* that ends the first half of the movement.

In music of the Baroque period the decisions regarding where a pattern or a group begins and where it ends, and consequent execution with or without slurs, are often based on where the voice changes, or where you close the lips of the note (an ending) before going on. Grouping relates to the harmonic aspect of dissonant notes resolving to consonant notes, and the non-tonic to the tonic, before beginning anew. It's always about relationships, about leading and completing. When you are unsure, sing the group of notes in question, stopping or pausing on what you think are destination notes—the notes the music just has to go to. Does it work for the ear? Try stopping a note earlier or a note later. Does that satisfy the ear to a greater extent? Sometimes it will be two-note groups, sometimes three, and sometimes four (made up of almost indiscernible two-note groups). This is subtle. You do not want to be drawing your listener's attention to *how* it is that you are creating this sense of forward motion, only that the music is alive, that it speaks.

Return to the Bach *A minor Violin Concerto* and revisit the opening with this illusory motion in mind. I will use my cello version here—this time with my bowings and other markings included—and you readers of the treble clef can practice reading tenor and bass clefs and also playing up an octave. Remember that in tenor clef the clef sign centers on middle *C*, the second line down.

**Excerpt 22 Bach *A minor Violin Concerto*, first movement, transcribed for cello**

My markings here are a bit different than in the Vivaldi. I used a dash with a dot over it to indicate a shortened note that has a bit of a lift to it so that it doesn't act like an arrival note. A simple dot indicates a short note that is more of an arrival note—one that separates voices rather than leading to the next note. I use accents to indicate the start of something—a bit of emphasis or more weight so that the ear hears the beginning of something—weightier than the following lighter note. I use the vertical slashes to indicate a closing of the lips of a note and the beginning of another pattern or group.

If you don't have a full version of this movement I suggest you buy a copy so that you can work through the entire movement on your own, applying these principles. Remember that most available editions will have extensive editing. In this version for cello, I too have included dynamics and slurs showing how I tend to play the music: ones which reflect what I understand the composer's intent to be.

## *MUSINGS ON MELODY AND RHYTHM*

Rhythm is such an intrinsic part of melody that it is hard to conceive of a melody without rhythmic relationships. This idea of leading and arriving is quite obvious when you have differing note values, but it may still exist within a sequence of same value notes. In a sequence of four equal-value notes often two and four need slightly more weight. In a triplet it might be the third note of the group that needs the emphasis. But never assume this to be true. Find out for yourself. Keep singing the music to find your answers.

In our Western culture we are attuned to certain sound relationships that we differentiate as consonant or dissonant, leading or resolving; they are part of our essence, almost a part of our DNA. If you make the effort to check it out, your ear will tell you which notes lead and which finish. Often there is a fractal pattern in which two notes relate as the four notes relate, as the eight relate, just as structurally the two bars relate like the four and the eight. The small units combine to form the larger units with one leading and one resolving.

The patterns in music can be as entrancing as the patterns in math and physics. A retired mathematician friend spends his days converting complex theoretical mathematical equations describing the sub-atomic universe into exquisite visual representations on his computer, which I have had the good fortune to view. The beauty is stunning. He is able to rotate these visual depictions, see them from all angles; they move, warp from one shape to another, and they remind me of music. Similar to the patterns that music creates in time, he is seeing patterns in multi-dimensional space and representing them on a two-dimensional screen. Fascinating. [121]

---

[121] Julie Rehmeyer has written an interesting article for *ScienceNews*, March 4, 2008 titled *The Geometry of Music*. The link is: https://www.sciencenews.org/article/geometry-music Also of interest is her June 6, 2007 article *Musical Illusion* available at: https://www.sciencenews.org/article/musical-illusions

## MELODIC MOTION

The other definition of motion in music (that technical definition found on page 117) refers to melodic motion, or the pattern of changing pitches: whether the melody follows a direction higher in pitch (up) or lower in pitch (down). We use the terms *up*, *higher*, and *ascending* to refer to frequencies that get faster; for example, the 880 hertz *A* is double the frequency or an octave *higher* than the 440 hertz *A*. *Down, lower,* and *descending* all refer to frequencies getting slower. This definition of motion refers exclusively to the motion up or down in pitch—the Y axis on my graph on page 118—generally perceived as vertical motion in space. How melodies use this vertical motion facilitates creating greater or lesser degrees of the illusion of motion in time.

There is even a term, *musical gravity*, used in reference to melodies. It is a term "implying that the 'natural' movement of a musical line is downward, while an ascending motion always has the connotation of tension and energy."[122] Please note that the adherents of this theory presented it as an absolute—that it is always true. It isn't of course. The concept is quite limited as it assumed that a downwards pitch sequence was more natural (and musically preferable) than an upwards sequence, and that an upwards sequence always implies a building of tension and energy. But as you will see with a later analogy of a diving board propelling an object upward, the opposite is also quite natural: the object loses energy and momentum as it ascends. And of course most melodies contain both ascending and descending melodic lines, so to consider one preferable to the other seems more of an analytical construct rather than a demonstrable truth.

The motion on this vertical pitch axis can occur step-wise—*conjunct* or *scaler motion*—or in larger intervals referred to as *disjunct*, or sometimes, *chordal motion*. Conjunct melodies are generally deemed more expressive and disjunct melodies more reserved. Melodies constructed in scaler fashion, such as in the second half of the Brahms *Sonata* theme we previously looked at, may provide more opportunities for an organic type of note-grouping—the tension of leading and resolving that is indeed very expressive.

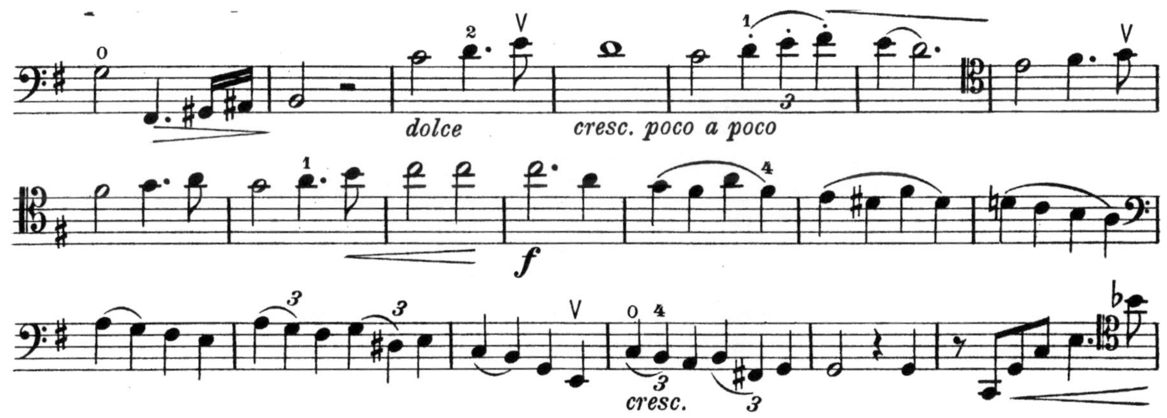


**Excerpt 23  Brahms *Sonata in E minor for Cello and Piano*, Schott edition, first movement**

This portion of the theme (starting in the third bar of the excerpt) consists of step-wise (conjunct) motion going to the peak at the *C*, then disjunct and conjunct motion are combined as it descends. It is one of the most expansive, emotional themes in cello music. Some of its

---

[122] *Harvard Dictionary of Music*, Fourth Edition, Willi Apel

emotional power comes from the rhythmic opportunities with the shorter leading notes in the rising line creating the sense of forward motion, each one adding greater intensity, the emotion peaking on the third of the *C*s. If you played this theme with all the notes the same time value, it would lose its powerful emotional and expressive content. Try it.

*HeartSong* provides an example of a disjunct melody that is more static since much of it is built on chord notes, giving it fewer opportunities for melodic expressiveness, thus making the harmonic and rhythmic illusions of motion essential to any sense of life. But the opening disjunct themes of both the first and third movements of the Barber *Sonata* (shown below) defy the idea of reserve and a static state. Though disjunct, both themes are expressive, dramatic and powerful, propelling the music and the ear onwards.

**Excerpt 24  Barber *Sonata in C Minor for Cello and Piano*, opening of first movement**

This disjunct first movement theme, as we have seen, is tremendously intense and expressive, but different emotions are being expressed than in the Brahms or in *HeartSong*. It is the opposite of static! The third movement theme, also disjunct to begin, is very powerful and dramatic—again a different expressiveness than what is contained in the Brahms theme.

**Excerpt 25  Barber *Sonata Op. 6 for Violoncello and Piano*, opening of third movement**

There is always value in noticing whether the lines you are playing are conjunct or disjunct. Noticing will give you more insight for what is needed to bring to life different types of melodies, how the rhythmic relationships will provide meaning.

## USING TEMPO ALTERATIONS TO CREATE ILLUSIONS OF MOTION

There is a physicality to music and its implied motion that must be honored. In many ways the perceived motion in music—the illusion and sensation thereof—relates to and follows the laws of gravity, acceleration, deceleration, and magnetism that objects in the natural world are subject to. Movement in opposition to gravitational laws also exists in the world and in music. Illusions of motion can be created through tempo changes referred to as "rubato,"[123] and through the interface of rhythmic and melodic patterns mimicking motions and energies found in the physical world.

### Rubato

The tempo modifications referred to as rubato generally happen without destroying the sense of meter. The meter is the stable playing field—the lines on the court, beyond which we don't go or play. Within those lines we have a great deal of freedom. Mozart wrote frequently about the need for rubato, the pushing and pulling of tempo needed to communicate the music more effectively, but always coming back to the basic sense of the meter, whether 3/4, 4/4, 6/8, or any other meter. However, views on rubato, even the definition, vary widely. One controversial view is that after any number of measures of complementary accelerandos and ritardandos, the player should arrive at the same point in time as if there had been strict adherence to the tempo.[124] Whereas in jazz (and also in the second half of the 18th century), it is considered that rubato may be applied to the melody but not the underlying accompaniment.[125]

These *ritardandos* (same as *rallentando*)[126] and *accelerandos* that are a part of rubato are most effective when they follow the same perfectly graduated slowing down or speeding up as you find in natural phenomena, such as something rolling unobstructed downhill or uphill. The rate at which an actual object in motion slows down or speeds up varies of course with factors such as the amount of friction and degree of slope. Sometimes our *ritards* or *accelerandos* must happen quickly over a short period of time; sometimes they happen slowly over many measures. It is that natural even rate of change that we can emulate.

The best ritardando I ever heard was from a Red-shafted Flicker (a type of Woodpecker common in western states) who was sure that he could drill a hole through the metal vent pipe coming out of my roof. His drumming—a lengthy series of pecks (perhaps ten in each series), repeated ad nauseam—was impeccable in its deceleration from first to last peck. He was mistaken however. He did not succeed in his drilling; my vent pipe remained intact despite his perseverance over some days. Alas.

---

[123] Rubato: "An elastic, flexible tempo involving slight accelerandos and ritardandos that alternate according to the requirements of musical expression." *Harvard Dictionary of Music*, Second Edition, Willi Apel

[124] *Harvard Dictionary of Music*, Second Edition

[125] Ibid.

[126] A *ritenuto* however is not a gradual slowing; rather it calls for an abrupt reduction in speed.

## Rhythmic Alterations

There can be rhythmic alterations within one beat, which in themselves do not change the tempo. These may happen deliberately or unconsciously. However we need to be aware of what we are doing because they do alter the emotional and energetic feeling of the music. Probably the written rhythmic pattern most subject to variation is that dotted-eighth/sixteenth-note one that was in the figures on page 172, as well as other dotted-note patterns. In some periods of music or with some works, under-dotting, over-dotting and standard dotting are practiced. There is still much controversy as to when each is appropriate. Under-dotting is when the figure has more the feel of a triplet, with the 16th note being played almost where the third eighth of a triplet figure would fall, hence a more relaxed feel than when the figure is played meticulously as written (standard dotting). Over-dotting creates the opposite effect by delaying the 16th, making it more like a 32nd coming just prior to the next beat, which may be hard to differentiate from double-dotting. This gives a more energized, aggressive feeling. A precise rendering of a dotted rhythm may seem a bit stodgy by comparison.

Notice your own tendencies with this dotted rhythmic figure and consciously decide what is appropriate to the music: as written, more relaxed, more energized. If you will let the content of the music be felt in your body, you will likely do what is appropriate for the mood or feeling demanded in the music. Do some research on your own on this subject of dotting and other performance practices of different eras, including that of *notes inégales* (similar to 'swing' in jazz). It is an entire field and musicologists have written reams of material debating various points.

> **Tip**: Be alert to the tendency to place a pickup eighth note a little too close to the next beat, which takes away from the sense of what the tempo is and minimizes the pickup's function. It will tend to sound swallowed and unimportant as a leading note—like stumbling into something rather than deliberately stepping there. An example of where an absolutely accurate rhythm is needed is in the three pickup eighth notes at the beginning of the Beethoven *Symphony No. 5*. Too often they sound like a triplet going into the downbeat, greatly diminishing the power of this opening.

Please treat the following descriptions and examples of tempo and energy alterations as exercises, where you play and experiment with the music excerpts and my suggestions. Choose other music as well and apply these concepts before continuing on to Theme E.

## Natural Laws of Gravity

In the art of diving at the moment you make that last jump on the diving board before soaring into space, the laws of physics take over and govern your momentum, the height you reach (amount of time on the upsweep before beginning the downturn) and thus the arc and speed at which you return to the water. An ascending passage in music—that is one where the pitches go higher in frequency—can mimic this. Often you must bounce or spring off a bottom or lower note with enough weight and energy to propel you upward to the height of the passage. In this case that top note will *not* be the strongest, as by now you have lost momentum; the peak is almost a still point before the changing of direction and the melodic movement turning down  (pitches going lower in frequency). There is a gain of momentum as you approach a new bottom jumping-off point. The upward flow of notes from such a springboard may need to slow somewhat and the downward flow speed up.

The exquisite opening of the first movement of the Debussy *Cello Sonata* provides a good example of this type of motion. (A more recent edition shows a crescendo through the first five notes of bar five; that edition is not in the public domain.)

**Excerpt 26  Debussy *Sonate pour Violoncelle et Piano*, Edition Durand 1915, first movement**

The first four bars of the cello line provide a wonderful opportunity to allow the music to freely follow natural motions. Capturing the *feeling* of a physical rising and falling in the natural world and equating it to the rising and falling melodic line allows you to play this luscious phrase in an incredibly expressive way.

The four 32nds which begin the phrase have to start with enough weight to allow you to float up to the *D*. Fortunately they are marked forte. The two 16ths at the end of the bar have to lead to the next downbeat *E* with enough emphasis to then kick off from that 32nd-note *E* and roll down, gathering momentum, to the longer *D* (the one below middle *C*) and then drop to the *G*. From there the music climbs 'uphill', to the top *Bb* in the *Cédez*[127] bar, losing energy the whole way up, but still overcoming the force of gravity. This loss of energy is indicated or verified by Debussy's diminuendo marking starting at the bottom *G* and extending to the *Bb*. Once on the *Bb* it is a balancing act on the top of a hill or a crest, then a tipping over the edge, gathering momentum going down, then swinging back up once more to end at the crest, and then doing it *again,* almost making it back up to the *Bb* crest, but not quite—totally spent, almost having defied gravity.

You must get the feel of motion in your body. Perhaps remembering the sensations of being on a swing will help. Or imagine being a bird diving and soaring, gliding effortlessly, using gravity and wind, not effort.

I had a favorite ride at an amusement park many years ago, which perfectly created these sensations. There was movement outward while circling a central pole, hence a centrifugal force, combined with rising and falling motions, all of which created the same sensations that can be created with music: speeding and slowing as the direction of motion dictates, soaring,

---

[127] Cedéz means to slow down.

gliding, falling. These organic, physically rooted changes in speed or tempo, as well as changes in the perceived weight and energy can take a passage out of the realm of a strict and plodding rhythm or tempo and give life to it.

## Movement Defying Gravity

Other physical motions may conjure up what a driver and car might do. I find that when I need to accelerate going up a hill there is a gradually increasing rate, and as I approach the crest of the hill the car finally surges forward and over the top. Sometimes that is what you must emulate, rather than the springboard effect. It will of course communicate a very different quality than the springing off of a low note. And, going downhill, rather than continuing to gain momentum it is possible to gradually run out of it, and roll to a stop. Sometimes this is what the music does.

Once again let's turn to the Bach *Concerto* to examine this illusion of motion.

**Excerpt 27  Bach *A minor Violin Concerto*, first movement excerpt from bar 158 to end**

This ending to the movement provides a good example of gathering momentum to surge up a hill, arriving at a peak and then bouncing downhill and rolling to a stop as the energy runs out. Though the dynamics are not Bach's, both the crescendo and forte at the peak *E* seem appropriate to me. The scale up, starting in bar 164 on the *E* (third note) gains energy all the way through the next bar, requiring that increase in volume and energy and perhaps tempo (at least a great increase in bow speed) to arrive at the top *E*. Then, maintaining the dynamic and energy, it goes deliberately to the next downbeat *A*. I make a retard on the last two eighths so that this bar of eighth notes and their resolution *A* sound like a final cadence, as if you were to remain here and not go back down. That *A* is the real end of the music and the peak of the energy. But—you have trembled too long on the precipice, and now plunge precipitously over the edge. To convey this, the 'lips of the *A*' close quickly—the sound is somewhat clipped—the music rushes on, in tempo, to tumble downhill *and* peter out calmly. You communicate this by becoming more gentle as you descend and holding back with a bit of retardando in the second half of the penultimate bar—not too much, as you have already had the dramatic ending in bars 167-8. What you do energetically mimics that energy required for the car to go up a hill and then coast down until the slope flattens and you come to a stop.

## Choosing the Appropriate Physical Motion Metaphor

The Schumann *Piano Quartet,* Op. 47 has a glorious third movement where the cello has the privilege of initially presenting the entire theme, which is so full of love that there are no words for it. (That, of course, is why Schumann expressed the feeling as music not in words.)

**Excerpt 28   Schumann *Piano Quartet in E-flat Major*, Op. 47, first edition F. Whistling, 1845, opening third movement**

When I most recently played this quartet I obsessed over how to shape the theme. That kept me awake nights as I sang the melody out-loud and in my head this way and that, endlessly. Ideally it would be played without any string crossings, the way it would be sung. But since that is not feasible, how to best finger it is also quite a puzzle. It could be shaped and fingered in multiple ways and be exceedingly beautiful. (I won't tell you my fingering—it's too good an opportunity for deep thinking.) As for shaping the beginning of the theme, I finally settled on what I felt mimicked natural motions and gravity.

The melody starts with two pickups to the *D* of bar 4. I treat that downbeat *D* as the springboard to the higher *C*, hence the *F* and *Eb* upbeats grow into the *D* giving it sufficient weight so that I can leisurely float up to the *C* arriving gently, rather than emphasizing the *C* as if it were the start of the melody. Because it is a higher pitch it is apt to stick out, regardless of intent, so care must be taken for it to sound like a rebound from the *D*. The end of the dotted *C* and the eighth-note *Bb* then grow into the next downbeat *Bb*—a momentary resolution. The *C* and *D* of that bar are upbeats to the next downbeat *D*, which falls to the *Eb* that is statically repeated twice before the next phrase begins. I view both the second and third versions of this melody in the same way. The subtle switching around of major and minor intervals in these three iterations of the theme lends incredible beauty to this extended theme. None of the three are quite the same in their interval sequences, but the shape and the rhythm stay the same.

The descending eighth notes that finish the theme simply roll tenderly downhill, running out of steam to end quietly and gently as the violin takes up the same melody. Schumann's decrescendo (and the fact that it is the end of the theme) makes that idea of running out of steam a clear choice, instead of the option of gaining momentum going downhill.

Let's return to Bach for another opportunity to apply these concepts, again keeping in mind that the printed dynamics and bowings are the editor's—so mentally cross out these bowings and dynamics.

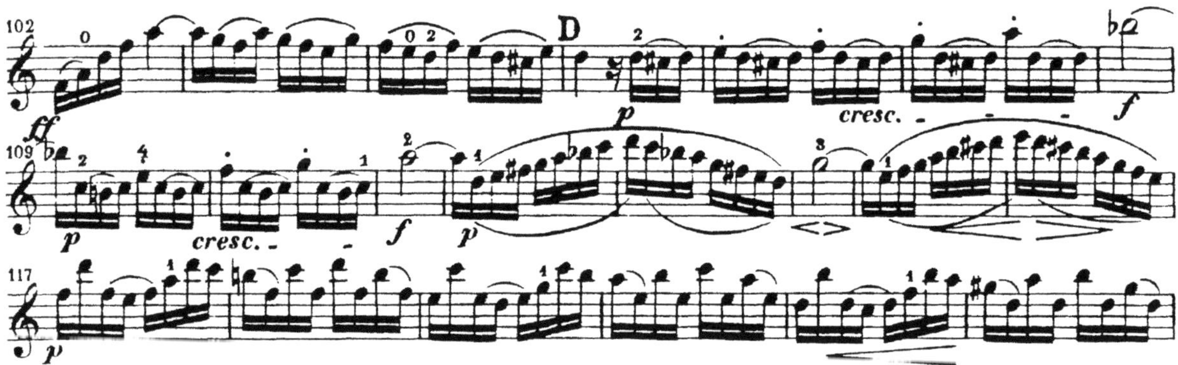

**Excerpt 29   Bach *A minor Violin Concerto*, first movement excerpt from bar 102 to 122**

In bars 112 and 113 and again in bars 115 and 116 of this excerpt, there is scaler progression up in pitch and then back down (melodic motion up then down). One possibility is that this flurry of motion needs to gather energy and accelerate to the high note, the peak, and then fall away. The top note is the destination and is loudest, the descent contains less energy and the music goes gently to the following half note.  There is also the possibility that the music does just the opposite: that it starts with substantial sound and energy and as it goes up to the top note it loses energy, and that it is only as the pitches roll downhill that they gain energy and speed propelling the music into the half note.

To help decide how you will choose, examine these bars in context starting back at letter D. From here there are two voices, or left and right hands if you play it on the piano, with the right hand taking the beat notes. Thus the right hand plays the progression *E, F, G, A, Bb*, then again *E, F, G, A*; then there is a flurry of motion with the left hand, the right-hand *G*, followed by another left-hand flurry, and the *F*. Because the right-hand notes are working their way down from the *Bb* in measure 108, I feel that the music needs to go rather gently into the tied-over half-notes *A* and *G*, and the downbeat *F* in bar 17. I am thus inclined to the first approach, in bars 112 and 115, of the left hand rushing to the top and relaxing downward before the *G* and *F*. In this edition the editor has thought likewise and added the crescendo-diminuendo, as well as some dynamics. Personally I like all separate bows (in the upper half of the bow) for these "left-hand" flurries, for the sense of energy that conveys and because it allows you to slightly emphasize more important notes, but that is *my* interpretation. Consider what makes sense to you.

Look now at these first ten bars of *Schön Rosmarin*, the charming violin piece by Fritz Kreisler.

**Excerpt 30** *Schön Rosmarin for Violin and Piano* **by Fritz Kreisler, B. Schott's Söhne, 1910**

This music is full of opportunities to apply these ideas. Almost all of the series of eighth notes cry out for rhythmic flexibility. The springboard/diving metaphor is applicable to some passages, and the idea of motion contrary to gravity can be applied to others. One possibility, for example, is that the opening pickup notes can spring off the missing downbeat *G*. That illusory note (tonic of the chord and key) is the springboard for the four written eighth-note upbeats leading to the downbeat *D*. The missing *G* is the heaviest and the *B, D, G, B* flow or float upward out of it, losing energy as they go to the *D*, but not speed. The springboard impetus must carry the music to the accented *E* in the next bar, and it is almost as if the upbeat *C#* (to the *E*) is an additional mini-springboard to ensure the motion carries to the *E* without getting stuck on the *D*. In bar 3 the eighths leading downwards can gain momentum, hence speed, letting the next downbeat *D* bounce effortlessly off the bottom *B*. The eighths in bars 5 and 6 fall to the bottom *A*, lose speed as they first rebound upwards, but then surge up to the peak *B* which can remain suspended for a moment before the motion turns around gaining momentum down to the bottom *B* and this time floating up to the *D*, losing energy and momentum.

You may choose a different interpretation, but the markings are Kreisler's. Regardless of any pushing and pulling of the tempo to mimic motions from the physical universe, this theme definitely needs to have the feeling of one beat to the bar, without being too fast to sound *grazioso* (graciously). If it is played absolutely straight rhythmically it loses much of its charm. However if tempo alterations are too obvious the piece becomes grotesque, no longer charming. Your intention, what you do with your internal sense of energy, is the most important factor. As always, what you choose to do should be informed by what is inherent in the music and those hints from the composer. We will look further at this piece in Act V.

**CONCLUSIONS**

Sometimes notes going up lose speed and energy—the springboard effect—and sometimes they gain momentum—the accelerating car. In the case of note patterns going down, there may be a gain of momentum and energy—like the last of the diver's arc just before cleaving the water, or the momentum and energy decrease like the ball rolling down the gentle slope that eventually flattens out. There is not a consistent correlation between the direction of melodic motion and the needed rubato, dynamic, and energy changes.

Because there *is* a correlation between speeding up and gaining energy and between slowing down and losing energy, it is quite possible to create the effects of motion without actually using *any* rubato. It can be done, and sometimes is more appropriate, just with energy and dynamics, adjusting the bow speed or placement between bridge and fingerboard, to simulate these things. You have to stay attentive to the inherent nature of the music to know which approaches are appropriate. The Debussy, for example, calls for much greater rubato and rhythmic freedom than the Bach, and the Kreisler more than the Schumann. The effects in the Bach can be created entirely with dynamics and bow speed.

Because an increase in momentum (speed) correlates with something feeling heavier, in music that sense of falling to the bottom of a sequence of notes or surging to a crest requires a change in weight regardless of whether or not you increase the speed. Heaviness requires more substance, and usually volume, in the sound. A loss of momentum or slowing in a passage requires getting lighter and softer. The terms louder and softer however do not totally correlate with heavier and lighter. There is a change in energy as well, which can be felt but not seen. It cannot easily be indicated in the music.

There are many frustrated conductors out there who when they ask an orchestra member to play something lighter (or heavier) will get back the impudent question, "So, do you want it softer, (or louder)?" Usually this is just an attempt to make conductors wrong, implying they have no clue as to what they want, when in fact these terms are not synonymous and any good musician knows that.

***MUSINGS ON PHYSICAL MOTION***

All of this unfortunately reminds me of my first, and last, experience downhill skiing. I knew nothing of it and was dumped (literally) on my own at the top of a Utah ski lift to make my way down. (And these are *real* mountains!) After the first immediate fall I had the misfortune *not* to keep falling, and so I picked up more and more momentum until I was finally going so fast that I feared a fall would kill me. Therefore I *had* to keep my balance as I hurtled straight down the mountain, unable to slow or traverse the slope, or even swerve. As I soared over numerous moguls and gained more and more speed I have never been so thankful for a good sense of balance! At the time I wasn't actually *feeling* the thankfulness, busy as I was being in the moment trying to keep myself from dying. Thankfulness came later. Fortunately there was a long stretch of nearly level land at the bottom of the slope before the area where people, objects, and other opportunities for collisions were plentiful, and so I did gradually come to a stop (like the Bach ending), still on my feet. Then I fell.

That's when I took up kayaking. (At the time our sick leave in the Symphony did not apply to skiing-related injuries.)

My whole point to all this discussion of the music's relationship to physical motion is that you must feel the music kinesthetically to understand what you need to do to add the illusion of motion to it. In addition to singing the music you need to dance the music: choreograph it, use your arms like a conductor, mime it, use big motions—take up the entire dance floor as you let you body inform you of how the music needs to be played, what it needs in terms of energy and motion. Be the diver or the mountain climber, the crazy driver, the out-of-control skier, the graceful dancer, the tender lover. Let gravity and the motions of the natural world dictate your playing of the printed rhythms. Don't be afraid to slow or speed as the music demands. This pushing and pulling of tempo and energy just needs to be organic, natural, as it happens in the physical world. The ball rolling downhill picks up speed gradually, not with a sudden bump. Rolling uphill the speed from the initial impetus decays gradually.

The composer can't put all these things down in print. The page would be too cluttered to read and your rendition might come off as being artificial if you have not internalized the actual sense of motion you have felt when your body is moving. You want the instructions to be coming from your body and kinesthetic sense, not just from the analytical mind. When you make use of rubatos it should be because the music *has* to do those things, an inevitability that drives these dynamic changes and the illusion of physical motion.

# THE ROAD LESS TRAVELLED
# —THEME E

This Theme is a significant diversion from what we have been addressing, but is included at this point to clarify that there is much music written since the 1920s where many of the tools discussed so far simply don't apply.

*"Music is a higher revelation than all wisdom and philosophy."*
—Ludwig van Beethoven (1770-1827)
German composer

## THE SPLIT

To understand music of the twentieth century and beyond (sometimes quite beyond—maybe other-worldly), it's important to understand the split that took place in the early 1900s. A superb description of this split and subsequent development of music along two different paths can be found in the lectures that were given by Leonard Bernstein at Harvard in 1973. The six-lecture series is titled *The Unanswered Question* (a reference to the work by Charles Ives with that title), and lecture five is *The XXth Century Crisis*.[128]

By the end of the 1800s, and definitively with Mahler's profound *Symphony No. 9* in 1908, the search for expression had carried to such an extreme with the use of chromaticism (that is going outside of the notes contained within a key) that music could barely be constrained by tonality. The need to resolve to consonances was being abandoned. The tonic tone was losing its importance. Symphonic works had gotten larger, longer, more complex and more ambiguous.

The composer Arnold Schoenberg followed in Mahler's footsteps long enough to write his passionate *Verklärte Nacht*, but he was convinced that music could go no further within the restraints of tonality. His last tonal work was a quartet, *Opus 10*, in which he added a soprano voice to the final movement; the text includes the words "I feel air from another planet"— prophetic for himself and those who followed him. A new language was needed.

Schoenberg abandoned both tonality and the type of symmetrical structure we examined in Theme A. As with beliefs, once you let them go something else can come in.[129] By the early 1920s he had developed a new language: an atonal one based on the equivalence of all the 12 tones in an octave, with no tone taking precedence over another—a true democracy of tones[130]—referred to as the twelve-tone system. But music without form is chaotic, not comprehensible, and having abandoned the classical forms, he now had to develop new rules of grammar for his music. Rather rigid rules resulted: an arbitrary sequence of *all* 12 tones was required before any repetition of a tone could occur; certain devices such as inversions[131] and

---

[128] These are available on YouTube; your next exercise is to listen to lectures five and six.
[129] Irina Tweedie in *Daughter of Fire* quoting her teacher Radha Mohan Lal: "If you let the belief go, then after a while you will discern something very different."
[130] I first heard this phrase and other ideas in this section in the Bernstein lectures.
[131] Inversion: the change of ascending intervals into corresponding descending intervals.

retrogrades[132] were to be used, and there were other conditions. Schoenberg's two disciples, Alban Berg and Anton Webern, continued to develop this twelve-tone school. Webern in particular left his legacy, adding many aspects, but there are only a few works from each of these men that have actually become part of the repertoire. This school of serial music (a rather general term that includes the music of many composers since 1945) became what I call "the road less travelled."

Postmodern or avant-garde music are other terms applied to the works of subsequent composers on this path, composers such as: Boulez, Cage, Carter, Stockhausen, Berio, Babbitt, Gorécki, Nono. These composers have introduced new ideas including electronically produced sound, unpredictability, general asymmetry, perpetual variation, chance (aleatory music), the use of noise and silence—a randomness that defies definition or categorization. The only common denominator may be the lack of any defining structure or commonality. Indeed it is music from another realm. For the most part little of the music written by these composers has made its way into the hearts of the public or of performing musicians. There are exceptions of course, but we will look at possible reasons for this lack of acceptance in the next *Musing*.

The road *not* taken by Schoenberg *was* taken by Stravinsky, who, rather than totally rejecting tonality, found new ways of expression while remaining within the tonality that is part of our physical universe: those relationships of the harmonic or overtone series. Stravinsky's great innovations were in the rhythmic freedoms he took, freedoms never before entertained, including frequently changing meters, multiple rhythms going on simultaneously, rhythmic figures crossing bar lines—freedoms that raised the tool of rhythm to an art form. He made use of ever more complex musical devices, including much greater motivic development, yet his music had a rootedness in the earth that reaffirmed tonality. *The Rite of Spring,* his powerful ballet score, though it stunned the public when first played, has a physicality and connection to life that was lost in Schoenberg's new language.

Stravinsky did flirt, rather seriously, with serial music from 1954 to 1968, but his music from that period is not what has been embraced. His earlier neoclassical works, along with those of Hindemith, helped inspire a whole trend in composition. His opera-oratorio *Oedipus Rex* from this period is a very powerful and moving work. The *Apollon musagète Suite* is equally moving in an exquisite and tender way. It was Stravinsky who primarily led the way for subsequent composers such as Prokofiev and Shostakovich to continue renewing music with their unique sounds but within a tonal and structural framework. Despite the normal cultural lag, most musicians and many audiences are now quite comfortable with Stravinsky's music. It has endured in our hearts, and, with his exciting rhythms, in our bodies.

---

[132] Retrograde: the playing of a melodic line backwards.

*"A genuine work of art usually displeases at first sight,
as it suggests a deficiency in the spectator."*
—Goethe

### MUSINGS ON THE AVANT-GARDE IN THE ARTS

Charles Rosin, well-known pianist and advocate of avant-garde music, feels that the Goethe quote above helps explain the cool reception that this genre of music has received. He acknowledges that music from composers on this road is very complex and difficult to play, and that one of the problems of acceptance is that such music is rarely performed well. Schoenberg supposedly said about his own music: "My music is not modern, it's just badly played." Indeed this is a problem, particularly in America where rehearsal time for orchestras on any one piece is very limited. This is less true in Europe, where Boulez—both a conductor and composer—was able to have the 35 or more rehearsals needed for an orchestra to play such music well.

Rosin himself has said: "I can't criticize what I don't understand. If you want to call this art, you've got the benefit of all my doubt." He points out in his lectures that it is always the more difficult and complex music from any period that survives best, for example: the music of Bach over Handel, Brahms over Dvořák, Mozart over Haydn. His implication is that this genre of music will survive; culture just hasn't caught up to its degree of complexity.

Randall Jarrell—American poet, critic, and novelist (1914-1965)—provided an expanded translation of Goethe's words as follows: "All great excellence in life or art, at its first recognition, brings with it a certain pain, arising from the strongly felt inferiority of the spectator. Only at a later period when we take it into our own culture, and appropriate as much of it as our capacities allow, do we learn to love and esteem it." Do Goethe's words apply to music that seems formless: without harmonic form, rhythmic form, structural form? Will this music be around in 300 years? Will musicians in that distant future wonder why such music wasn't popular in its own time? Will performers and audiences ever embrace this music?

Even in the 1800s as composers ventured beyond the classical forms, music was being written that seemed formless at the time, music that now seems quite traditional—Chopin's Ballades for example. This should give us caution before we dismiss any music as having no meaning or value to us. There have always been cultural lags before new ideas are broadly accepted. It seems possible that one element in cultural lag and lack of acceptance is that the amygdala— the fear center in the brain—is activated by uncertainty and unpredictability,[133] both of which are part of new experiences and certainly new music. Perhaps it is anxiety more than deficiency that makes acceptance difficult. Or, perhaps it is something else, as yet unidentified.

Some of this music reflects a philosophy found in art as well: that it is more important to take the ordinary or awkward, or even the ugly, and find a way to represent it beautifully, than it is to represent obvious beauty beautifully. This is a more difficult task, and many artists (as well as composers) fail miserably. But a great artist can succeed. It is important to differentiate the successes from the failures. Every work, whether a painting or a composition, must be examined independently of how it may be categorized.  In the case of music, because the

---

[133] Research published in *Processing of Temporal Unpredictability in Human and Animal Amygdala*, from the *Journal of Neuroscience* (2007).

technical difficulties may greatly exceed capabilities called for in the past, it may mean devoting significant time to studying a work before you even know if you resonate with it (that is, if it has anything to say to you).

I have an abstract painting that I very much enjoy, but even after 20 years all I can see is splotches of color beautifully intertwined in ways that please me. I consider this to be art, even though I find no discernible form or theme. Something about it touches me. I also have my own beautiful photographs adorning my walls, and I enjoy them too, but anyone can take something beautiful and represent it beautifully. I don't consider these photographs to be art, but rather wall-hangings. They are pretty, but they just capture pretty scenes. There is nothing more there. To my friend Arthur, who does stunning black and white photography, these must seem no different than New Age music seems to me.

Arthur is a true artist; he can take the ordinary, or even the ugly, and photograph it in such a way that you see the beauty that is hidden there. His photographs take you deeper into yourself, into understanding and compassion. It is the same transformation internally as happened for me when I studied the dead just-hatched parakeet. Close inspection showed me beauty. I've had a similar experience with a human being—a man who was so homely that at first meeting I thought he was repulsive. Thirty minutes later, after talking with him and sensing his profound compassion for life, I thought he was beautiful—not the wall-hanging type of beauty but the great art type—Arthur's kind of art.

I have also seen paintings that are totally random, not even with the paint applied directly by the human hand, but rather through machines, and, selling for over $30,000! I have yet to find such a work with which I resonate. I feel the same about most of the music produced electronically. Ansel Adams[134] in referring to the spread of sophisticated machines to do the work of the human eye and hands and heart said: "The sheer ease with which we can produce a superficial image often leads to creative disaster." Because someone who understands little of music or art can yet manipulate a machine and come up with something of superficial interest is indeed a disaster to true creativity. On the other hand, taking the sounds of the world, even ugly ones, and incorporating them into a work of music, is not unlike what Arthur does.

In the dedication of this manual I wrote that Sally Peck could move me with a one-note viola solo. As I don't wish to retract that, I have to acknowledge that this formless avant-garde music, even when partially random and electronically produced, is apparently capable of moving the listener—if played well. Perhaps it comes down to the performer being totally present with each sound or note and having an intention for the sound, regardless of the nature of the sound. Possibly the performer's intent is the only intention behind the sound.

---

[134] Renowned American photographer (1902-1984)

## REVISITING MORPHIC FIELDS

Experiments done in the 1920s at Harvard first indicated the existence of morphic fields. These early experiments were done with rats. The rats had to find their way through a maze. The first generation of rats averaged 230 errors. After 22 generations the average error rate was down to 25. Later when the experiment was repeated in Australia, the first rat generation started off making 25 to 30 errors, but that same generation got quicker and quicker, eventually dropping their error rate to zero. It appeared that all rats of that same breed had benefitted from the earlier learning of the Harvard rats, though now separated in both time and space. [135]

This passing on of learned behaviors from past generations is one example of morphic resonance. It is the same phenomenon that allows current generations of musicians to play with ease music that was difficult 50 years ago. We benefit from morphic resonance and the morphic fields that form around specific life forms, ideas, belief systems, types of music, etc. Tonal music has its morphic field. We can all tap into that because it is based on our shared experience of the natural world.

The ground-shifting developments in music that began with Schoenberg have since evolved (perhaps devolved) into greater and greater complexity. As mentioned, little of this music has made its way into the active repertory even though it has been around for more than 75 years. The time period for cultural lag is generally 40 or 50 years, not 75, so are there other aspects than fear and cultural lag involved? Is the lack of acceptance an issue of complexity for its own sake, that is, the writing of music primarily for the intellect rather than for the ear or heart? [136] Or, is it the ignoring of the morphic field of tonality that creates difficulties? The question that arises in my mind is: can a morphic field form around music that is essentially atonal and formless? With every piece a world unto itself, it seems doubtful, which would mean that this music will not get easier to play and will not get easier for audiences to understand.

Tonality in music has not disappeared and can probably never disappear as its morphic field is intrinsic to this universe. Leonard Bernstein considered tonality—that natural harmonic series—to be the root of music. Tonality, as he put it, is too connected to the earth itself to ever disappear. [137] It is not a question of taste.

---

[135] From Rupert Sheldrake's talk on *Morphogenetic Fields of Body and Mind* given at the World Summit of Integrative Medicine 2015
[136] *Facing the Music* by Harold C. Schonberg (paraphrase)
[137] *Dinner with Lenny* by Jonathan Cott

*"Metaphors have a way of holding the most truth in the least space."*
—Orson Scott Card (b. 1951)
American novelist

## REVISITING METAPHORS

Of all the metaphors that fill our lives music is the most powerful. Music is the metaphor we use in the physical world when we have no words, pictures, stories, ideas, or other linear understanding.  Even when we use speech metaphors to describe how to play a passage, the chosen metaphor will always be just one of many possible metaphors. The music has no absolute analogue in the physical world.

The meaning of the music is never in the story we tell about it, or even in a story the composer may attach to it, as in program music. The meaning of the music is in the feelings it evokes in you. One tone alone *may* mean nothing to you. Two or more sounds in relationship will likely have meaning, and probably as many different meanings as there are human beings to hear. That meaning is metaphorical; it represents something for you.[138] Aldous Huxley[139] expresses this as follows: "Music 'says' things about the world, but in specifically musical terms. Any attempt to reproduce those musical statements 'in our own words' is necessarily doomed to failure. We cannot isolate the truth contained in a piece of music; for it is beauty-truth…."

There is ambiguity in art, and often the greater the ambiguity the greater the art. This is true for all art forms. In literature it is poetry that draws most on metaphor and is the most ambiguous. Think also of how ambiguous a great painting can be, the *Mona Lisa* for example.[140] Music is the most ambiguous of all. When we decide on a particular interpretation of a work, it is one of many possibilities represented by the blueprint. Sometimes we come close to what the composer may have felt.

Music acts like a metaphor to create an entire gestalt of something that we may have never experienced, something we may never be able to describe in words, color, or movement, but something that is known and can be felt in the heart.

---

[138] Leonard Bernstein
[139] English writer (1894-1963)
[140] Leonard Bernstein

**207**

### THE CANARY IN THE COAL MINE—A MUSING

Bernstein expressed the belief that the movement started by Schoenberg was an effort to expand music's metaphorical speech or language. The desire to find new ways of expression is strong in artists, so we must assume that to be the underlying motivation, even in music that seems complex merely for the sake of complexity. The question arises: for what is this musical road less travelled a metaphor? Is this music a 'canary in the coal mine'[141] telling us something about where humanity is headed?

Is it possibly a metaphor for humanity's loss of connection to the earth, a severing of our rootedness in the earth itself, evidence of a dangerous separation from the natural world? Such a separation is reflected in how we have allowed the earth to be treated as an object to be used and abused without reverence and without regard to consequences. It is also evidenced, at least here in America, by the increasing lack of contact with nature endemic to generations younger than mine, in the increasing absorption of consciousness in electronic devices and virtual realities—all a separation from physicality.

In contrast, during those years when I was a child, my neighborhood friends and I spent every possible moment outdoors. We sought out the remaining wild places in the neighborhood: the natural springs, the over-grown gullies, the hidden and heavily fruit-laden trees to steal from, the open spaces, the untamed areas. We played in the dirt and mud, dug caves, made toys and tools out of what was at hand. We were a part of our physical environment. This is far from what I see of children's lives today.

Atonality is foreign to our dualistic physical world; music without structure may sound foreign to our ears. Freedoms without boundaries result in chaos. Formlessness indeed seems like "air from another planet," or, more accurately, another dimension. Is humanity evolving in a direction where one day we will simply be brains floating in nutrient tanks, as suggested by science fiction writers? Will virtual realities be our only reality—having severed our connections with the physical universe? If this is humanity's future then perhaps the music of the road less travelled will be the music most easily related to, and future musicians will play it with ease.

---

[141] This idiom refers to miners taking a live canary down in the mine with them to detect dangerous buildups of gas. If the canary fell over dead—being highly sensitive to toxic gases—it was time to escape the mine.

**IN THE MEANTIME...**

When you encounter music that makes no sense to you, before you pass judgment on it you have to acquire excellence in the playing of it. Once you do that you might find that it indeed has value and a beauty that you will have come to love.

When I was a student at Juilliard I had a close friend who was a composition student. She wrote a five-minute piece for solo cello that she asked me to perform. It was the most difficult and un-cellistic piece I had ever attempted; it took a lot of experimentation to even get the sounds being asked for out of the cello. But because she was a friend I put in the needed work and performed it numerous times (to less than enthusiastic audiences). In the end the music made sense to me; I came to like it and believe that it had something to say. I had other similar experiences over the years, but there were no common denominators between the works. I could not build on what I had done before. Each piece was a journey of discovery and experiment. Some I regretted spending the time on; others were worth the time and energy.

Perhaps you, my reader, probably of a later generation than my own, find or will find no difficulty in playing and liking music from the road less travelled. Perhaps you will find, not randomness, but patterns that have indeed become new morphic fields. Perhaps you will sense what the metaphor is, and you will bring that metaphor to life.

Because there are few similarities or rules shaping such music, it is difficult to point you in directions to assist you in bringing it to life. The materials on harmony and rhythm are of little help. There are other ways of course to bring music to life, but as always your starting point will be that effortless excellence. Be aware that the blueprint—the written music—will be much more detailed and precise than music from earlier composers, and your adherence to the print will need to be greater. That is your starting point. There will still be relationships, groupings that you might find, or shapes that relate in non-traditional ways, different rates of motion occurring in different voices. Maybe there won't be a sense of motion through time. Maybe it will be only your presence and intention that will communicate. The ideas in the next theme—Motion and Emotion—may be of help. You will find you own path, building on all the skills you have been developing.

If after achieving excellence with the music, you have no resonance with it, then I suggest you do not perform it. Your love, or lack of love, for the music will communicate to the listener.

If you find this entire Theme ambiguous, that's because it is (that doesn't make this writing great art however).

**Exercise 27.**

**Purpose: to understand the twentieth century split**

Listen to the Bernstein lectures five and six from the Harvard 1973 lecture series: *The Unanswered Question* (if you can find them on YouTube or elsewhere on the internet).


**Exercise 28.**

**Purpose: to give aleatory music a chance and have 'fun'**

The terms aleatoric, chance music, and music of indeterminacy are all applied to music where chance or unpredictability are introduced—sometimes choice on the part of the performer as to when to play something, sometimes involving what to play, or how to play it, or chance involved in how the music was composed. John Cage's *Music of Changes for Piano* (1951) is the first well known work where aspects of the written music were determined by chance.[142]

I have performed symphonic works where at various times the music instructs all players to play whatever they want. This usually resulted in cacophony, but because we were a true group, sometimes we listened and played off each other and maybe created something of interest. I have also played a work for electric cello, *Broom Street* by Sydney Davis, where the sequence and duration of the written material was left to my discretion. This inspired my own minimalist foray down this road, limited to the simple chant on the next page where some discretion on the part of the performer is involved. Use it to make some choices of your own. Read the instructions before you begin to play; they set up the rules, or 'playing field.'

Because so much of the music we play is dictated by a blueprint, we do need opportunities to co-create music in a more obvious manner. It is freeing in a way, and if you are one of those players reluctant to improvise or make up anything on your own, this is your chance to sneak into the arena. The liberating aspect is that you can't make a mistake. Whatever you do within the instructions is legitimate, so experiment. At times you may make a choice that you won't like as well as other possibilities, but don't try to 'set in stone' a specific way of playing *Chant*, or any work for that matter. Be in the present moment when you play. Don't try to think your way to something 'good' or right. Come back to *Chant* from time to time.

---

[142] *Harvard Dictionary of Music*, Second Edition

Chant is to be played straight through, phrases [A] through [G], once; at the end of [G] return to a phrase of your choice, playing it and then continue playing phrases in any order that seems appropriate to you. Continue in this fashion until the desired meditative~almost hypnotic~effect has been created, then end the piece with phrase [G]. This is to be played almost without expression—no vibrato, an unchanging dynamic except for the trailing off of sound at the end of each phrase.

copyright © 2016

**FLOW**

Flow in music-making is always pertinent, regardless of genre.

The following definitions of flow apply to music. As a verb: "to manifest smoothness, continuity, and ease." As a noun: "the form or artistic arrangement of something flowing,"[143] as in the flow of the sculpture by Camille Claudel (*La Valse*). Additional definitions from *Webster's New International Dictionary*, Second Edition, as a noun: "any gentle, gradual movement or procedure of thought, diction, music or the like, resembling the steady movement of a river." As a verb: "to glide along smoothly without harshness or asperities… to sound smoothly to the ear; to be uttered easily." The word "flow" has also been used for the phenomena that people refer to when they say "being in the zone."

These definitions of flow are pertinent to what we do, from the flow of the music itself to the flow of a performance. This exercise is to provide you with just a taste of a way of thinking not constrained by predictable bar lines and meters. We do need to go beyond the typical morphic fields.

**Exercise 29.**

**Purpose: to be able to perceive the flow in music that has an irregular rhythmic unit or structure**

We will use my piece *Flow* (next page) for this exercise. It is not constructed with a uniform two or four measure unit, but rather with an irregular number of beats in each building block. It is the flow of the music that you need to be aware of, and not get confused by bar lines or time signatures. Here it is written with no time signatures or slurs, and only an occasional bar line to give you a bit of a hint. Your task is to see how the music fits together—where a unit starts and where it ends. For purposes of determining the tempo, consider that the quarter note is about 90 on the metronome.

1. Play or sing the music enough to be able to hear it in your head as you read the blueprint on the page.

2. Use brackets to group the notes that belong together. For example, the first group goes through the dotted-quarter *F* plus eighth rest. Regardless of what time signature is used or where bar lines are put, these notes belong together, and there must be a flow from the beginning through the eighth rest that clearly establishes this. If you were conducting this or dancing it you would want to feel these first ten quarter-note beats, not in quarters but in half notes, so you would have five big beats, instead of ten quarter-note beats. It could be written as one long measure in 5/2 time with the half note at 45 on the metronome, but that is awkward. Instead, as you will see later, I have used time signatures that maintain the quarter note as the note value that gets the beat; however the number of beats per measure is not constant.

---

<sup>143</sup> *Webster's New Collegiate Dictionary*

3. Work through the entire piece grouping the notes that belong together. Now begin moving to the music in a way that makes these groupings apparent. You can use your entire body or just your hands and arms, with or without your voice, but breathe in a way that facilitates the flow of the music. Do your groupings feel natural and authentic? If not, try something different.

4. When you are satisfied with your groupings, and using the quarter note as the beat, go through the piece and put in what you think might be appropriate bar lines and time signatures. Feel free to change the number of beats per bar, but keep the quarter note as the beat.

5. As you no doubt experienced, it is difficult to find what makes sense. Compare what you arrived at with what the composer arrived at (see complete score page 341 in the Addendum). As it turns out I had to go through exactly what you just did. I heard or sang the music first, wrote down the pitches and note value relationships that I was singing, and then figured out a way to notate the meter—fit the melody into our musical framework of measures and time signatures.

There is an arbitrariness to what I did—sometimes I opted for fewer changes of meter rather than logic or consistency. For example, the beginning could have been written as two bars of 4/4, then a bar of 2/4, then a repeat of that, then maybe two more bars of 2/4 before arriving at my 3/4 bar. I opted for fewer changes in time signature. It could also have been written as two bars of 5/2 time followed by a 3/2 bar and then a 1/4 bar for the two eighth-note *C naturals*. However arrived at, I did want the two eighth notes to feel like upbeats to a following downbeat, so what I did makes sense in that regard. Likewise I wanted the *C#* just before going into treble clef to have an upbeat feel. Might your version do a better job of communicating the flow of the music?

6. Look through the piece one more time and see if you think the indicated slurs in the Addendum version facilitate the flow. Someone else might have slurred the first four beats, and then the next four to help indicate the need for the melody to be felt in a big two. I did not put in long slurs because I didn't and don't want the piece to sound constrained in any way. Trying to play too many notes in one bow can definitely dampen the sense of freedom and flow, which, as I have already told the player in the beginning instructions—"freely and flowing"—is what I want. [144]

There is another reason not to have too many long slurs, and that is for the physical well-being of the player. Because *Flow* basically has the same quality and feeling throughout, the bow speed is not going to vary dramatically. Our arms can get very tired when there is not an opportunity to play different bowing styles and speeds, and the more sustained the sound, the worse the pain. Generally this is more of a problem in orchestral music than in the solo repertoire. Holding the same note for a long time at the same dynamic is the worst!

In one contemporary symphonic work that I have played, the cellos hold a low *D* for the entire piece. Agony! As I remember, we (the cellists) came to an unspoken agreement with our stand partners to switch back and forth playing the note, as in handing off a baton in a relay race. Of course we had to keep a close eye on the conductor and quickly jump back in should he glance in our direction. Conductors don't always understand the physical limits of playing an instrument, and they tend to ignore the cellos and basses, giving most of their attention to violins and winds. This is not a good thing overall (it ignores the importance of the foundation) but it was a blessing in that piece.

There is a place for freedoms (discussed in Act V).

---

[144] See page 250 in Act V for further discussion of slurs.

The end purpose for this section is to have you be comfortable connecting physically with your feeling-state, so that you allow your outer physical motions to be congruent with and expressive of the inner emotions the music evokes in you, free of inhibitions.

*"Music is an outburst of the soul."*
—Frederik Delius (1862-1934)
English composer

## EMOTION

In this discussion I wish to use the broadest, most inclusive definition of the term "emotion." Our modern word has origins in Middle French from *esmovoir,* meaning to set in motion, to excite, move the feelings, and from the Latin *emovere*—to disturb, and from *movere*—to move. Various scientific disciplines will define emotion more narrowly, but for our purposes it includes all those internal feelings. The word *affect*, as a noun, has a similar meaning, referring to the conscious, subjective aspect of an emotion considered apart from bodily changes.

## MOTION AND EMOTION

Motion and emotion then are correlated, as we have touched on previously. Thanks to this alignment, to create the illusion of motion we can use emotion, and to create emotion we can use motion. When we allow our bodies to be congruent with our emotions, there will be an expression of the emotion through the motions we use. Emotions have corresponding types of motion that capture the energy of that feeling-state.

Content or meaning can be considered in terms of emotions, attitudes, and less well-defined qualities evoked in you, nostalgia for example. You may attach a storyline to that particular feeling, but that differs from the feeling itself. The use of appropriate physical motion—with your bow (or air stream), vibrato, tempo, dynamics, and yes, body motion as well—is critical in communicating the content of the music, the meaning you give the sound.

Harking back to Prelude No.1, the android from the *Star Trek* series, Data, was viewed as a technically perfect violinist whose playing was nevertheless devoid of life. In that fantasy world (to which we are fast catching up), androids are essentially robots who can only be distinguished from humans by their lack of feelings and emotional expression, their lack of affect.[145] In Data's case it is this lack of capacity to communicate any meaning in the music that makes his playing dead. This is the crux of what we are dealing with in bringing music to life.

We humans primarily communicate our emotions through voice and body motion, but there is the unseen, unique frequency that is intrinsic to each emotion, which we broadcast as well. When we feel an emotion various vibrational, chemical, and other physical changes occur in our bodies: changes in heart beat or blood pressure, respiration, body chemistry (glandular activity), skin conductivity, etc. These internal changes may coincide with or manifest in outward physical ways, unless we have learned to thoroughly suppress any visible signs.

Perhaps Data was even able to capture and reproduce the correct motions that correspond to a specific emotion: the right changes in bow speed, vibrato, volume, intensity. But, if these motions were merely a mimicking of what he had observed and deduced, the music still would not come to life. These motions have to be driven by the emotions and corresponding frequencies that they are consistent with. You have to create the emotion before those motions you use for communication will be perceived as authentic.

---

[145] Unfortunately there are types of brain damage or disorders in humans that manifest in the same lack of affect.

"If I don't become Brahms or Tschaikovsky or Stravinsky<br>
when I'm conducting their works,<br>
then it won't be a great performance."[146]<br>
—Leonard Bernstein


## *BE* THE MUSIC

There are always paradoxes in life. Here I have started to speak of motion, and now I will ask you not for a motion—a 'doing'—but rather for a 'being.' There are multiple things I have asked you to *be*: *be* present, *be* the carrier wave of love, *be* in communication, and now *be the emotional content of the music*. The ultimate tool for communicating is to simply *be* the content—or as I phrased it in Illusion of Motion, page 121, *be* the music.

You have to *be* the nobility or the protest or the sadness or the joy that you wish to communicate. You have to create something in your own universe before you can communicate it to others. It is the same skill an actress needs in order to play different roles convincingly. Watch a number of Meryl Streep films, or those starring Helen Mirren or Judi Dench, and you will see actresses truly becoming the characters. This is what you must do. Create the character and feelings within yourself; your body will do the motions needed to convey that.

But you might ask, how *do* you *be*, or create, an emotion? Intent is paramount. We are used to responding to a stimulus before feeling an emotion, but it is quite possible simply to intend that emotion, make a decision to feel it. At first you might need to recall a time when you felt that particular emotion, to put yourself back to the time you felt that way. Once you have called up that feeling again, which is really an energy state, pay attention to your body. Let your body move as you re-experience the emotion, notice sensations and how your body motions change with the different emotions. Know, however, that we don't actually have to have experienced something to be able to create it, possibly because there are morphic fields to tap into. Exactly how we do all this can go in the category of *the not yet understood—the mysteries*.

As you have experienced by now, there is always that annoying prerequisite of having to attain effortless excellence with the music you are working on before much else can happen. Once that physical playing of it is in your body—your muscle memory—and your body is doing what is needed to accurately produce the sound you are intending, you are freer to add meaning to the intention behind each note. You continually create the appropriate feeling and morph it into the next feeling, and the next, and the next—and your body manifests appropriately. Trust it.

Emulate the great opera singers. They can't get by with just singing the part; they have to totally *be* the part. As Joyce DiDonato said in a Juilliard master class:[147] "You don't have to do anything; it's an energetic thing." The doing is not where it starts. It starts with being.

---

[146] From *Dinner with Lenny* by Jonathan Cott
[147] January 25, 2013 master class—one you should listen to—available on YouTube

217

**Exercise 30.**

**Purpose: to become comfortable using your voice, your body, or both to communicate an emotion**

As we grow out of infancy we usually learn to repress or suppress various emotions. We create internal barriers to free expression—a must to live in the external world. However in music there need be no such barriers, so being able to dismantle those barriers at will is an essential skill.

Much of music is about that which is inexpressible other than through the metaphor of music, thus the emotions and feelings in music that we actually have names for are in the minority. We will use some of the more obvious named ones for this exercise.

Steps one through six are to be done using three contrasting emotions: sadness, anger, and exhilaration. Keep in mind that the energy behind each expressed emotion will have a directional flow. For example, with anger, the direction energy flows is outwards from you. Likewise with exhilaration. Sadness is introspective; its energy is held or directed inward.

1. Use your voice only, no body motion. Make up a short sentence or just a few words that make sense but which have no inherent emotion. It could be something as simple as *I am going to the store.* Say the word sequence while feeling the emotion of sadness. Do this very softly, then medium volume, then as loud as possible. Repeat as needed to feel comfortable and be convincing. Do the same thing with the emotion of anger behind the words, then with the feeling of exhilaration.

Notice if you are uncomfortable with a loud volume. Or perhaps a soft volume doesn't feel comfortable. Does that transfer over to your playing? Keep in mind that both your loud and soft dynamics have to reach the furthest away of your listeners. Notice also if you are more, or less, comfortable expressing a particular emotion. Also notice if it feels incongruent to express an emotion at certain volumes. Is there a volume level that seems appropriate for each emotion?

2. Now use body motion only, no voice or sound. With motion only communicate the feeling of sadness. Continue to hold your words in your mind, or not. Repeat as needed. Go on to communicate anger and then exhilaration. As in step one, use different volume levels, as they translate into the amplitude of your body motion.

If you have any trouble correlating your body motion and emotion in an obvious way, first try walking in ways congruent with these emotions. First-graders, by the way, are very adept at this. They understand that when you are angry your motions are harsh, rigid, loud, and very angular; that when you are sad your head droops, your whole body droops and your motions are slow and heavy; that when you feel exhilarated you might skip. So, be a first-grader and demonstrate the freedom to move in different styles. Set aside any inner censor that might be inhibiting you relative to motion. You are doing this in the privacy of your practice space.

3. Now use your voice with the words plus body motion to communicate these emotions. Practice at the different amplitude levels.

4. Begin switching back and forth between the emotions very quickly, using different volumes or amplitudes of the emotions as well, and then even more quickly. You need to be able to switch in the blink of an eye. Get comfortable at speeds as fast as you can say the words.

5. Repeat steps one, three and four using the following nonsensical phrase: left when super downtown spinach.

6. Repeat these same steps using the three pitches of either a major or minor chord rather than words. You can use the note names as you sing or just a syllable like *ma*.

7. When you are comfortable with all of the preceding steps, it is time to move on to a freer motion and expression than you may have used. Now dance around the room—preferably a large room—in the manner of many different characters and emotions: the loving one, the angry one, the light-hearted one, the noble one, the ecstatic one, and so on. Notice how differently you use your body and how different your hand and arm gestures are. Feel the changes in energy in your body as you become these various feelings. Remember: *be* that emotion, that feeling, that character, that attitude, and allow your body to respond appropriately. This is not an exercise in thinking or analysis, but you might sometimes observe the differences in the quality of motions you use. This will translate into how you apply these motions to your instrument—bow speed, weight and placement, speed of shifts, vibrato (discussed after the next exercise).

> **Tip**: If you get stuck on any of these steps, back up a bit and redo earlier steps, or try doing the exercise by throwing a ball or Frisbee (no hammers please) with these energies. There may be fewer inhibitions that way.

*"You **make** music. I just advise students to look at the score and make it come alive
as if they were the composer. If you can do that you are a conductor…
and if you can't, you're not."[148]*
—Leonard Bernstein


**Exercise 31.**

**Purpose: to be able to aptly choreograph a piece of music as a conductor**

Practice conducting a work you have studied with imaginary players. Use your body to create
the music the way you want it to sound. Mime it. Show the shape and dynamics, rhythm,
motion, and emotion with your hands and arms. Let the entirety of you be involved: dance it,
sing it, *be* it—the whole of the music, not just one line. Follow the advice in the Leanin' Tree
birthday card I just found for a Buddhist friend. There is a funny picture of a cat in a
meditation pose—looking quite zoned-out—and then the message:

*Feel the Birthday
Embrace the Birthday
Be the Birthday*

If you will just substitute "Music" for "Birthday," that is what I am asking for. This is your
private exploration so don't be concerned about how silly you look. There are no orchestra
players present to do caricatures of you or ask questions designed to trap you, as they have
been known to do.

---

[148] Ibid.

**Exercise 32.**

**Purpose: to be able to create different emotions at will on your instrument**

You are the mercurial chameleon changing colors at will. You want the entire palette of emotional colors available to you in any moment. The composer gives many clues as to the emotional content by the type of motion written into the piece. A fast tempo, or short quick notes, or jerky rhythms obviously do not correlate with sadness, nor a slow tempo or long, soft notes with exuberance. The emotional content is inherent in the music to a great extent. There are always other hints and guidelines too. There are many shades of color in each broad emotional band, and you will be the one determining the shade you find appropriate (more on that in Act V). In this exercise rather than creating a finely nuanced emotion, stick with broad categories of emotion.

Focus on the *intent to be* the emotion as the causative force for expressing the emotion.

1. Play a simple scale on your instrument while creating different emotions. Do not use vibrato in this exercise. (We will get to that soon.) Let your bow motion and the dynamics reflect what your body wants to do. Perhaps sound quality and intonation will suffer at first, but it is valuable to exaggerate until you feel quite free to use the motions needed to communicate various emotions. Subtlety is not what you want here. Be sure to practice the emotions that are hardest for you to express.

2. Find out what happens when you create within yourself a particular emotion but use your bow and dynamics in a way appropriate to some other emotion. For example create the sense of sadness, but use a very fast bow speed. What does this contradiction and conflict feel like? Have you experienced that feeling before? Is it easier to be congruent?

3. Repeat step one but this time confine all motion just to what happens with your bow. Play with no extraneous body motion.[149] Make the creation of emotion entirely internal; let it be communicated strictly through fingers, hands, and arms. Get comfortable and competent before moving on to step four.

4. Now incorporate body motion into this exercise. Let your body do more of what it did in Exercise 31. First, exaggerate your body motions to the point where they are absurd. Then use body motions that feel very inappropriate to that emotion. Finally, find the body motions that feel natural and coherent, that help you communicate the emotion, but are not so exaggerated as to hijack a listener's attention.

---

[149] We will do more with this in Exercise 36 page 231

**Exercise 33.**

**Purpose: to have conscious understanding of the correlations between motion and emotion**

The use of dynamics and changes of bow speed are critical tools to convey different emotions. This exercise uses an analytical approach, with conscious decision-making determining how you move your body to communicate emotion.

1. Practice using different bow speeds on a short sequence of notes, or a scale, and listen for what the different speeds tend to communicate. Does each quality of bow use elicit a certain feeling in you? This is reversing the cause and effect that you did previously (being the emotion and letting your body respond). It does work both ways. Truly it is easier to just *be* the emotion, but I do want you to analytically understand the correlations because if you are feeling emotionally stuck you can help yourself off that stuck point by the deliberate use of appropriate motion. This approach can succeed in helping you communicate if you allow it actually to pull you into the desired emotion.

2. Create a list of emotions/moods. Be the mood and play the scale or note sequence and notice how you use your bow and dynamics and make an indication by the emotion of what you did. You must be both creator and observer here.

3. Now once again try communicating the emotion using inappropriate motions. Note the results.

4. Alternate between appropriate and inappropriate bow speed and placement, and dynamics, until you feel a certainty about what works.

5. Using my piece on the next page, which is minus the title, dynamics, and other hints as to how I intended it, experiment with playing it using different bow speeds and dynamics. Did any approach strike you as being more appropriate than others? Do not read on until you have done this step.

6. Now, find the version of this piece (page 321 in the Addendum) that contains the dynamics, etc. When I wrote this I had in mind a rather bold, noble feeling—something appropriate to my concept of Don Quixote, hence the title and subtitle *Tilting at Windmills* (*Quixotic*). This concept demands a very free use of the bow and mostly big dynamics until measure 37 when the figurative Don Quixote begins to run out of steam. Play from the beginning with these concepts in mind and notice how you use your bow. You cannot be timid and succeed in communicating what I had in mind. But remember, Don Quixote is merely a storyline, not the meaning of the music. I could have picked a different title to fit the same feelings; in fact I didn't decide on this title until years after writing the piece.

♩=96-100
Poco meno
accelerando
♩=112
♩=92
Meno Mosso
copyright 2016

*"To control the hand you must be able to control the emotions."*[150]
—Bernard Greenhouse (1916-2011)
American cellist and teacher


## THE TOOL OF VIBRATO

Vibrato is a tool to enhance what you want to communicate. It is not a uniformly colored blanket to be thrown over everything. In fact you don't really want a listener to notice your vibrato. If someone tells you what a lovely vibrato you have, you had best reconsider how you use vibrato. What such a comment tells you is that your vibrato was a distraction preventing the listener from really receiving the content of the music, from having the emotional/spiritual response that you want. Having someone notice what a beautiful sound you make is not the goal. Just as, I imagine, a very handsome man or beautiful woman would prefer to have others notice *who* they are, not just their outer beauty. The same with our music: exterior beauty of sound is not enough. *And,* if the being in that beautiful body, or in our case the content of our music, is not in synch with the exterior beauty (the vibrato), it will set up a disturbing dissonance.

Vibrato should never be the same from piece to piece, emotion to emotion, phrase to phrase, and sometimes even note to note. It should never be all one color. If it is, then you will tend to communicate one energy or emotion only: that which corresponds to the motion of your vibrato. It would be like having a home with many different qualities and rooms and then painting everything the same color. It might be a beautiful red, but is it appropriate everywhere? Doubtful. Red has a wonderful enlivening quality, but probably you don't want red walls in the room where you sleep, or in the kitchen where you eat and need your digestive system to be functioning calmly. Perhaps you will want red walls in a game room where you play ping-pong.

If all the world were red you would stop registering any distinctions; a person and a horse would become indistinguishable from each other and from the background. Just so, when our sound remains the same for very long—often due to an unchanging vibrato—a listener stops listening. Vibrato is a color to be used and altered to enhance what you wish to communicate.

You can vary the width of the vibrato, the speed of the vibrato, how you use your body to produce it, the consistency of it on one note, whether you use it at all, or the pitch direction that is emphasized—does the alteration of the pitch go only below the true pitch or both above and below[151]—and no doubt other subtle factors. You want it to be driven by the content you are communicating, and if your intention behind the creation of the content/emotion is strong enough, most likely you will intuitively use the vibrato appropriate for creating that feeling. In other words your vibrato will be coherent with the emotional content. For example, if you are intending to communicate deep sadness, you will not use a fast narrow vibrato, which would more likely communicate anxiety or fear. It will be slower and probably not very wide. There is not a lot of active energy in sadness, so there cannot be very active energy or motion in the vibrato, any more than in your bow motion or shifts.

---

[150] This is an approximation of Greenhouse's comment to a student in a master class—as I remember it.

[151] The ear tends to hear as the dominant pitch the highest of the frequencies of the vibrato being used, hence it is usually best to have the vibrato go only below the specified pitch.

If you have a habitual vibrato that you use all the time, on every note, this is your opportunity to reconsider the subject. I would recommend starting with no vibrato at all, until you have released the physical habit[152] of a certain type of motion on every note. This may have been a compulsive motion, so don't be dismayed if it is not easy to give up. Indeed it can be like any obsessive-compulsive behavior. If it is difficult to let it go, then first take conscious control by intentionally doing the motion, until you can start and stop at will. Then you may need to focus your attention on having no extraneous motions in your fingers, hand, and arm for a while. As should always be the case no matter what you are working on, maintain awareness of the quality of sound and the physical contact you have with the instrument. If you do this, the sound should remain pleasing, never deteriorating into something unpleasant that you don't love.

It is like meditation. Just as you would still your mind in meditation so that something else can be present, here we wish to still our fingers. Once you have achieved that (when it is effortless to be still), you can choose the motion you wish. Just like with your mind—once it is still, you can choose what thoughts you will entertain and identify which ones are unneeded in the present moment.

It may be that for a time you will need to decide consciously how the vibrato should be in any particular passage. Ultimately this should not be an intellectual activity, but rather your vibrato motion, along with all the other motions involved in playing your instrument, will be driven by what you are creating through intention. You won't be thinking about it. Thinking is not the same as being present; when we get into a "thinking" state we stop creating and effort sets in.

There are however, style/period-appropriate uses of vibrato. Vibrato was rarely used in performance during the Baroque period. Then, it was reserved for longer notes, where a touch of vibrato might be added. As the nature of Baroque music is more in the vein of speech rather than singing, vibrato muddies the 'words,' meaning, and purity of pitch, just like an overuse of slurs. To a slightly lesser extent this is true in Classical period music as well. Even in the Romantic period the use of vibrato was more judicious than it is today. Use it when it serves a purpose, not to cover up poor intonation or the lack of presence or an intention for the music.

---

[152] Habits trap you. Just because the prison you are in is a lovely one, or even one you chose, doesn't mean you aren't in prison—trapped

**Exercise 34.**

**Purpose: to observe and hear vibrato in a different setting.**

Are you familiar with these electronic instruments: theremin and Ondes Martenot? If not, do a little research. They are similar, both developed in the 1920s, and both producing a potentially very pure sine wave timbre—amazingly beautiful. The theremin is controlled without any physical contact; the sound depends on what the player does with the two hands relative to two antennas. Harold Schoenberg, the New York Times critic (who was confident that the road less travelled would perish) is said to have described the sound of the theremin as that of a "cello lost in a dense fog, crying because it does not know how to get home." It can have a very ethereal sound, particularly when played without vibrato.

The Ondes Martenot is similar and was invented by the cellist Maurice Martenot. It has a keyboard but also can be controlled by a glide of the hand in front of the keyboard. Both instruments have been used in avant-garde music.

I actually prefer to hear them played without vibrato, but what I want you to see and hear is Katica Illényi playing the Puccini aria *O Mio Babbino Caro* on the theremin. I hope this is still available on YouTube. She uses vibrato the way a singer would, and it is worth seeing the correlation of her hand movement with the type of sound she wants. Enjoy.

**Exercise 35.**

**Purpose: to be able to match your vibrato to the desired emotional content of the music**

1. *Be* the emotion you want to convey—let's say anger—and play a note using a vibrato that is appropriate to anger. Probably it is going to be fast and wide: lots of motion that matches how you move your body when you are angry. When you are satisfied that you have a vibrato coherent with anger, try playing an entire scale with that emotion, using vibrato on every note, making sure that a weaker finger doesn't result in a weaker vibrato that no longer conveys anger.

2. Try another emotion, perhaps sorrow.

3. Continue working in this fashion until you feel like you can change vibratos at will, to convey anything you choose.

4. Play scales with different emotions with a listener present. Ask your friend to tell you what emotion or mood she or he perceives you to be communicating. Work as needed on different emotions until you and your friend are on the same wavelength, so to speak.

5. Use these pieces of mine, found in the Addendum, to experiment with the vibratos that work best to convey the content. I composed these pieces in part to convey specific emotions, making them useful for teaching appropriate motions. For now go with the emotions and metaphors I suggest:

> *After the Storm* – try a wider, but not too intense or fast motion to communicate the general feeling of calmness and contentment—*be* the peace after the storm (the metaphor).

> *Off-Leash* – try a faster, slightly narrower motion to communicate more excitement—*be* the dog running excitedly off-leash, very extroverted.

> *Lament* – try a slower, not too wide motion—*be* the sadness and introversion indicated by the title.

> *HeartSong* – try very little vibrato, neither fast nor wide—*be* heartfelt and gentle.

Remember: *be* the new emotion first. If not, what you do with your tools will likely sound un-authentic, artificial.

**Tip**: Sometimes we need to do a less logical fingering to better convey the desired content. As I have gotten older and my fingers less athletic, I find that I might need to use my second or third fingers, rather than first or fourth, when I want great intensity on a note. Rarely can you perfectly match sounds with all fingers, so finger selection, like vibrato, is a tool to help communicate content.

Also, having just one finger down on the string gives a freer, more vibrant sound, but when you need the greatest intensity on a note, supporting the vibrating finger with an adjacent finger is helpful, done by 'gluing' it to the vibrating finger, not to the string.

## ANOTHER LOOK AT BODY MOTION

We looked at physical movement of bow and body appropriate to different emotions; now let's look at body motion from a slightly different point of view: what and how much motion is appropriate in an actual performance.

I commented on this aspect in Act III and on the vast difference—yet individual internal congruence—between Artur Rubenstein and Joshua Bell. I liken Rubenstein's stillness at the piano to a lake where motion deep in the lake never perturbs the surface calm. With Bell's playing the entire lake has been set in motion, as it is below so it is on the surface, one body moving as a whole. Both are right; both extremes work to fulfill the purpose of music; both artists touch the soul with their playing.

In some players Rubenstein's stillness would not be stillness at all, but rather a lack of movement, a rigidity, an inhibition or fear—not a choice. But with Rubenstein there is a quality to his stillness that speaks of intention, certainty, trust, and… choice. Like Rubenstein we need to be capable of creating all of the meaning of the music internally, expressing only through fingers, hands and arms. This forces you to hone your intention. Once you can do this you have a choice whether to remove the restraint on other body motion.

Stillness however doesn't mean that the unmoving parts of the body are not involved. Providing the stable support for what is moving is crucial. This means understanding principles about congruent use of the body, which can be learned from *Feldenkrais* or *Alexander Technique* practices. Visible motion that is congruent will be initiated from the core of the body, not just from an appendage.

Like Bell we want to allow the music to move us without reservation or inhibition. There is a quality of oneness with the violin, his body, and the music that is remarkable. I have colleagues who object mightily to his motions, but some who object tend to be those musicians who can't move, not physically with the instrument, not emotionally with the music. They are a bit frozen. There will always be conflicting opinions regarding body motion, but rather than putting energy into asserting an opinion, our energy is better spent examining our own behavior: whether what we do is unchosen habit, or choice coming from options.

It's my contention that motion incongruent with the music will show in the sound, detracting from control and ability to express the music, and that certainly isn't the case with Bell. I may not always prefer his interpretation of the music; I just don't think his motion interferes in any way with his playing and interpretation, or my enjoyment. In part it has to do with that oneness with the instrument—the violin is simply an extension of his body. The whole moves together, not separately, one part against another. Motion is who he is. Making him hold still would be like telling my dog, Mari, not to run full out.

So, what is incongruent body motion? Some guidelines:

> 1. Foremost would be any motion contrary to the decided upon emotion or metaphorical meaning of the music.

Example: part of your body moving wildly while you're playing something tender and introspective.

2. Any motion where one part of the body is doing something in conflict with the whole or other parts.

Example: a foot or leg keeping the beat or other body motion that is keeping the beat.

Example: bopping of the head, or dipping the knees to show every downbeat or beat.

Rhythm needs to be internal—felt in the core of your body—not as an appendage doing something separate from the whole.

3. Moving the instrument separate from or incongruently to the body.

Example: bobbing the violin up and down relative to your body.

These are all motions that separate the body from the intention, the music, and the instrument.

Let's turn these around and frame things in the positive. Appropriate body motion is:

1. Body motion congruent with the emotional content and metaphorical meaning, including use of the bow and vibrato.

2. All moving parts of the body are in synch, moving with the same energy and intent.

3. The instrument moves with the body, as an extension of the body.

This last aspect is perhaps the answer to why Rubenstein's quietness seems so congruent. The piano after all is fixed in place, so a wildly moving pianist seems incongruous. A pianist can't become virtually one with the instrument on the physical level the way a violinist, cellist, or oboist can, where we essentially are embracing the instrument. For us it is like having a dance partner where you move together beautifully as one. For a pianist the oneness is created strictly on the intentional level. It's an energetic embracing.

Congruence between body motion and breath is essential when giving a preparatory beat to begin a work. For others to know the tempo and when to begin, all of you has to give that invitation to play. As H. I. Khan said, when you turn in a direction all of you has to go in that direction, or as with the lion, everything in you prepares for the leap. And, always the intake of the breath must be in the tempo of the music to come. Leading in this way is like a conductor's preparatory beat telling everyone what tempo and energy is desired. You can't just bob your head; the right energy and tempo of the music start before the sound.

If you have the opportunity, study the art of conducting.

**Tip:** Often knee joints will lock up without our being aware. If you are playing in a standing position, a slight bend in your knees can allow them to act a bit like shock absorbers. If you sit to play, generally your entire body will be more relaxed if your feet are forward enough that your knees are at an angle slightly greater than a right angle (a bit more than 90 degrees). Having feet tucked behind chair legs is counter-productive and hard on the back. If you have a difficult passage coming up try relaxing your feet even further out from the right-angle bend. Jaw, mouth, and neck muscles are also ones that tend to tense. Let your lips be parted slightly, so that you can sing under your breath as you play. Keep your eyes soft rather than staring fixedly at the notes or elsewhere. As much as possible soften everything in your body—with or without motion.

In summary, the relationship between your body motion and the music you are playing must be a congruent one, each communicating the same energy. Otherwise body motion will be a distraction.


**Exercise 36.**

**Purpose: to gain the freedom to move or not move in accord with how the music moves you to be—find the motion, or lack of, that feels congruent as you play**

1. Using a piece that you know well, work through the guidelines given previously of what is incongruous, and intentionally apply these movements to your piece. Notice how this feels to you. If anything feels comfortable or habitual then work with that motion consciously until you can do it or not do it at will. Our unconscious habits *will* feel comfortable so be on the alert for that.

2. Play your piece with no extraneous movement—only what is essential. Work with this until it is effortless to remain still while creating and communicating the content through intention, being the music, and the appropriate bow and vibrato motions. Challenge yourself as in Exercise 32 to achieve all the appropriate intensity of emotion while maintaining quietness of body. (The body is loose and relaxed, not rigid.)

3. Now play your piece allowing the entirety of body and instrument to move together in a way that feels congruent and expressive. Work with this step until you sense what feels most coherent, which could be no extra motion. Don't decide ahead of time what you *should* do; let it evolve over time. Remember: you and your instrument are one.

**ACT IV REPRISE**

*"Genuine music fills the soul with a thousand things better than words."*
—Felix Mendelssohn (1809-1847)
German composer

**Exercise 37.**

**Purpose: to be able to apply the ideas in this Act, creating the illusion of motion, bringing life to the music**

1. Write a sequence of at least 32 notes (preferably in a specific key), but with no rhythm (all notes the same value). Use the blank manuscript paper on the next page.

2. Note the interval relationships.

3. Is your sequence conjunct, disjunct, or a mix of both?

4. Play or sing the sequence.

5. Did you create the sense of being in a specific tonality with its tonic note, or do the notes simply orient around a tonal center without that sense of a larger framework of a major or minor key, or did you follow the road less travelled? Is there a discernible difference as to which notes seem to be leading you on?

6. Play the sequence again bringing out any notes which help to lead the ear on. Within the scale, if you created that framework, how do the various notes function (tonic chord notes, leading tones)?

So far you have worked with the tonally-based illusions.

7. Now create a time signature and add rhythm to your 32 notes, so that you divide them into a correct number of beats per bar. Mix up the various time durations if appropriate. If you feel the need, add to your sequence of notes.

8. Check to see if you have created a structure that naturally falls into units of two or four bars, or some other structural unit that can be made obvious to the ear.

9. Play what you have written and listen for where the emphasis needs to fall rhythmically and structurally for the notes to propel you forward. Did you end up with any rests (silence), or more than one voice? Did you tend to put shorter notes on the beat or after the beat? How do the notes group? Play your sequence as needed to find all the possible ways of leading the ear onward.

10. Did you write with descending or ascending lines that need to mimic natural laws of motion? Does your sequence need to gain or lose energy in a way contrary to gravity and natural motion?

232

11. Add all the features you know in terms of emphasizing or bringing out certain notes to give your sequence its maximum sense of forward motion. Use rubato if appropriate, or simply change the energy to help with the illusions. Make use of dynamic changes.

12. Add emotional content congruent with what you have written, suiting your physical motions including bow speed, vibrato, and dynamics to the emotional content decided upon.

13. Feel free to create other longer sequences of notes and take them through this process.

14. Play my piece *Protest* with all the appropriate motions. As discussed in Extreme Motion (page 182), much of the piece *is* a protest, very loud with tremendous energy, but the middle section from measure 21 through 29 has a different quality—one of resignation and sorrow. The energy dissipates along with the volume. Then the music returns—almost—to the feeling of extreme protest, until bar 41. The low *C* in that measure is a turning point. Part way through the note the feeling changes from protest/anger to one of gentleness and tenderness. Hold the note as long as it takes to accomplish this transformation. How you use your bow, dynamics, and vibrato must change during the course of this one note (the low *C*) to communicate a changing mood. The piece then finishes quietly and with great tenderness.

15. Go through this process on the first 25 measures of the first movement of the Brahms *Sonata No. 1 in E minor for Cello and Piano* (page 185 of this Act). Transcribe this for your instrument if you are not a cellist. The first eight measures of this long, expanded opening theme are dark, mysterious, almost secretive, filled with longing, so suit the motions you use to that concept. Apply all that has been discussed in this Act.  Notice which notes compel movement. Your vibrato will need to be a bit faster than a lush relaxed sound. There needs to be something fervent, though subdued, here. You may perceive the character of the music differently than I do, but for now go with this description.

The remaining measures of this opening change character and color. The ascending, step-wise progression of notes has a more expansive, open-hearted, and optimistic quality. A wider, more lush vibrato will be appropriate—not too passionate at first—but building in intensity and energy to the peak of the phrase, coinciding with the forte marking, then dying back down with the pitch-wise and dynamic descent of the music.

16. Go through this process on a piece of your choosing.

Always, always, always… intention comes first.

INTERLUDE

**Figure 23**

## UNDERSTANDING THE GAP BETWEEN KNOWLEDGE AND CREATIVITY

At moments of major creativity or insight scientists and artists both report similar physical and mental changes, including heightened alertness, bursts of energy, and increased clarity of thought.[153]

Oddly, these are also hallmarks of a fear response. In both cases there is a release of adrenaline from the adrenal glands,[154] a response we musicians tend to identify as 'nerves.' Because the physical responses to creative surges and to fear are so close in nature, it behooves us to reframe our supposed fear response as being one of creative excitement. So the next time you have a case of 'nerves' before playing, remember this is the close cousin to creativity, and something you can tap for a better performance.

Before a creative interpretation can occur there has to be the step of gathering all the information, doing the hard work. In the case of musicians that includes learning to play the instrument, and learning to both play and understand the piece. The period of preparation may be lengthy. Then that step has to be let go of, allowing an opportunity for everything you have done so far to simmer on the back burner. When you bring conscious attention back to what was studied so diligently, something will have jelled. For the scientist often it is at this point—rather out of the blue—that the "eureka" moment occurs. For the musician perhaps it will be the sudden insight into exactly what needs to be communicated, or a degree of ease will be there that wasn't there before, or without thinking about it you start going beyond what is printed on the page.

Looking at what happens in the brain, our first lengthy step primarily involves what we have come to commonly (if not entirely accurately[155]) refer to as left-brain activation and skills. Then when the left brain steps aside—you having stashed the project on the metaphorical back burner—the right brain quietly goes about its job: perceiving the emotional content, the needed kinesthetic components, the shapes.  However there is still the necessary communication between the two brain hemispheres, and this is where the corpus callosum comes in. It is the

---

[153] *Leonardo's Brain* by Leonard Shain is my source for this information.
[154] Ibid
[155] I am using the concept of left brain versus right brain somewhat metaphorically to refer to types of functioning which may or may not ultimately be found to reside in a specific brain region. Research is ongoing and results are ambiguous.

part of the brain connecting the two halves. It is the least understood part of the brain, but without this unique band of brain tissue the two hemispheres don't communicate.[156] In the case of individuals where the corpus callosum has been severed,[157] the various functions of the two hemispheres are still intact, but there is no relationship or coordination between them. For example, speech is cold and emotionless, like an automaton, like Data, and the right hand literally doesn't know what the left is doing. There have been many cases where the left-brain speech centers have been so damaged that a person cannot speak, yet due to an intact right brain they may be able to sing and curse, both being right-brain functions (swearing usually being motivated by strong emotion).

With an intact corpus callosum and proper connections, the two halves of the brain and their respective functions integrate. In most people the analytical style of functioning does tend to dominate as we are a culture that emphasizes left-brain skills over right, submerging and devaluing right-brain skills. But it is those right-brain abilities that we need to unleash in performance to *be* the music, so it is critical that musicians have effective communication and a balanced exchange between the two hemispheres. In other words we need a well developed corpus callosum.

 Do not get caught up in the popular thinking that you can only function in one of these modes. As with everything else in life, you get more of what you practice.

One danger of allowing the left-brain focus to dominate is that it destroys much of the pleasure in life. I just got home from a classical guitar concert (yes, even here in my remote corner). Before going to the concert I had been working on this section of the manual, which put me very much into the analytical left-brain mode. And I got stuck there. I didn't much enjoy the performance, thinking about all the ways the guitarist did *not* create illusions of motion, or communicate emotion. The listener (me in this case) has the responsibility to show up in a receptive (right-brain) mode, ready to be touched and moved by the music. That of course doesn't happen if you are busy analyzing. Mea culpa.

---

[156] There is still debate as to whether the corpus callosum is just the bridge between the two halves or whether it is the seat for the integration of the two, forming a whole greater than the sum of its parts.

[157] Known as split-brain patients, this procedure is sometimes done in desperate cases to control otherwise unstoppable seizures

Sometimes you have to ignore what conductors, composers, and teachers say and pay attention to what they do. If you have listened to the six Bernstein lectures you might get the impression that, for him, how the music is constructed is the most important aspect of a work. If you also listened to and watched the performances in those lectures then you might think otherwise.

Ultimately for you, the performer, it doesn't matter if an eight-bar passage of music is the retrograde inversion of the second theme, or simply a string of notes relating beautifully. Yes, the analytical knowledge may help inform how you will play the notes, or not, but still your job is to touch the hearts of your listeners, and that does not happen if you are busy thinking "here comes the retrograde inversion." You have already decided how to shape the phrase, now it is your business to *be* the music. The meaning you are communicating isn't: "Listen, do you hear the clever use of an inversion here?" It's the meaning that can't be expressed in words. It may be that the inversion was required to create that exquisite moment in the music, but that inversion is the tool, not the message. If the tool used allows something from the unseen world to come into the 'seen' world through our playing, then it is a useful tool.

Listening to and watching Bernstein (or other great conductors) conduct, it is clear that it is the metaphorical meaning of the music that he is feeling and conducting. Despite his great intellect and analytical understanding of the music, he is not conducting the tools or compositional devices of music; he is conducting the meaning—what it is he feels. The music is in his body, his face, his hands, his carrier wave. And what is that meaning? We can't name it, there are no words for it, but it is not the intellectual understanding. Bernstein feels it, the orchestra feels and reflects it, we feel it; it is what he conveys through his body motions, facial expressions and the energy behind those. It doesn't need a name. He was one of those rare humans who could totally integrate the analytical and expressive sides of himself and the music.

Most composers, with notable exceptions, when they speak of their music, they speak of the metaphorical content, not of the architecture (structure). It is the inner purpose, as with the cathedral analogy, that is of greater interest than the outer form. They trust that performers will bring their own creativity to the blueprint provided. C.P.E. Bach was apparently scornful of those "who astound us with their prowess without ever touching our sensibilities."[158]

Then there is Stravinsky. Recall from the Bernstein lectures that in his autobiography Stravinsky said: "Music is essentially powerless to express anything at all… expression has never been an inherent quality of music." He never quite retracted his words, but as Bernstein pointed out, his music, so full of expression, was evidence against his words, which he did modify over the years. Humorously, his scores are full of verbal instructions as to how the music is to be played: dolce, tranquillo, espressivo. He also had strong associations with ballet and the theater, many of his works being written for dance and stage collaborations. His music, throughout his different stylistic periods, is powerful and very expressive, and musicians have no problem finding and communicating that expressiveness and metaphorical meaning.

The *Apollon musagèti Suite* is an example of how very lush and expressive Stravinsky's music can be. This is one of those recordings you need to buy (my old favorite Toscanini recording is probably unavailable), and then listen to it until you fall in love with it. That happened to me over the course of a day about 40 years ago. (That story is in the next Act.)

---

[158] *Facing the Music* by Harold C. Schonberg, page 74

## BRIDGING THE GAP

The activities of reading and studying (anything) tend to take you into left-brain mode.

Because of this vast gulf between analytical and intellectual knowledge (left-brain) and *being* or experiencing that knowledge (right-brain), there is a danger in a manual like this that the reader—that would be YOU—leaves on the page what has been read without taking the steps to live the material. This tendency to leave matters with the left brain is exacerbated by the necessary, mostly left brained, first steps toward a creative performance—studying the score, understanding structure and relationships, learning the notes. So you must find a way to balance that intense study of the music (left-brain) with experiencing the music (right-brain) as you proceed.

Fortunately, the very playing of an instrument combined with the study of music has been shown to increase the size and complexity of the corpus callosum. Musicians do develop much better connections or integration of the differing sets of skills of the hemispheres than the average person. A more developed corpus callosum makes for greater ease of learning, and this is the rationale behind why the teaching of instruments and music in schools is so valuable. As musicians we definitely have the capacity to achieve the desired gestalt. We just need to nudge this integration a bit. Many of the exercises in this manual are designed to help bridge that gap, particularly the ones in the sections on Motion and Emotion and Vibrato. Merely reading this manual won't suffice.

The more you practice using your body to communicate emotion, the quicker the bridge is built. Singing and dancing are right-brain functions and this is why I place importance on both the singing and dancing of the music. These activities speed the integration, hence my repeated requests to you to do those things. It doesn't matter that you are not a trained singer or dancer; in fact it is probably better. Due to the intimate connection between your voice and body motions, and emotions, making use of this connection, strengthening it, will help you internalize all the concepts that have been presented. These right-brain activities form a critically important tool for taking the information and ideas you have studied and integrating them all into the gestalt of an artistic performance that may deeply touch and move another human being.

The process of internalizing knowledge takes time. It is a process. To truly communicate also takes desire and the willingness and courage to let others peek into your soul—the core of who you really are.  At this point much of what is needed is to let go of all the concerns you may still have about what others might think, find the freedom to trust your body, and *be* the music.

### *We Should Talk About This Problem*

*There is a beautiful creature*
*Living in a hole you have dug.*

*So at night*
*I set fruit and grains*
*And little pots of wine and milk*
*Beside your soft earthen mounds,*

*And I often sing.*

*But still, my dear,*
*You do not come out. I have fallen in love with Someone*
*Who hides inside you.*

*We should talk about this problem---*

*Otherwise,*
*I will never leave you alone.*


Hafiz
translated by Daniel Ladinsky

Part of my intent with this book is to help bring you, the beautiful creature, out of your hole.
Let's talk some more.

# ACT V

## Singing *Your* Song

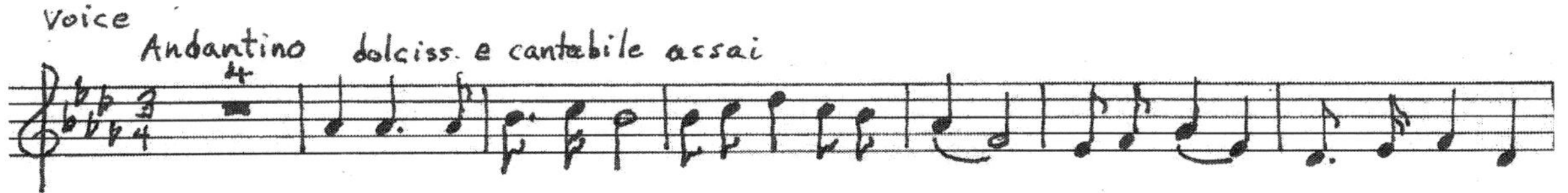

**Figure 24**

## OVERVIEW OF INTERPRETATION

The basic definition of interpretation simply refers to a person's conception of a work of art. The *Harvard Dictionary of Music*[159] elaborates: "The personal and creative element in the performance of music, which, as in drama, depends on a middleman between the composer and the audience… The player or conductor, while studying a composition, absorbs it and, consciously or unconsciously, models it according to his own general ideas and taste… A personal interpretation is a performer's great privilege, granted him by the composer. A really fine performer is always aware of the responsibility toward the work that this privilege imposes."

You arrive at *your* song through a multi-faceted process combining analytical study, intuition or instinct, and your effortless excellence.

At some point you need to ask: Why was this piece written? What was it that needed 'saying' that compelled the composer to write this piece? What metaphorical content was being expressed that is common to all humanity, and, have I gone deeply enough into my own heart to find it? Without this commonality the music would probably not have remained in the repertoire.

Answering these questions requires some analytical study. The more you understand what informed the mind of the creator the better your chances of finding resonance with the creation. Study the life of the composer, understand the time in which the composer lived—the culture, what was happening in other arts, in the greater world. What were the strong influences on the composer? Did the composer leave writings and opinions you can consult? Was there a specific philosophy? Comments about this piece?

If you study Debussy's life, for example, you will discover that he didn't consider himself to be an impressionist in the sense of the impressionist art movement of the time. Rather than representing nature in this new way as artists like Claude Monet were doing, he considered that he was representing the human emotional response to nature. Understanding this gives you a deeper picture of what Debussy was saying with his music.

---

[159] Second Edition

Once you have a sense of the Mind behind the creation, you need to examine how the composer notated that intent. What guidelines are there? What is there inherent in the music, such as running 16ths at a fast tempo, that tells you about the motion and emotion desired?

For example, if the music on the page appears static to the eye, like my *HeartSong,* that is a huge hint. You can assume that the music is not meant to feel angry or exhilarated. The preponderance of 16th notes in the Bach *A minor Violin Concerto* tells you a lot about the energy and emotion needed in that work. You can assume it is not an introspective piece. So your understanding of the correlation of motion and emotion is one of your tools.

You have looked at the evidence in print, and gotten an idea of what the composer wants you to feel. In the process of acquiring the physical effortless excellence, you come to intuit more and more about the music. You incorporate that within the context of your experiences and the language of your own heart. How will I express the message I have found? Am I ready to *be* that content? Do I have something to say with this music?

You have applied all your musical tools to begin to manifest the content in your sound. You have used your knowledge of tonal centers and rhythmic groupings and physical motion to understand what elements of the music to bring out that contribute to the meaning you have arrived at. Now you simply must *be* that content. Once you have something to say and know what it is, then you go with conviction, total commitment to your concept. There is no place in performance for doubt. You sing *your* song.


*"I think… if it is true that*
*there are as many minds as there are heads,*
*then there are as many kinds of love*
*as there are hearts."*
—Leo Tolstoy (1828-1910)
Russian novelist
from *Anna Karenina*

*"A personal interpretation is a performer's great privilege, granted him by the composer.
A really fine performer is always aware of the responsibility toward
the work that this privilege imposes."*
—*Harvard Dictionary of Music*, Second Edition

## INTERPRETATION AND RESPONSIBILITY

Responsibility entails the ability to respond—appropriately. Interpretation comes from your response to the blueprint recorded in the language of music by the composer.

All privileges entail responsibilities, and the first responsibility in the interpretation of another's creation is to bring integrity to it, which means you need to study the score. For those of us who play an instrument where we mostly have a single line of music to play, it is tempting to learn only one's own part and not study the score. But there is an obligation to understand the whole, which may include a piano part, several other instruments as in trios or quartets, or an entire orchestral accompaniment. Don't give in to a temptation to bypass this crucial step.

Great artists such as Pablo Casals speak of first learning a work through study of the score, then through work at the piano, playing and hearing the whole of it, and only then taking it to the cello to learn the skill of playing it. This way your musical decisions are not made on the basis of your comfort level with the instrument. You make the musical decisions first, then figure out how to realize and become comfortable with them on the instrument.

The study of a score includes examining and understanding all those aspects of a piece that we discussed in Act IV. You must also understand how your part dovetails with the other lines, including: understanding the context for your line, what to bring out, when to play a supporting role, how to balance dynamics. Know when you need to sound like a trombone, or flute, rather than a cello,[160] or if you are a pianist, when to sound like a cello.[161] Know when you can bend the intonation for greater expression, and when you can't because it conflicts with what is in another part. By understanding that there are near-impossible passages for another instrument, you will not take the liberty of pushing a tempo faster than your colleague can play it. Recognize also that there are limitations as to what your listeners' ears can grasp, and a too-fast tempo becomes a blur, while a too-slow tempo makes it difficult for you to create a flow and for your listeners to sense the motion.

Your study of the music should be as thorough as that of a good conductor; it is the foundation for your unique interpretation.

In choosing fingerings go with what makes the most musical sense, even if it increases left-hand difficulties. Melodies for example generally sound better if you can maintain the same string color. But artistry really lies in the bow arm; it is your bow arm that must respond to your artistic intent. That's where all the subtleties happen, and, most of the difficulties. If it is

---

[160] Remember: everything starts with intention. You must intend to sound like a trombone, and hear that quality in your mind, before physically producing it.

[161] Gregor Piatigorsky said of Rubenstein that he was the only musician who had a cello tone like his (i.e. Piatigorsky's): *Facing the Music*, page 329.

musical "sixes" between alternate ways to play a passage, choose left-hand difficulties over complicated bowing. Left-hand problems are easier to resolve.[162]

Your responsibilities as a section player in an orchestra differ from those as a soloist, and in that scenario your decisions may be different. When it is necessary to blend with nine or ten other people you may not be able to make the best musical choices if that causes your sound to stand out. Good section players in an orchestra will often use open strings and stay in first position more than you would choose as a soloist. Sometimes left-hand simplicity is a plus, particularly if you haven't had adequate time to learn a complicated fingering and are under the pressure of having to be absolutely in synch with others.

> **Tip**: If a passage doesn't reach excellence with what should be adequate practice, it is probably a bowing issue. Try practicing just the bowing pattern on the equivalent open strings, and eventually at much greater speed than will be needed, until that is effortless. Then add the left hand back in.

An additional responsibility during performance is the maintaining of good communication with both your colleagues and listeners. To the extent possible do not turn your back to the audience or to your colleagues. Know the music well enough that your eyes never need be glued to the page. Keep your hair out of your face and your clothing in good repair. You don't want anything flapping in the breeze to distract. One of my colleagues kept his orchestra tails together with black electrical tape. Unfortunately the tape reflected light differently than the cloth. There are other stories I could mention, but I won't. In other words do not put up barriers or create distractions. The most stunning interpretation will be worthless if you don't have communication with colleagues and the audience's focus on your music.

---

[162] Emanuel Feurmann purportedly said that he could teach a horse to play with the left 'hand.' However he didn't make the same claim about the bow arm.

**REVISITING ALEC**

Do you remember my comments on the movie *The Black Stallion* and my upset at how the young man Alec was portrayed in the movie? I believe I am correct in thinking the creator of the book series would not have been pleased, as the many clues he gave about Alec were ignored by the people who made the movie.

Since first writing about the movie, I have gone back to that first book of the series to reacquaint myself with Alec. The author stated that Alec was a redhead, with blue eyes and freckles, and he had lean, hard arm muscles after working in the jungles of India with his uncle all summer. We can infer from other information in the story that he has had at least one year of high school, probably two, maybe three. This is all the information we have to construct the image of the physical aspects of Alec, but there is certainly adequate evidence that he is not the pudgy, dark-haired, pre-puberty young boy that I remember from the movie. If I, the audience, found this to be upsetting, what must the creator feel? The author fortunately wrote a great deal more about the inner qualities of Alec—his character.

Like writers, a composer first has a concept, however arrived at (intentionally or via sudden inspiration), then manifests it as accurately as possible through notes. A composer can put down on paper the outer appearance of the music, but the language of music is less precise about the inner character and qualities. Composers and authors both must feel despairing about performances when the most obvious of guidelines that are included in the blueprint are ignored.

## ARTICULATION

Like other guidelines, articulation marks provided in the score need to be honored. They provide clues as to the unseen content of the music.

The basic definitions of "articulate" include: "expressed or formulated clearly or systematically; distinct; able to speak; especially able to speak intelligibly or expressively." "Articulation" then is: "the act or manner of jointing" (or joining in the case of music as opposed to body joints).[163] In music the term is used to denote clarity in musical performance, involving breathing, phrasing, the use of the bow or breath in legato and staccato, silence, accents, attacks, etc.

Articulation marks are sometimes indicated and sometimes not. Staccato is generally indicated, but there is a broad spectrum of sound within each category of style. Accents may also be appropriate where not actually indicated, such as in the Barber *Sonata* discussed in Act IV. In the case of music for strings, slurs are often actually phrasing markings, not bowings. (There is a need for adequate bow changes to allow the music to flow.) But articulation can't be looked at in isolation in your part only, ignoring other lines of music. When you are playing with others these decisions have to be made together so that everyone expresses the same concept of the music. It is reasonably easy when you are playing with instruments in the same family—all strings, or all winds. Then you will be speaking the same language in terms of the tools at your disposal to create the marked and agreed upon articulations.

When you play with piano, you must understand the sound produced by the different articulations called for in the piano part, and you may need to match that style. Generally string players have a larger selection of tools; we can match the articulation the pianist is being asked to produce. It can work the other way too, of course. This is an aspect to discuss with your musical partner. A good example is the third movement of the Brahms *E minor Sonata*, where the piano and cello trade the same themes back and forth. In this movement the piano starts with the fugue theme. When the cello enters it needs to be with the same quality of sound, the same degree of separation between the notes, the same clarity. Keep in mind that on a lower string you may have to use your bow quite differently and play physically somewhat shorter notes than on a higher string, to create the same effect. It's always the sound that you want to be comparing, not how it feels physically. Just keep intending and listening for the sound you want and your body will adjust.

There is an interesting problem in another great Brahms work: the *Piano Concerto No. 1 in D minor*, first movement, which is marked *Maestoso*. The opening theme[164] in the orchestral accompaniment, played initially in octaves by just the violins and cellos, is one of the most powerful, insistent, and majestic themes in the entire piano literature. (Perhaps the only theme of comparable power in the cello literature is the opening theme of the Dvořák *Concerto*, which when the cello finally comes in is marked *risoluto*.[165]) In the Brahms the piano doesn't actually play the first theme in its entirety until the recapitulation, almost three quarters of the way through the movement, but I believe that the articulation of the strings in the beginning, and in other instruments as they take the theme or parts of it, must duplicate the sound of the

---

[163] *Webster's New Collegiate Dictionary*
[164] That's the theme quoted in Figure 5, page 77.
[165] This is the theme quoted in Figure 3, page 44. To help students get the right feeling for this theme, Irene Sharp—superb cello teacher—suggests the idea of the words "I am the king" to fit the opening notes. This seems a quite fitting metaphor.

pianist. This articulation would be something for the conductor to discuss with the pianist before rehearsal with the orchestra.

The percussive hard start to each of the first five notes and the clipped sound of the two quarters in the second bar have to be imitated as well as possible in the strings, which is doable. It is the last two eighths in that second bar, and the following bar, that are problematic. There just doesn't seem to be a really good bowing for this. Usually the second of the two eighths tends to get swallowed and the two 'grace' notes at the end of the trill tend to sound different than in the piano. My sister tells me that pianists are quite used to trills having prefix notes and, as is the case here, suffix notes (not grace notes), and that the convention is that these suffix notes are the ending of the trill leading seamlessly from the trill to the next beat, sounding as if the trill were slurred through the suffix into the next beat. This is *not* how it usually sounds played by the cellos and violins. The bowings I have seen in the cello part are usually separate bows on all these notes,[166] which I think actually weakens the sound as it becomes rather awkward for the needed strength and creates a slight break between the trill and its suffix notes. I have yet to find a satisfactory bowing that approximates what pianists do.

Sometimes approximating is all we can do.

---

[166] This is the case in the original manuscript as well.

**FREEDOMS**

Now that I have harangued you about being faithful to the composer's guidelines, let's examine exceptions other than the rhythmic ones discussed in Act IV. Composers C.P.E. Bach, Mozart, and others had things to say about the printed score: essentially that it was only a part of the music. Nineteenth-century composers were used to and expected the altering of tempos by performers. Prior to the twentieth century the printed manuscript was more an approximate guide—not fixed for all time. Mozart professed that he never played his music twice in the same way. There is ample evidence supporting the idea that we are not bound to the literal *letter of the law*; yet we must stay within the *spirit* of the music.

Slurs or bowing markings in a piece may or may not be the composer's. As mentioned, sometimes they are simply phrasing marks, not actually bowings. Often bowing suggestions are added by an editor, along with fingerings and sometimes additional dynamics. If the work includes a piano part, the composer's original markings may show in the cello line included in the piano score. This is another reason for studying the full score and multiple editions: you want to check for discrepancies. It is not unusual for the editing to diverge significantly from what the composer indicated, particularly if the editor is from a different time period than when the music was written. For keyboard players a comparable, but certainly more complex issue, is the pedaling. Again, an editor's suggested pedaling may diverge considerably from the composer's original markings.

To resolve slurring issues and find what works for both you and the music, keep in mind what purpose slurs serve. They are generally a tool for telling you about note groupings—the notes that belong together without interruption. If the composer is a fine cellist, then they need to be taken more literally, but this is rarely the case. If I can achieve what I believe to be the composer's intent with different bowings that work as well or better, then I feel free to do so. This is a valid interpretive tool. Often the flow of the music is better communicated with more bow changes rather than fewer. This assumes of course that you know how to make smooth, almost imperceptible bow changes. (See Tip, page 175.) Using shorter slurs may give you the freedom to make more changes in bow speed, and thus color the sound to suit the music. You never have carte blanche to change bows indiscriminately, but if the composer's slurs result in too slow a bow speed for the emotional content—resulting in a constipated sound that doesn't move—then consider revising what is in the part.

If you are a cellist playing with violins or violas, don't feel that you have to use the same bowings. What you want is the same effect, however you attain that. A frustrating aspect of orchestral playing is that often the cellos are asked to use the same bowings as the violins. This means that string crossings, which are the most natural and work best on the violin, will be backwards for cellists—down-bow string crossings for the violins might be better as up-bows for cellists. Likewise the slurs needed to optimally express a line may be quite different. Once again it is the issue of the tool needing to serve the purpose.

It is interesting to view different cellists playing the first of the Schumann *Fantasy Pieces* (try YouTube) to see what they do with the bowings in the beginning and in the section starting at the end of bar 26 (see Excerpt 31). As you can see there are long slurs in the music, and adhering to these makes the music somewhat difficult to bring off in a way that sounds flowing. However, having done your homework, you know that this work was originally written for clarinet, thus making these not bowings, but phrase or breath markings. In the cello and viola versions, which were apparently approved by Schumann, these phrase markings were kept, but clarinetists have more length of breath than we have length of bow. It is possible, and I think desirable, to break up these 'slurs' in ways that sound organic and accommodate string crossings.

**Excerpt 31  Schumann** *Fantasy Pieces, No. 1*

The fingerings you choose will impact the bowings that work best. I try not to end a slur at a point that doesn't sound like a completed group when I sing or play it. For example, I would not slur only through the first four notes following the upbeat *A* in bar 27. You might sneak in a bow change after the fifth note. However sometimes a slur across a bar line or group ending *can* facilitate something else such as hiding a string crossing, taking care of course not to obscure the end or beginning of a group. Do some experimenting with this passage, including the possibility of slurs going across bar lines. There are many valid possibilities, including Schumann's phrase markings of course.

In the Act IV discussion of rhythm, I mentioned various situations where the rhythm and tempo need to be 'played with' to better create what we perceive as motion. Freedoms are in order when the printed language of music is inadequate to convey the rhythmic intent. In *Musings on the Limitations of the Language* I discussed the reoccurring rhythmic motif in *Protest*, and how hard it was to notate as I conceive of it. Finally I settled on that division of the beat into six parts at the beginning of the piece. When I considered writing it with the beat simply divided into four parts (16ths), I was thinking other players would just distort it appropriately. But if it were played literally that would totally fail to capture the intensity I had in mind, so I used the sextuplet rhythm. This difficulty in notating my intent made me wonder how often that rhythmic pattern (16th /8th /16th) is truly what a composer has envisioned. I think it within the bounds of interpretive privilege to exaggerate or distort these rhythms according to the emotional content you find in the music, provided doing so doesn't conflict with other parts. If the rhythm has to line up with what is in another part, such freedoms are curtailed—another reason to know the whole of the music, not just your own part.

The distortion can go opposite to how I play *Protest*: the dotted-eighth/sixteenth figure being interpreted as the lazier sounding triplet figure—quarter plus eighth under a triplet sign. Some conductors do consider this as an accepted standard with certain music. Once again I believe the emotional content of the music must drive such decisions.

Tempo markings are guidelines, even when accompanied by a metronome marking. Metronomes in the past were not consistent, and appropriate tempos are very dependent on outer conditions, acoustics for example. Search for the tempo that expresses what you sense as the metaphorical content—that potential of the music that creates resonance within you.

## MUSINGS ON SINGING YOUR SONG

There are many thorny questions to consider. What makes our concept of the music personal and unique? What happens that allows us to bridge the gap between our analytical study and the integrated whole understanding of the music? How do we account for the experience of listening to various artists playing the same piece of music in dramatically different ways, and yet being touched by each version? I think of my own experience of hearing Gregor Piatagorsky and Zara Nelsova each perform the Dvořák *Concerto*, quite differently, and being totally convinced and moved by both versions. Or Joshua Bell playing the Tschaikovsky *Concerto* versus Joseph Heifetz. How many 'right' ways are there to play a piece? How deep does our obligation run—we musicians who bring a composer's music to life—to seek to understand the composer's intent and to honor that? How can we possibly know that intent without being in the composer's mind and heart?[168] How much liberty do we truly have?

If we look at artistic creations that manifest in a physical form, such as a beautiful cathedral, it is obvious that it would be sacrilege to plaster over marble or tack on vinyl siding. We wouldn't consider touching up a Picasso to make it less abstract and more realistic. We honor the intent of the creator. Similarly we have the same responsibility to honor a composer's intent. But we are working from a blueprint only! We can't hear what is in a composer's head, and even if we could, is that version the only valid one? A piece of music is such a complex creation that even a simple piece like *HeartSong* can have multiple interpretations, all of which are valid. I certainly don't play it in a consistent way, even though it is my creation. Yet, I would not play it, and would not like to hear it played, with the indicated tempo doubled, or played with an aggressive attitude. That simply doesn't go with a piece named *HeartSong*.

If we are sincere in our desire to communicate and uplift, there is no need to depart drastically from any of the composer's instructions throughout the piece—tempo markings, dynamics, articulations, perhaps an aspect of the title as in my pieces. If ego takes over then what we hear from a performer may be a major departure from the composer's expressed intent. A piece marked andante (a moderately slow but still flowing tempo), is not intended to be played at breakneck speed. A molto allegro (very fast) rendition of such a piece may be quite impressive, but it will communicate about the musician's ego, not the composer's vision.

There is ample room, infinite room in fact, *within the composer's guidelines* for each soul to sing a unique song. Sometimes the guidelines are rather loose—perhaps just the instruction allegro at the beginning of the piece and very few dynamic markings. Or, dynamic markings may be plentiful and there may be a precise metronome marking for tempo, but even in our age of electronic precision this is not an absolute. With my own pieces I often change the initial metronome marking after living with the piece for awhile, and I certainly never play my pieces in the exact same tempo from performance to performance. The tempo will change, and

---

[167] The central text of Rabbinic Judaism

[168] The book *Beyond Words, What Animals Think and Feel* by Carl Safina contains interesting views on what we can know and what we can't know, both with our fellow humans and other animals. With other species we can know a lot more than some scientists claim we can know. Real observations provide more insight than non-pertinent experiments.

dynamics too, to enhance the aspect of the music I am emphasizing or resonating with at that moment, and to suit the acoustics of the space in which I am playing.

Once again you can use the analogy of a cathedral, likening it to a work of music. As you walk all the way around the cathedral, it will appear different from every single angle. You will create different concepts of the cathedral depending on where you stand to view it, yet there are certain fixed aspects: a basic structure visible from every angle, component parts visible from every angle, an overall color scheme, etc. But maybe the stone is very rough over here, the mortar more yellow over there, and some moss where it's shaded, and so on. With music your in-depth study of a piece is the careful walk around the cathedral, noting the overall characteristics as well as the unique properties. As you go deeper into the music, the meaning and content you find in a piece will differ from what another finds. Music indeed has a kind of plasticity, a malleability that allows it to be performed with differences yet retain the essence intended by the composer. Those nuances that you find in a piece, which differ from what another finds there, are essentially what you are most in tune with. *You* choose to bring out the moss on the stone, the yellowing mortar. Something in you that is unique will resonate with some potential in the music. Something in you will be stirred by the music and then you find the way to express that and communicate it to your listener.

Just as people will hear different messages from identical words, each of us will hear a piece of music differently in our inner ear. We do perceive the world through our individual filters, as if through different colored glasses, be they rose, amber, grey, or green. You may notice the arches of the cathedral; I may notice the spire. You notice the rough stone; I notice the yellow mortar. The Picasso you see is not identical to the one I see.

The exuberant energy of *Off-Leash* gives way to moments containing a tinge of sorrow (after all in the city the leash goes back on, or, if viewing the title metaphorically as in a release from the body at death, there is the sorrow at leaving something precious). You may find not sorrow, but a tinge of gratitude (one can be quietly grateful for brief periods of freedom). Regardless of the differing shades of emotion brought out in a piece from one performance to the next, the music must always retain a recognizable identity. We always recognize a tree to be a tree, the cathedral a cathedral, the Picasso a Picasso. Variations in mood that I may create in *Off-Leash* will not be confused with the energy of boredom. The basic exuberance is always there. We may bend a piece somewhat, but if the music is 'colored' exuberant we have an obligation to recreate exuberance, not fear or boredom. There are infinite shades of exuberance. One of those shades will be the song of *your* heart at that moment.

Everything about the music, whether it is the shape of the melody, the dynamics, the structure, the tempo, informs your concept of the whole, giving it a dominant energy or quality and creating a resonance within. You may express only one thread of a feeling-state, but that thread is representative of an entire gestalt. As with a metaphor the listener perceives something greater than the actual words.

Ultimately it is the culmination of the experiences of your soul that colors your performance in a unique way. Tomorrow will be different. Don't try to repeat yesterday. That way spells death to the music and your creativity.

It is possible to sing your unique song despite an exacting blueprint. The score is still only a blueprint, from which you are building a completed edifice imprinted with your soul's stamp.

## A STORY OF THE UNATTAINABLE—PERFECTION

I have encouraged you *not* to make perfection your goal as it is unattainable, being an absolute. But in true paradoxical fashion there are experiences and moments that from a subjective point of view are indeed *perfect*, if not flawless. I am including one such story about a performance many years ago at Juilliard, but first some anecdotes to illustrate what perfection can mean in this subjective way.

Years ago when a somewhat older friend's hair had turned a beautiful silver color, she found a bumper sticker for her car that said "AGED TO PERFECTION," a take-off of course on the meat industry's practice of aging meat. I was never sure if she meant the slogan to refer to herself, or her somewhat aged vehicle. I thought it applied to her as I watched her become more and more beautiful as she grew older—stunningly so.

Now if the sticker were on my car it would definitely refer to the car. To anyone else my 1998 minivan might seem rather weather-beaten and worn, with its peeling paint (it has gotten sun-burned from sitting out in the intense desert sun at 7200 feet), different-colored hood, and the 270,000 miles clocked so far. This is my 'new' car, and for me it is just right. It looks just shabby enough that no one would ever break into it or steal it. It is dependable and runs beautifully. The car can easily carry a small (9') kayak, a dog crate, my cello, the dog, myself, all our gear, and still have room for a passenger. I keep it in good running condition; it is an excellent tool. It is in fact the *perfect* car for me.

The different-colored hood is its own story. I will digress even further from music to inform you that when you live in a location where chipmunks, mice, and pack rats are always in need of warm and dark nest locations, they have a fondness for engine compartments—and chewing on wires. They can be quite industrious too, even in one night. (Rodents also like to stash dog-food in a safe place, like in tailpipes, to my friends' chagrin when they kept complaining to the mechanic about their car's loss of power.) I finally made the brilliant discovery, after most of the insulation on the underside of the hood had been torn away to contribute to various nesting attempts, that the only sure-fire deterrent was to leave the hood propped open a foot or so at night. There is enough ambient light—in fact, enough to read by at times from just the stars and moon, no city lights—to dissuade these creatures from nesting under the hood. However we can also have intense winds, and one time the wind caught the hood and blew it open and back violently enough to smash the windshield and twist the hinges. So now I prop up the replacement hood from the junkyard (the insurance company totaled the car), but also chain it to whatever metal I can find underneath the car. It does look rather funny—almost like a large, discolored creature with an open maw and a chain around its teeth—or a grand piano with the lid open on the small stick. I think it quite amusing, including the expressions on people's faces when they drive by. It is the *perfect* solution: no toxic chemicals, nothing smelly, no traps nor harm to anything… and it makes people smile.

Experiences of perfection also come when I take people kayaking on a not-too-distant lake. The weather here is never predictable in the summer—it's our monsoon season. But once we set a date to go, we go regardless of the weather when we set out. We have started out, shivering, in cold rain, and ended up with warm sunshine. Or a still morning here can mean wonderful breezes, clouds, and wavelets on the lake or a short and spectacular storm. Regardless, it is always a *perfect* experience.

I think this subjective sense of perfection is that you wouldn't want something to have been or be any different than it was or is. And that would indicate that you were/are truly in the present moment with the experience—a good place to be.

The following musical story is a subjective one, but one shared by hundreds of people.

The year was 1966, or thereabouts, and the occasion was the Juilliard opening night performance of Beethoven's opera *Fidelio*, with Jean Morel conducting. Maestro Morel was another extraordinary conductor, not always an easy one to play for in rehearsal, as he would do heart-stopping things like asking individual string players to play some impossibly difficult passage alone. But in performance he was quite inspiring.

This was the first-ever *Fidelio* production at Juilliard, and all those involved including the orchestra were in that creative state of excitement/anxiety (nervousness). The opening overture and the first act went quite well. Then it was time for the familiar *Leonore Overture No. 3* introducing the second act. The lights dimmed, we began the *Adagio*, the cellos and basses then exquisitely setting up with our last three notes and fermata the transition to the *Allegro*. As the cellos and violins, playing in octaves, began that well-known allegro theme,[169] it was apparent that Morel had found the *perfect* tempo and energy for this music. We didn't know there was such a thing as a *perfect* tempo until that moment. It was electrifying, and the remainder of the overture was incredibly exciting. The audience went wild. Morel had us stand to receive the applause. It didn't quit! Finally he seated us, realizing that the only thing he could do was to repeat the overture. This had been the custom in earlier times, but such an interruption of the flow of the opera most certainly wasn't in vogue in 1966.

We orchestra players felt that it would be impossible to repeat such a feat—nervous glances were flying around the pit—but we did. If anything the performance was more exciting. Of course it is impossible to improve on perfection—an absolute—but somehow we did. And, it is quite possible that Morel didn't take the exact same tempo! Maybe it's like the concept of infinity. There is an infinity of even numbers just as there is an infinity of odd numbers, but the infinity of all numbers—even and odd together—obviously must be larger, but then maybe it isn't. This isn't a concept easy to wrestle with and neither was this experience. Once again at the finish the audience, *and this time the players too,* went wild. It was a long time before the opera could proceed. Magical! Drug-free ecstasy! I count this as one of my top orchestral memories.

In retrospect what made the performance *perfect* was the incredible underlying energy that was expressed through the right tempo—for that moment in time—and the controlled pianissimo dynamic, which has to hold all the inherent energy in the music in check until it bursts forth— explodes—at the fortissimo when the woodwinds and brass join in the theme along with the strings. I played it many times over the years but never again with that perfection of tempo and underlying energy, and the perfect connection from the *Adagio* to the *Allegro*.

---

[169] It is the theme quoted on the Overture title page of this manual.

## Exercise 38.

### Purpose: to be able to recognize a right tempo

I won't suggest that you find the perfect tempo for each piece that you play, noting it down and returning to that tempo with each performance. Then that tempo of course could no longer be perfect; no moment in time can ever be repeated. What you can do is find the right tempo—right for that moment, in that hall, with that instrument and those acoustics, those colleagues and conditions. It is a challenge to find that tempo.

The right tempo is primarily dictated by the underlying energy and emotion inherent in the piece, which it is your job to communicate. It will be a tempo that allows the music to come to life and move, no matter how slow it is. This is not something that can be arrived at intellectually. It has to be felt. The body is involved; you experience it in your body, not your head. Finding the tempo is really a part of the needed body motion in music.

When you are the one setting the tempo, you must feel the desired tempo in your body before you begin a piece. There will be subtle muscle movements in the core of your body while you're feeling out the tempo, finding when it feels right. When you have it, then you use your whole body and breath to indicate that tempo and the start of the music. The rhythm has already started in your body; you are already playing during the silence preceding the sound. Your colleagues should have no trouble picking up the tempo and entering correctly.

This is mostly a listening exercise, so let's go on to some specific examples.

We will use Saint-Saëns' emotionally powerful, mezzo-soprano aria *Mon coeur s'ouvre a ta voix (My heart opens itself to your voice)*, from the opera *Samson et Dalila*, to compare different tempos from different noted singers.[170] (Recordings should be available on YouTube.) Two extremes of tempo are from Maria Callas—quite fast—and from Jessye Norman—quite slow. Please listen to these two artists before continuing on. It's quite possible that you will find different performances by these artists than those I heard, and that my comments won't apply. Check different versions.

Neither performance I heard captures the maximum emotion or quite the right flow, even though both artists are magnificent singers in their unique ways. Now listen to Montserrat Caballé, Renata Tebaldi, Elina Garanca, and Marilyn Horne. These are all concert stage performances, out of the context of the entire opera. Do your listening before continuing.

From my point of view Horne is the one who finds a tempo that seems to make everything work. For me Caballé's version lacks a flow, and the others don't convince in the way that Horne does. I have heard different recordings of her singing this aria; I can't remember the date of the one I like best, and it is probably not on YouTube. Sorry.

The slower tempo used by Norman requires that the artist stretch the phrases and still have them hold together. I don't think they do in this case. Horne's version, though not as slow, is on the slower side, but her pacing and connection of phrases is very beautiful and heart-opening for me. She pulls and stretches the music like taffy, never leaving holes. Horne continues the emotion and tension even during the rests, and her transitions are done with

---

[170] The beginning of the theme is quoted on the title page of this Act.

exquisite control, gluing the entire aria together. In her performances I simply hear the music (if I'm not trying to analyze as is the case here). With others I hear the quality of the voice, or what they are doing to be unique, the special effects, etc.

As for performances in the context of the opera, listen to Shirley Verrett with Jon Vickers from a 1981 Covent Garden performance, and to a 1998 performance by Olga Borodina and Plácido Domingo. Do this before reading on.

Within the staged opera context I find Verrett's tempo and performance to be 'perfect,' with Borodina's a little too comfortable—lacking the emotional tension Verrett gives it. Borodina's version is lovely; Verrett's is wrenching. She doesn't just open your heart, she tears it open![171]

Tempo and pacing have to be driven by the emotional content, the energy you want to convey, those metaphors from the unseen world.

---

[171] One internet commentator (see foropera on YouTube) refers to Verrett's singing as "molten lava"–an apt description.

## BEYOND THE GUIDELINES—A MUSING

The guidelines we have discussed tend to deal primarily with the external aspects of the music: tempo, articulations, phrasing, slur markings. Some of these also give us indications of the internal aspects of the music, by which I mean the emotional and metaphorical content. Titles, tempo markings, verbal instructions, rhythms used, also shed light on the metaphorical content. However a composer cannot indicate so clearly as does an author what the invisible qualities are. Walter Farley painted a clear picture in words about Alec's character. A composer can't paint so precisely, leaving us with wonderful ambiguities to decipher for ourselves and choose among. They are inherent in the music, there for you to find as you study a work.

If the composer has written about the piece then there might be images or metaphors you can create for yourself based on the composer's words, as is the case with *Off-Leash*. Or, you can simply try on different qualities and emotions to see if any of them fit the printed music. It can be difficult to express the right content with a new piece if you haven't achieved effortless excellence. You do not want your interpretation to be limited by technical issues. The early study of the score along with the singing, dancing and miming of the music will be an immense help in discovering what in the music you resonate with, what content you wish to express. And knowing the content you wish to express also helps in achieving the excellence. Remember my story that as a child I had trouble getting the flowing quality of sound needed in the first of the Schumann *Fantasy Pieces*, until I was given the metaphor of the broad, smoothly-flowing river. This metaphor created for me what I call a feeling-state, and then my body knew how to respond physically to that state.

Let's return to the idea of a carrier wave. Using the analogy of speech, if you take a word like *beauty*, which denotes something pleasing, and if you were to speak it, not with love as the carrier wave, but with anger, the word would lose its meaning. This underlying vibration would now be in conflict with the very significance of the word. It is the same with our music: a note played with a carrier wave of anger, boredom or fear can no longer communicate the composer's intent, even if the composer wishes to communicate those feelings. We still have to maintain the pristine carrier wave. A part of you must always be emanating the desired carrier wave, while you are simultaneously being the emotion or mood of the music.

Before you can find your song, or this carrier wave of love, you may need to take steps to be sure your heart is open. There are many ways to do this, including listening to music or sounds that you know always and quickly result in an open heart. You want something that touches you deeply, makes you cry or gives you goose bumps, makes you want to hear the music or sound over and over and over. Then you will be more open to what the music you are studying is telling you.[172] Be totally invested in the music you are studying. Treat it as your child, your progeny. Love it the way you would anything you have assumed responsibility for, such as a pet.

---

[172] My list of music that quickly opens my heart includes *Wolf Eyes* by the Paul Winter group from his early recording *Common Ground*, much of the Verdi *Requiem*, both of the Brahms piano concertos, the second movement of Paul Schonberg's *Café Music for Piano Trio*, most any movement from a Mahler symphony, much of Piazzolla's tango music from the album *Zero Hour*, the cries of Western Grebes, the Beatles' song *Because* recorded by The Modern Mandolin Quartet, *Gymnopedies* by Eric Satie recorded by pianist William Masselos, *Flos Campi* by Ralph Vaughn Williams with Sally Peck as soloist with the Utah Symphony, Fleming singing most anything. There are many more of course, but within a few notes these help me to reach that state.

Is it possible to imbue music with qualities greater than what the composer may have envisioned, to bring out beauty beyond what the composer thought possible? David Popper's *15 Easy Studies* for cello, as well as my own pieces, can be quite mundane. But, if all the concepts in this manual are brought to the playing of these pieces, then they can be very moving.  His *Study No.1* needs lots of dynamic variety and rhythmic freedom, changes in string color and bow use, and revised bowings to really bring it to life. Did he realize how lovely it could sound? I think if he had realized the full potential of some of these studies he had written, he might have added more dynamics and musical instructions, though perhaps he wrote the studies merely to develop certain skills. Over time I have come to play my own pieces differently than what I first heard in my head. As a performer I found more in them than I had consciously intended as I wrote them, and so the versions I have included in this manual may have additional markings that the original manuscripts did not, to indicate more of how I actually play them.

Listening to multiple recordings, after you have done all your initial study, can be helpful as it may allow you to rule out certain approaches. You do want to find your unique approach, so take care not to copy someone without genuine conviction and understanding of why you are doing what you are doing. Picasso purportedly said: "Good artists copy, great ones steal." I think by "stealing" he was referring to the borrowing of an idea and truly making it your own, almost to the point of forgetting its origin. (I suggested in the Acknowledgments that you do so with the material in this manual.) Merely copying would mean just capturing the outer appearance of something, a facsimile of the real thing devoid of inner conviction.

Perhaps you will have a similar understanding of the music as someone else. If you are creating the feelings anew, in the present, your interpretation will be an original, not a copy. There are shades of color in each broad emotional band, and you have the privilege of finding the shade you think appropriate, regardless if someone else has found that same shade.

Nor do you want to be copying yourself in repeat performances. The importance of being truly present and creating the music anew in every performance cannot be overemphasized.

## REVISITING *SCHÖN ROSMARIN*

Let's look at some of the ways in which you might approach this piece by Fritz Kreisler to find your interpretation, but first review the discussion on page 199 of Act IV.

The title is the first hint Kreisler gives you: it translates as fair or lovely Rosemary. Then he provides the instruction at the beginning of the piece—*grazioso* or graciously. He writes in 3/4 time, not in one, though ultimately it is apparent that in order to flow the first theme has to be felt in one, regardless of tempo. So, already you know that this piece is not about showing off with a fast tempo that would not sound gracious; nor should it sound harsh or clipped with a dry spiccato sound more appropriate to a bowing study rather than to fair and lovely Rosemary. You want to create within yourself this feeling state of gracious and lovely, and let's add tender. If this piece has been motivated by an actual person, the composer must have been moved by this person. He finds a sweetness in her that you will want to communicate.

Do your initial steps of study away from your instrument. Once you bring it to your instrument the romanticism and charm will emerge more readily if you first quietly play what you see on the page, getting very comfortable with the piece technically, before 'interpreting' it. Good-natured, smiling outpouring of love is inherent in the blueprint Kreisler provided. You will hear it. It will become obvious to your heart if you don't impose opinions or beliefs about the music prior to knowing it intimately and actually giving what's there a chance to speak to you or resonate with something in you. Start with an empty mind, note the guidelines, study the score, learn the notes, apply principles discussed in Act IV, sing and dance the music. As you become increasingly comfortable with the music, you will realize for example that the many passages of eighth notes need to flow in a way that sounds natural, rather than how they literally appear on the page. You begin to bend the tempos[173] to create the illusion of motion and to communicate the charm. But the bending must feel natural, not like an imposed, attention-grabbing, incongruent artifice. Other aspects of creating the illusion of motion will begin to insinuate themselves into how you play the piece.

From a quick look at the score (excerpts on next page), it is apparent there are only two themes in this piece, and that the piano part is a true accompaniment, not an equal partner. The first section simply is repeated intact after the middle *meno mosso*. The accompaniment is strictly chordal and the waltz-like rhythm prevails. Bringing this section to life will depend to a great extent on the illusions of motion created by the rubatos taken in the solo line.

The *meno mosso* section (Excerpt 33) is more complex. The solo line seems to be in units of two beats each, with three such units over two bars creating a feeling of one long bar in three/two time over the space of the written two bars. The printed accents lead the ear to this conclusion. Meanwhile the piano part emphasizes with accents the downbeat of every bar—every three beats. The piano right hand briefly plays the melody in thirds with the violin in two spots, but otherwise continues with chords. I think of the music as being in six/four with a hemiola in the melody line (three half notes instead of two dotted halves). I think it important for the two rhythms to be heard, so the pianist shouldn't be timid in this section.

---

[173] See Act IV regarding rhythmic freedoms that mimic physical universe motion.

**Excerpt 32** *Schön Rosmarin* by Fritz Kreisler, Schott's Söhne, 1910, 1911, opening theme

**Excerpt 33** *Meno Mosso* theme

Perhaps this is the time to listen to a dozen or more recordings (easily available these days), since by now you have a concept of the music. Notice whether the interpretations fit Kreisler's guidelines. If they don't, they lack musical integrity, no matter how impressive they might be. The main purpose here in listening is to discover what doesn't fit the music, what doesn't resonate, what you don't want to do. This kind of listening is like sculpting, where the artist is removing what doesn't belong to the finished work.

In order to coach my young violinist friend on this piece, I went through these steps and then had her do the same. We listened to many performances: one, by a virtuosic Russian violinist, was so amazingly fast that I concluded Rosemary might have been a cheetah. It was strictly an exercise in technical virtuosity—nothing lovely in it at all. There were other versions meant strictly to show off an up-bow staccato—that was what drew one's attention—not the tenderness and warm feelings evoked by fair Rosemary. Still others emphasized a methodical correctness completely devoid of any sense of motion—dead. Another was so aggressive that I thought Rosemary was not lovely at all, but perhaps the ugly step-sister from the Cinderella story; there was certainly nothing graceful in the *rendering*.

Sadly, many performances are really about ego on display. Why else take a charming, tender piece and turn it into a vehicle for showing off? Remember the adage that just because you can do something doesn't mean you should? Because you can play a piece faster than anyone else, doesn't mean you should, and doesn't mean it will communicate *more*. So, first, be as true as possible to the composer's intent, as best you understand it.

Within the given guidelines there is still room for much that will be unique to each person who plays this piece, but you need to manifest feelings appropriate to "schön Rosmarin," whoever or whatever[174] she is, and the composer's feelings about her. You have to *be* the graciousness, the fairness, the tenderness. When you become those qualities, you won't play too fast, or harshly, or dryly, or erratically, and your interpretation will be authentic and mesmerizing.

---

[174] I don't know for sure that Kreisler had in mind a person, but I haven't found anything to contradict that assumption. The piece was first published as part of a set—*Old Viennese Melodies*—the other two pieces being *Liebesfreud* (*Love's Joy*) and *Liebesleid* (*Love's Sorrow*). It seems safe to conclude that Rosemary is a woman, not a river or nymph.

**Exercise 39.**

**Purpose: to differentiate the emotional intent behind different artists' interpretations and whether it matches the composer's.**

This is similar to what we just did with *Schön Rosmarin*. Now listen to various versions of Strauss' *Morgen!* and decide what various artists are communicating and how close they come to what you feel Strauss' intent to be. Go back to the text of the song on page 166 in Act IV, and review that. Find a copy of the composer's score for his orchestral version and study that.[175]

The initial tempo marking is *Langsam* (slowly). Notice that the only dynamic markings for the orchestra are *p, pp,* and *ppp*, including for the solo violin, plus several diminuendos. All strings are muted. When the voice enters, the part is marked *sehr ruhig* (very calm, gentle, quiet). The last entrance of the voice is marked *immer ruhiger* (always calmer, gentler). All parts have slurs or phrasing marks indicated—rather long lines. The final notes of the voice descend in pitch making for a slight natural diminuendo. That's it on the composer's guidelines, outside of the very important text he chose.

Listen to numerous recordings of this version with orchestra, including Anna Netrebko with Joshua Bell on violin (available on YouTube), Domingo with Perlman, Fleming with the English Chamber Orchestra (you should buy her CD, *A Beautiful Voice*, which includes this), Jessye Norman, Elizabeth Schwarzkopf, and others you may find. Listen from the viewpoint of the extent to which the performance—the whole of it, not just the singer—touches your heart. Now listen a second time. Listen for the performance that best captures what you perceive to be the composer's intent. Listen for whether the performers observe the guidelines. What about tempos? What do you pick up about the various artists' purposes? How about the pacing, the flow, the silences?

Of the suggested recordings, my personal favorite (which I think is truest to the guidelines, reflects best the feeling I get from the text, and touches me most deeply) is the Renée Fleming recording. Here the singer, the conductor, and the solo violinist are all on the same page. (Other versions on YouTube with Fleming as vocalist do not create for me this sense that the conductor and the violinist are on quite the same page with her gentle, introspective take on the music.) In numerous recordings the violinists' vibratos and connections between notes and bow changes are not gentle enough—the part is treated very romantically and with lush connections between all the phrases. Surges in sound in the music do not seem appropriate to me, nor do obvious slides between notes. Likewise I have reservations about various singers' interpretations. Some I think are too fast, some too melodramatic and outwardly passionate, some simply aren't being the music in the way that Fleming is, or the performance is more about demonstrating their skills.

Not only is it Fleming's beautiful and sensitive interpretation that makes me prefer the recording with the English Chamber Orchestra, it is also what the violinist does with vibrato, bow changes and with that almost silence I mentioned between the second and third notes of the final six melody notes: the second note being stretched, with a diminuendo to almost nothing—a pregnant wait—before continuing on to the final four notes. (The conductor may

---

[175] You can look at scores on the imslp web site. Please abide by copyright laws. Musicians and those who support our art need to be compensated.

be the one to thank for that.) This stretched diminuendo is not actually in the score. Nor is it indicated to be played that way in the original version for voice and piano:[176] there is no diminuendo marked and the piano pedaling change is indicated as a legato one. If you listen to recordings of the piano version—Janet Baker with Gerald Moore is a lovely one—you will hear however that the piano sound dies out on the long note, duplicated sound-wise by the violinist's lengthy diminuendo. The indicated pedaling change could translate into the same effect as the violinist achieved. (The pedal does not hold through the final six melody notes; instead two notes are slurred, then three, then just the one.) Moore is quite the illusionist! The English Chamber Orchestra likewise creates a mood that is quite special. I find that this liberty or interpretative choice captures the mood dictated by the poem and reflects the ending of the poem very well.

Listening to some of these recordings should show you that being world famous—a great name in music—doesn't guarantee that you will best achieve the purpose of touching someone's heart. You don't have to be famous to have something to say, to be able to say it eloquently, and to fulfill the purpose of music.

---

[176] Strauss wrote another version at the same time for voice, piano, and violin. He later orchestrated this—the version on the recording.

### *MUSINGS ON CONNECTIONS*

As so many artists have said, the music happens in the spaces between the notes. In line with my comments about connections between notes in *Morgen!* I think it valuable to listen to singers for this aspect of music-making.

When my colleague Robin and I get together, we usually share the latest great recordings we have found, and writing this I realize that they are always of singers, often not from the classical genre. And, as Robin pointed out, what makes these singers invariably stand out for us, is how they make connections between notes. The nature of a singer's instrument allows for the most varied and exquisite connections, connections that are difficult to duplicate with other instruments. But we can listen and learn. Part of what amazes me with Fleming's voice is her ability to go to a high *C* so that it sounds effortless and controlled at any dynamic, with a fluidity that keeps focus on the music, allowing the listener to be touched by the beauty, rather than hearing just the technique.

Connections are also a matter of timing and dynamics, and energy of course. Maestro Abravanel, in his conducting of the music of Strauss and Mahler, made 'perfect' connections between sections of these enormously expressive works—breathtaking connections. These moments stay with you forever, as has that connection we made from the *Adagio* to the *Allegro* in the *Leonore Overture No. 3* in the 1966 performance. In the *Samson et Dalila* aria, part of what I like about Horne's singing is her way of connecting gently and leisurely to the high notes, and her timing in going from a held note with a diminuendo to the next note, never having to belt anything out to be sure of it. This is in part superb vocal control, but it is also her congruence with the musical intent.

The composer writes the notes he wants, but it is up to the performer to create the relationships between the notes. This can't be indicated on paper. If every shift made from position to position on a string instrument is made the same way, per a formula, once again the music will lose life because of the sameness. How we connect the notes is another tool to serve the expression of the music. We can make those connections beautiful, authentic, and natural, or when done poorly, harsh or vulgar.

Due to the nature of our instruments, we instrumentalists (keyboard players most of all) have to deal in illusions more than vocalists do. But once we have a concept of what could be, we can most likely achieve it.


> *"The thing always happens that you really believe in;*
> *and the belief in a thing makes it happen."*
> —Frank Lloyd Wright

**Exercise 40.**

**Purpose:  to be able to discern, in a variety of works, interpretations true to the composer's intent, from those that are not.**

Find or acquire the score for a piece that you are familiar with but have not played—one for which you can find multiple recordings on the internet or in your library.

1. Thoroughly study the score until you have a good grasp of how you think it should sound. Sing it, dance it.

2. Now listen to some of the many versions of the work available. Evaluate each performance as to whether you think the performer has captured the composer's intent.

3. Note which performance is closest to how you would play it. What differences are there between this version and your imagined ideal? What would you do differently?

4. Do all this with as many different works, as you have time. This is an on-going project.

## SOMETHING TO SHARE

Think back to the two quotes from Jaron Lanier and to the Hafiz poem in the Overture. This manual through Act III is about helping you to become that person who has something to share and is willing to share it, and we will look further at this in the final Act. Playing from the heart doesn't happen if you haven't something to share about the music you are playing.

Renée Fleming stated in an interview that she wasn't willing to sing the complex and difficult role of Violetta, in the Puccini opera *La Traviata*, until well into her career. She declined singing the role until she felt she had something to say. By that I believe she refers to wanting to have her own deep understanding of the music and the role, the very character of Violetta, not just something copied from traditional versions but rather a totally convincing personification of the music—able to *be* the part *and* the music. It takes integrity to resist the pressure to perform what you aren't ready to perform.

Wisdom would suggest that you not program works about which you have nothing to say. It doesn't mean that you can't learn the notes and acquire the effortless excellence with the music, but wait until you have *your* song to sing with that music before programming it.

**The Listener**

"We were sitting in the veranda facing the beach and the sea, watching the moon just risen, low on the horizon, yellow and large. The sea was dark. Then Wagner's introduction to *Parsival* was played, then the Good Friday music, and the *Liebestod* from *Tristan and Isolde*, and Siegfried's journey on the Rhine from *Götterdämmerung*. It all seemed so unbelievably lovely. The sea, the moon, the beach, patches of moonlight on the white sand, fresh fragrance of the sea and the flowers, and I was experiencing in myself a curious phenomenon: I was LISTENING WITH THE HEART. Yes, it was just so; the music was reaching me through the heart. The mind was still. The heart was wide open to receive the sound, and the sound went into it. The sound was, but the mind was not there… never experienced anything like that! Of course it was a magnificent recording directed by Toscanini, but even so, I could not explain how I could listen with the heart. Of course, I could switch over and listen with the mind too, but then it was as it used to be before—enjoying the music, appreciating it—and this gives much enjoyment too. But if I just listened, through the heart, just listened, and no thinking was involved in it, then the heart sang with the violins, it WAS the trumpet call, it WAS the woodwinds, and I WAS THE MUSIC."[177]

—Irina Tweedie *Daughter of Fire*

[177] Excerpt from *Daughter of Fire: A Diary of a Spiritual Training with a Sufi Master* by Irina Tweedie, pp. 89-90, copyright 1986/2016 The Golden Sufi Center UK Charitable Trust, published by The Golden Sufi Center, www.goldensufi.org.

**Exercise 41.**

**Purpose: to listen to and experience great performances where the artist is truly communicating**

Listen to well known opera arias and art songs by famous singers. Usually there is a good reason that they are famous—people such as Jussi Bjöerling, Renata Tebaldi, Franco Corelli, Jon Vickers, Maria Callas, Marilyn Horne, Luciano Pavarotti, Leontyne Price, Renée Fleming, Beverly Sills, Elizabeth Schwarzkopf, Victoria De Los Angeles, Kiri Te Kanawa, Plácido Domingo.

I suggest opera arias because the emotional content of the music tends to be so apparent and powerful. You will hear that a great singer can communicate the essence of the music even in a language that you probably don't know, and the language matters not. The content is not just in the words; the words help to inform the singer of what she needs to communicate, but the music itself and the performer have to express the same feeling-state that the words convey.

Opera singers, because they are also acting the music, and because singing is so intertwined with right-brain emotion, perhaps do a better job of communicating the meaning of the music—the metaphor—than most instrumentalists do. There often is a sense of greater directness, immediacy, and involvement. It seems that singers 'become' the music more easily, or at least more frequently, than instrumentalists.

Specific suggestions are:

- Maria Callas singing *"Vissi D'Arte"* from Puccini's *Tosca*
- the *Pie Jesu* movement from the Fauré *Requiem* sung by Lucia Popp
- José Carreras singing Puccini's *"E lucevan le stele"* from *Tosca* (*An Enchanted Evening* album)
- José Carreras' 1988 recording of Frederico Mompou's *"Damunt de tu només les flores"*
- Victoria de los Angeles singing *"Damunt de tu només les flores"* with Mompou at the piano
- Montserrat Caballe singing *"Damunt de tu només les flores"*

(All versions of the Mompou are very different and all very heart-felt.)

- Marilyn Horne singing Saint-Saëns' *"Mon coeur s'ourve a ta voix"*
- *"Vesti La Giubba"* from Leoncavallo's *Pagliacci* sung by Pavarotti, as well as his *"Nessun Dorma"* from Puccini's *Turandot*
- Franco Corelli singing *"Che Gelida Manina"* from Puccini's *La Bohème* (1966 recording)
- Leontyne Price singing *"Ritorna Vincitor"* or *"O Patria Mia"* from Verdi's *Aida*, and don't overlook her *"Summertime"* from Gershwin's *Porgy and Bess*

- Inessa (or Inese) Galante singing the *Ave Maria* supposedly by G. Caccini (the version with orchestral accompaniment)[178]

There might be multiple recordings by the same artist of many of these works, varying greatly. If you search a bit you should be able to find the recordings I have listed.

As you listen to these artists you will hear that there are vast differences, and you won't like everything about each voice. The actual quality of Callas' voice for example was on the harsh side, but if you are simply present without analyzing, I have no doubt you will be touched by her singing. You will also have to ignore some of the poor recording quality. Part of this exercise is to practice being a good listener: being present, being open to whatever might happen, being willing to be touched, being receptive with that same empty mind that the player starts with. Listen to the music, not the quality of the tools. Listen with your whole body and Mind—not just your analytical mind. Feel the music in your body, feel where it resonates. Perhaps it evokes a physical response?

The best singers are very thoughtful about their music-making, and there is much to be learned from them through their comments about music as well as their singing. For example, Maria Callas had this to say, or variations on these words, in different interviews:[179] "You can't persuade the public of a preposterous thing. And to persuade the public I try to find truth in the music. Give it the most credibility possible." Also: "When you want to find how to act on stage all you have to do is listen to the music. If you take the trouble to really listen with your soul—the soul and with your ears—you will find every gesture there." Birgit Nilsson said: "An artist who cannot forget themselves in the moment when they are creating art, they are no artist." Fleming in an interview with Edward Seckerson speaks of setting everything aside and finding the magic. Leontyne Price said: "It comes down to beauty."

I must throw in a more current instrumental example: Stephen Isserlis playing the slow movement of the Schumann *Cello Concerto in A minor*. His interpretation rivals in beauty and sensitivity what I heard in that lesson with Nelsova those many years ago. Of course I can't deny the possibility that what is similar is the impact the music has had on me. Memory can be deceptive, but the feeling-state created in me is not forgettable. He finds the magic of beauty and the heart opens.

---

[178] As you will hear, this music is quite romantic and was apparently written by a Russian composer who passed it off as the work of the early Baroque composer Caccini.

[179] The interviews available on YouTube with Lord Harewood are particularly noteworthy.

## MORE TOOLS

How your fingers touch the strings is another tool to influence expression. If you hammer your fingers down, pushing the string to the fingerboard, you get one kind of sound. If the fingers and joints are soft and you have more of the sense of pulling the string to the fingerboard you get a different quality. When you want a pristine clarity, or greater articulation, you might use the former; a more lyrical, smoother passage requires the latter. Once again if you go beyond beliefs and convictions that there is one way to best play the cello (or any instrument) and allow your body to be congruent with what you wish to express in the music, you will chose from a vast array of possible sounds and physical approaches. Experiment.

The emotional content of a single note doesn't necessarily stay the same throughout, and you will have noticed from listening to these great performances how much color change is possible on one note. Singer Carolyn Sampson has defined coloring for vocalists as: "the way we choose to say the word, sing the word…" You too can color notes, with how you choose to touch the string, how you use your bow and vibrato, all dictated by the emotional expression you want. This is often what separates a dull performance from a touching one. As opera star Joyce DiDonato said: "Make your sound serve your expression." As the expression changes so must the sound. Listen to DiDonato's exquisite performance of *La barcheta* by Reynaldo Hahn, as well as her version of Strauss' *Morgen!,* both available on YouTube. Pay attention to the color changes. Also listen to Fleming's recording of the *Song to the Moon* from Dvořák's opera *Rusalka*, (the performance with the BBC, Last Night of the Proms 2010—available on YouTube). Connections, coloring, and being the music—a recipe for touching the heart— yours and your listeners'.

*"If you hear a voice within you say,*
*'you cannot paint,'*
*then by all means paint, and that voice will be silenced."*
—Vincent van Gogh

### MUSINGS ON 'GIFTS'

Most of the great artists I suggested you listen to are of an older generation. There are reasons for this. One reason is that I have grave reservations about the availability of music on the internet where there is no exchange of anything with the artist: neither applause, energy nor money. Often the artist's work has been pirated and made available in this way without permission. For artists of the current era endeavoring to make a living, this easy availability over the internet works against their livelihood.[180] Society needs to have an exchange with its artists. Expectations that we give our art without recompense are simply wrong, which is another reason I am opposed to referring to excellence and artistry as a 'gift.' When people view what we do as a 'gift,' they tend to think that we should give it freely, since it's *not a product of incredibly hard work*. We need to have the choice to give our music. I like to give my music, freely much of the time, but that desire would soon vanish if it were compelled.

The other reason behind these specific suggestions is that I think there was a greater interest in expression and presenting one's unique interpretation in earlier times. Certainly there are great voices and great instrumentalists currently, but I am not so sure that there are as many great artists.

Let's go outside the realm of classical music and performers and look at some other genres and performers (both living and dead) where great art exists. American jazz of course has its greats and can be enormously expressive, but what have you listened to in the way of Fado and Flamenco music, Ragtime, Klezmer music, Middle Eastern music, Morna (the music and dance genre from Cape Verde), Cabaret, Tango, and countless other musical styles or genres in the world? I mention Morna because Cesária Évora was a great artist of this genre. She was of international fame, known as the Barefoot Diva. Her recording of *Partida* is must listening. Listen to the young Fado singer Gisela João sing *Voltaste*. Listen to Astor Piazzolla's Tango music played by his ensembles (the album *Zero Hour*), and listen to Hungarian violinist Katica Illényi[181] play *Libertango* with her three siblings and orchestra. (Also *El Choclo*, and *The Godfather*, and while you are at it *Schindler's List*.)

Another stunning singer is Sister Marie Keyrouz, singing liturgical music of the Near East, particularly the chant of the Melchite Church (Imperial Byzantine Church). Listen to the album *Soeur Marie Kerouz Chants sacrés de l'Orient*. (Please buy this if need be.) She is quite extraordinary—her purity of purpose is reflected in her purity of sound. These chants and her singing can soothe the soul.

Then there is French chanteuse Édith Piaf, and the German singer Ute Lemper—singing the cabaret music that so influenced Kurt Weill—and French jazz violinist Stéphan Grappelli. In America we have had great jazz musicians such as Ella Fitzgerald, and countless others, artists well known to Americans and whose music I hope is familiar to you, such as Shirley Horn

---

[180] Jaron Lanier discusses this significant issue in *Who Owns the Future*.
[181] Yes, the same Katica who played the Theremin

singing *"Here's to Life."*[182] Then there are the great popular artists—Barbra Streisand and Judy Collins immediately come to mind.

What have you picked up about the carrier waves of these artists? How about the amount of space they occupy (or expand into)? Listen to the Illényis play *Libertango* again. Compare the carrier waves and space of these siblings. What do you perceive? Who do you want to 'steal' from?

All these genres and artists are quite capable of opening the heart. They have something to say, and they say it powerfully. Humanity is richer for what they have given to the world. I hope they have been well rewarded.

---

[182] Notice how she uses silence between her phrases to create a sense of anticipation. Find a video of her playing the piano as she sings (one possibility is Shirley Horn and Trio, the Heineken Concerts 99, *How Insensitive*) for an example of total congruence.

**Exercise 42.**

**Purpose: to become more aware of differences in interpretations**

We will make one more use of YouTube to listen to different versions of Rachmaninoff's *Vocalise*, which I talked about briefly relative to the intonation needed for optimum resonance. Now let's look at it in terms of tempo, flow, feeling-quality, color, and phrasing — or appropriate breathing. First listen to recordings by four superb vocalists: Anna Moffo (posted by The voicemonkey9), Kiri Te Kanawa (posted by Dame Kiri Lover), Natalie Dessay (posted by Jean Florenzano), and Kathleen Battle (posted bynapat14). Then listen to three cellists: Mischa Maisky (bluicc01's channel), Daniil Shafran (posted by Alex cello), and Rostropovich (posted by Nathanael Saint-Cyr). And last, violinists Joshua Bell (the version with orchestra uploaded by violinmusicfan with the Orchestra of St. Luke's, Michael Stern conducting, or the upload by StarStruckFilms101, Dec.7, 2010), and Itzhak Perlman (posted by wmd10).

It's a bit of an overload to listen to all these versions at once, so you can stretch this out a bit. Prior to listening find the original score (imslp website) and study it. Please do the study and listening before continuing on.

Now that you have listened to all of these versions, let's examine the different approaches of the artists. Keep in mind that the music is marked *Lentamente. Molto cantabile*. Lentamente means slowly, molto means very and cantabile means in a singing style. In the hierarchy of tempos only a largo is deemed to be slower than a lento; adagio is faster.[183] Also, if you looked at a version transcribed for your instrument, instead of the original, the dynamics may have been changed, making it harder to grasp the composer's intent. For example in the cello version transcribed by Leonard Rose dynamics differ somewhat from the original score, and in the original there is no register change as there is in the violin versions I've heard. Go to the original to best understand the composer's intent. In this case the Urtext score will show you that the dynamic peak in the piece occurs in bars 28 and 29 where a fortissimo (very loud) and crescendo are marked. It is the only fortissimo in the piece. There are several prior brief fortes, but no other fortissimo. That needs to mean something.

Anna Moffo gives a highly inward interpretation with a significantly slower tempo than anyone else. This gives her ample time to really be present with the 16th notes, and to be more in tune, but overall the tempo seems a fraction too slow. The long phrases in the beginning are more broken up; she takes additional breaths not needed with a faster tempo. That isn't necessarily distracting as it adds to the introverted feeling she is communicating, and mostly the music still moves forward, but I do think more movement is needed at the *poco piu animato* section. She allows the peak of the music to be in bar 28, and keeps the ending in the nature of an afterthought, not the peak of emotion. To me, her performance seems congruent and heartfelt, despite my reservations regarding tempos.

Dame Kiri Te Kanawa takes a much faster tempo and generally expresses a more outward feeling. The second of the 16ths often seems swallowed. At times there is a lovely introspective quality, but it gets interrupted by fortes that seem overwrought, too extreme within the context of the line. The long notes with crescendos are clipped, cut off abruptly, so that the connection to the following notes doesn't feel congruent. Her passionate quality of

---

[183] Though faster than a largo, adagio is still defined as slow, at ease. In the 17th and 18th centuries, presto merely meant fast, not the breakneck speed appropriate in later periods.

voice seems too much for this music, despite that she does some beautiful vocal coloring at times. She makes the dynamic and emotional peak in the coda, not as marked in bars 28-29. It is a rather dramatic interpretation.

The Natalie Dessay version has a mix of inward and outward energy, and the 16ths are done with more presence than some; it's very reflective and quiet when indicated and more passionate when indicated by the printed dynamics. I think the tempo is 'right;' it allows the music to flow, not get bogged down, and at the same time keeps the indicated *Lentamente* feeling. The quality and relative purity of her voice seem appropriate. She changes the quality and color of the sound throughout. I like her control of the longer notes in the opening section where she makes them face both directions, making the diminuendos as marked, but then giving an increase of energy just before connecting to the next note, thus tying the long phrases together. In the *animato* section she breathes in a very organic way. However, again I think the fortes are too much, not allowing room for the fortissimo to be the peak of the music. I found this performance touching nevertheless.

Kathleen Battle also takes a faster tempo and clips the endings of the longer notes as did Kiri Te Kanawa. Her version lacks a lentamente feeling; mostly she seems in a hurry, until she makes major unmarked tempo changes. Again this interpretation has a rather outward energy and for me lacks the expression of the others. It seems a little shallow or matter-of-fact, as if the singer did not relate to the music in a deep way.

The three cellists you listened to have very different interpretations also. Maisky's version is very individualistic (idiosyncratic perhaps), in a way that I think detracts from the music, drawing attention more to the devices he uses than to the content. I like the very beginning, but the first time through, before the repeat, this opening section seems rather too sustained, lacking color changes, and indulging in rubatos that don't feel organic—artificial, done for the sake of effect, not driven by the music. The repeat of the section has some lovely qualities with more color changes, however the *poco piu animato* could breathe more, as the singers do. I find that overall the music is too erratic and driven, even forced, and again with dramatic tempo changes that seem non-organic. Watch his bow arm. He really presses rather than letting gravity and weight produce the sound. He can get beautiful color changes, but it seems very studied, not actually spontaneous. He simply rewrites the music. For example, on the repeat, the *poco piu mosso* starts painfully slow and later speeds up painfully fast.

Russian cellist Daniil Shafran is unique amongst these artists—not the same as what I mean by individualistic. His music-making seems the most heartfelt—nothing done out of the desire to impress. He, like Rostropovich, gained early fame, but stayed primarily in the Soviet Union. One gets the sense that life was very serious for him. Certainly his version of *Vocalise* seems more sober, poetic, and sincere than other versions. His use of changing tone colors seems totally authentic. I find the vibrato a bit too tight or fast, but I like the mix of vibrato and no vibrato. The tempo facilitates his more introspective approach. For me he captures the vocal quality of the music, is true to the composer, and simultaneously sings *his* song.

Rostropovich, for all his cellistic greatness, doesn't communicate in the same heartfelt way. He takes a slower tempo, which could be fine as with Moffo, but it has a static feeling, partly because of his relatively unchanging, sustained sound. More breaths, changes in vibrato and dynamics—particularly on the long notes—would create more life. If you sing this (as you should if you are planning to play it on your instrument), I don't think you would chose to sustain the longer notes all the way through as he does, without a sense of breathing or something happening to give more life and shape to the phrases.

Joshua Bell, depending on which of many performances you listen to,[184] seems to relate more intimately with this music. His pure tone at the beginning, with little vibrato, creates a more vocal sound. The tone coloring seems very appropriate to the music and counters what might be a tempo on the fast side. His playing seems true to the meaning of the music. The only arrangement, besides voice and piano, made by Rachmaninoff was for voice with orchestra. All the instrumental arrangements were made by others, and for me the register changes in this violin version seem a bit incongruous, but Bell plays beautifully. He doesn't overwhelm the music with thick sound, and overly romantic connections.

My comments about Rostropovich apply also to Itzhak Perlman's version: too much of the same sound, a lack of color changes, too loud throughout, and with slides between some notes, which in this case strike me as incongruous.

I think there may be a downside to great fame, or fame too early. It can lessen the understanding that needs to be brought to the interpretation of music. Kiri Te Kanawa speaks of this problem in her own career—not having the time to develop all the potential artistry, the depth and breadth of musicianship, because of the early excellence of one's tools and consequent fame. Both she and Callas have suffered for this I believe, and in listening to all these artists, I think others have suffered from it as well. Or, there was just insufficient thought and care put into the interpretation—a resting on one's laurels perhaps.

Of all these interpretations, when I listen without being analytical, my heart is most touched by Anna Moffo's and Daniel Shafran's versions, despite any reservations I have expressed. Both versions seem to be free of 'self.' They are just about the music, not about how good you are, or what special effects you can create with the instrument. But also these are the two, who for me, come closest to what I believe would have been Rachmanioff's concept based on the written guidelines. I really love Shafran's ending. It clearly is a shadow of the climax that came before, not usurping that role.

Those are my responses. Regardless of whether you agree, these versions should have made you more aware of the possibilities to be considered in coming to your own interpretations of music.

---

[184] I particularly like the one with the Orchestra of St. Luke's.

## REVISITING BELIEFS

You are not your belief structures and your life is not about beliefs — it is about singing your song.

We were not born with beliefs. We acquired them. And what we acquired we can also let go of. Beliefs are filters through which we perceive the world. They prevent us from being in the moment, perceiving the world as it actually is in this *NOW*. This is true regardless whether the belief is an accurate picture of the world, or not. A belief is an added something, a layer that exists between us and what is. We don't need them. They obscure what might otherwise come to us as inspiration.

We tend to treat our beliefs as beloved collections that we are loathe to part with. But they clutter the space that needs to be empty so that something else can come in. As long as we think it is valuable to have such a collection, or that our collection is more valuable than someone else's, it is hard to let go. So, the first belief or attitude that has to change is the idea that our collection has value and serves us in some way.

A Zen master illustrates this point to a Buddhist scholar in the following story. The scholar had an extensive background in Buddhist studies and was an expert on the *Nirvana Sutra*.[185] He came to study with the Zen master and after making the customary bows, asked her to teach him Zen. Then, he began to talk about his extensive doctrinal background and rambled on and on about the many sutras he had studied.

The master listened patiently and then began to make tea. When it was ready, she poured the tea into the scholar's cup until it began to overflow and run all over the floor. The scholar saw what was happening and shouted, "Stop, stop! The cup is full; you can't get anymore in."

The master stopped pouring and said: "You are like this cup; you are full of ideas about Buddha's Way. You come and ask for teaching, but your cup is full; I can't put anything in. Before I can teach you, you'll have to empty your cup."

This, of course, applies to how you approach a work of music.

I've incorporated a process of inquiry into beliefs in my own life, my approach gleaned from many different and effective systems. When I have unpleasant emotions, don't feel happy, find myself being critical of others, or things aren't going well, I start by looking at the beliefs I'm holding that could be causing this sort of discomfort, making my life look the way it does. Once I have spotted the belief, often more than one, that is the probable cause behind my feelings and emotional responses to situations, I ask myself a series of questions and write down in detail what I come up with.[186] Sometimes I have a trusted friend help me with the process, which expedites it. I use the following questions or variations thereof:

---

[185] A type of literary composition or text in Buddhist traditions

[186] The questions I use bear a significant resemblance to what Byron Katie uses in her work, which she calls *The Work* (see www.thework.com). However, various approaches to clearing negative beliefs and substituting more useful beliefs have been around for a long time, and my approach has drawn on many things that I have studied over several decades, including *Psyche-K*, the *Sedona Method*, *EMDR*, *NPL*, *and others*.

**Do I know with total certainty that _______________________________(the belief) is true?**
(When I look honestly the answer is always *no* because our knowledge can never be absolute.)
**Do I know with total certainty that _____________________________ (the belief) is not true?** (No.)
**What thoughts, opinions, actions, and emotions are based on this idea that____________ (the belief)?**
**What reasons are there for holding this belief when I don't know with certainty if it's true or not?**
(This question helps me look at how I use the belief. Do I use it to make myself right about something and others wrong—a way of feeling superior? Does it give me an excuse to do something or not do something? Does it allow me to hold on to some type of prejudice? What would I lose if I gave up this belief? This one is often the key to why I am hanging on to something.)
**What would my life look like without the belief?**
**Is there a belief I would prefer to hold?** (Actually not a belief, but more of a new attitude, since it is now a conscious choice.)
**What would my life look like with this new belief?**

The wording of my questions isn't set in stone. From my point of view the important thing is to bring to conscious awareness through questioning the unconscious beliefs and the energy behind them that have been running (maybe ruining) your life. Once you are aware of a belief, even if you haven't entirely let go of it or replaced it with something more constructive, you can at least acknowledge that it is there, as in: "Oh, there's my belief that I can't do anything right." Or some such belief. Maybe it's the equally destructive one: "I *have to* do everything right!"

An example of why and how I have worked with these questions follows.

Recently I had to break an important commitment. Even though it was imperative to do so, and I had figured out how to make everything work out for others, I still agonized over it and felt tremendous stress—not a new experience. Throughout my life I have endeavored to keep all commitments, no matter how trivial, even if that meant harm to myself. This time I had the wisdom to realize that my agonized reactions were way out of proportion. After all there are appropriate and ethical ways to change a commitment—all involving communication with the others involved. Given the power of communication to resolve almost anything, why couldn't I just take the necessary steps without the unnecessary distraction of painful emotions?

When I really started examining my feelings and responses, I realized that it always felt like a betrayal if I or others changed a commitment, regardless how trivial. I realized the belief behind that feeling was that *breaking a commitment equals betrayal*—a belief coming from a childhood experience. For well over half a century I had carried with me the sense of having betrayed a stray dog that I had befriended and given my heart to. My parents had made me turn this dog over to the Humane Society (and in those days that generally meant death). This caused me untold grief and loss and the conviction that I had betrayed the dog—broken a commitment of the heart.

As I examined the incident and the concept of betrayal from my present, wiser point of view, I came to the realization that the only true betrayal would have been withdrawing my love from the dog, which I did not and would never do. Sometimes in life and especially as a child, we simply do not have the power to make things the way we think they should be. We can't save a loved one from a terrible disease or accident or death itself. Things happen in the world that we cannot change. What we are in charge of is *our* response. Do we stop loving, or keep on loving? I had no power to affect my parents' decision, but I kept on loving this dog. There was no betrayal.

The examination of what actually took place, the consequent realization, and the inspection of how I have used the belief, have allowed me to finally let go of the belief that any break or change in a commitment is a betrayal. Since then I have been able to negotiate changes of agreement without the terrible angst and without judging others harshly when they need to make changes.

Now—in conjunction with the following exercise—would be a good time to go to your journal and address again your beliefs about creativity, as well as any others that catch your attention. The ones that stand out are ready to be examined more closely.

**Exercise 43.**

**Purpose: to be able to examine and understand familiar works from a new point of view**

1. Return to Exercise 2 on page 37 and do it again. Are there now more beliefs that are apparent to you than those you identified previously? If not, please widen your lens—look more broadly. What about beliefs such as not liking a certain artist's playing? Could that be a generality, a vague statement that might have been true for the one time you heard that artist play, but if you were to listen further you might like the bulk of that artist's performances? What about a belief that: You are too ___________ (fill in the blank) to___________________ (fill in the blank)? A belief could be something as innocuous as "I am too young to play this piece," or the very likely misguided assumption that "the audience is too unsophisticated for my music." (Don't underestimate your audience; sometimes the least sophisticated and educated are the best listeners and the most responsive.)

2. Create some type of review process for yourself and frequently examine your life for the beliefs you have been acting on. Perhaps every evening before sleeping take a look at the beliefs that determined your behavior that day. Pay particular attention to the behaviors that capture your attention and consume energy, that hold you back from carrying out your intentions. The beliefs behind the behaviors that most capture your energy are the ones that you are feeding, the ones that will grow stronger.

3. For this step use a piece that you learned very thoroughly a long time ago. The notes will be in your fingers, as we say, and you can play it on automatic. It is not unlike a belief that has incarnated in your physical body. Listen to how you play it. Reexamine it with your new knowledge and see if you might change anything in how you play it. Take it off automatic but know that if the music is deeply embedded in neuromuscular and aural memory, it will be a challenge to change the way you play it. (When I revisit a piece, to help with this process I approach the music as if it were entirely new, first studying the score, and then when I bring it to the cello I start just with pitches played slowly and gently, without vibrato, listening for all the beautiful relationships that excellent intonation produces.)

As you grow and mature, your understanding of the music needs to grow and change with you. Don't just rely on old patterns or your teacher's version that you may have unknowingly copied. It is enlightening to listen to multiple recordings of the same work by a great artist, made over many decades, to see how their interpretations change with time.

## A Story from the Road *More* Travelled

In Act IV I mentioned falling in love with Stravinsky's *Apollon musagète Suite* over the course of a day. That experience is an example of how *not* to find your own interpretation, but paradoxically it had great benefit.

It was early in my years with the Utah Symphony and we were scheduled to perform the work, but the orchestra music had not arrived in time to pick up a cello part and study it before the first rehearsal. I have always wanted to be well prepared, and as I had never heard the piece, I borrowed a recording and played it while I worked on my project of building a music cabinet. I worked all day—at least twelve hours—hammering and sawing and drilling and sanding, while playing the recording over and over and over, the entire time. Only the first time did I sit and consciously listen to the music, but by the end of the day that Stravinsky piece was my new favorite music. The next morning at the first rehearsal it was as if I had played it many times. It was totally familiar despite sight-reading the actual part. I could hear in my head every sound to come; more importantly I felt passionately about the music.

This is *not* the way I recommend learning new music. That one particular interpretation becomes deeply embedded, like a belief, and any other interpretation will definitely feel wrong. Nevertheless in an emergency it is a great aid. Because I was carefully focused on the construction work I was doing, I assume the music went in strictly on a right-brain level. My body knew the music, my ear knew the music, my heart knew the music. It has always been a favorite, and it is a joy to share it, to introduce people to the work.

**Exercise 44.**

**Purpose: to differentiate between when you are playing a piece without *heart* and with *heart,* and to be able to do both at will**

1. Play my piece *HeartSong* without any interpretation, exactly as it appears on the page, just the blueprint. Don't *be* anything other than an instrumentalist playing the notes on the page.

Played thus, without heart—nothing of you, no interpretation, not going beyond the notes, no carrier wave of love—you will notice that it sounds meaningless and is not apt to touch anyone's heart.

2. Now play it with everything you have practiced and learned up to this point.

It will be a very different piece. Might it touch someone's heart played in this way?

3. Play pieces of your own choosing, alternating playing without heart and with heart. Get very comfortable with switching back and forth. You want to get to the point where you can easily tell when you are only playing the notes, and then have the tools to drop into that wonderful space where you are playing from the heart.


**Exercise 45.**

**Purpose: to incarnate the intention behind the music**

*You will notice that this is almost the same as Exercise 31 in Act IV. In repeating it I hope that you will dig a little deeper, be a little freer, and move from the heart.*

Practice conducting a work for which you have studied the score, with real players if possible. Use your body to create the music the way you want it to sound. Mime it. Show the shape and dynamics, rhythm, motion, and emotion with your hands and arms. Let your entire body be involved: dance it, sing it, be the whole of the music—not just the melody line.

The composer has had an intention. That intention is manifested through written music. The musician (you) duplicates that intention as closely as possible. By holding that intention as you play or conduct, the composer's intention becomes incarnate.


*Feel the Music*
*Embrace the Music*
*Be the Music*

> *"If your mind is empty, it is open to everything.*
> *In the beginner's mind there are many possibilities;*
> *in the expert's mind there are few."*
> —Shunryu Suzuki (1904-1971)
> Japanese teacher of Zen Buddhism

### MUSINGS ON SPONTANEITY

Never think that your interpretation is fixed or finalized. When you create each performance as if it were an original—the one and only—you will bring a freshness to your playing that is needed for the performance to sound alive, not canned. You have a concept, but as you might do when speaking on a favorite subject, the words you use this time could be very different from those used last time—chosen to express the same basic concept, with a twist.

Your interpretation is your unique creation. The blueprint on the page that you have brought so much thought and love to is not unlike a balloon lying there empty of air. When you blow air into it—the breath of life—it assumes a shape that no one else has ever given it. Until you 'inspire' it, it is no more than a deflated balloon lying on your music stand. You don't know for sure exactly what shape that balloon is going to take this time as you blow life into it. Just as *your* existence has brought into the 'seen' world what was merely a potential in the 'unseen' world, so your unique interpretation brings into the 'heard' world a potential from the 'unheard' world.

# ACT VI

## Finale

# THE KITCHEN SINK

In the Overture I promised you I might throw in some unexpected things and asked you to follow my digressions. It's time to go further afield and pull many of these threads together.

**Figure 25**

## WEAVING THE TAPESTRY

We have looked at communication and examined the carrier wave that we use to convey the content of the music. As discussed, this will be one of those frequencies not detectable by electronic equipment but very noticeable to many people and responded to by almost everyone, even if it is registered below the threshold of awareness.[187] You *know* when someone is fearful, or anxious or uneasy, and generally you will begin to reflect these vibrations—mirror them, become ill at ease yourself—particularly if you are unaware that this can happen. Being forewarned about resonance and that such things occur helps you avoid getting caught up in these feelings that have originated elsewhere.

My opinions about the purpose of music are strong. I don't think music should serve the goal of dragging people down to a lower level of vibration—into hate, rage, or violence. Our art should be used to bring people to a heightened state of awareness, love, and compassion. I have little liking for 'music' created or performed with a contrary intent, and I prefer not to have those vibrations, sounds, or images impinge on me.

There is a powerful book—*Beauty* by Sheri S. Tepper—that deals with the subject of how art can influence a culture and what happens when all the "magic" (beauty) is gone from the world. It is a book for adult readers only (there is ugly stuff in it). Reading that book, which combines fairy tales, fantasy, and science fiction to look at social issues, made me think twice about what I allow into my 'space.' As I said before this doesn't mean that art shouldn't portray ugly, angry, or sad things, as does this book at times; it is the intent behind the portrayal that is important. The symphonies of Shostakovich are a good example of powerfully moving music that sometimes portrays the horror and terror of suppression, and simultaneously opens the heart. Where does the music, the book, the poem, the painting, the sculpture ultimately leave the one who perceives? Does the heart open? Or, does the heart close down in coldness and indifference? And yes, as you may have experienced, the heart opens more readily through sadness than pleasure or excitement. Indeed music should open you to the possibility of growing as a person.

---

[187] Discussed further in A Last Look at Love, page 299.

Examine for yourself how you feel and act after listening to various types of music, including some where the intent is to drag you into hate or fear. Make some decisions about what you will allow in your space. And this leads inevitably into the field of ethics and integrity.

What, you might ask, have ethics and integrity to do with playing music? It has little to do with playing the notes and a lot to do with playing from the heart. Acting unethically and without integrity shuts the heart very quickly. Ethics is not the same as morality. Morals are generally a specific code of conduct dictated by a particular religion or culture, often having little to do with any universal truth. Ethics and integrity go beyond to universal truths. Ethics generally are concerned with the nature of the "highest good," and ethical choices come from within—freely chosen. Integrity has to do with wholeness, which is what we want in our music-making. Morality can be likened to *equal-tempered* tuning (there's no flexibility) and ethics to *just* tuning. Just as there is a subtle beauty in just intonation, there is a beauty in ethical behavior absent from the behaviors imposed by moral codes.

Developing a sense of ethics and integrity goes hand in hand with the development of the individual. Children usually think mostly of their own desires and needs, and their worldview is very small. As the individual matures and grows in experience and wisdom, the sphere of awareness and responsibility continues to grow and become more inclusive: first, limited to immediate family, then expanding outward to encompass more and more of life and the universe. At least that is how we seem meant to grow. But sometimes people get 'frozen' at a certain stage and fail to evolve to maximum potential. This can result in the self-centered behavior of a narcissist, where, like an infant, the person is still the center of the universe, everything revolving around him or her. Or, the colleague who wishes ill to others, hoping they will make mistakes. We musicians often have tendencies in these directions. Nothing is *so* important as our next performance, how our practicing is going, whether we like the conductor, etc. As the musician who never left the practice room said, "Enough about me; how did you like my latest recording?"

An artist has to evolve as a person before there will be something worth sharing. And then there is the necessity of being present and touching your instrument with love. Hazrat Inayat Khan speaks beautifully to the marriage of these two concepts: "The effect of instrumental music also depends upon the evolution of man who expresses with the tips of his fingers upon the instrument his grade of evolution; in other words, his soul speaks through the instrument."[188]

In that Jan. 25, 2013 Juilliard master class,[189] Joyce DiDonato speaks of how opera and music are "about life, breath, energy, passion, forgiveness, betrayal… you need to know what life is to communicate all that." She also tells of understanding more about performance skills from observing the focus and superb mental game of George Brett—exceptional third baseman for the Kansas City Royals—another type of performer who has to bring all of who he is to the 'stage' to succeed. The same principles and psychology applicable to sports are applicable to music. She encourages students to explore more of life than just the practice room.

Ethical behavior and integrity come with understanding the inter-connectedness of all things and living the innate desire to do no harm. Sometimes ethical behavior corresponds with the

---

[188] *The Mysticism of Sound and Music, The Sufi Teaching of Hazrat Inayat Khan*, page 164-5
[189] Posted to YouTube on Feb. 13, 2013

culture's moral codes and sometimes it does not. Ethical decisions are arrived at by looking at the whole and the purposes one serves, not out of fear or cultural programming or even laws.

A personal, rather mundane example of arriving at the type of ethical decision I am describing occurred after I had been a member of the Symphony for about twelve years. The then-conductor decided that it would make the section stronger if everyone other than the first-stand players rotated—sitting with different players in different positions periodically. He left it up to the section to decide. My contract, when I was initially hired, was for the third chair position in the cello section, and at the time there was a bit of prestige attached to the position as well as other contractual advantages. I was quite happy sitting there. I felt I had some degree of responsibility to make sure that what the principal cellist was doing got reflected accurately back to the rest of the section, and I enjoyed my stand partner.

My initial response to rotating was negative because I felt it would lead to a diminishment of my satisfaction in the job. My stand partner was also happy with the status quo. The remainder of the section was eager for this change, for a variety of reasons. I thought about it quite a bit, even thinking I could insist on my contract being honored. On the other hand I was aware that some players were always unhappy with their stand partners, and that where you sit defines what you hear and tend to play with, even if that differs from those in front of you. Rotating would give everyone a chance to listen from the different positions, relieve pressure on those always sitting with someone not compatible, and in general spread out discontent more equally. Presumably all this would cause the section to improve.

In my mind I really couldn't argue with these observations, but emotionally it felt like a loss to me. It was necessary for me to look carefully at what were my purposes in playing in the Symphony. There was the income of course, but my passion, reflecting the impact of the Abravanel years, was in playing great music from the heart, united in that purpose with others doing the same. Focus on this overriding purpose allowed me to move beyond my sense of loss and really look at which scenario would contribute most to that purpose. The rotating section won out, and both my stand partner and I agreed to the switch. Knowing that others were happier was a good tonic for opening the heart.

Your music-making will grow as you grow as a person. The more ethical you become, the more depth you will have in your playing. So don't neglect all the other aspects of your life. They don't develop while you are shut in a practice room. Understand what is going on in the world, but don't dwell on what is wrong. Get a dog. Volunteer, preferably for something dear to your heart. Read widely. Read books like *The Different Drum* by M. Scott Peck, *Flow* or *Creativity* by Mihaly Csikszentmihaly, *A Soprano on Her Head* by Eloise Ristad, *Brown Dog of the Yaak* by Rick Bass. Contribute to the world in other ways than through your music-making. Have fun along the way. Be with friends.

## HUMMINGBIRD WARS

Something is wrong in the world of hummingbirds. The vanguard of black-chinned hummingbirds (two to be exact) that arrived a couple of months ago was never joined, as in the past, by hordes of the less adventuresome ones. Additionally the rufous variety which I had expected weeks ago is just appearing—not many yet, possibly just one. If you have had the opportunity to observe this species, you know that just one can give the impression of a multitude. They are remarkably aggressive with a tendency to drive the other species away. They are larger, their flight is loud, and their antics crazy. Other than that they are obnoxious! Nevertheless, fascinating to observe. What is truly unusual today is that one of the black-chinned vanguard is protecting its territory and holding its own against the mighty rufous. I have never seen a black-chinned put up such resistance to being driven away from the source of nectar. It's too bad they haven't all learned the idea of sharing. I suppose though that if humans have trouble learning that lesson—as seems apparent from the state of the world—it would be foolish to expect more of hummingbirds. But maybe not. The bonobo, an uncommonly altruistic primate, generally would rather share a treat with others than selfishly keep it.

Let's be the bonobos of the human species and share our music—without aggression to our fellow musicians. Competition is not nearly as much fun as cooperation. Support your fellow musicians, rejoice in their successes, encourage them.

## THE HEAD *VERSUS* THE HEART

Here are examples of what can happen when the focus on tools overrides attention to purpose, and why we must develop as humans, not just technicians.

In our digital world there is much interest in inventing ever more clever software—tools to carry out some purpose. Two research teams from the University of Massachusetts at Amherst and the University of Washington spent two years working together to figure out how to use a mobile phone to stop a pacemaker connected to someone's heart—knowledge which potentially could be put to use to contribute to a death. They then publicized the research at tech conferences, almost in its entirety, including enough information that someone with murder in mind could probably figure out the missing information and indeed put it to use.[190] Such research gets justified in a rather convoluted manner, but I believe something has gone very awry.

It is the same story with many violent videos, or other media products, that invent new ways of torturing and killing people, and are then justified with elaborate rationalizations. The images created stick in viewers' or readers' minds and become part of morphic fields of violence, which impressionable minds do then tap into, as we regularly experience in this culture.

There is always some justification for ignoring the purpose something serves.

A young man I knew had studied diligently for many years with a highly esteemed cellist, who however had failed to achieve status as a great artist. There was a reason: this cellist's playing was impressively correct, tasteful… and colorless. His student had acquired a high level of technical excellence, a level we might all aspire to, but this young man's playing also was devoid of life. Eventually the student realized it was time to find a different teacher and gain a new perspective. At the first lesson with another esteemed cellist and teacher, she said to him, "There is nothing more to teach you about playing the cello, but you seem to hate it so. Where is the joy?" She had identified exactly the issue. His focus had been directed solely to developing the tool of technical excellence, never to the purpose it might serve. That lack of the connection to purpose will ultimately close the heart—very effectively. His carrier wave became anger, not love, and it was the anger that got communicated. Sadly, he gave up cello and music and turned his capacity for disciplined study to the field of law. I hope his mentors have put his focus on the purpose served by the law, not just on the facts and the letter of the law.

When you are learning and practicing your music, the head must of course be involved, but always with the consciousness of purpose. You use your mind when you have technical problems to solve, structure to understand and relationships to see, an intention to set. But, the

---

[190] Paraphrased from *You Are Not a Gadget* by Jaron Lanier. Lanier is considered the father of virtual reality technology. In this book he details his fears concerning the inflexibility of software (both internet and other) that is actually molding human beings in ways that diminish our capabilities and our creative works.

diligent acquisition of 'tools' also demands awareness and understanding of their purpose, lest this focus on tools be devastating to the heart, as was the case with the young cellist.

As for the university researchers who figured out how to stop pacemakers with cell phones, I don't for a minute think that they actually ever wanted someone to die as a result of their research, but I believe they didn't think through their purpose very carefully. I wonder how their hearts have fared. An excellent mind is a wonderful thing, but it is a tool that must serve the purposes of the heart.

The world desperately needs your focus on the purpose of touching people's hearts (not stopping or polluting them) and bringing beauty into the world. Be passionate about this!

I just read what turned out to be a very negative book about life in the music world, and it compels me to offer the following thoughts.

When or if you come across material of an 'exposé' nature about the classical music field, or any other field for that matter, rather than letting it negatively impact you or change your passion for the subject, first consider H. I. Khan's wisdom that hidden in every created thing is a voice telling you for what purpose it has been created. If the purpose you detect doesn't contribute to or further *your* purpose, then ignore the message and the messenger.

Your experience will not be the same as another's. In fact they can be worlds apart even in the same environment. We tend to draw to ourselves those people and situations that are in tune or resonate with who we are and the vibrations *we* put out. And, for purposes of sensationalism and marketing, or even for unconscious reasons, an author may cherry-pick information, telling you story after story that proves the author's premise. Rarely does the author tell you about all the things that don't reinforce the message. Don't let another's beliefs and underlying vibration determine your experience, and don't assume or anticipate the worst in life because of others' experiences.

Of course, as we have seen, not everything that is shocking or upsetting has a negative purpose behind the relating of it. Derrick Jensen's book *A Language Older Than Words* exposes many of the evils of this world, but they are things we need to be aware of, as the awareness could change beliefs and behavior in a way that would be better for the reader individually and for the greater world. Discernment is always needed.

There *are* problems in the field of music, and a professional's life is not easy. I expect readers of this manual to be students, teachers, perhaps professionals and even non-musicians. But if you are still young and aspiring to be a professional musician, unless you believe you can't live without music as your main focus in life, I would not encourage you to seek to become a professional. Jobs are scarce, competition is great, monetary gain is limited for most of us, and artistic control is rare.

The sense of satisfaction for professionals can be scarce when so many people are involved in the 'product.' Still, satisfaction is largely an inside job. If you decide to pursue a professional career, or are already in music, it is vitally important to play every performance of a work (even if it is the 100th) as if it were the first. Bring presence and all of who you are to every performance and play from the heart even if no one else is. You have one standard and only one: your best. No excuses. Your best may not always be wonderful, but as long as it is your best for that moment, you never need to apologize, or feel guilty, or feel less than the beautiful soul that you are. Immerse yourself in the music, not the politics of the music business or personalities. Always, always, always keep your focus on your purpose.

If you remain an amateur you may actually have greater say in what and how you play. You too can fulfill the purpose of music.

## CRY OF THE EARTH

My piece *Cry Of The Earth* was written after reading Jensen's book *A Language Older Than Words*. As I mentioned earlier it is a devastating book, but written from great caring and love. He chronicles many evils and wrongs that have been done to people (individuals, entire groups, cultures), to the planet itself—our Mother Earth, and to other life forms, mostly in the name of greed and for power

Most of us are not in a position to go up against these forces that effectively control our world, but we can't hide our heads in the sand and pretend none of this destruction is going on. There are things we can do. To begin with, it is important to be aware of what is happening and to do so without hatred or judgment—this is called witnessing. In his talks, many of which are on the internet, Sufi teacher Llewellyn Vaughn-Lee speaks of the importance of this step in our response to all that is happening today, and then to follow this by feeling the sorrow, grieving and praying. All this must occur before any actions we take are apt to be successful.

*Cry Of The Earth* is my way of doing these things.

I live in a place where I feel very connected to the Earth. It is like a living body, with the flesh stripped away—unnecessary—leaving the bones visible and the soul uncovered. Most people who visit experience a strong spiritual sense about the area. Something about the type of beauty opens hearts, or perhaps there is a special energy here that many find easy to resonate with.

My house is nestled into a huge rock formation with a tall, stately Ponderosa improbably growing out of the base of the cliff. I play *Cry Of The Earth* to the rock wall and the tree (Sacred Wall and Noble Tree in my mind) and to all the Earth most days—outside, if the weather permits. It is my way of talking to Mother Earth, expressing my sorrow, feeling her pain. It is a sacred act.

If you choose to play this piece, I encourage you to play it with this intention.

## ON-TRACK

Environmental activists get off-track when they only fight *against* something, whether that something is corporate greed or a culture obsessed with consumption and dependent on fossil fuels. Fighting against something tends to strengthen that which you oppose, often bringing about an equal and contrary reaction—hence the polarization we see on virtually every issue in this country. A more effective way to make positive changes in the world is to be passionately *for* something, something that you love.

Rather than opposing, we should be advocating for two critical things: a return to an ethical stewardship of the planet and a return to the once understood concept that all of creation is sacred. This would mean moving away from the dominant cultural attitude that everything outside oneself is an *'it.'* (This, by the way, is how the military has succeeded in getting soldiers to actually aim and fire at another human being: turning opposing soldiers into *'its'* through deliberate programming.) We see from the daily news how pervasive and lethal this attitude has become. To change would mean moving towards the concept that everything other than self is *Thou*—sacred, like each of us.

Humans have the responsibility to take care of the planet from which we have grown. Our physical bodies exist because, through an alchemy almost beyond our comprehension, nutrients from the earth combining with sunlight, oxygen, and water have produced the plants and animals that are then transformed within the body of a woman into a human baby. Truly miraculous. All this from Mother Earth. No test tubes needed.

Leaving aside the question of the existence of the soul, we *are* the children of the Earth in this physical sense. Ironically, even though we are the children of the Earth, we are also the stewards of our Mother. Usually stewardship is from the parent to the children—a responsibility to care for the child, not to abuse the child, and to protect that child from those who would do harm. Stewardship entails these things. Most parents understand this and do the best they can for their children. Many of us however fail to extend that same understanding of stewardship to the greater family of which we are a part—our Earth.

This responsibility to Earth ultimately is an ethical issue. Will we continue to view Earth as an 'it' that we can desecrate at our whim, or will we begin to see that we have an ethical obligation to take care of a *Thou*: a *Thou* that is a part of the universe, which like us, is sacred? The level of consciousness or animation, in any part of creation, is immaterial. It is the sacredness that matters. Any part of creation, regardless of how it came to be, cannot be less than sacred. Perhaps the underlying issue in our world today is this loss of the sense of sacredness of all things. We, the only stewards of our world, are allowing—perhaps through ignorance, perhaps through denial, perhaps through other negative influences—our family to be abused.

Can you imagine going to your mother's home (or your child's home) and gorging on all the food in the house, running the well dry, spraying poison in the air, leaving an empty propane tank and no firewood?[191] That would be unthinkable, particularly if you were the one charged with the responsibility to look after your mother.

Matthew Scully put it very effectively in his book *Dominion*. He brings the issue of how we care for the other creatures on this planet back to ethics. An ethical person doesn't destroy what he has stewardship over and what his existence is dependent upon, not simply because that would ultimately mean his own demise, but because it is the right thing to do, the ethical thing—because love, compassion, and gratitude are the companions of good people. Those qualities shouldn't stop at the front door. Our culture has become blind to such a degree and fallen to the level that we see no inherent worth in the remainder of creation outside immediate family. Earth, like a sow in the factory farms that Scully investigated, has become in our eyes merely a production unit—a large factory. Scully makes a powerful plea for human benevolence towards the rest of Creation.

My hope is that we humans will become passionate advocates for the sacredness of all creation: humans, animals, Mother Earth, and music.

---

[191] This essay was originally written for my rural area newspaper, an area where we have such things as wells, propane tanks and wood stoves.

## 'GIFTS' AND GRATITUDE

Though I don't believe (and it is just a belief) that there is a gift for music per se, certainly some people have more natural physical facility than others or a greater intuitive grasp of the music. It may be the 'gift' of larger hands—helpful on many instruments—optimum vocal chords, more physical coordination or athleticism, or an advantageous mental makeup. If you are one of those people who does have a natural aptitude and better equipment for the physical aspects of playing your instrument, this story is for you (lest you become a trifle arrogant).

It is *Maestro* Olav Roots' story, as promised in the page 42 footnote. He was the conductor of the National Orchestra of Colombia in Bogotá during the years when I was there. Like Maestro Jean Morel at Juilliard and Maestro Abravanel, he was deserving of the honorific Maestro.

In the aftermath of World War II, to save his own life, Maestro Roots had walked from his Russian-occupied native country of Estonia to Sweden, leaving in the middle of the night with only the clothes he wore. He sought asylum in Sweden and eventually made his way to South America, and the conductorship of the Colombian National Orchestra. There, like Abravanel, he fashioned an amazing orchestra out of a ragtag bunch: European refugees from the war (both Jewish and Nazi musicians), Colombian musicians, students at the Conservatory, and me—the one American. Nobody *ever* spoke of or asked about the past! Music was our only common denominator. Olav Roots was a true Maestro in our eyes, and we all addressed him as such. (It didn't hurt that he was fluent in seven languages.) He had gotten quite used to it.

One day, walking down a neighborhood street, he saw some laborers resting by a brick wall they were building. He heard one say, "Here comes the Maestro." Well, his ego began to swell a bit, and he was thinking what a fine impact he was making in his adopted country that even a brick-layer would recognize him. He came to a stop eager to engage his admirers. Just then an older laborer pushed past him to be greeted warmly as "Maestro" by the others. Ego deflated, he walked on. As it turns out, in Colombia any fine craftsman was addressed as Maestro, which makes sense as the word derives from the verb *to master*, and also means *teacher*.

Keep in mind that excellence rarely comes without diligent work, though sometimes it is facilitated by a physical gift. There is no such thing in this world as being born onto an even 'playing field.' Some of us are born to greater advantages, whether it be to parents of greater means, or who value the arts, reading and education, or who encourage us in our dreams. Or we are born with an exceptional brain or body. If you have had such advantages remember to feel gratitude, and if you haven't had those advantages, feel gratitude anyway for what it is in you that has allowed you to excel.

Perhaps one of the greatest gifts is the capacity to feel gratitude. It is a powerful vibration.

## INVOKING THE KITCHEN SINK CLAUSE

I have another story for you, included here for no other reason that I am aware of other than my desire to share it. As hard as I have tried I can think of no way to tie it in musically, but fortunately there is the kitchen sink clause that I included at the beginning of this manual to justify this sort of thing.

After Mari[192] had lived with me for about a year she had a bad fall, landing on rock and apparently separating her pelvis and tearing muscles. Fortunately in a young dog the pelvic joints are not yet rigid and she could heal. She could still get around and even run if she spotted one of our ubiquitous rabbits, but rather than use her hind legs separately she was using them together, looking a bit like a kangaroo. Her rehab therapist (just four hours away) wanted her to strengthen the torn and damaged muscles by exercising with a controlled walk or trot where she would have to use her hind legs separately, hence a treadmill was prescribed (and donated to boot). She, as do many dogs, quickly learned to walk on one, and thereafter for almost seven months she exercised daily on a treadmill for up to 40 minutes.

Each morning I would get her started at a slow pace, then over the session vary the speed and slope so as to gradually build the needed strength. I could go off for a bit or sit close by and she would diligently continue on. She was very serious and dutiful about it. She appeared to concentrate totally on what she was doing—being mindful one might say—and really seemed content to do this new job she had been assigned. Actually her seriousness was quite hilarious.

Then one day she refused to stay on, jumping off as soon as I started the machine. That was it. She was done. And she was right. Her gait was completely normal; she could run effortlessly again without any sign of a limp. She returned to her preferred exercise of chasing rabbits or tennis balls. Try as I might on brutal cold and windy days, I couldn't persuade her to get back on the treadmill in lieu of ball playing. No way. Nothing convinced her—not treats, cajoling, or me getting on the treadmill with her.

Until… I had hip replacement surgery. As part of my own rehab therapy I decided to use the treadmill. I got on, rather cautiously, and started it up. Mari immediately hopped on with me and shared my 'walk.' All of it… but only once. It was as if she wanted to show me how to do it, and once she was assured of my competence and safety, she had no further need to shepherd me. She did always stay in the room with me though.

That's what we do for those we love.

---

[192] I trust you remember Mari: the dog who loves Mahler.

## A LAST LOOK AT LOVE

The frequency or vibration of love is so high that it is well beyond the capacity of our machines to register. It is part of our unseen universe, but as we have discussed, humans perceive it through our capacity to feel.

*You* are indeed capable of perceiving the difference between being sent a flow of hatred or a flow of love. Even if you have talked yourself into believing that no such thing is possible, your body/mind knows the difference and responds accordingly. You can test this with a simple experiment with a group of friends.

Hold your arm out straight, to the side, and contract your muscles to resist the medium downward pressure that someone else will apply to your arm just above the wrist. Notice how easy or difficult it is to resist the pressure. Only do this for a couple of seconds. This will be your neutral muscle strength. Relax your arm for a moment. Now have everyone else in the group send a silent flow of disgust and hatred at you, and have your accomplice test again with the same amount of downward pressure and the same degree of resistance on your part while that flow is coming at you. Notice your muscle strength. Rest your arm again and then have the group send you silent flows of love and admiration, and retest muscle strength.

Normally there will be a huge difference in muscle strength, with your muscles weakening with the flow of hatred and strengthening with the flow of love. A flow of hatred creates dissonance in the body, which weakens muscles. This apparently has to do with the interference with electrical impulses from the brain to the muscles (dissonance) when you receive a flow of, or the energy of, hatred. The inverse is the enhancement of those impulses (resonance) with love.

If there is no difference in muscle strength it most likely means that your body is dehydrated, or you might have worked to put up more resistance. You want to stay neutral in your perceived expenditure of energy in resisting the push. Don't try harder or less hard. If you get a reversed response it tells you something about how your two brain hemispheres are relating—or not relating—at the moment. (To help with that try crawling on the floor, reversing your normal pattern of how arms and legs coordinate. That should get your brain hemispheres talking to each other. If you haven't crawled for awhile and don't sense a habitual pattern, then switch back and forth between patterns.)

Merging, or the sense of oneness, is the nature of love. In a way you borrowed the strength of others when love was flowed to you.[193] Mystics speak of the macro universe holding together for love, as well as the infinitesimal atom holding together for love. Love is the magnetic, attractive force. Pay attention to your own attraction toward what you love. You are drawn to that; it is as if a magnetic force pulls you to what you love. That desire to merge and be one

---

[193] Do you remember my story of the Mozart Quartet cello solo going better when the other players mentally created it with me? I piggy-backed on their love. Everything was enhanced.

with what you love is a powerful force. It is that force that allowed the pilot and plane in Richard Bach's story to fly out of an impossibly small space. The pilot merged with his plane, became one with it; they were of one mind and the intention to take off was without reservation, without doubt.

Make love your constant companion and the carrier wave for all your communications.

Last night I attended another guitar concert. The guitarist was quite excellent, but the evening had no flow to it, and that took away from over-all enjoyment. The venue was small and hadn't been prepared to contain all the people attending. Time was wasted finding chairs and fitting everyone in. Once most people were seated, the presenter spoke at length. Next came the person introducing the guitarist. And when the guitarist was finally on stage, he too spoke before beginning to play, demonstrating no awareness of how long people had been waiting for the music. Additionally he spoke about each piece in a somewhat rambling fashion, which was interesting, but too much for an evening that got off to such a slow start. The intermission was lengthy and people were slow to return to their chairs. Once they did, there was more talking from the presenters and the artist. Continuity and smoothness, from coming into the venue until the end of the concert, was lacking. It was like being stuck in rush-hour traffic: now we go, now we stop, now we go, oops—slow down, and so on. Pace, meaning "the rate of tempo and timing in the presentation,"[194] can refer to this aspect of a performance. The right pacing heightens the dramatic effect, and keeps people's attention.

Effective pacing is something to think about when you plan a performance. It involves programming the right amount of music (not too much) and providing contrasts in style or moods. Optimum pacing includes a purposeful walk onto and off of the stage, an intermission just long enough for everyone in need to use the bathrooms, exiting the stage after a lengthy work but staying on stage after a short work, making sure you are off the stage after taking bows *before* the applause dies out, etc.

A request beforehand to the presenter, to minimize comments, can be a good idea. In an informal situation rather than be introduced, I prefer coming on stage directly and speaking as needed to welcome the audience, briefly introduce the group or myself, and if there are no program notes then to speak briefly of the music (three or four minutes total will do). Remarks about the music are most effective if you share something about yourself: what the music means to you, something about the concepts you feel the composer was expressing, rather than words about the form or style of the music. Listeners will be able to hear those formal aspects, or not, and once again the intent is to touch the heart, not educate others on the subject of music.

The entire performance needs to be congruent: appearance, pacing, and the quality of music-making. These form a triangle, where if one corner of the triangle droops, it tends to pull the other corners down. Last night another incongruity was the appearance of the performer. He is world-class as a guitarist, but his choice of attire was more suited to someone hanging out at the pool hall after school. Clothing too should suit the venue and the audience. I like that we have moved away from the extreme formality of classical music concerts, but looking attractive or smart, or at least neat, still has its merits. It is quite easy to dress comfortably and yet not be an eyesore. Why would you not want to create an overall aesthetic impression when you are dealing in the realm of aesthetics?

Back to the music itself—flow! We previously talked about this in terms of needing to feel music in larger units than the time signature may indicate, so that a two-bar unit might be felt as two big beats, a four-bar unit as being one long measure in four. This is so very important in keeping the flow of the music going—not getting bogged down in emphasizing every beat.

---

[194] *Webster's New Collegiate Dictionary*

Using your body to feel the flow of the music is always helpful. I can't over-emphasize the importance of dancing to the music you are learning to play, by which I mean simply moving your body with the music. Feel it in your body, feel that inherent flow. The flow is in the blueprint, but only as a potentiality. Closely read the blueprint, but find the flow that works and manifest it in the sound.

There is no absolute correct tempo for a piece of music. But regardless of the tempo you choose you must find the flow. When I teach I find that if I dance around the room to the music or move appropriately—no matter how silly I may look—it always helps the student get the feeling of flow. As with the kinesthetic experience when you do the dancing, this visual input seems to register in a way that allows the flow to be more easily grasped and expressed. That input apparently bypasses the analytical mind and registers directly in the body. Seeing the dancing, like doing the dancing, seems to act in the same way as does a metaphor: it communicates something very directly to the entirety of who you are.

Even something as mundane as typing out these words can have a flow to it that facilitates the work. I am not a fluent typist, but if I let my hands and body move in a way that has a gentle, rhythmic quality to it, the typing goes much faster. When I move my hands, fingers, entire body in curving, rounded ways, rather than as harsh straight up and down finger motion with a rigid body, it is much easier and a lot more fun. Just like a smooth bow change involves all the joints participating in the change of direction in a non-linear way, I am finding that approaching typing in the same vein makes for fewer errors and less physical tension. I am virtually dancing in the chair. You might try bringing this concept to everything you do, from washing dishes (ah, at last we really get to the kitchen sink—you knew it had to be here somewhere!)[195] to walking.

---

[195] No doubt you have heard the adage that we teach what we need to learn. My friend Carol, the Feldenkrais Practitioner, pointed out to me that when standing at the sink doing dishes, my back was holding as much tension as if this were a life-threatening situation.

**Exercise 46.**

**Purpose: to bring the concept of presence and flow to life (as well as music).**

You have begun a process of growth: by being present, perceiving your body, feeling the sensations in your hands, encompassing an entire room and audience in your space, and more. As a flower knows to open to the sun, your heart knows what to open to, what makes it sing. And then you see the beautiful creature that you are. Now it is time to bring this awareness and these skills to all of life and your activities.

Find an activity that is a regular part of your life, one that you find tiresome, annoying, boring or otherwise irritating. The next time you engage in this activity notice the way in which you carry it out. How do you use your body? Is there unnecessary muscle tension in your body as you do it? Where on the effort scale (1 to 10) are you? What are you doing with your breathing? Where was your attention before noticing these things? How do you feel when doing it? What is your attitude or emotion? Are you experiencing joy, happiness, resentment?

Flow, or the lack thereof, applies to all of life, so the bottom line question is: are you doing this activity with or without flow.

If flow has been missing from this activity, find ways to incorporate it. There are varied aspects of flow, as with our playing. Are you present, aware of your surroundings? If not, ground yourself through your breathing and the sensations of physical contact with your environment. Is there a valid and valuable purpose in the activity? Make a note to yourself of what it is. What would be the consequences of not doing the activity? Is it indeed something you can freely and consciously choose to do? What underlying carrier wave do you want? Love? Fear? Resentment? (If you are cooking food for yourself or others, doing so with love rather than without love has positive, if unseen, health effects according to many schools of thought. Best to err on the loving side.) Can you improve your communication with the tools you are using for this activity? Or choose better tools? (Don't use a shoe to hammer a nail when you have a hammer handy). What else might you have become aware of through your study of this manual that you could apply to your task?

Now look specifically for ways to use your body to bring greater physical ease to the activity. Can you create a flowing motion? Incorporate the entire body? Dance it?

What about your interactions with other people? Are there ways you could incorporate ideas that we have considered into those relationships? The flow in communication is important. In conversation the flow needs to go in both directions. If something flows too long in one direction it can get stuck, or something snaps back like a rubber band stretched too far. How about just the idea of silence—so that something else can be present, like understanding? How about starting with presence and awareness? What's the carrier wave you are using? (If something unpleasant needs to be said, it doesn't have to be devastating to another if the underlying carrier wave is love.) What else might be applicable?

Can you live from the heart in all the same ways we have discussed about playing from the heart? If you were to do that, might it bring flow and ease to your life—greater joy and satisfaction?

Let the art of being present with love pervade all aspects of your life.

*"Lost time is never found again."*
—Benjamin Franklin

### MUSINGS ON BEAUTY

Sufi thought holds that there are two primary aspects of Absolute Truth: beauty and majesty. In this paradigm beauty correlates with mercy and majesty with justice. Beauty and majesty are qualities found throughout the music we play. Most humans, perhaps all, resonate with these qualities—part of why music is so universal in its appeal. I told you my stories of the Berlioz and Verdi Requiem Masses, works that are superb examples of music that communicates both beauty and majesty (or mercy and justice). Where I live the land also reflects both these qualities. It is *so* very beautiful… but the majesty is also quite harsh at times. Both aspects attracted me to the area. However even great beauty is inconsequential if you don't give it your attention.

In 1986 I first heard the tango music of Astor Piazzolla. It was late at night; I was driving home from somewhere, turned the radio on and heard the most exquisite heart-rending music imaginable. It was nothing I had heard before and defied categorization. I was mesmerized. I *had* to know who the composer was, which meant sitting in the car for 20 minutes once I got to my driveway, until the set was over, and the disc jockey came on.

Thereafter I looked for cello music written by Piazzolla and found *Le Grand Tango for Cello and Piano*,[196] which I have since performed with my sister multiple times. It is 12 minutes or so of unrelenting passion and beauty—that's how I perceive it. It's one of the few pieces that I like to listen to when I am driving. Normally I prefer silence, but I had just started listening to Yo-Yo Ma's recording one winter day—as I was driving on a snow-packed highway from St. George to Cedar City, Utah—when the long uphill pull began. A very slow moving truck was in the right lane, and the U-Haul vehicle that had been behind it had just pulled ahead of me into the passing lane where I was. I slowed down to give it some clearance, and it labored to pass the truck on this long climb. The driver in the car behind me however decided to tailgate me, blink lights, create various gestures and otherwise be obnoxious. I got rather angry with that driver and had my attention thoroughly fixated on him. There was nothing to do, nowhere to go, until the U-Haul finally made it past the truck and was able to pull back into the right lane. I quickly passed the U-Haul and likewise moved over, still angry. I did my share of blinking of lights and ranting as the tailgater passed, but then turned my attention back to the music… only to realize that the piece was all but over. The road episode had lasted a good ten minutes, and during that time I had heard none of the music.

I realized then that I had just wasted ten minutes of beauty that could have been in my life—exchanging it for ten minutes of anger. Ten minutes of beauty permanently gone from my life, ten minutes that I could never retrieve. Not a good bargain. It was a powerful lesson. Now I do a better job at considering what responses I will choose, and where I wish my attention to be. Beauty is much more enjoyable than anger.

---

[196] Bérben Edition, which is the one recorded by Ma; the music quote, Figure 25 on page 287 of this Act, is from *Le Grand Tango*.

**305**

**beauty**

beautiful desert
clean, pure, inspirational
love of land and place
how i cherish the feeling of awe
of taking my breath away
with the beauty of the clear, thin, sparkling air and
the crispness of the atmosphere
and how everything is so close
and real and alive
and nothing is dead
devoid of spark or soul
magic and beauty

rabbits run hop
faster than any predator
even the human with his gun is hard pressed
to follow the rabbit

what feeling in the air is this
that the heart expands
the soul pours forth
and the desert is alive
with soul and spirit
and all things magical

it is real
it is here
you are here
and everything is present
there is no past
no future
only now and endless time
and everything exists in now and forever
and nothing can be hidden or lost
or buried in guilt or shame

all is beauty
and magic is beauty
and beauty is the god in all things

and it takes your breath away

to wake up in the desert
is to awaken to soul
and life and light
and truth and glory

this is god and you are god
and god is the rabbit
and the gun
and the bush
and the thorn and the grain of sand
and it is all you
and you are all these things
and all time
and all love
and that is all

world of light
and color and sound
and music

and music above all

only music
can paint the beauty
of god and love
and the desert
and magic


Bonnie Mangold
2006

**Figure 26** [197]

## MUSINGS ON JOY

The intent and desire to find beauty in small things, perhaps what some might call inconsequential things—such as the blossom of a plant, or the flight of a hummingbird—and the capacity to experience joy and feel gratitude are concomitant with our development as human beings and musicians.

Those qualities don't develop just by sitting in a practice room, always being focused on work. They develop by engaging and interacting with life. We need both the 'notes' of life and the quiet spaces 'between the notes' to create music in our lives: music that encompasses beauty and joy as well as sorrow and passion. Gratitude and compassion are handmaidens to beauty and joy, attitudes intrinsic to a whole human being and to a whole musician.

This morning, as I am writing this, I am sitting outside listening to bird chatter and songs, watching for hummingbirds to come around and feed from the lovely hibiscus blooms of the latest houseplant to make its home with me. For the first time since the plant arrived, it is bursting with vibrant, electric pink flowers. It had occurred to me, sitting here on the deck admiring, as I do daily, the vast and magnificent landscape, to bring the plant outside and let the hummingbirds enjoy the blooms too. And they are. I am sitting a mere three feet away, and one (the rufous) has come up to check out the purple-colored ballpoint pen in my hand just in case it is a source of good things. Alas, no—at least not eatables.

Developing the capacity to find joy in such observations, as of blooms and hummingbirds, helps to counter the vicissitudes and inevitable sorrows of life. It is not necessary to be pain-free, or even happy, to experience joy. Joy is not noisy; it sneaks up on us; it is quiet. But there is no room for joy if we are always busy, always doing, always talking, always thinking. First we must create the empty space for it to enter into. Then we feed the joy: listening, feeling gratitude, helping it to grow.

Co-existing with the hummingbirds, a pair of red-tailed hawks has nested once again on the cliff behind my house. Now is the time of the year for their lone, recently fledged off-spring to master its wings. The youngster spends the days gliding off the cliff, soaring out over the meadow, riding the thermals, developing an incredible flight capacity. The parents have a strident, even raucous call, easily recognized. The immature one has a call too, quite different

---

[197] From the fourth movement of the Beethoven *Symphony No. 9*; text is from Schiller's *Ode to Joy*: "Joy, beautiful spark of divinity, Daughter from Elysium."

from that of the mature birds. The cry is short—a rising shriek of exultation—repeated over and over almost as if screaming to the world: "Look at me! Look at me! Look at me! No hands, Mom!"

The freedom to fly like that—wings unfurled, unafraid, joyous—is a quality to emulate in our music-making.[198] Essential also is the courage to explore and the trust of the hummingbird—trust in its own abilities and trust in the safety of the universe, even to the point of an occasional landing on my finger, secure in the knowing it will not be harmed, at least not by me.

These are the attitudes towards life and making music that cannot be cultivated in the practice room. Observe and learn. Everything in life is your teacher. Cultivate the joy and bring it to your music-making.

---

[198] The music excerpt on the title page of this Act has to flow and soar as if on wings. It is a cello line from Richard Strauss' *Der Rosenkavalier Suite*.

### CADENCE—THE FINAL MUSING

Music unleashes the soul—from the limitations of the body, from material form, from identity, from boundaries. It can take you anywhere. If this is unreal to you listen to the third section of Piazzolla's *Le Grand Tango*. Better yet, find a willing pianist and play it if it's within your capacity. The music pulls out all the energetic stops.[199] It truly demands something beyond what the physical cello and piano can deliver. Without that added *something*, those tools can't possibly be adequate for communicating the unbearable intensity of this music.

But with that something—the heart—Piazzolla's intent can be expressed despite the limitations of the instruments, despite that the energies and feelings may not have been experienced by either you or your pianist in life. Once your hearts are involved and grasp the meaning behind the music, then together you can manifest it, bring it to life. Two hearts 'on the same page,' in resonance, are more powerful than one plus one. You can go anywhere with the music.

"For everything there is a season…"[200] You have done the work; now, when you perform you are 100% the music. There can be no room for thinking about how you are doing. Have the attitude that the great singers do: "I've done the work, trust the work." Trust yourself and know that you can manifest what you desire. If you can conceive it, even if you haven't experienced it in life, you can attain it, despite apparent limitations. The dream, the desire, the intention come first.

As I alluded to in Prelude No. I, it has been a struggle for me to discover how to truly communicate through my playing what I could sense about the deeper content of music. The key has been learning to be in my heart, and keeping it open not just to music but to life in general. It is my hope that through my personal stories and poems, the exercises and theory, I will have evoked some similar discoveries on your part that will help you to be the musician you want to be.

---

[199] I have yet to hear it played, however, with all the intensity and wildness I perceive to be inherent in this music.
[200] Ecclesiastes 3:1 *The Bible, New Living Translation*

# CODA

Since I began writing this book I have been much saddened by the death of my friend, Dottie, who so loved Mahler, and a short time later by the death of my beautiful Mari. I must go now and play music. It is time.

Our talk is over. Be the beautiful creature that you are. Sing your song—from your heart. Scream it to the world like the hawk, whisper it like the hummingbird—let the world hear it.

Best wishes.

Bonnie Mangold

# ADDENDUM

## Twenty Short Pieces for Solo Cello
## with Commentaries

# DISCLAIMER

No "self-help" book would be complete without a "Disclaimer," but rather than tell you to consult your doctor before implementing my suggestions, I'm going to advise you to consult your own knowing when studying and playing these pieces for solo cello. I have written about some of the pieces in the text of the manual, however that material and the commentary accompanying each piece are pertinent to how I viewed it the day I wrote the comments and may not be accurate for how I play the piece the subsequent time. There are of course guidelines to be observed in the printed music—more perhaps than you will generally encounter—but I have endeavored not to be *too* detailed in the accompanying commentaries in order to avoid taking away your right to your interpretation. Feel free to ignore my written words but pay attention to the guidelines in the music itself.

## *Inner Reflections*

Refer to page 141 in the manual for other comments.

This piece was conceived while I was at a six-week-long seminar in northern Wisconsin late one fall. Snow was already on the ground and the distant sun barely warmed the fallen leaves, much less me. I was staying in a cabin in the woods, and I hadn't expected to be sharing, but there was a surprise coming. It was dusk when I first arrived at my cabin in the woods, and for a moment I thought the large creature suddenly sticking its head in my car window was a bear. It wasn't. It was actually a massive Saint Bernard—my primary companion for the duration of the retreat. This dog had a habit of pressing up against any door I attempted to exit from (or enter), and I spent a great deal of time persuading him that I wouldn't run away if he would only let me through. In return, he got to slobber all over me. I never learned his name. In due course I simply addressed him as Mr. Slobber. Even though I was actually a bit lonely there— one of the few times in my life—this dog just didn't make the cut as good company.

After class would end for the day I would return back to my isolated cabin, trying to outwit Mr. Slobber. I had my cello with me, fortunately, and would spend the evenings playing, once I made it inside and wiped off the drool. This is when I first began to do what I call "fooling around on the cello," improvising, if you will. These weeks were a time of stillness—enforced meditation. The opening theme of this piece came to me as I was contemplating the nature of a human being—my own nature. There were words in my mind that compelled the notes of the theme, but rather than share those, you can make up your own if you wish.

I didn't put the blueprint on paper until sometime later, after I had written *HeartSong*, but I consider *Inner Reflections* to be the first song I wrote. The open string double stops were added recently, to make it a bit more interesting for a student. You are welcome to include them or not. They were not in the original morphic field of this piece.

To add interest to your playing of this piece you might ask some questions about your own nature, and let the music be your answer. Try starting your answer with "I am…" You might just have an ah-ha moment, or even recognize your own beauty—that you are a wondrous being.

Inner Reflections
Solo Cello
Bonnie Mangold
Play with a sense of wonderment
♩=88-96
mp tenderly
mf
p (tenderly)
mp
mf
più forte
f
dim. poco a poco
mp
mf
mp
mp
P
dim. and rit.
copyright © 2016

## *HeartSong*
### (Carol's Song)

The subtitle, Carol's Song, refers to how this piece came about. My friend Carol, the Feldenkrais practitioner, had written a lovely song about the sea, and I was trying to write a counterpoint second voice for the cello. I gave up on that goal after a measure or two, as there was no blueprint to work from (the music was in her head and heart and subject to variation). However my initial efforts and subsequent ideas became *HeartSong*. Please refer to the various comments in the manual on pages 132, 177 and 227.

I truly vary how I play *HeartSong,* every time, with many more dynamic changes than indicated in the part—sometimes subtle, sometimes more outward. I find this to be a good warm-up piece because it is quiet, demands presence, impeccable intonation, and control of both hands, in order to communicate. It is one of those very simple pieces that in reality requires excellence to bring off successfully.

# Heart Song
## (Carol's Song)

Cello

Bonnie Mangold

### *Tilting at Windmills*
(Quixotic)

The title and subtitle of this piece, as well as the metaphor I am about to give you, came well
after the writing of it—many years later. When I wrote it my intent was to create a theme that
would be heroic and noble in nature, something easy to play that would yet communicate those
qualities. This requires a use of the bow that is confident, definitive, and somewhat marcato.
The left hand has to reflect those attributes as well. Congruence. The overall energy is
extroverted.

Only recently did I consider that the Don Quixote story contains this noble, heroic feeling, and
that it is an appropriate metaphor for the piece. I further realized that the way I played the
piece there was a second somewhat different voice contained in the music. So, to use the Don
Quixote metaphor, we have our *knight errant* making his initial bravura statement from the
beginning through beat two of bar 12. Then a second voice briefly interrupts, one that is a bit
placating, a bit more rational, or doubting, or warning of impending doom. It could be the
voice of his squire Sancho Panza, or more likely that of his lady-love Dulcinea. At beat three
of bar 16 the first voice returns—the Don—and restates his intent to do battle with the
ferocious giants (windmills), which he then does in the 16th-note passage (hence the title).
Defeated in his battle with the windmills the Don continues to keep a brave, heroic face on
things, but there is an element of defeat present now. The four-bar tag at the end of the piece is
the second voice, in sad agreement, echoing the sentiments of defeat, or pleading to give up
this quest, the impossible dream. The final note would be the Don stomping his foot in refusal
to accept defeat—an emphatic "no!"

Using this metaphor, or another of your choice, will help you find the feeling in your body of
what I intended the music to communicate. The opening theme is to be played marcato, that is,
with a decisive bow stroke and stress or accent at the beginning of each sound, and with a
slight separation in sound between notes. When the second voice enters, a more legato sound
is appropriate with only the indicated two accents, which are emphases rather than attacks.

The "tilting" section of 16th notes requires as much bow as possible to help communicate this
flurry of action and energy. The *Poco meno mosso* section that follows is still meant to be
heroic or noble sounding, but now without the marcato. The sound remains strong, but requires
playing through, or sustaining, each note more than in the opening bars. Bars 39 and 40
communicate the exhaustion following such an outpouring of energy. The second voice's four-
bar tag at the end, pleading to give up the quest, requires a smooth, even bow speed. But then
the Don takes over during the crescendo in the final bar and the emphatic final note gets as
much bow as possible, coming off the string with an increasing speed.

It has taken you longer to read this than to play the piece, so go *be* Don Quixote and convince
your listener.

Solo Cello
Tilting at Windmills
(Quixotic)
Bonnie Mangold
♩=96-100
f marcato (bold)
mp   f marcato
Poco meno
f
accelerando
♩=112
ff
♩=92
mf (Meno Mosso)
mp
p III
rall.
p   sf
copyright 2016
322

## *Chant*

Because this piece is a chant and is meant to bring about stillness in the listener—not a sense of movement and emotion—much of Act IV does not apply.

You will see that it is in *E* minor and makes use of all three minor modes: natural, melodic, and harmonic. Tension is not to be emphasized; do not push the *D sharps* closer to the *E*s, or the *C*s lower, when you have the step and a half interval of the harmonic minor mode. The pitches should sound as they do on the keyboard.

To maintain the steady, calm sense of stillness the bow speed needs to be unvarying, the bow changes and shifts inaudible. The sound should shimmer like gold threads spun in sunlight: pure, clear and beautiful, sans vibrato. A comfortable, even tempo is needed: never hurried or dragging, no tugging at the rhythm, no note standing out. There is true democracy here—every note of equal importance.

*Chant* gives you an opportunity to ensure that you are not making compulsive or habitual motions with either vibrato or bowing. Playing this will also enlighten you about the quality of your shifts and bow changes. Tranquility must prevail. Like a placid lake, nothing on or below the surface disturbs the still waters.

# CHANT

Chant is to be played straight through, phrases A through G, once; at the end of G return to a phrase of your choice, playing it and then continue playing phrases in any order that seems appropriate to you. Continue in this fashion until the desired meditative — almost hypnotic — effect has been created, then end the piece with phrase G. This is to be played almost without expression — no vibrato, an unchanging dynamic except for the trailing off of sound at the end of each phrase.

Copyright © 2016

### *After the Storm*

Once again this title—*After the Storm*—didn't come to me until years after I wrote the piece. Here my intent was to communicate an optimistic, relaxed, out-going feeling. In bar 24 the energy increases, and the calm joy turns into a more exuberant, expansive feeling. The ending, from bar 32 on, steadily winds down until like wisps of clouds the music vanishes into thin air.

The piece is clearly in *C* Major so the triad *C-E-G* must be well in tune, with other pitches orienting to those. As there are not a lot of rhythmic or pitch-relationship opportunities to create tension and a sense of movement and flow, it is important to feel the 6/4 meter as if it were in two, or even in one, and make clear to the ear the two-bar units that predominantly make up the phrases.

Using the bow freely—faster bow speed rather than weight or density of sound—will help to create the needed feeling of openness and flow. Even at bar 24 the sound should be produced by greater bow speed with just enough weight to balance the speed. The sound should never be forced. The vibrato, likewise, need never draw attention. It should be fast enough to avoid any hint of sorrow and slow enough not to sound nervous. It is a middle-of-the-road sort of vibrato—neither too wide nor too narrow. The mood you wish to communicate will dictate all this if you will just *be* that feeling-state.

# After the Storm

326

## *Improvisation in G*

This is a contemplative piece, an exploration of modes, to be played with an attitude of reverence and love—qualities you now possess as your underlying carrier wave. It has a rather dreamy aspect, never pushing forward, never hurried except in the *ad libitum* sections where the tempo can be varied. I intended it to communicate a mindful quality, like Mari on her treadmill with all her attention on what she was doing.

Make use of expressive intonation to emphasize dissonances and the pitches that characterize the different *G* minor modes, and *G* Major when it appears. In the eighth-note sections for example, bring out the *B flats* and *B naturals*, and the *F naturals* and *F sharps*. Most of the dotted-eighth-note/sixteenth-note figures should be on the lazy side, trending slightly toward a triplet feel. However bars 11 through 17 require exact 16ths plus greater emphasis on them to create more sense of motion and emotion—a feeling of being more in this world and less in a dream-state.

Bars 18 through 25 can be played freely. I gain a lot of speed and a sense of urgency by bars 22 and 23, then start calming and slowing in bar 24, bringing the music back to the initial tempo and calm by bar 26. I treat the last eighth-note pattern similarly.

# Improvisation in G

Solo Cello

Bonnie Mangold

## *Based On Blues*

After I acquired my electric cello I studied briefly with a jazz pianist to help me make use of the low *F* string and the bass sound I could get with it. I've always loved the sound of a blues scale and wanted to create something with that quality. The optional pizzicato sections sound great on the electric cello where I can exaggerate the resonance, but may not work well on your acoustic instrument. When I play it I anticipate certain notes, coming in with them before the actual beat. Where I do this I've put a little forwards-pointing arrow over the prior note that is cut short, thus bringing in the next note a bit early. This is not short-hand for an accelerando. The tempo does not change; I just go to certain notes a little too soon. A slash between notes indicates a clean break in sound without a time delay.

Feel free to play around with other rubatos. You want a loose, jazzy feel—no uptight classical approach insisting on fidelity to the print. I've put in some portamento lines where I want a nice slide between notes. But just because I haven't put in such a mark doesn't indicate that every other connection between pitches must be pristinely clean. A little sloppiness is appropriate.

Take a look at how the notes group in terms of beats. As you can see the time signature and bar lines are irrelevant. The piece starts with a 10-beat group, then a 6-beat group, a 7-beat group, a 5-beat group, a 6-beat group, then 8, 5, another 5 and another; then comes the other voice—the response—with a 7-beat group, which on the electric cello I always do as pizzicato. And so on.

If you choose to do the pizzicatos, sometimes try plucking the string then starting the vibrato immediately after the pluck—not before—for a different sound. Make your vibrato over-the-top wide and fast to help with resonance. Where there is one star (*) over a portamento line connecting two pizzicato notes, pluck both notes, but pluck the second note near the beginning of the slide. Two stars over a slide indicate that only the first of the two notes should be plucked, then slide into the second note on the same finger while the string is still vibrating. You will need to be plucking fairly loudly for this to work. Also use a bass player's pizzicato where you get plenty of flesh on the string; pull it more sideways than upwards and allow the first joint of your plucking finger to be flexible.

In your music-making if joy is taking a back seat to seriousness, then this piece provides a good opportunity to let go of that attitude. In language appropriate to the genre: you want to be laid back in your approach to this piece.

Solo Cello
Based On Blues
Bonnie Mangold
♩ = 100
(pizz)
ARCO
mf
III
ARCO
MP II
Livelier
f
ARCO (jazzy)
mf
MP II
freely
P (uh)
mf
III
ARCO
mp
molto rit.
PP
* Start the pizz at the beginning of the slide
** Pizz only once on the note before the slide
Go early to the next note
Clean break in sound
copyright © 2016

## *Elegy*
### (For all the vanishing clans)

This is a song of mourning as the title indicates. Living all these years in Utah has made the plight of the "downwinders" [201] quite real to me. So many human families have been devastated by the cancers resulting from the radiation exposure, and so many animal families as well. They have vanished from our lives, hence the subtitle. But the subtitle and the story came after the initial intent to simply write a piece communicating sorrow.

The energy and motion needed for this piece fall into the category of *beautiful-sadness*. This sorrow is not of the same 'color' as the personal type of grief that can overwhelm. Perhaps there is a bit of distance—you are the watcher, the observer, the one who records the tragedies. Perhaps you see the beauty of those lives as well as the sadness of lives cut short. Perhaps the sadness you feel is for the hubris of a species that plays with fire, thinking we know more than we do. You are free of course to supply your own metaphor, whatever helps you to feel this energy in your body.

From the key signature *Elegy* appears to be either in *F* Major or *D* minor. The minor key is more in keeping with an elegy, but maybe the music goes back and forth, or maybe the beginning is really in *A* minor. By the end of the piece a *D* minor tonality becomes more definite, particularly after I rewrote the final bar to end on a *D*, not an *F*.

The first part of the piece is chordally based with disjunct melodic movement, allowing few opportunities for expressive intonation. What is important in terms of intonation is simply to be aware of the chords that you are playing and ensure pristine intonation within those. The middle section, beginning with the pickup eighths at the end of bar 16, has more conjunct melodic motion and provides more opportunity to bend or emphasize pitches for expressive purposes. The section from bar 29 to the end relies on color changes—dynamics and vibrato, or lack of it—for expressiveness.

As you have experienced, the energy needed to communicate sadness or sorrow is slow and heavy. Even though the piece begins forte, the bow speed must be contained. A dense sound is needed; the first note requires no more than two-thirds of the bow. If the speed is too great you are more apt to communicate anger. Look for the shorter notes that can be emphasized in some way to create emotional tension—in particular the eighths following the dotted quarters. The 16ths don't function in this way, but don't let them feel static. They need to be spun out without being overly precise or hammered in sound.

---

[201] Downwinders is the term for those who lived within the radioactive fall-out pattern of all the nuclear tests during the Cold War.

Cello
Elegy
(For all the vanishing clans)
Bonnie Mangold
Lyrical
♩=60
f
IIf
5
P
8
Piu Mosso ♩=70
I mf
13
poco dim...
mp
poco cresc - - - - - -
18
P
22
mp
f
Tempo I
26
PP (non vib.)
30
vib. poco a poco
mp
34
p
rit...
II
mf
rit - - - - -
© Feb. 1992   Bonnie Mangold
All Rights Reserved

## *Whistling in the Wind*

Though most of the pieces I've written are in a minor mode, I did make an effort to write occasionally in major so as to explore the different usage of bow and vibrato to communicate more upbeat music. This is one of those, and the feeling I wanted to communicate is that energy which correlates with the action of skipping. Do you remember skipping? Try it if it has been a while. No excuses—consider it an assignment (your next to last). It's really quite wonderful for body *and* spirit. Do it with a friend, holding hands. I bet you break down laughing in short order.

The dotted-quarter/eighth/quarter-note figure, which is the rhythmic basis of the piece and best conveys the skipping energy, needs to be played more like a double-dotted quarter followed by a 16th. It isn't exactly that; somewhere in between you will find the right relationship. Definitely do not play this faithful to the print. You want great abandon and expansiveness, not carefulness. Be the happy-go-lucky character who ignores all adversity, which correlates with free use of the bow: full bows every stroke with adequate weight to makc thc strings speak clearly, substantial but not forced sound. Pair the bow use with a vigorous vibrato: fast and wide. In the *Piu Mosso* sections, float the bow more, using less weight but ample bow to produce a less solid sound. When you play it, feel that skipping energy in your body with its corresponding mood.

Whistling in the Wind
Solo Cello
Bonnie Mangold
Carefree
Tempo I
Piu Mosso
Tempo I
piu forte
meno forte
accel. and cresc
Tempo Piu Mosso
marcato
poco rit.
copyright ©2016
Alfred

## *In the Nature of a Cadenza*

Hmmm. I have to admit that there was not a clear intent behind the writing of this. My idea
was along the lines of writing something requiring a great deal of freedom to find what will
make the music exciting to the listener. I do like the gypsy-czardas sort of feel, which I wanted
to capture because it exemplifies musical freedom to me. But mostly this was an exercise in
how to play a cadenza, bringing your own ideas to it. Keep in mind that for music to sound
free there has to be a lot of motion, so use plenty of bow, wide and fast vibrato, and play the
16th-note passage at the end with more bow than you think possible. I leave it at that. You are
on your own. Experiment.

In the Nature of a Cadenza
Solo Cello
Bonnie Mangold
♩=100
f
5
mf
>
mp
<
>
f
9
f IV
III
rit
14
mf
Ad lib.
<
>
cresc.
18 tempo
f
Cadenza
20
Ad lib.
fp
rit.
Start slow and accelerate
P
cresc.
21 tempo I
f
I
Cadenza-ad lib.
f
2
4
II mp gradually slower and softer - - - - - - PP accel. poco a poco a - - - - tempo
♩=116

ARCHIVES

2
24 ♩=116
mp
27
cresc. poco a poco — — — — — — — f III
32
II
36
Cadenza
fp slowly
accelerando and cresc. poco a poco to
39 tempo ♩=132
f
On the string
41
43
♩=126
Meno mosso
45
ff f cresc. + accel.
pizz.
fff
copyright © 2016

## *Oblivion Improvisation*

The appropriate energy here is quite opposite from the previous two pieces. This piece is inspired by Astor Piazzolla's *Oblivion*, which I find immensely expressive and moving. If you consider what oblivion means—a state of being forgotten, non-existence—you will immediately know that this needs to be played deliberately with a slow, steady bow, gentle vibrato (narrow but slow) if used, and a very introverted sort of energy. I think that this state of nothingness is nevertheless not devoid of all feeling. There is a questioning, almost curious or quizzical aspect to it, as if waiting to see what comes next. I do not equate it with sadness— tenderness and gentleness yes—and perhaps a quality of remembrance.

The technical challenge is to ensure that the pitch and quality of tone on the arco notes being sustained during the left hand pizzicatos remain unaffected, unperturbed. On those arco notes, get the note well established before bringing in the pizzicato. Sometimes I will start those notes with a bit of vibrato and then drop the vibrato when I bring in the pizzicato. You don't want a lot of conflicting sound, so pure pitches are better. The *B flats* and *F sharps* all need an expressive, plaintive emphasis. There is no key signature, which is the case in some modern music, but clearly *G* is the tonal center for most of the music, so orient your pitches to the *G*. You have to use the open *G* and *C* strings, so you haven't much choice but to be in tune with those strings. The opening pizzicatos should feel very static and deliberate, setting up the unhurried calm. You might want to take those notes with the left hand so that the arco voice can come in totally prepared and undisturbed.

Oblivion Improvisation
Solo Cello
Bonnie Mangold
Largo ♩=100
+ left hand pizzacoto begins
Optional mute
ARCO
pizz.
mf
+
mp
5
II
3
8
mf
3
12
I
16
21
II
3
mp
24
III 2
III
I
II
2
rit. + dim.
27
2
right hand
pizz
copyright © 2016
340

***Flow***

Refer to the comments in Exercise 29, page 212.

I wrote this piece during a period of being unable to play in the Symphony due to an overuse injury (a frozen shoulder this time). When I felt ready to return to work, I had to play for my rehab doctor to prove I was capable of doing so. I had been challenging myself with playing *Flow*, repeatedly, because it requires a sustained sound and similar bow use throughout the piece—a very tiring use. I played for the doctor for over an hour, without any real break, repeating this piece numerous times. *Flow* was indeed tiring, but I found that the more flow and congruence I could bring to my playing of it the less I hurt. Younger bodies should do fine.

# FLOW

Solo Cello

Bonnie Mangold

# A SUITE OF SONGS FOR ZACHARY
## (A DOG)

**Sweet Zachary**

**Protest**

**Lament**

**Off-Leash**

**Epilogue**

by

**Bonnie Mangold**

Copyright © 2016

# SONGS FOR ZACHARY

These five pieces form a Suite. Zachary was an Australian Shepherd, and he preceded Mari in my life; he also loved music and the cello, and liked to lie on the floor so that my endpin would be touching him as I played. Need I mention that he was a wonderful, noble spirit? He was a dog who, besides this very noble side, also was sweet, people-smart, and a bit of a trickster (whimsical and impish). He had a sense of humor, and he did like to play tricks on me, including bringing in the fallen walnuts to leave me gifts here and there. We had finally agreed that he wouldn't crack and eat them inside, staining the carpet, but he couldn't resist leaving them uncracked inside the front door for me to find when I came home. He liked to play and he had his girlfriends, as I described in *Off-Leash* Metaphor.

We lived in Salt Lake City during his life, and he was a neighborhood favorite. He would lie for hours at the retaining wall separating my property from the narrow (12-foot wide) street. More people walked than drove on our block, and everyone coming by would stop and engage with him. Not everyone knew his name, but he would respond to "Pumpkin," "Sweetheart," "Honey" and any other word said with great affection. He gloried in the attention. There were people who would walk through our block whom I sometimes judged harshly, confusing external appearances (the scores of piercings and tattoos and body language attitude) with essence. But when I saw their open-heartedness with Zachary I retracted my judgments.

Sometimes I play these pieces separately and sometimes I include *HeartSong* as the first piece if I am playing them as a Suite.

## *Sweet Zachary*

As you can hear and see from the opening theme, I have borrowed liberally from Dvořák to communicate Zachary's noble quality. I used separate themes for each of his primary qualities: the nobleness, the sweetness, and the trickster. You can decide what's what in the music and play accordingly, and also decide if you think I captured the energies of those qualities with the themes I chose. This piece could definitely be called program music. The qualities I wanted to communicate came directly from a real life character. I tried to capture Zachary's attributes. The music however is still a metaphor, as you could simply recreate the energies that I hope are inherent in the music, never knowing anything about Zachary.

Zachary too, died prematurely, and the reprise of the themes from measure 33 to the end of the piece is intended to get quieter—echoes of the original energy—and to fade away, as he did.

Solo Cello
Sweet Zachary
Bonnie Mangold
= 92
f (noble)
mp
mf
f
cantabile
mp
mf
dolce
mp
mf
mf
mf
cresc.
mp
rit.
tempo giocoso = 108
f
poco
f
Tempo I - dolce
Tempo giocoso
f
mf
rit - al - tempo I
P
Tempo I
mf
mp II
f deliberate
mp
346

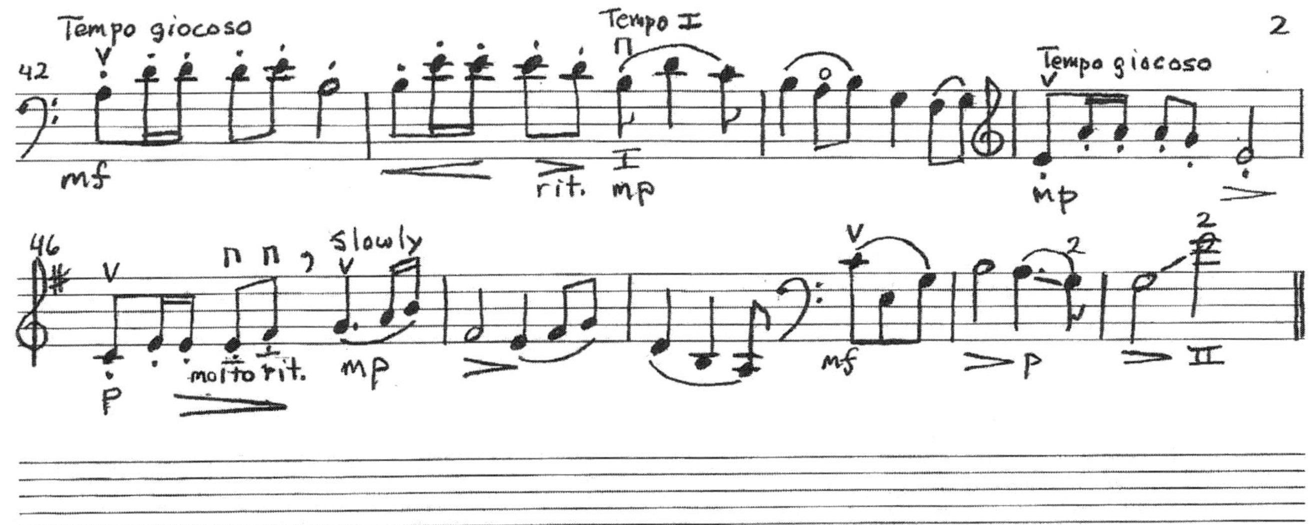
2
Tempo giocoso
42
mf
Tempo I
rit.
mp
Tempo giocoso
mp
46
slowly
P
molto rit.
mp
mf
p
copyright ©2016

## *Protest*

Refer to pages 182, 183 and 232 in the manual for my various comments and suggestions regarding the playing of this piece. It is meant to capture *my* feeling of protest of Zachary's too-soon death from lung cancer (brought about most likely by exposure to the cancer-inducing toxins we humans dump on our world). Zachary however was very stoic, as all dogs seem to be, rarely complaining or indicating how sick he was. Because of the quality of energy required to communicate real protest, it will be necessary to muster your own energy in great quantity. Like most things this is a matter of intention. Do not hold back on this piece. Ask everything of yourself, and ask everything of your instrument that it can possibly give, stopping just short of a forced sound. Besides the energy in your bow motion, your vibrato too needs to be very energized—fast and wide.

# PROTEST

Cello
Ronnie Mangold
♩=84
fff
accell..
a tempo
accell... ... a tempo
dim. poco a poco-
Slower (♩=72)
P con rubato
poco piu mosso
accel.
rall
Tempo I
ff
fff
dim poco a poco a
ff
f

legato
f
3
3
3
rall.
ff
Adlib.
6
2
P
2
copyright © 2016

## *Lament*

*Lament* was written as an expression of my grief at losing Zachary—a very personal grief, no distance here.

We don't generally get through much of life before we encounter real loss that brings us to our knees with grief. It is important to feel that grief and give voice to it one way or another, especially through actual sound. (There is a reason that wailing is a part of the expression of grief in many cultures. It provides a great release.)

And then we move on… in our own timing of course. But it is important not to get stuck in the grief, which is usually primarily for oneself. I know my dogs well enough to know they wouldn't want me to remember them for how they died, but rather for how they lived. This is why *Lament* is followed by *Off-Leash* in the Suite.

As with *Elegy* the motions of bow and vibrato must correlate with an inward, heavy, and mostly subdued energy. I have not marked many bowings after the first section, as I want players to use their own judgment regarding appropriate bowings, following in the vein of my initial suggestions indicating a legato approach. Even though the slurs would indicate a desired smooth sound, many of the eighth notes benefit from a slight articulation of each note to make them sound more deliberate—more like speech, as in the second bar where I have put lines above the notes. I have included string/fingering suggestions, which are pertinent to the color of sound I want—in this instance more important than the slurring choices. I also did not include many dynamic markings as I wish for the player, including myself, to have the freedom to interpret as the mood of the moment dictates. The string changes tend to achieve what I had in mind dynamically.

Lament
Solo Cello
Bonnie Mangold
copyright © 2016

## *Off-Leash*

Refer to pages 54 and 253 in the manual.

When I wrote this I truly had both the literal and metaphorical meanings in mind. I wanted to capture Zachary's exuberance at the off-leash dog park and, more importantly, what just might be the freedom that comes with death. We'll see. I'll reserve judgment for a while on that one.

The bow use in this piece needs to be fast and not dense, so not too close to the bridge; don't 'dig' into the string and squash the sound. The vibrato is correspondingly fast and fairly narrow. In the ad libitum sections (the little cadenzas) both bow use and vibrato change accordingly, matching the bit of regret, or other feeling, that you find there. I did have the intent to interrupt the joy with the thought of the goodbyes being said, and so the piece is in a minor key.

The four-bar quote on page 54 shows a slight difference from the full version here, in that the last notes of bars 2 and 4 change pitch to that of the next downbeat. More often I play it as I have written it here.

Off-Leash
Solo Cello
Bonnie Mangold
Animated
♩= 126
f (L.H.)
p legato, dolce (U.H.)
marcato
legato
marcato
f (freely)
marcato
legata
II mp dolce
Tempo I
Lento
III
P
II mf
legato
Animated (as the beginning)
f
356

copyright ©2016

## *Epilogue*

This piece, which concludes the song cycle for Zachary, is based on the poem I wrote after
Zachary died, titled *Dance Improvisation*. My poem is inspired by a short poem I once came
across attributed to Rumi.  I don't know who translated it, so I will not quote it here.


### *Dance Improvisation*
### *for Zachary*
(inspired by Rumi's poem *Dance*)


*Dance when your heart is broken open~~*

*Dance when you rip the bandages away~~*

*Dance when the pain cannot be borne~~*

*Dance in your own heart's blood*

*Dance when the clouds are darkest~~*

*Dance when the zia shines through~~*

*Dance when your heart melts from love~~*

*Dance for the beauty of what is~~*

*And dance for no reason at all*


Bonnie Mangold
January 2007

(zia – a ray of sunlight shining through a cloud)


My wonderful step-mother, whom I had the privilege of knowing for too short a time,
suggested I set the poem to music and so I did. Every note in the first section is a syllable of
the poem. The reprise, beginning in measure 20, is a wordless one in my mind, simply echoing
the sentiments of the poem.

# Epilogue

Solo Cello
Epilogue
Bonnie Mangold
♩= 46
with resignation
Mute
P II
mp
mp
mf
tenderly, holding back slightly
mp
p
tempo
uH
As an echo until the end
Ever quieter
deliberate II
pp
copyright © 2016

## *Cry Of The Earth*

We have looked at this piece in terms of how the intonation can be molded to make the music more poignant, and you have read what it means to me personally. It is a lament. It is meant to have a free-sounding, almost improvisational quality, which implies rhythmic rubatos and freedoms that are not actually written into the part, but that are necessary to make the music as expressive as possible. The *D* harmonic minor mode lends itself to a plaintive, middle-eastern sounding, almost wailing, voice. I have added a few markings, such as lines over notes that can be lengthened slightly or otherwise emphasized, some portamentos (slides) and breaths, all of which ordinarily a composer might not bother to put in the part, assuming that a player would automatically do these things. These departures from the print, which by now you will have started to internalize, help in making the music expressive. You can use this piece to focus on expressive intonation and the rhythmic distortions needed to communicate the feeling of lamenting.

Where there are two or more consecutive eighth notes I doubt if I ever play them equal in value—some may get lengthened, others hurried. If all the eighths were played arithmetically correct, the piece would sound square and dull. For example, I lengthen the first eighth note just to set things up and establish that the piece has really started—giving some depth or substance to the note before bringing in the open *A* string. Once I bring in the *A*, I hurry a bit to get to the *C#*. In the second bar I 'sit' on the first *G#*, making it important to the ear, as well as the second *G#*, then I make up the time by hurrying the next three eighths, though not evenly, to arrive at the dotted-quarter *E*. At the end of bar three I take time if needed to get rid of the energy and emotion, and I breathe before going on with a softer, more inward and tender plaint.

Almost all *C sharps* and *G sharps* need to be brought out—made more important to the ear— particularly when they are part of that minor third sound that is so poignant. (Technically I should call it an augmented second or an interval of three half steps, but I said sound, not interval, so I am off the hook.) It's the *Bb* to *C#* or *C#* down to the *Bb* and the *G#* to *F* that I refer to. The *G#* is the augmented fourth of the scale and is a very dissonant note and can be emphasized on that account as well, desperately needing then to resolve.

The little slide or connection in bar nine between the *C#* and *Bb* can be made by dragging the fourth finger down a ways before going to the second finger on the *Bb*. In bar ten the slides on the first finger are not metronomic. I hurry the eighths to get to the quarters, which are correspondingly lengthened. All the *Fs*, being the lowered third of the scale, have greater significance than adjacent notes, as do the *B flats* (the lowered sixth).

As you work to find how to make this piece speak to the heart, play around with all these ideas. Find out where they might apply, and even if they do apply. Remember that what you end up with needs to sound and feel organic, not contrived or studied. You know the concept I had in mind. You can feel all these same feelings, so in the end *be* those feelings.

Cry Of The Earth
Solo Cello
Bonnie Mangold 
Lento
♩=52
p II - until bar 8
mp
cresc.
mf
P
mf
mf II
f
mp
P
poco
cresc.
mf
P
Agitated
gently
f marcato and deliberate
piu mosso
rit
P
poco
mf
rit
copyright ©2016

## *Mari's Song*

If you have read through to the end of Act VI, then you know that Mari is no longer with me. Her song is one I started while she was still alive but had never put the finishing touches on. I didn't know how to end it, and still don't. If it seems to be unfinished, with a too abrupt ending, perhaps that is the right metaphor for her life. It ended much too soon.

This is a high-energy piece, bold and impulsive as marked. Mari loved to run free, with a top speed of at least 25 miles per hour. She would leap over anything in her path, figuratively giving any obstacle a disdainful dismissal. She was also a bit of a princess—I think she knew how beautiful she was and how much everyone admired her. Mostly she was just optimistic, joyous energy, until she started to fail.

Free, fast bow-speeds are needed to communicate this energy, with marcato attacks except in the few softer measures. A wide, fast vibrato is appropriate. *Mari's Song* needs to be played with utmost confidence and conviction, like her certainty that she could jump anything, catch any ball, and out-run my car. She couldn't quite do that but I never let on. She gave herself multiple opportunities to try, as she had this bad habit of escaping the fenced 'yard' (sand, cactus, sage, junipers, lizards and such) and running free through the mostly wild, adjacent land. Eventually she would tire, return to the county dirt road, and find me, who of course had been out in the car looking for her for way too long. But she wouldn't then just jump in the car. She had to race down the road ahead of the car, to prove her point, until finally she took pity on me. (The road is rather rough.)

She was a brief but bright star in my firmament. Make this piece reflect that bright spirit.

Mari's Song
Solo Cello
Bonnie Mangold
Bold and impulsive
♩ = 96
marcato
legato
poco meno mosso
mp marcato
Tempo I
marcato
Poco piu mosso
mf jauntily
legato
(U. H.)

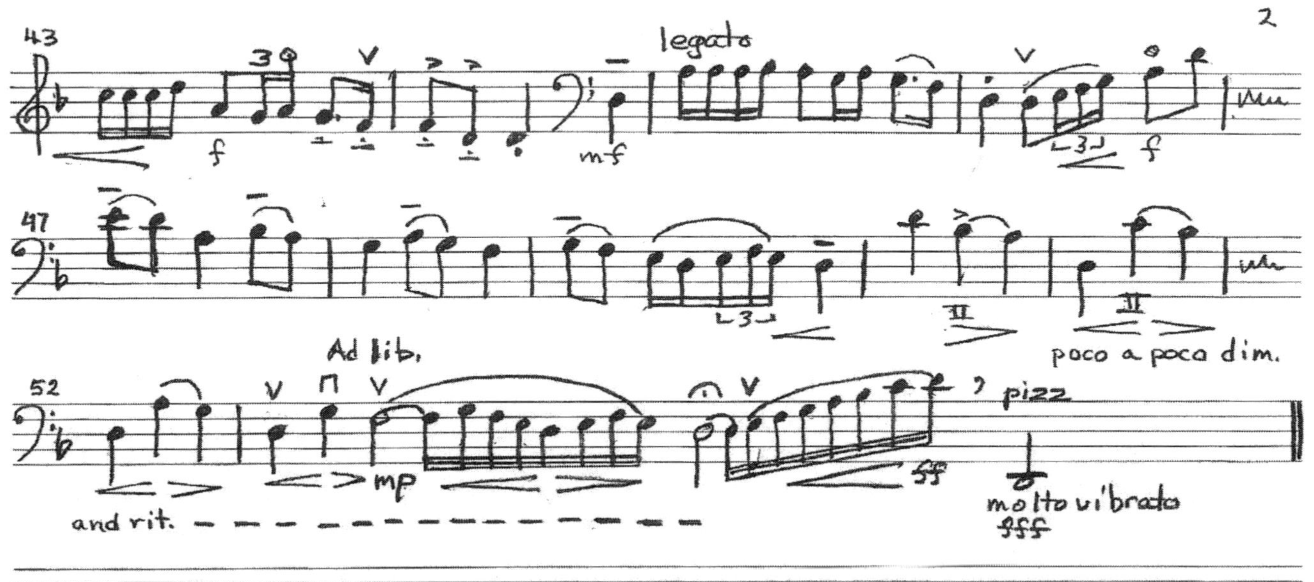
43
legato
f
mf
f
47
poco a poco dim.
52
Ad lib.
mp
pizz
and rit.
molto vibrato
sff
sff

# *Your Song*

Surprise! This blank music manuscript is for you to write something that has meaning for you. It needn't meet anyone else's criteria. It needn't be 'good'; it needn't be long; it just needs to be yours. Start with an intent: decide the quality or feeling you wish to communicate. Wait for the right theme to come to your mind (it will appear in due course—don't hurry it) and build from there. Play it with love.

# REVIEW SECTION

## Fundamentals of Music

# OVERVIEW

This section is a review of music fundamentals that music students ideally learn early on in their studies. If for some reason you didn't get this background, then this review will provide you with the minimum understanding needed to utilize the information I've included in Act IV. It does not cover basics of rhythm since rhythmic relationships are more likely to be taught when students first learn to read music. If you are weak in this area the internet will provide you with many resources. If you are a serious student of music your knowledge of music theory needs to go a lot deeper than what this review covers, but an  understanding of the fundamentals presented here of how music is constructed will be adequate for continuing on in the manual.

The material in this section will be useless if you leave it on the page. Play and sing everything. It is your ear as well as your mind that needs these basics. Obtain music manuscript paper and write out the drills in the clef appropriate for your instrument as well.

<><><>

## INTERVALS

"Frequency" refers to the number of vibrations or cycles per second. Audible frequencies are in the range between 16 and 20,000 cycles per second.

"Pitch" refers to the specific frequency of a tone, such as 440 vibrations per second for what we call concert *A*.

"Interval" refers to the difference in frequency of two tones.

The smallest distance, or *interval,* between pitches normally used in our Western musical language is what we call a half tone, half step or semitone (synonyms).[202] If you look at the partial piano keyboard drawn on the next page, it is the distance from one note to its closest neighbor, whether up or down, white note or black note. Know the sound of this half step.

Example: *C* up to a *Db* (same as *C#*), or *C* down to a *B*

---

[202]There is such a thing as a quarter tone, which you will encounter in modern music. It cannot be played or represented on the keyboard, but you can hear that interval, which is half the distance of the half tone (or a quarter the distance of the whole tone), and you can play it on a wind or string instrument. If a composer uses quarter tones there will be an explanation in the music of the symbols being used to indicate them. You probably won't encounter it often, and none of the basics discussed here will deal further with quarter tones. They are used more frequently in music from other parts of the world, as are even smaller intervals.

**371**

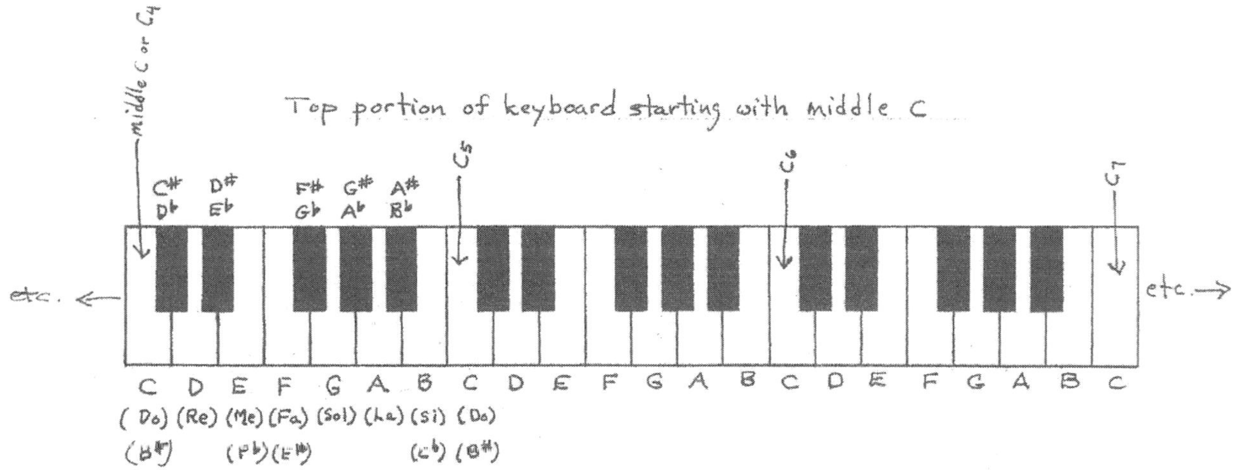


**Figure 27**

Skipping a key (or tone) on the keyboard results in the interval of a whole tone or whole step (synonyms).
Example: *C* up to *D*, or *C* down to *Bb*.

The interval of a half step can also be called a minor second, and the whole step a major[203] second. To have this designation of a second, the two notes must be written with a different note name, as in *C* to *Db*, (referred to as a diatonic half step—different pitch plus different alphabet note name). The same interval can be symbolized, in terms of sound, as *C* to *C#*. Here the basic note name is the same, but there is a change in pitch. This is referred to as a chromatic half step.[204]

The general principle then is: Different note names and different pitches are diatonic intervals; Same basic note names and different pitches are chromatic intervals. To label half steps as minor seconds, they must be written in the diatonic way. A whole step, to be called a major second, must be written diatonically. A major second then is written as *C* to *D*, not as *C* to *C double sharp*.

For the ear, the sound is the same whether you call an interval a half step (half tone) or a minor second. Likewise, whole step (whole tone) and major second are the same to your ear. I will generally use the word *step* rather than *tone*, and may use *seconds* when written diatonically. All the other intervals can be built from these two. When I use the phrase *step and a half*, or *1½ steps*, it means a whole step plus a half step. Or you can think of it as three half steps. Two steps means two whole steps or four half steps. Later, I abbreviate further and just write whole or half.

To build the other intervals, base them on how many whole and half steps are in that interval. Following the major second (abbreviated as M 2nd), the next largest interval is the minor third (m 3rd).

---

[203] For clarity the 'M' in Major *may* be upper case, but the 'm' in minor remains lower case. When referring to a specific scale or chord the 'M' is upper case, as: the key of *C* Major. Commonly used abbreviations are shown on the next page.
[204] See discussion of enharmonic tones on the next page.

**Interval Composition in Steps:**

    minor second (m 2nd) = ½ step—Example: *C* to *Db*, or *C* down to *B*
    major second (M 2nd) = one whole step—Ex: *C* to *D*, or *C* down to *Bb*
    minor third (m 3rd) = 1 ½ steps—Ex: *C* up to *Eb*, or *C* down to *A*
    major third (M 3rd) = 2 whole steps—Ex: *C* up to *E*, or *C* down to *Ab*
    perfect fourth (P 4th) = 2 ½ steps—Ex: *C* up to *F*, or *C* down to *G*
    augmented fourth (A 4th) = 3 whole steps—Ex: *C* up to *F#*, or *C* down to *Gb*
    perfect fifth (P 5th) = 3 ½ steps—Ex: *C* up to *G*, or *C* down to *F*
    diminished fifth (d 5th) = 3 whole steps (same sound as the augmented 4th, but uses the diatonic spelling in order to be referred to as a 5th), hence *C* up to *Gb*, or *C* down to *F#*
    minor sixth (m 6th) = 4 whole steps—Ex: *C* up to *A b*, or *C* down to *E*
    major sixth (M 6th) = 4 ½ steps—Ex: *C* up to *A*, or *C* down to *Eb*
    minor seventh (m 7th) = 5 whole steps—Ex: *C* up to *Bb*, or *C* down to *D*
    major seventh (M 7th) = 5 ½ steps—Ex: *C* up to *B*, or *C* down to *Db*
    octave (P 8ve) = 6 whole steps—Ex. *C* up to the higher *C*, or down to the lower *C*

Intervals larger than an octave are referred to as compound intervals, as in a compound sixth. The terms ninth, tenth, eleventh, and twelfth are also used for the first four intervals greater than an octave.

To augment means to make something bigger; to diminish means to make something smaller. Besides the common references to a diminished fifth or augmented fourth, the terms may be applied to other intervals as well, such as a diminished octave (d 8ve)—*B* to *Bb* for example. Figure out how you would write those on the staff. Remember, if you call an interval a fourth there have to be four alphabet names involved in the separation of sounds, as in *C* is one, *D* is two, *E* is three, *F* is four. *C* to *F* is a perfect fourth; *C* to *E* is a major third. How would you write an augmented third, and what would it sound the same as?

Your assignment now is to write out, play, and sing the intervals shown above, beginning from every available pitch within an octave. You just saw and practiced all the ones based on *C*. Now move to *C#* and figure out the intervals: seconds, thirds, fourths, etc.

Then start from *D* and figure all the intervals from *D*. The last set will start from *B*, so you will have:

    minor second = *B* up to *C*, or *B* down to *A#*
    major second = *B* up to *C#*, or down to *A*
    minor third =
    etc.

As suggested in the text of the manual you really need to know the sounds of these different intervals. If you see a written *F* down to a *C*, you need to recognize instantly that this is a perfect fourth, and you need to be able to hear in your head what that sounds like. Be sure to take into account that *E* to *F* is just a half step, as is *B* to *C*.

Find the system that works best for you to truly learn these sounds. You might need to focus first on just differentiating half steps from whole steps, then major thirds from minor thirds.

**Enharmonic Tones**

Enharmonic is the term for the tones that sound the same but which can be written differently, such as the *C#* and *Db, or G#* versus *Ab*. On the keyboard there is just one physical key and one sound for notes written with either symbol, so we cannot differentiate between these *enharmonic notes*. However theoretically there is a slight difference. The distance or difference in frequency encompassed by a whole tone can be divided into nine parts, referred to as commas. The difference between enharmonic notes is one comma, or one ninth of the frequency difference of a whole tone—a slight difference but one you should train yourself to hear. You achieve this distinction on non-keyboard instruments when you push a pitch slightly closer to the note above, as in *C#* going to *D*, or a flatted note played a bit closer to the note below, as in *Db* going to *C*. Thus, the *Db* sounds slightly lower than the *C#*. Making these distinctions when possible is part of what adds expressiveness to your playing.

There are other systems of tuning in addition to the commonly used well-tempered (or equal-tempered) tuning of the piano. In these systems different terminology and descriptions are used for dividing an octave or whole tone into parts. In one system the difference in sound of enharmonic tones can be as much as a fifth of a whole tone. In earlier centuries there were also enharmonic instruments made that had extra keys, strings, or pipes for the different sounds of enharmonic tones.

## SCALES, TONALITY, MODES

*Scale*: a series of generally adjacent notes within an octave, adhering to a particular pattern of intervals, known as the mode of the scale. The root or starting note of any scale is referred to as the tonic note or keynote.

*Tonality*: loyalty to a tonic or keynote

*Mode*: scales can be constructed according to different patterns. A mode is a specific pattern. The most widely used scales in Western music are constructed according to the major and minor modes.

### Major Scales

*Major scales* have the following interval relationships between the notes: **whole, whole, half, whole, whole, whole, half.**

When *C* is the tonic, then the notes are: *C, D, E, F, G, A, B, C*. On the piano that happens to be all the white keys—no sharps or flats. When *G* is the tonic, then the pattern is: *G, A, B, C, D, E, F#, G*. The *F* must be made sharp to get the required whole step between the 6th and 7th notes (or *degrees*) of the scale. By following this sequence of whole and half steps you can build a major scale starting on any note.

Finish the major scales below, based on the indicated tonic notes, in the same fashion. Write these out on the staff as notes, but also write out the pitch names below the staff. As you play or sing them, say the pitch or note name as well. You want to make use of all levels of perception to absorb this information.

As you construct the scales be sure you always change the note names sequentially. Don't skip or repeat a note name. By following this rule you won't mix sharps and flats in the same scale. In other words, write them diatonically not chromatically. For example in *C* Major you would not write: *C, D, E, E#, G, A, B, C*. That would be a chromatic spelling.

### Major Scale Charts

| Tonic | Whole | Whole | Half | Whole | Whole | Whole | Half | Name of scale and alterations |
|---|---|---|---|---|---|---|---|---|
| *C* | *D* | *E* | *F* | *G* | *A* | *B* | *C* | *C* Major  no sharps or flats |
| *G* | *A* | *B* | *C* | *D* | *E* | *F#* | *G* | *G* Major 1 sharp (*F*) |
| *D* | | | | | | | | |
| *A* | | | | | | | | |
| *E* | | | | | | | | |
| *B* | | | | | | | | |

| Tonic | Whole | Whole | Half | Whole | Whole | Whole | Half | Name of scale and alterations |
|---|---|---|---|---|---|---|---|---|
| *F#* | | | | | | | | |
| *C#* | *D#* | *E#* | *F#* | *G#* | *A#* | *B#* | *C#* | *C#* Major 7 sharps *(F,C,G,D, A,E, B)* |

**Table 1**

You have constructed all the major scales that have sharps.

Now build the ones with flats—same pattern.  Start again with *C* Major so that you can see the relationship sequence.

| Tonic | Whole | Whole | Half | Whole | Whole | Whole | Half | Name of scale and alterations |
|---|---|---|---|---|---|---|---|---|
| *C* | *D* | *E* | *F* | *G* | *A* | *B* | *C* | *C* Major no sharps or flats |
| *F* | *G* | *A* | *Bb* | *C* | *D* | *E* | *F* | *F* Major 1 flat *(B)* |
| *Bb* | | | | | | | | |
| *Eb* | | | | | | | | |
| *Ab* | | | | | | | | |
| *Db* | | | | | | | | |
| *Gb* | | | | | | | | |
| *Cb* | *Db* | *Eb* | *Fb* | *Gb* | *Ab* | *Bb* | *Cb* | *Cb* Major 7 flats *(B, E, A, D, G, C, F)* |

**Table 2**

You will have noticed that *C#* Major and *Db* Major use the same tones or keys on the keyboard. Just as there are enharmonic notes there are enharmonic scales. *F#* Major and *Gb* Major use the same tones, as well as *B* Major and *Cb* Major.

You may also have noticed that with the sharp scales, to get to the tonic of a scale that adds one additional sharp, you start on the fifth note of the scale you are currently on, i.e: *C* to *G* is a perfect fifth, *G* to *D* is a P 5th, *D* to *A* is a P 5th, and so on.

With the flat scales, to get to the next scale in the sequence, you can think down a perfect fifth from the tonic (or up a perfect fourth if that is easier), i.e: *C* down a P 5th to *F*, *F* down to *Bb*, *Bb* down *to Eb*, etc.

### Cycle of Fifths

This relationship between all the scales and their sequences of sharps and flats is known as the *Cycle of Fifths*. Life as a musician is much simpler if you simply memorize these sequences of scales, sharps, and flats. The *key signature*, which is usually repeated at the beginning of each line of music, shows you what sharps or flats to play, which helps tell you what key[205] is indicated—that is to say, what scale is the basis for this piece of music. If you see three sharps in the key signature, you need to immediately know that they will be *F#, C#* and *G#*, and that five sharps are *F#, C#, G#, D#,* and *A#*. The three sharps tell you that the music is either in the key of *A* Major, or in a minor key with the same sharps. With sharps you have a quick extra hint as to the key, provided it is a major mode not minor: the last sharp shown on the staff is the 7th or leading tone of the scale. That third and last sharp (*G#)* in the first example is the 7th of *A* Major.

### Minor Scales

There are three minor modes in common use. Let us first look at the **natural or Aeolian minor**, also known as Pure minor, Ethiopian, and the Mohammedan.

The pattern here is: **whole, half, whole, whole, half, whole, whole.**
When *A* is the tonic or key note, then the notes are *A, B, C, D, E, F, G, A*. Again, these are all the white keys on the piano. The intervals are correct without needing to add sharps or flats. Thus there is a relationship to *C* Major, which has neither sharps nor flats. Since the scale started on an *A* instead of a *C*, the relationship of *A* minor to *C* Major is that they share the key signature and all the same notes, but the minor scale starts on a note a minor third lower. The scale of *A* minor is thus called the relative minor of *C* Major, and vice versa: *C* Major is the relative major of *A* minor. They are related, sharing the same pitches but starting on different notes and having a different pattern of the whole and half steps.

Finish constructing all the natural minor scales as you did with the major scales and include the name of the related major scale. Play or sing them of course, and use your manuscript paper.

Table 3 contains the minor keys that have sharps. Notice that once again the next scale in the sequence of adding sharps always starts on the fifth of the current scale.

---

[205] Key (besides being the word for the mechanical device you press to produce a sound on keyboards and wind instruments) has come to mean the tonal center of a composition, to which other notes relate.

# Natural Minor Scale Charts

| Tonic | Whole | Half | Whole | Whole | Half | Whole | Whole | Name of scale and alterations | Relative Major scale |
|---|---|---|---|---|---|---|---|---|---|
| *A* | *B* | *C* | *D* | *E* | *F* | *G* | *A* | *A* minor no flats or sharps | *C* Major |
| *E* | *F#* | *G* | *A* | *B* | *C* | *D* | *E* | *E* minor 1 sharp (*F*) | *G* Major |
| *B* | | | | | | | | | |
| *F#* | | | | | | | | | |
| *C#* | | | | | | | | | |
| *G#* | | | | | | | | | |
| *D#* | | | | | | | | | |
| *A#* | *B#* | *C#* | *D#* | *E#* | *F#* | *G#* | *A#* | *A#* minor 7 sharps (*F,C,G,D, A,E,B*) | *C#* Major |

**Table 3**

Now construct the minor scales that have flats. Again *A* minor, which has no sharps or flats, appears first to show the pattern and the relationship to the next scale.

| Tonic | Whole | Half | Whole | Whole | Half | Whole | Whole | Relative Major Scale | Name of scale & alterations |
|---|---|---|---|---|---|---|---|---|---|
| *A* | *B* | *C* | *D* | *E* | *F* | *G* | *A* | *C* Major | *A* minor no sharps or flats |
| *D* | *D* | *F* | *G* | *A* | *Bb* | *C* | *D* | *F* Major | *D* minor 1 flat (*B*) |
| *G* | | | | | | | | | |
| *C* | | | | | | | | | |
| *F* | | | | | | | | | |
| *Bb* | | | | | | | | | |
| *Eb* | | | | | | | | | |
| *Ab* | *Bb* | *Cb* | *Db* | *Eb* | *Fb* | *Gb* | *Ab* | *Cb* Major | *Ab* minor 7 flats (*B,E,A,D, G,C,F*) |

**Table 4**

As with the major scale sequence, for the minor scales with flats go down a perfect fifth from the tonic of the prior scale to get the new tonic, or think up a perfect fourth.

There are two other modes of minor scales: harmonic minor and melodic minor. They have in common that they always have the lowered third, that is a minor third from the tonic to the third degree (or pitch) of the scale, as in *C* to *Eb*, or *A* to *C*. Be sure to play all these different scales, so that you can identify the modes by ear—not just by sight.

**Harmonic Minor**
The difference between the natural minor and the *harmonic minor* is that the harmonic minor has a raised 7th, thus creating the *sound* of a minor third or three half steps between the 6th and 7th tones of the scale. The pattern becomes: **whole, half, whole, whole, half, one and a half, half**. The *A* harmonic minor scale is thus spelled: *A*, *B*, *C*, *D*, *E*, *F*, *G#*, *A*. Look at the minor scales you have written out and determine how to convert them to the harmonic minor form.

## Melodic Minor

The classical *melodic minor* scale goes up one way and comes down differently. (In jazz use, it is the same coming down as going up.) The ascending pattern keeps the lowered 3rd degree, but raises the 6th and 7th as in a major scale; the only difference from major is the lowered 3rd. However it descends like the natural minor with lowered 7th, 6th and 3rd. The pattern going up is: **whole, half, whole, whole, whole, whole, half**. The pattern coming down is: **whole, whole, half, whole, whole, half, whole**. The *A* melodic minor scale going up is thus spelled: *A, B, C, D, E, F#, G#, A*. Going down is: *A, G natural, F natural, E, D, C, B, A*. Work with this a bit so you can recognize this scale and construct one starting from any pitch.

Let's look at some other scales you may encounter, often referred to as modal scales or church modes, as they formed the tonal basis for Gregorian Chant. I will spell out some of these modes using *C* as the tonic. You can figure out the patterns and translate those to other keynotes. Play these scales so you can hear the unique sound of each.

## Phrygian

*C, Db, Eb, F, G, Ab, Bb, C*

## Lydian

*C, D, E, F#, G, A, B, C*

## Mixolydian

(**A**lso known as Dominant Scale)

*C, D, E, F, G, A, Bb, C*

Other interesting scales are the whole tone, major pentatonic and blues scales.

## Whole Tone

*C, D, E, F#, G#, A#, C*

## Major Pentatonic

(**A**lso known as Mongolian or Chinese Scale)

*C, D, E, G, A, C*

## Blues Scale

(This spelling is for the hexatonic, or 6 note, minor blues scale. There are others.)

*C, Eb, F, F#/Gb, G, Bb, C*

## Chromatic scale

Every pitch within the octave: going up the notes are spelled using sharps as needed (*C, C#, D, D#*, etc.) and coming down using flats (*C, B, Bb, A, Ab*, etc.)

## KEY SIGNATURE

Going back to the *key signature* (the collection of sharps or flats at the beginning of the line, shown after the time signature and repeated generally on each line of music), you now know that it could indicate either a major or minor key. Three sharps in the signature denote either the key of *A Major, or the key of F# minor*. With a brief look at the music you will quickly figure out which it is, based on the use of notes from the tonic chord (coming up next).

In a minor key the sharps or flats included in the key signature are those used for the natural minor scale. The alterations needed to make the sounds of harmonic and melodic scales are inserted as accidentals in the music score. Accidentals hold good for only the measure in which they occur and usually for any octave of the note. Twentieth-century practice may differ on whether an accidental applies to all octaves of the altered note or just the octave where it is written.

## CHORD

A *chord* is three or more notes built of thirds.

### Terminology for Naming Chords Based on Degrees of the Scale

As mentioned, each diatonic note of the scale may be referred to as the degree: 1st, 2nd, 3rd, etc. There are other terms as well, which are used in the naming of chords. The 1st degree is also referred to as the keynote or tonic. The normal way of writing the degree is using Roman numerals, hence: I, II, III, IV, V, VI, VII, VIII. They can be referred to as the tonic, supertonic, median, subdominant, dominant, submediant, leading tone (when it is a half step below the octave), or subtonic (when it is a whole step below the tonic as in the natural minor scale).

### Structure

"Chord" implies a vertical structure, including at least three notes built using every other note of the scale (thirds). They can be arranged in sequence from the bottom, or root, of the chord up: *C-E-G*. They can also be inverted as in *G-E-C*, or other arrangements of the chord notes can be used. *C-E-G* is the tonic chord of the key of *C* Major, with a root tone of *C*. The tones of the scale used are I, III, and V, in any arrangement. When the root of a chord is built on the 5th degree (V or dominant) of a scale, the chord is called the dominant chord—in this case spelled *G-B-D*. When the chord has the 4th degree or subdominant note of the scale as its root, then it is called the subdominant chord, spelled *F-A-C* in *C* Major.

When the chord has three tones only, arranged either in thirds above the root or in an inversion, it is often called a *triad*. Triads can be either major or minor. As defined, chords are built on thirds, but the type of third varies. In a major triad (or chord) there is a major third followed by a minor third, as in *C* to *E* and *E* to *G*. In a minor triad it is the reverse: a minor third followed by a major third as in *C-Eb-G*. The distance from I to V does not vary in the major and minor triads. That remains the interval of a perfect fifth.

It is important that you are able to hear, see, and spell thirds. To spell a chord on the staff (one that is not inverted) you use either sequential spaces or lines. Learn to rattle off thirds effortlessly, both up and down. This is a big help in identifying the arpeggiated chords often found in melody lines, where the chord notes are played one after another, melodically, instead of simultaneously.

You can build a major or minor chord starting on any note, but, as described above, within a particular key they assume the name of the root note. So, in *C* Major the triad built on *C* is the tonic triad, the one built on *D* is the supertonic triad, the one built on *E* is the median, on *F* is the subdominant, on *G* is the dominant, etc.

Construct triads on each of the notes of the *C* Major scale and identify whether they are major or minor.

**Chord Charts**

| Chord Name | Triad | Type |
|---|---|---|
| Tonic (I) | *C-E-G* | Major |
| Supertonic (II) | *D* | |
| Median (III) | *E* | |
| Subdominant (IV) | *F* | |
| Dominant (V) | *G* | |
| Submediant (VI) | *A* | |
| Leading tone (VII) | *B* | |
| | *C* | |

Table 5

You will notice that the triad built on the leading tone *B*, in the key of *C* Major, is neither major nor minor as it consists of two minor thirds. This is called a "diminished triad." A triad consisting of two major thirds would be an "augmented triad," such as *C-E-G#*. The major and minor triads are considered to be consonant, and the diminished and augmented are dissonant. You will see that in a major key the sequence of triads is: Major, minor, minor, Major, Major, minor, diminished and back to Major.[206] The all important I, IV and V chords (tonic, subdominant and dominant) are all major.

---

[206] Here I did use the upper case for the 'M', of Major, just to make this sequence more obvious.

Now construct triads on all of the notes of the *A* minor scale and identify each.

| Chord Name | Triad | Type |
| --- | --- | --- |
| Tonic (I) | *A-C-E* | minor |
| Supertonic (II) | *B* | |
| Median (III) | *C* | |
| Subdominant (IV) | *D* | |
| Dominant (V) | *E* | |
| Submediant (VI) | *F* | |
| Leading tone (VII) | *G* | |
| | *A* | |

**Table 6**

The sequence here is minor, diminished, Major, minor, minor, Major, Major, and back to the minor tonic chord. The I, IV, and V chords are all minor.

When the chord has more than three notes it continues to build in thirds, adding the 7th tone, then the 9th, then the 11th, etc. The chord of four notes is called a seventh chord, five notes is a ninth chord, and so on. A frequently used seventh chord is built on the dominant (or 5th) of the scale and is called the Dominant seventh chord (V7). In *C* Major that would be *G-B-D-F*.

## CADENCE

"A melodic or harmonic formula that occurs at the end of a composition, a section, or a phrase, conveying the impression of a momentary or permanent conclusion."[207]

A variety of formulas that create the sense of finishing, or finality, have been used in compositions over the centuries. In the Classical tradition the tonic chord is the final chord with either the subdominant (IV) chord or dominant (V) chord preceding it. There are other conditions for the various types of Classical cadences, but the final chord almost always is the tonic chord. Identifying this chord when looking at a piece allows you to quickly interpret the key signature—whether it is that of a major or minor key. If the key signature is three sharps and the final chord is *A-C#-E–A*, you can assume *A* Major to be your key. If the final chord is *F#-A-C#-F#*, you know you are in *F#* minor. Additionally, you will generally find the notes of

---

[207] *Harvard Dictionary of Music*, Second Edition

the tonic chord at the beginning of the work—in the piano part if there is one, and in your melodic line as well. Often a piece will start with an upbeat on the dominant tone, going to the tonic on the downbeat.

## MODULATION

This is the process of music transitioning from one key to another, either major or minor. The usual method is by going to a closely related key, such as to the key of the dominant, i.e. *C* Major *modulating* to *G* Major. This is done by using an alteration—or accidental—*F#* in this instance, leading into the new key. You might have a sequence of notes such as: *C, D, E, G, E, F#, A, G*. Clearly this starts in *C* Major, but then the *F#* going to the *A* leads the ear to the *G*— the new tonic note. Modulations also easily go to the relative major or minor key (*C* Major going to *A* minor for example), and to the Subdominant (*C* Major to *F* Major). The minor scale with the same tonic is another possibility (*C* Major to *C* minor). Scales related in this way are referred to as homotonic scales.

## CONCLUSION

The study of harmony will take you much deeper into all the topics addressed in this review— classical rules of chord progressions and other intricacies—but if you have come this far you are ready to return to Act IV of the manual. Congratulations!

# APPENDIX A

## IDENTIFICATION OF MUSIC QUOTES

Listed here are all of the music quotes that were not identified where they occurred in the manual.

Overture: Nuts and Bolts of the Manual title page quote, page 1, is from the Beethoven *Leonore Overture No. 3*.

Act I: The Philosophical Underpinnings for Making Music title page quote, page 11, is from the Verdi *Requiem*, Agnus Dei.

Figure 1, page 16, is from the Mahler *Symphony No. 1*, first movement.

Figure 2, page 29, is from the Schumann *Cello Concerto in A minor*, 2nd movement.

Figure 3, page 44, is the first movement theme from the Dvořák *Cello Concerto in B minor*.

Figure 4, page 60, is from *Don Quixote for Cello and Orchestra* by Richard Strauss.

Figure 5, page 77, is the opening theme of the Brahms *Piano Concerto No.1 in D minor*.

Figure 7, page 123, is from *Vocalise* by Rachmaninoff.

Figure 9, page 150, is the opening of the Courante from the Bach *Cello Suite No.1*.

Figure 23, page 235, is from the C.P.E. Bach *Cello Concerto in A Major*, second movement.

Act V: Singing *Your* Song title page quote, page 241, is from Saint-Saëns' aria *Mon coeur s'ourve a ta voix* from the opera *Samson et Dalila*.

Figure 24, page 243, is from the *Gymnopedie No. 1* by Erik Satie.

Act VI: Finale title page quote, on page 285, is from *Der Rosenkavalier Suite* by Richard Strauss.

Figure 25, page 287, is from the *Grand Tango for Cello and Piano* by Astor Piazzolla.

Figure 26, page 308, is from the Beethoven *Symphony No. 9*, fourth movement.

# APPENDIX B

## SUGGESTED READING

The books listed below (mostly not about music) are the ones mentioned in the manual that I believe to be the most helpful in developing a broad perspective and full humanity—developing a heart that is open and capable of holding (as Piglet would say), a "rather large amount of gratitude" and love.

*A Language Older Than Words* by Derrick Jensen

*A Soprano on Her Head* by Eloise Ristad

*Art's Cello* by James N. McKean

*Beauty* by Sheri S. Tepper

*Beyond Words, What Animals Think and Feel* by Carl Safina

*Brown Dog of the Yaak* by Rick Bass

*Dominion* by Matthew Scully

*Facing the Music* by Harold C. Schonberg

*Flow and Creativity* by Mihaly Csikszentmihaly

*Stand Up Straight and Sing* by Jessye Norman

*The Basic Code of the Universe* by Massimo Citro

*The Biology of Belief* by Bruce Lipton

*The Boys in the Boat* by Daniel James Brown

*The Brain's Way of Healing* by Norman Doidge

*The Different Drum* by M. Scott Peck

*The Inner Voice* by Renée Fleming

*The Road Not Taken* by M. Scott Peck

*The Sense of Being Stared At* by Rupert Sheldrake

*Who Owns the Future* by Jaron Lanier

*You Are Not a Gadget* by Jaron Lanier

# About the Author

Bonnie Mangold began her music studies in her native California, growing up during a time when the schools provided instruction for all interested students in the musical instrument of their choice. She chose the cello, despite it being unknown to her (she just liked the sound of the word), years later moving to New York City to study with famed cellist Zara Nelsova at the Juilliard School of Music. After graduation from Juilliard she moved to Bogotá, Colombia where she played three seasons as principal cellist of the Orquesta Sinfónia de Colombia and was professor of cello at the National Conservatory. From there she travelled to London to study with master teacher and cellist William Pleeth.

She returned to the States to join the Utah Symphony under the direction of Maestro Maurice Abravanel. In addition to her lengthy symphony career Mangold taught and continues to teach privately and has performed extensively in various chamber music groups, including the long-lasting Mangold Duo with her sister—pianist Marilyn Mangold Garst.

She continues to maintain her lifelong interest in the healing arts and sports and has additionally learned the arts of bow-making (French school), being an activist, and now writing. Her next contemplated book is *The Reluctant Advocate*—a manual for citizen activists. These varied interests and experiences have all contributed to her unique understanding of life and music.

At present she lives in South-Central Utah: playing music, teaching, writing, giving workshops, and enjoying the majestic beauty of the land. You may contact her at bonscello@gmail.com.